The Bro Code

Extending from the belief that masculinities are multiple, consisting of complexities and constructions that make up the traits associated with each, this book explores the various ways in which boys and men are conditioned to view women as inferior to themselves and predominantly sexual objects—and the deleterious effects this has on both women and men, society, and culture at large.

Beginning in childhood, the book provides a critical framework to understand one form of masculinity referred to as "bro culture," and how it is reproduced and reinforced through popular culture, social institutions, and patriarchal forms of religion and politics. Weaving together current research with illuminating historical and contemporary examples, Thomas Keith unpacks the attitudes, beliefs, and behaviors that constitute this subculture and reveals the ways in which traditional and outdated codes of manhood, power, and gender relations have evolved into problematic forms of sexism, misogyny, and abuse. For as much as popular culture is revealed to be a contributing factor in the passage of bro codes, the book also includes examples of cultural forces that are challenging and seeking to overthrow the core tenets in powerful and lasting ways.

Timely and thought-provoking, *The Bro Code* addresses the implications of an enduring social problem and moves us to reflect on ways to empower men away from this toxic form of masculinity.

Thomas Keith teaches philosophy and gender studies at Claremont Graduate University and California State Polytechnic University, Pomona. He has wrote, directed, and produced the bestselling Media Education Foundation films *Generation M: Misogyny in Media and Culture* and *The Bro Code: How Contemporary Culture Creates Sexist Men*, which are used in classrooms around the world. His latest film, *The Empathy Gap: Masculinity and the Courage to Change*, was released in 2015 and has been met with sensational reviews. He recently published *Masculinities in Contemporary American Culture* (Routledge 2017).

"Thomas Keith possesses keen insight and a precise and illuminating lens when examining men and masculinities in the 21st century. He helps readers understand how antiquated codes and tropes of masculinity have grown old and even toxic to men's humanity and that of others. The radiant illumination provides an opportunity for individual men and the culture of masculinity to change, evolve and become better versions of themselves."

Randy Flood, Director, Men's Resource Center of West Michigan

"*The Bro Code* is an incredibly comprehensive and informed analysis of the many ways that our culture continues to indoctrinate young men with a set of misleading and misogynous ideas about manhood, gender and power. It's a must-read for anyone who wants to help these young men develop healthier, more inclusive, and more adaptive identities and behaviors for their lives in the 21st century."

Jackson Katz, author of *The Macho Paradox: Why Some Men Hurt Women and How All Men Can Help*

The Bro Code

THE FALLOUT OF RAISING BOYS TO OBJECTIFY AND SUBORDINATE WOMEN

Thomas Keith

First published 2021
by Routledge
52 Vanderbilt Avenue, New York, NY 10017

and by Routledge
2 Park Square, Milton Park, Abingdon, Oxon, OX14 4RN

Routledge is an imprint of the Taylor & Francis Group, an informa business

© 2021 Taylor & Francis

The right of Thomas Keith to be identified as author of this work has been asserted by him in accordance with sections 77 and 78 of the Copyright, Designs and Patents Act 1988.

All rights reserved. No part of this book may be reprinted or reproduced or utilised in any form or by any electronic, mechanical, or other means, now known or hereafter invented, including photocopying and recording, or in any information storage or retrieval system, without permission in writing from the publishers.

Trademark notice: Product or corporate names may be trademarks or registered trademarks, and are used only for identification and explanation without intent to infringe.

Library of Congress Cataloging-in-Publication Data
Names: Keith, Thomas, 1958- author.
Title: The bro code: the fallout of raising boys to objectify and subordinate women / Thomas Keith.
Description: New York, NY: Routledge, 2020. |
Includes bibliographical references and index.
Identifiers: LCCN 2020034328 (print) | LCCN 2020034329 (ebook) | ISBN 9781138624740 (hardback) | ISBN 9781138624757 (paperback) | ISBN 9780429460524 (ebook)
Subjects: LCSH: Masculinity. | Men—Identity. | Sex discrimination against women. | Misogyny.
Classification: LCC HQ1090 .K445 2020 (print) | LCC HQ1090 (ebook) | DDC 155.3/32—dc23
LC record available at https://lccn.loc.gov/2020034328
LC ebook record available at https://lccn.loc.gov/2020034329

ISBN: 978-1-138-62474-0 (hbk)
ISBN: 978-1-138-62475-7 (pbk)
ISBN: 978-0-429-46052-4 (ebk)

Typeset in Palatino
by codeMantra

CONTENTS

Preface vi

Chapter 1 **Raising Boys on Sexism 1**

Chapter 2 **Bro Culture in the Age of #metoo 29**

Chapter 3 **Frat Life: A Continuum from Honor Societies to Toxic Bro-hood 54**

Chapter 4 **The Bro Code-of-Silence: How Men's Silence Harms Women and Men 85**

Chapter 5 **Advertising's Sexist Call to Men 104**

Chapter 6 **A Bro Manual to Movies, TV, and Games 124**

Chapter 7 **Musical Misogynists: The Beat of Bro Culture 151**

Chapter 8 **Pornography: Sex-Ed for Bros 178**

Chapter 9 **Trump and the Bro World of Political Sexism 206**

Chapter 10 **Religious Bros 233**

Index 258

PREFACE

The first thing to note is that this book is not a traditional textbook nor is it a traditional nonfiction narrative. It is more of a hybrid that provides information that can be used for didactic purposes, but that also includes argument of the kind often found in books that are nonfiction narrative in nature. The idea is to provide readers with information and thought-provoking challenges that can translate into class discussion, class projects, presentations, or simply individual self-reflection. Points will be made that will create disagreement and debate, which is often crucial for learning and growth.

The bro is a social construction. The training to become a bro begins in childhood and is reinforced throughout a young man's life by a culture that socializes boys to adopt sexist and even misogynistic tropes, the most common being that women and all things feminine are inferior to men and all things masculine. By the time boys reach adolescence, many have been groomed to believe that the value found in girls and women is mainly aesthetic and sexual. Much of popular culture reinforces this lesson.

However, *The Bro Code*, as a code of attitudes and behaviors that train many boys to view women in one-dimensional and often demeaning ways is not restricted to the bro as a stereotypical white, middle-class, college-aged man to the exclusion of all other demographics. In fact, many men avoid bro culture altogether, while others adopt milder versions of the bro persona. But for others, being a full-fledged bro becomes a way of life, and is not constrained by age, race, ethnicity, culture, economic class, or sexual orientation. As we will see, the beliefs and behaviors common to bro culture are found throughout a variety of groups, and in some cases, can even extend to women.

For educators, you may want to couple this book with an anthology or other materials that are more comprehensive in nature. Since this book weaves through intersectional identities within the context of what we will be calling *bro culture*, it should work nicely with anthologies that investigate the experiences of boys and men from very different backgrounds.

The chapters follow a path that begins in boyhood and takes us through the many influences in men's lives that include for some fraternities, advertising, movies, TV, games and gamer culture, music, pornography, politics, and religion. Even physical and mental health are covered, since many men notoriously avoid seeking help when help is needed. This is part of what I term *the bro code of silence*, which can be found in sports culture, the military, and throughout the day-to-day lives of millions of men.

What is hopefully obvious to readers is that *the bro code* is not just detrimental to women; it is detrimental to men, to LGBTQ individuals, to relationships, to families, and to culture at large. There are forces in popular culture today that threaten bro culture such as the #metoo movement and the slow, but increasing power of women in academics, business, politics, and many other areas of life. As women gain power, bro culture will recede or, like the

Make America Great Again platform, attempt to rebel against the progressive changes of the 21st century. We have seen this sort of rebellion from men's rights activists, the so-called *incel* rebellion, white supremacists, and other reactionary groups that are petrified by the notion that women, and particularly feminists, LGBTQ people, and people of color are slowly beginning to increase social, political, and economic power.

Bro culture, therefore, can be viewed as a Trumpian call for a return to a mythical utopian America of the past when white, heterosexual men had a stranglehold on the power of the nation. It is a regressive form of masculinity that seeks to return to the days when men could sexually harass women with impunity, or were able to produce jokes at the expense of LGBTQ people and others without pushback. Today, the blanket bro-Trumpian rejection to criticisms of bigotry is to state that all criticism of bigotry is simply an appeal to political correctness. This is a strategy taken straight from *the bro code*, which mocks and bullies any form of critical assessment. Simply put, *The Bro Code* is based on sexist, but also racist, homophobic, and xenophobic bigotries that have been socialized into many, many boys and men throughout their lives.

1 RAISING BOYS ON SEXISM

Key Points

- Male Privilege and Entitlement
- The Asshole Effect
- The Gendered Clark Experiment
- Gender Essentialism and "Mansplaining"
- The Boy Code
- Cultivation Theory and Mainstreaming
- The Maisy Test
- Blurred Lines: Misogyny in Music
- Digital Heroin: The Sexist Instruction of Gamer Culture
- Pornography: Sex Ed for Bros
- Proud Boys
- The Incel Rebellion
- Gay Bros and the Non-Binary Challenge

INTRODUCTION TO BRO CULTURE[1]

Before diving into a book that takes up bro culture, as it will be defined throughout, it is important to note the goal of this book, which is to expose problems within a segment of larger male culture that create harms to both women and men. Sometimes books about men and masculinities can appear to be engaged in male-bashing when those books expose detriments in the ways that boys and men behave without also exposing favorable qualities in men. But by exposing longstanding problems in the ways that many boys and men are trained to think about manhood, the goal is to reveal how this training often comes at the expense of boys and men, as well as at the expense of women and healthy, more fulfilling relationships. Ultimately, the goal of this book is to expose some of the more toxic elements of bro culture that trap men into very limiting and even tragic lives, with the further ambition of helping boys and men recognize and hence avoid these pitfalls.

    Like racism, sexism is taught. Sexism is sold to boys across lines of race, ethnicity, culture, socioeconomic class, age, and even sexual orientation. From media indoctrination to the many who continue to preach gender essentialism to shared experiences in sports, religion, and other areas of interest, to sexist validation from fathers, uncles, coaches, brothers, and other influential men, boys are systematically instructed that girls and women are of less value than boys and men. This chapter, as well as the entire book, will focus on a large subculture of boys and men termed "bros" in popular culture, since these are the boys and men who create the greatest obstacle to gender equality. That bros represent a subculture of boys and men, even a large subculture, means, of course, that not all men are part of bro culture. Many boys and men are raised in different environments or face challenges or choose different paths that avoid bro culture. But many boys and men succumb to the training that creates bros, and many of these bros move on to become political and business leaders who shape policy, create hiring and advancement protocols, and influence the next generation of boys to become bros.

The term "bro" is a neologism and abbreviation of the word "brother" and is thought to have been appropriated by white boys and young men who wanted to emulate what they believed to be cool about black boys and men. More recently, the expression "bro" has been attached to a range of expressions commonly heard among young men:

Bromance
Brogrammer
Brohug
Don't tase me, bro!
What up, bro?
That's the way I roll, bruh.
Bros before hoes.

Essentially, a "bro" is considered to be a friend, pal, or confidant, but can also be used in a neutral sense as a synonym for "guy" or "dude." It is slang, but the connotation, whether as a friend, acquaintance, or stranger, is that a bro is male, even though pop cultural vernacular has converted the slang term "dude" into a non-gendered youth idiom.

At the same time, the term "bro" has become synonymous with the stereotype of young, heterosexual guys who are always on the prowl for sex, who do not seem willing to grow up, who often drink alcohol or smoke pot to excess, who are often, but not always, big sports fans, and who view their male friends as being more important than women. While this is certainly the common media construction of a bro, it is a caricature. To constrain the boundary conditions of a bro too narrowly can create the stereotype of the bro as a white, middle-class, heterosexual frat-guy who is preoccupied with sex and partying, and certainly there are young men who fit the stereotype. But bros are a more diverse lot.

The bro universe can be witnessed through the words, attitudes, and behaviors of boys and men from a variety of backgrounds and shared interests. Each day, whether found in the multicultural realm of boys' and men's team sports, the male dominated domain of STEM, the male-friendly spaces of games and gamer culture, the boardrooms and meeting spaces of business, politics, and the entertainment industry, or the made-for-men realm of online pornography, boys and men from different socioeconomic backgrounds, different races and ethnicities, different ages, different occupations, different regions of the world, and even different sexual orientations participate in the beliefs, attitudes, and behaviors of bros.

The key to much of bro culture revolves around the idea that women are to be viewed principally as sexual opportunities, as having value only in terms of their physical looks and sensual appeal, and as otherwise being inferior and incompetent when compared to men. In essence, bro culture is a reflection of pop culture, where these same sexist tropes are proliferated each day. With respect to some gay men, while there may not be a sexual interest in women, there is often an underpinning of sexist ideology that will be explored in these pages. But bro culture is a culture most readily observed among heterosexual boys and men, where sexual interest in women is a preeminent part of their lives, which contributes to the one-dimensionalizing and therefore devaluing of women overall.

Consider sexual harassment and sexual assault. The high-profile cases of sexual harassment and sexual assault that have been reported in news accounts across the country document the fact that there is not one age group, ethnicity, or socioeconomic class that monopolize these cases. The only commonality among the vast majority of cases of sexual harassment and other forms of sexual misconduct is that the perpetrators are overwhelmingly men. The allegations are now a matter of public record. Of course, the more newsworthy cases involve celebrities. From older men such as Bill Cosby, Harvey Weinstein, Donald Trump, Kevin Spacey, Matt Lauer, Russell Simmons, Dustin Hoffman, Charlie Rose, and Morgan Freeman to younger men such as Kobe Bryant, Casey Affleck, Nick Carter, Junot Diaz, Nelly, R. Kelly, Ryan Seacrest, and James Franco, no isolated variable of age, race, ethnicity, or socioeconomic status determines who commits sexual misconduct. The only isolated variable is that they are all men. Those men who are not rich and famous often fly under the radar of public scrutiny, but research documents the fact that the majority of all cases of sexual misconduct of one kind or another are perpetrated by men.[2] The question is, *where are boys and men getting the idea that sexual harassment and nonconsensual sexual contact is permissible*, or at a minimum, *where are boys and men receiving the view that it is permissible to engage in these behaviors if they believe they will not get caught?* This chapter explores those early sources from boyhood to late adolescence that instruct boys to view women as having less value than men, but in particular, instruct adolescent boys that women's primary value lies in terms of their looks and sexual appeal to men.

MALE PRIVILEGE AND ENTITLEMENT

One thing all of the men listed above share is that they enjoy wealth, fame, and power. With wealth, fame, and power comes a feeling of invulnerability. Writing for *The Guardian*, social philosopher Anne Manne argues that wealth leads to feelings of entitlement, which leads to the further sense that one can or should exploit others when opportunities arise.[3] U.C. Berkeley psychologist Paul Piff calls this phenomenon, **the asshole effect**.[4,5,6,7] This is the view that wealth and power often lead to narcissism. Five separate studies were undertaken where people of higher socioeconomic class reported a greater sense of entitlement and narcissistic personality tendencies.[8] The men on the sexual harassment – sexual assault list above certainly qualify as men with wealth and power, but of course this does not mean that everyone who enjoys wealth and power automatically becomes narcissistic and exploitative of others. So, there is more to the story. This effect also does not account for the many men who sexually exploit women in various ways, but who do not enjoy wealth and economic power. In these cases, male privilege and entitlement must be explored as likely candidates for men's exploitative treatment of women, since enjoying privilege and feelings of entitlement are forms of power.

Male privilege and male entitlement are concepts that are thought to attach to most and perhaps all men, but in different ways. That is, since men occupy positions of executive power at much higher rates than women, and particularly in those occupations known for male dominance such as the banking industry, politics, military and police departments, federal judgeships, engineering, construction, television and film industries, and many other areas of endeavor, men have a considerable statistical advantage over women in terms of power.[9] In fact, there are more men named "John" who are Fortune 500 CEOs than all women taken collectively who are Fortune 500 CEOs.[10] These male advantages often place women in positions of dependency upon men when decisions are made about who gets hired and who gets advanced to positions of authority. On the other hand, society is undergoing change such that women are slowly and finally beginning to enjoy careers that offer them economic independence from men. With past generations, women were often utterly dependent upon men for economic solvency. This is no longer the case, although much is left to do before anything resembling gender equality has been achieved.

Some may argue that there are boys and men who possess little to no power due to any number of intersectional circumstances. For instance, a gay, Black man who is differently abled and who possesses few economic resources has very little power and privilege when compared to a heterosexual, able-bodied white man who enjoys economic privilege. Some boys are bullied, while other boys are bullies. Some boys are abused at home, while others are not. There is little doubt that boys and men do not possess the same amount of privilege and power, but if you exchange the word "men" with "women" and "boys" with "girls," the privilege assignment is even less, and this is the point. An economically challenged man still possesses privileges that an economically challenged woman does not, including an ability in many cases to physically intimidate others. Those boys and men who do not enjoy the traditional power of wealth and executive authority can nonetheless enjoy power over others, including most women, through physicality that can include sexual harassment, physical intimidation, controlling and bullying behaviors, physical and sexual assault, and rape.

In 2014, for my film *The Empathy Gap*, I was interested in discovering how old boys and girls are when sexist ideation first becomes the norm. We know that gender identity begins to form in children at around ages three or four.[11] But I wanted to see whether boys and girls, ages five and six, were already internalizing the notion that boys are more powerful and in some ways superior to girls. To accomplish this task, I organized a number of interviews with five-year-old children in which dilemma-based questions were asked that emulated the famous study conducted by Kenneth and Mamie Clark with the focus, this time, on gender.

GENDERING THE CLARK EXPERIMENT

In the 1940s, Dr. Kenneth B. Clark and Mamie Phipps Clark conducted experiments using dolls to show that African-American boys and girls had internalized feelings of inferiority due to racial segregation and white supremacist propaganda.[12] The experiment was conducted using 160 African-American girls and boys aged five to seven. In case after case, Black boys and girls identified the white doll as possessing positive traits (Which is the nice doll?) and the black doll as possessing negative traits (Which is the mean doll?). The results of the Clark experiment actually helped persuade the Supreme Court to desegregate public schools in the famous ruling of *Brown v. Board of Education*.[13] It was determined that Jim Crow segregation and the negative stereotyping of people of color that went with it created a sense of self-loathing in the minds of Black boys and girls. In 2005, filmmaker Kiri Davis replicated the Clark experiment in the film *A Girl Like Me* by asking the same questions asked by the Clarks and obtained very similar results.[14] Reflecting on the doll experiment, Davis noted that Black youths are still struggling with self-image in a culture where white skin is celebrated as preferable.[15]

I decided to emulate the Clark experiment for gender by using a boy doll and a girl doll.[16] A total of 132 boys and girls aged five and six took part in the experiment, 71 boys and 61 girls (Figures 1.1 and 1.2). The children were drawn from college day-care centers that cared for children of different economic backgrounds, different ethnicities, and different ages and educational levels of parents. Referring to the dolls, children were asked questions like "which one is nicer?" or "which one is smarter?" Of the 132 child responders, only 14 claimed that the girl was smarter than the boy and all 14 of these responders were girls. As a safeguard, I interviewed half of the children, while a female colleague interviewed the other half to see whether they would give us different answers, but the results remained consistent regardless of the sex of the interviewer. We also isolated each participant so they would not be influenced by the responses of other children. In each case of a question designed to identify power (Which one is smarter? Which one will be president some day? Which one is rich?), the boy doll was overwhelmingly selected by both girls and boys; whereas, in each case where the question was selected for traditional roles assigned to women (Which one cleans the house? Which one is poor? Which one is nicer?), responders replied with very gender-traditional

Figure 1.1 Gendered Clark Experiment with a Boy. Film still courtesy of the author, from *The Empathy Gap*.

Figure 1.2 Gendered Clark Experiment with a Girl. Film still courtesy of the author, from *The Empathy Gap*.

responses by selecting the girl doll. Every single boy, except one, claimed that the boy doll was smarter than the girl doll, the one exception claiming that they were "equally smart." The boy examining the dolls in the image below was the one exception.

In 2014, filmmaker Lauren Greenfield created a video-short entitled "Like a Girl" where boys, men, and women were asked to do certain things "like a girl." Predictably, boys, men, and women performed their tasks in over-the-top clumsy ways. However, when Greenfield asked little girls to perform these same tasks, the girls feigned for the camera throwing, fighting, and running as fast as they could. When one little girl was asked, "What does it mean to you when I say *run like a girl?*" she responded, "It means run as fast as you can." The implication of Greenfield's film experiment is that while little girls do not find doing something "like a girl" awkward, clumsy, or incompetent, boys and adults do. But why assume that girls are awkward and clumsy? Why assume that boys are more adept? Why assume that women are incompetent? Why assume that men make better leaders? Why assume that boys are smarter than girls? Why is it that boys and men believe the worst insult one can aim at a boy or man is to call him a name associated with femininity? The many influences in boys' and girls' lives intersect to form a confluence of narratives, scripts, and normative instructions that shape boys' and girls' beliefs, attitudes, and behaviors. Taken collectively, these influences help guide one's orientation or conformity to societal expectations of appropriate behaviors in what is often termed the process of ***socialization***.[17]

Thought Box

View the video "Like a Girl" and then answer a couple questions: https://www.youtube.com/watch?v=XjJQBjWYDTs

Why do you believe people in the video performed exaggeratedly uncoordinated behaviors to imitate what they believed is to do things "like a girl?" Even women performed their assigned tasks in silly and demonstrably bumbling manners. Why do you believe this is?

Since girls are raised in the same sexist culture as boys, it is unsurprising that girls also begin to believe that boys are more adept at some things than girls, and particularly in those traits commonly coded for leadership. This is part of a traditional gender-binary that has been reinforced for millennia that boys are built for one set of skills, while girls are built for another set of skills. The gendered inequality found in leadership roles is part and parcel of a culture that reinforces this inequality. We live in a nation where a woman has never been president or vice-president, where women make up a fraction of Fortune 500 CEOs, where women lag far behind men in careers as writers, directors, and producers in the film and television industry, where women are greatly outnumbered in STEM fields, where women are rarely found in policing and military command positions, and where women are greatly underrepresented in executive positions in the banking industry or on Wall Street.[18] Since media join many parents and others of influence in reinforcing these inequalities, it is not surprising that children pick up on these gendered narratives at early ages and consider these inequalities to be *normal*.

GENDER ESSENTIALISM AND MANSPLAINING

One of the foundations of gender inequality in society is found in the theory known as *gender essentialism*, which is the view that boys and girls, men and women are, beyond sexual dimorphism, fundamentally different, that men and women possess different behavioral traits, aptitudes, and interests and it is usually believed that these differences are caused by nature. Many gender essentialists also commonly normalize essentialism as the way men and women *should* be. An old-fashioned way of viewing gender is through a binary lens of masculine–feminine and then assume that masculinity is typified by physical strength, autonomy, leadership abilities, independence, and emotional stoicism, while femininity is epitomized by physical weakness, nurturance, kindness, dependence, and emotionality. These traits are then socialized into boys and girls, respectively, by parents and other influential adults and peers. But this gendered binary also reinforces a hierarchy whereby men are allegedly *designed* for positions of leadership and authority, while women are allegedly *designed* for positions of support and subordination.

One of many observable consequences of raising boys to view girls and women with less value and authority than boys and men is to witness men speaking over women when women are speaking, or in some cases, explaining concepts to women for which women need no assistance. The phenomenon often occurs because boys have been instructed that girls know less than boys about many subjects, but particularly subjects that men pride themselves in knowing whether technical in nature, economic in nature, sports-related, or political or scholarly in nature. It is the height of condescension, of course, to assume that women are less knowledgeable than men, but men will often defend this style of *mansplaining* by claiming that they were simply trying to be helpful. We find the roots of this condescension in the ways that boys are instructed to think about girls. As shown in the "Like a Girl" video, boys are taught that girls are awkward and lacking in athletic ability, but also lacking in knowledge about subjects that include most sciences, politics, economics, and technologies.

Gender essentialists, past and present, assume that certain areas of endeavor are naturally more suited for men. However, with women now succeeding in every undertaking once considered to be naturally suited to men, we see that these views and instructions to boys and girls were based entirely on gendered stereotypes. In fact, one of the main reasons why women did not pursue areas of science, technology, politics, or business in the past is due to the fact that women were neither encouraged nor in many cases allowed to pursue career paths thought to be suited to men. Today, women are still discouraged from pursuing careers in STEM and other male-dominated fields, even though the American Society of Civil Engineers notes that the discouragement of women in STEM fields violates the fundamental code of ethics that guides STEM hiring practices.[19,20] Yet, when women pursue STEM-based careers despite the disapproval of many, they have succeeded. As just one indicator of this success, the number of women earning Ph.Ds. in physics, biosciences, engineering, computer science, and mathematics continues to grow steadily, more than doubling over the past 20 years.[21]

Still, many men will insist on explaining to women the most basic things. Studies have also shown that men are more likely than women to interrupt others who are speaking,[22] and women have been found to respond more agreeably when interrupted than are men.[23] As sociologist Elizabeth McClintock notes, interrupting another person who is speaking is linked to social power.[24] McClintock writes:

> When a man explains something to a woman in a patronizing or condescending way, he reinforces gender stereotypes about women's presumed lesser knowledge and intellectual ability.[25]

Boys and men who practice this sort of patronizing behavior have likely been raised with the essentialist notion that girls and women are less competent and therefore need guidance. Of course, there are men who do not practice this sexist behavior and it also true that sometimes women talk over men or other women.[26,27] An ongoing problem, however, is that men who *mansplain* to women are often viewed as practicing assertiveness, while women who *womansplain* to men are often viewed as practicing bossiness.[28] If you are a woman trying to succeed in a professional career, these double standards can serve as obstacles to success.

Thought Box

Perhaps the funniest or at least most egregious account of mansplaining occurred when a man at a party attempted to explain to author Rebecca Solnit the meaning found in a book actually authored by Rebecca Solnit.[29] In another example, a man attempted to teach writer Dana Schwartz about the Twitter account @GuyInYourMFA, explaining, "It's really something you can only relate to as a male writer."[30] The problem is, Dana Schwartz runs this particular Twitter account.

Is this something you have an encountered as a woman? Men, have you ever caught yourself mansplaining to women? After reading the criticism of using expressions like "mansplaining," do you think critics have a point? Can you think of ways to respond to these criticisms?

Along with "mansplaining," there are a few other portmanteau terms that capture the idea that male privilege spills over into speaking down to women. The term "manterrupt" is meant to capture the phenomenon of men interrupting women when they speak, while "bropropriate" is meant to capture cases where men take credit for work and ideas created by women. Another common expression is the "manspread," where men spread their legs when seated in a way that invades the space of people sitting next to them.

However, there has been some pushback to the term *mansplaining* and other similar expressions. Some argue that terms like "mansplaining" is man-shaming that undermines the feminist goal of equality.[31] Writing for *The Guardian*, Liz Cookman argues that these expressions create harms.[32] First, they trivialize and one-dimensionalize problems that women face in the workplace. Challenges for women in pursuit of many different career paths extend far beyond concerns over men explaining things to them, interrupting them on occasion, or spreading their legs too wide. Cookman views this overly narrow concern as distracting to the more serious and debilitating obstacles that women face in landing careers, getting paid the same amount as men for the same job, and receiving advancement at the same rates as men. Second, Cookman argues, these terms reinforce gender essentialism by assuming that these traits are universally found or at least exclusively found in men. Would we want to the use the term "womanterrupt" in cases where a woman interrupts a man? How about in those cases where a woman interrupts another woman? Writing for *Think Progress*, Annie-Rose Strasser adds that the term "mansplaining" attempts to point out privilege, in this case, male privilege. But Strasser notes,

> A white woman can't "mansplain" to a black woman what it means to be discriminated against, but she can certainly be patronizing about the experience that a black woman endures, approaching that interaction with all of the privilege of a mansplainer.[33]

If pointing out privilege and condescension is the central goal of using terms like "mansplaining," terms of this kind miss the point of intersectional privilege by universalizing the phenomenon to one and only one group of people.

THE BOY CODE

In 1999, psychologist William Pollack published the book *Real Boys: Rescuing Our Sons from the Myths of Boyhood*, where he argues that from early ages, boys are instructed in the societal expectations of how boys should think and behave, resulting in what he terms **the mask of masculinity**.[34] This "mask" creates what Pollack identifies as **the silent crisis**, whereby boys hold their feelings inside and are careful not to show any outward signs of pain, fear, loneliness, self-doubt, or sorrow. Instead, boys are taught to exhibit outward signs of confidence, bravado, toughness, independence, and emotional stoicism regardless of their actual feelings. A crisis emerges when boys feel they have nowhere to turn to express themselves or to emote in ways considered to be weak, and weakness is usually defined as any and all traits considered to be feminine or gay by those policing the code. Pollack notes that the boy code is policed heavily by peers, but also by older men of influence who use shame to assure that boys adhere strictly to a code of behaviors considered to be properly masculine.[35]

Pollack points to four harmful instructions given to boys over and over again by those who take it upon themselves to shape boys' behaviors:[36]

- <u>Be a sturdy oak</u>: Boys are instructed to keep all emotions inside so as to resemble an object. Remain calm during a crisis and show no outer signs of fear, loneliness, pain, or vulnerability.

- Give 'em hell: Take risks, behave with bravado, and resolve differences with anger, aggression, and even violence.
- Be a big wheel: Achieve power and status by placing a high priority on becoming wealthy, owning and displaying expensive possessions, and always emit a sense of confident cool in everything you do. You are in charge, in control, and your power is on display.
- No sissy stuff: Be self-reliant and never behave in any way that could be interpreted as being feminine or gay.

It is this last instruction, in particular, that causes the boy code to become perspicuously sexist in nature. As soon as boys are taught that by contrast to themselves, girls are weak, emotional, and need guidance, the code explicitly notifies boys that they are superior to girls. Since heteronormativity is the rule for most bros,[37] gay men are lumped in with women as possessing feminine traits, which undermines their masculinity and makes them targets of derision and abuse. By adolescence, boys add the trait *sexual* to the list assigned to girls, which is reinforced by mass media and sold to both boys and girls as the trait providing value to girls and women. When President Donald Trump judges women by assigning to them a numeric value based on how he believes they look, for instance, the sexist reinforcement that women matter mainly in terms of their physical appearance gains support from the highest authority in the land.[38] But Trump himself is the product of a lifetime of socialization that instructed boys and men that women are essentially of value depending on their sexual appeal to men. In addition to older men who boys and young men view with admiration such as fathers, uncles, older brothers, music artists, pro athletes, and coaches, media provide a host of sexist narratives in movies and TV shows aimed at young, male audiences, music and music videos, video games, men's magazines, and pornography.

CULTIVATION THEORY AND MAINSTREAMING

In 1968, communications professor George Gerbner founded cultivation theory, which states that long-term media consumption has the power to *cultivate* or influence one's perception of reality:[39]

> Television is a medium of the socialization of most people into standardized roles and behaviors. Its function is in a word, enculturation.[40]

By viewing the same media, Gerbner believed that people of different backgrounds can develop similar world-views. He termed this phenomenon, **mainstreaming**.[41] In this way, boys of varying backgrounds can consume similar media and over time develop similar views about girls and women, including views about consent, value, emotion, rationality, competence, incompetence, and normative gender roles.

Mass media aimed mainly at male audiences, which include certain films, TV shows, advertising, video games, pornography, men's magazines, and web-based programming are at the forefront of training boys to view girls and women in one-dimensional and highly sexist ways. This is not, of course, to say that every instance of media aimed at boys reinforces a sexist script about women, but much of it does. This is particularly true for pornography, certain men's magazines, video games, and many summer films aimed at a teen, male audience. A prime example of this is found in the comedy hit *Hot Tub Time Machine* (2010) where themes of women's sexualized bodies on display for the male gaze and homophobic jokes pervade the script and visual content of the film. The boys and young men who consume these sorts of films and other similar media come from divergent backgrounds and cannot simply be reduced to white, middle-class boys from the suburbs. Yet by consuming similar media, the effects of mainstreaming can draw those whose intersectional identities may be very different into common ways of thinking. In these cases, boys and young men who may not share racial or ethnic identities, or cultural histories for that matter, can be found bonding around the same sexist beliefs and behaviors.

THE MAISY TEST

Inspired by Alison Bechdel's famous test of women's representation in media, Kehoe Rowden, a blogger and parent, created the **Maisy Test for Sexism** to test film and TV programming aimed at kids.[42] The test gets its name from the cartoon mouse "Maisy" by British illustrator Lucy Cousins.[43] The Maisy test is structured around four basic themes:[44]

1. **Gender Balance:** Are there roughly an equal number of male and female characters?
2. **Gender Freedom:** Do boys and girls get to do the same things? Do they all get to have adventures?
3. **Gender Safety:** Are body shapes healthy and realistic? Is everyone safe? Are boys and girls treated respectfully?
4. **Social Justice and Equality:** Can every kid see someone like them? Is the show free from materialism and violence?

Gender balance has been a concern for media aimed at children for decades. A study of TV programming for children noted that 68% of protagonists are male, and even in cases where the character is an animal, 75% are male.[45] This gender imbalance is found in media programming around the world.[46] In the media realm where male characters are overwhelmingly the protagonists, and often take on a heroic, savior persona, boys and girls are repeatedly subjected to the notion that men are responsible for defending and protecting women, but also that women are weak and in need of being protected from a hostile world.

With respect to *gender freedom*, boys are found to be much more active than girls in ads targeting children and as early as preschool, boys are happier with the ads targeting them, demonstrating adherence to stereotypes provided by advertisers and this phenomenon has been shown to increase with age.[47]

This is particularly true during the Christmas shopping season where toys are gendered to reflect the roles that advertisers expect boys and girls to assume. *Common Sense Media* reports that television characters are often starkly gendered with male characters depicted as "strong, emotionally restrained, risk-takers, and leaders," while female characters are usually portrayed as being "agreeable, virtuous, demure, concerned about their physical appearance, and more likely to be shown crying than male characters."[48] After reviewing more than 150 articles, interviews, books, and social-scientific research, *Common Sense Media* issued a report with the following findings:[49]

- Media reinforces the idea that masculine traits and behaviors are more valued than female traits and behaviors.
- Boys who consume media are more likely to exhibit traditionally masculine behaviors and hold traditional beliefs about there being a strong gender binary with associated gendered traits.
- Media promote the view that girls should be concerned about their appearance and should treat their bodies as sexual objects for others' consumption.
- Media aimed at adolescents construct more tolerant views of sexual harassment and more support for the view that women are in part responsible for the harassment aimed at them.
- Youth of color may be more vulnerable to the effects of media as applied to gender role development.

Media usage within the 8–18 age group has doubled in 4 years with 8-to-12-year-olds spending 4 hours and 44 minutes viewing media each day, and teens averaging 7 hours and 22 minutes viewing media, not including screen time spent on school purposes.[50,51] This time commitment has surged even though consumer groups have issued warnings about safety and development concerns that include increased impulsivity, negative effects on sleep and weight, exposure to inaccurate and inappropriate content, and compromised privacy.[52]

One of the measurements used by the Maisy test, *Gender safety*, is sometimes measured by body image and in study after study, girls and women report less satisfaction with their bodies than boys and men.[53,54] With the advent of very tall, very slim models, coupled with the introduction of digital editing tools, girls and women often feel compelled to emulate the beauty styles of fashion models who literally don't exist. Predictably, girls and women suffer from higher rates of body dysmorphic disorder than boys and men, which also lead to higher rates of anorexia, bulimia, and elective cosmetic surgery.[55,56] However, this does not mean that boys and men do not struggle with body image or that media do not target boys and men with body imagery that is, for many, unattainable.[57] It is very likely that the future of marketing will target boys and men with similar ads that currently target girls and women, with an emphasis on body-shaming to ignite sales.

Socioeconomic class also appears to play a role in media consumption. Kids living in lower socioeconomic neighborhoods view approximately three and a half hours of television each day, while kids living in more affluent neighborhoods view about two hours of television each day.[58] As parents struggle to earn enough money to survive in times of gentrification where rent costs have soared, it is not surprising that media have taken up a more prominent place in children's lives. Against this background, most media fail the Maisy test, subjecting children to sexist tropes on a daily basis. What is more troubling, according to a new study by the Global Early Adolescent Study, is that by age ten, most kids begin to believe the gender stereotypes they are consuming in media.[59]

BLURRED LINES: MISOGYNY IN MUSIC[60]

An interesting thing about contemporary pop music is that it reflects the sociopolitical times in which we now live. There are now numerous instances of music artists who are writing and performing songs that empower women. Yet, almost all of these empowering songs come from either female artists or LGBTQ artists. From the iconic song "I Will Survive" by Gloria Gaynor in 1978 to "Beautiful" by Christina Aguilera in 2002 to "Scars to your Beautiful" by Alessia Cara in 2015, women, for decades, have been producing music meant to uplift and empower girls and women around the world. Today, LGBTQ music artists are also changing the script by creating music with empowering messages. From Indigo Girls, k.d. lang, and Culture Club in the 1980s and 1990s to Sam Smith, Pablo Vittar, Azealia Banks, Frank Ocean, and Meshell Ndegeocello, among many others today who celebrate LGBTQ identities, music artists are becoming much more diverse and socially conscious in their lyrics.

By contrast, far too many heterosexual, male artists continue to live in the past by producing lyrics and videos that treat or talk about women as sexual objects, existing only for male gratification. Or they sometimes shame and demean women through hostile and highly degrading lyrics. Consider the song "No Lie" by 2 Chainz where women are reduced to being identified as *pussy* and things to be *fucked*.[61] This is simply one of thousands of titles in a decades-old legacy of music that treat women as interchangeable sex objects or things to be used by men. Another example among thousands is found in the song "Bartier Cardi" by Cardi B where artist 21 Savage boasts about giving *bitches molly* in anticipation of sex.[62] "Molly" is slang for the drug, ecstasy, or MDMA, which makes this a song about rape. The unapologetic misogyny found in the lyrics and videos of some hip-hop artists has been well documented for over 30 years, but the theme of using, abusing, infantilizing, controlling, and sexually dominating women has been part of rock, country, and metal for an even longer period of time. From The Rolling Stones' "Under My Thumb" to Motley Crüe's "Girls, Girls, Girls" to Trace Adkins' "Honky Tonk Badonkadonk" to Cannibal Corpse's "Stripped, Raped, and Strangled," generations of boys have been raised on lyrics that promote everything from the softer sexism of Burt Bacharach's "Wives and Lovers" to the violent misogyny of Devourment's "Fucked to Death."

A perfect example of the wanton sexism in music was found in the video to the 2013 hit by Robin Thicke, "Blurred Lines." The video, which came in an uncensored version where the women in the video were completely nude, depicts Thicke, and music artists Pharrell and T.I., positioned around scantily clad female models who defer to the men's wishes by frolicking about, bending over, getting on all-fours, lighting cigarettes, and emulating the women found in porn, while the men take traditional positions of power, while explaining to the women that their true nature is to be an animal. One of the female models actually murmurs "meow" into the camera. All of it is packaged around the idea of sexual liberation, but is more about women serving men as well as infantilizing women by first claiming that she is a "good girl" and then repeating the phrase "I know you want it." EUSA president Kirsty Haigh points out that while the male lead states over and over, *I know you want it*, You can't know they want it unless they tell you they want it."[63]

Assuming consent without explicit consent is sometimes called "gray rape," since consent is blurry, hence the song's title "Blurred Lines." Thicke, himself, defended the song by asking the Spinal Tap-esque question, "What's wrong with being sexy?"[64] This compounds the problem by making critics of the song's message appear prudish, while others defended the video by noting that a woman produced and directed it as though that fact alone immunizes any work from being sexist.[65]

Thought Box

If a woman produces or directs a work of art, whether film, TV-show, music video, or even pornography, does that fact eliminate the artwork from being sexist?

Blurred Lines is but one of thousands of songs that celebrate men's control over women, that women are play-things and sexual commodities. Sexism and often unequivocal misogyny is found in music that crosses lines of race, ethnicity, socioeconomics, age, genre, and political affiliation. For many bros, the music they grow up listening to becomes the soundtrack to their lives, including their hopes of living like the artists they hold in high esteem. The womanizing lifestyles of rock, country, and hip-hop stars have also been documented and glamorized in films, books, countless music publications, TV reality shows, and behind-the-scenes exposés. Unfortunately, too many male music artists and record company executives have enjoyed unbelievable financial success by producing music that undermines and demeans women, music that is ultimately consumed by boys and young men who are coming to their own understanding of what it means to be a man.

DIGITAL HEROIN: THE SEXIST INSTRUCTION OF GAMER CULTURE

In 2018, The World Health Organization (WHO) recognized gaming disorder as a mental health condition.[66] The WHO describes gaming disorder as:

> characterized by a pattern of persistent or recurrent gaming behaviour ('digital gaming' or 'video-gaming'), which may be online or offline, manifested by: 1) impaired control over gaming (e.g., onset, frequency, intensity, duration, termination, context); 2) increasing priority given to gaming to the extent that gaming takes precedence over other life interests and daily activities; and 3) continuation or escalation of gaming despite the occurrence of negative consequences.

While girls are entering gamer culture in increasing numbers, it is still considered primarily to be a boy-zone.[67] Beyond the fact that boys and young men are playing video games for durations of time that harm other areas of their lives, the games themselves and the culture that has been spawned by millions of gamers worldwide are some of the more toxic masculine environments in pop culture. When writer Anita Sarkeesian crossed the bro world of gamer culture to author a critique, she was assaulted by a barrage of attacks that culminated in an online game where players could digitally "beat up Anita Sarkeesian" by virtually punching an image of her face until it turned black and blue from bruising.[68] Sarkeesian also received death and rape threats culminating in her cancelling a speaking event at Utah State University after university officials received an email warning that a shooting massacre would take place at her talk.[69] These attacks, as well as attacks on game developers Zoe Quinn and Brianna Wu, collectively became known as *Gamergate*.[70]

The games themselves feature female avatars and characters that have been pornified with exaggeratedly large breasts and extremely revealing outfits. Even though many of the female characters act out as violently as the male characters in games, the hypersexualizing and fetishizing of female bodies found among female characters do not find an equivalence in male characters. If anything, male avatars are stereotypes of hypermasculinity, featuring hulking bodies of immense muscularity, while possessing personas of invulnerability, relentless ferocity, and sociopathic violence. The idea is to give boys and young men a pornified experience. While their male avatars commit acts of violence, the female characters act as highly sexualized automatons who are created to arouse. Studies have shown that playing games with highly sexualized female characters increases male gamer acceptance of rape myth and tolerance for sexual harassment.[71] It isn't as simple as there being a direct casual connection between playing video games and holding sexist views toward women, but when calculated alongside the many other influences in boys' lives that offer a similar assessment of women, a template of perspective is reinforced over and over that promotes a stereotype: men are *and should be* violent and invulnerable, while women are *and should be* seductive and sexually available to men.

One study conducted on the *Grand Theft Auto* (GTA) series of games revealed that those boys and men who identified with the male characters in the game also showed the least amount of empathy toward the female victims of violence.[72] Grand Theft Auto is one of the most successful game-series ever. As a player option, boys can beat, rape, and murder prostitutes, while receiving extra points for doing so. To illustrate how these game-choices can influence boys' views about women, at a talk I gave several years ago, one young man who self-identified as an avid GTA fan challenged the idea that these player options were highly sexist by shouting from the back of the auditorium, "you can't rape prostitutes, bro!" His idea of a prostitute had been influenced, in part, by a game that marketed the view that prostitutes were not fully human, as though any mistreatment toward them is permissible and defensible.

Writing for *Time Magazine*, Alexandra Sifferlin notes that the female characters in the game are mainly strippers and prostitutes, but that the interactivity between a game and the boy playing the game creates opportunities for choice and fantasy fulfillment that is different than that found in films where the content is unchangeable.[73] Ohio State University research scholar Brad Bushman states, "When you watch a TV show, maybe you don't identify with the character, but in a game you have no choice. You are the one who controls the character's actions."[74] This interaction and choice of behavior provides boys and young men a sense of power that they probably do not possess in their actual lives. Video games provide young, male gamers the opportunity to choose to fantasize about being a violent misogynist, while giving rewards to players for making these choices. When challenged about the misogyny of such choices, gamers often attempt to justify those choices by noting that "It's just a game, no one is actually getting hurt." But it is certainly unclear whether "no one is actually getting hurt." For those boys and men who wish their fantasy lives and real lives were more alike, how can we be certain that virtual harm does not convert into actual harm for many, if not through physical and sexual violence, perhaps through different forms of sexual harassment or viewing women in very limiting, one-dimensional ways that contribute to preventing women from attaining positions of leadership and authority? If men view women as having value primarily through sexual appeal, it is not a great leap to assume that men of this type do not view women as cutout for the task of executive management, but rather as those fit for positions of subordination.

PORNOGRAPHY: SEX ED FOR BROS[75]

The American Psychological Association reports that the average age for boys to be exposed to pornography is around age 11 and that the younger a boy is in his first exposure to pornography, the more likely he is to desire power over women.[76] There are variables, of course, that mitigate or strengthen this connection such as a boy's religiosity, sexual performance anxiety, and whether his first sexual encounter was positive or negative.[77] According to the American College of Pediatricians, porn usage by boys and young men increases a host of potential harms including increased rates of depression, increased risk of teen pregnancy, and a distorted view of relationships between men and women.[78] In studies conducted on the effects of porn usage by young men compared to the control group, men who consume porn demonstrated an increased callousness toward women, viewed rape as a less serious crime, and became less satisfied with their sexual partners.[79] Further negatives include the fact that steady porn usage by young men leads to an acceptance of rape-myth ideology, the belief that women either cause rape or enjoy being raped, and that usage of aggressive or violent forms of pornography was positively correlated with sexually aggressive behaviors in both adolescent and adult males.[80]

Not coincidentally, much of mainstream media aimed at men include the very same narratives and imagery found in pornography: that men should be assertive and even aggressive in their pursuit of sex with women, that women want sex all of the time, and that "no" is part of a flirtatious game women play with men, but not something to be taken literally or seriously. These messages can also be found occasionally in film and television scripts, but most notably in the visual displays of many consumer ads. For instance, in the ad for the Tom Ford cologne *"For Men,"* the bottle of cologne is positioned between the breasts of a woman to symbolize a penis. This particular ad's call to men highlights a theme in advertising aimed at men, which is the pornified view that product use gets women to be more like the women of porn, who are willing to do anything to serve men's sexual desires. Ads of this nature are strewn throughout pop culture, where women's bodies are displayed as decorations and props for the male gaze. But this also means that pornography is no longer content reserved for "over-18" websites and magazines. Between ads, music videos, music lyrics, feature films, video game content, and even some TV shows, porn proliferates popular culture and sells more than product; it sells normative beliefs about women, sex, and what constitutes consent to young, male consumers.

At the same time that we want to be *sex positive* and want women to feel sexually empowered and liberated, boys and young men consume female bodies in ways not radically different than the way they consume fast food. Women's bodies are disposable and interchangeable in pornography. A young man can peruse hundreds of sexualized women or women's body parts in the course of a day by consuming pornography. Moreover, we want sex to be fully consensual, but porn voids consent by assuming that women consent to any and all forms of sex all of the time, regardless of the sexual activities engaged in or the aggressiveness and hostility of the man or men in the scene.

In porn, women are receptacles. They are props who are interchangeable with one another and hold no value other than to be sexually compliant to whatever wishes or demands men require of them. Writing for *Psychology*

Today, author Alexandra Katehakis notes that while adolescent boys are learning to navigate an uncertain realm of sex and relationships with women, "pornography shows us a world where relationships mean nothing and immediate sexual gratification means everything."[81] This, Katehakis argues, creates the view that sex and relationships are separate from one another. Famed psychologist Philip Zimbardo adds that porn consumption wires the brains of boys to desire levels of novelty, stimulation, and sexual excitement that are not realistic projections of actual-life relationships.[82] In addition, boys who consume porn have no experience with affection, intimacy, or sexual boundaries.[83] Instead, pornography provides an on-demand, virtual sex experience that places men's desires above all else, including whatever interests, desires, and concerns about safety, consent, and sexual autonomy women may have. For many bros, porn becomes de facto sex education, but with wildly unrealistic scenarios and no sense of the emotional power of sex, let alone any boundaries set by participants.

PROUD BOYS

Founded in 2016 by writer and far-right provocateur Gavin McInnes, *Proud Boys* are an all-male group that has emerged as a radicalized men's organization aligned with alt-right politics that feature anti-Muslim, anti-Semitic, and misogynistic rhetoric.[84] Their name comes from the song "Proud of Your Boy" in the Disney Film *Aladdin*.[85] Identified by the Southern Poverty Law Center as a hate group, Proud Boys have spread racist propaganda, although their literature claims that they are not racist, white supremacist, nor anti-Semitic. Yet, when one of their core members, Brian Brathovd, also known as Caearalus Rex, was asked about the charges of racism, he responded, "If the Proud Boys were pressed on the issue, I guarantee you that like 90% of them would tell you something along the lines of 'Hitler was right. Gas the Jews.'"[86]

The bro significance of Proud Boys is their gender-exclusive brand of misogyny. In 2013, McInnes wrote what would be the forebearer of Proud Boys' guiding principles in a piece entitled, "Everything I Learned in College was a Lie," where he pretends to explain why racism and sexism aren't real features of society until college professors make them so by constantly bringing them up as challenges we must overcome.[87] With this as background, Proud Boys reject feminism in favor of what they term "the veneration of the housewife," which is the view that women should remain at home attending to domestic chores and the wishes and desires of their husbands.[88] These retrograde views capture a bro-friendly version of gender that centers around one fundamental principle: that women are inferior to men. This principle is witnessed in the roles and activities of Proud Boys, where men are visible leaders while women are invisible and do what they are told. When members of Wisconsin Proud Boys were scheduling an interview with a female journalist, they responded by asking whether they should bring condoms.[89] McInnes then told the journalist that she should quit her job and find a man, noting that there is a war on masculinity that runs contrary to nature.[90] Framing gender as conforming to natural roles with men as leaders and women as followers is a bro tonic that is found throughout conservative political rhetoric, where feminism is mocked and attacked as being responsible for what they view as the downfall of society. But McInnes and his group of Proud Boys also display a superb example of damaged and insecure masculinity, where a return to an era when men's domination and unquestioned authority was ubiquitous and considered *natural* is a restorative aid for those men who feel their power and unearned privilege slipping away.

THE INCEL REBELLION

A disturbing men's movement has sprung up among men who identify as "involuntarily celibate or incels." These are men who harbor anger and resentment toward women for not allowing these men to have sex with them. In what is the epitome of aggrieved entitlement, incel bros feel that they are entitled to women's bodies, a belief that is rooted in bro culture. In 2014, in what may be the most abhorrent actions of an incel bro to that point in time, 22-year-old Eliot Rodger filmed a video of himself lamenting the fact that he was a virgin, while aggrandizing himself as someone who women *should* find attractive.[91] He seethed with anger, claiming that women had rejected him, while accepting other men he viewed as less attractive candidates for sex and relationships. Rodger then went on a killing spree stabbing to death three men at his apartment and then driving to a coffee shop near the campus of U.C. Santa Barbara where he began shooting people, including three Delta Delta Delta sorority women. When he finished his killing spree, Rodger killed six people, wounded 14 more, and ending the carnage with a self-inflicted gunshot wound. Rodger's rampage killing inspired 25-year-old Alek Minassian, who, in 2018, drove a van into a crowd in Toronto killing ten people and injuring ten more. On his Facebook page, Minassian referenced Rodger:

> The Incel Rebellion has already begun! We will overthrow all Chads and Stacys! All hail the Supreme Gentleman Elliot Rodger.[92]

Writing for the Southern Poverty Law Center, Keegan Hankes notes that to incels, "women who deny them sex are committing a crime. Elliot Rodger is glorified among these people. They praise his 2014 attack and reference potential copycat violence as "going ER."[93]

In the bro universe, women are mainly sexual objects. Among incel bros, the denial of sex by women is a personal insult to their sense of entitlement. However, writing for the misogynist-exposing web-blog "We Hunted the Mammoth," David Futrelle uncovers an ironic tension in their view:

> Incels hate women, but they also hate themselves, and many of them convince themselves they're too ugly or too short to ever be attractive.[94]

This feature of self-hatred is a different twist on the more common frat-guy version of bro culture where bros place themselves on pedestals of desirability such that women should be honored to have sex with them. Certainly there are fraternity-affiliated men who do not conform to this pretention, but for generations, fraternity affiliation was considered to be a path to increased sexual opportunity, whether consensual or not.[95,96,97] But with incels, there is a misogynistic anger fueled by insecurity and self-hatred that drives their sense of aggrieved entitlement to women's bodies.

Much like *men's rights activists*, incels are driven by the passionate view that they are victims who are owed something by women. They consume porn where women are sexual with men without obvious regard to a man's physical appearance or socioeconomic status, but in their experiences, women do not behave as they do in pornography. Incels view this sex-denial as a form of injustice. These are bros in a very robust sense, but filled with rage at real-women who refuse to be porn-women. Just how many incels are out there is anyone's guess, but as long as bro culture is defined by *sexual conquest*, and women are viewed as valuable only in terms of their sexual appeal, there is no reason to suppose that the incel rebellion, if even in a less violent way, will disappear anytime soon.

GAY BROS[98]

Boys who become aware that they are GBTQ face challenges that heterosexual, cis-gender boys do not. In fact, it is common for homophobic slurs to be used by many bros to police the gender and sexual practices of their bro friends. This is not to say that gay or queer boys and men cannot be bros. In the piece, "From Oppressor to Activist: Reflections of a Feminist Journey," Chief Diversity Officer Amit Taneja for College of the Holy Cross states:

> I was hanging out with some gay, male friends, when one of them stubbed his toe and let out a cry of pain. One of the other men in the group yelled, "Stop being a pussy and take it like a man!" Later that evening, another queer man claimed that he was "allergic to vagina in every way possible." Another one responded that he could "barely tolerate the dykes at the pride marches."[99]

Taneja explains the sexist jabs by noting that queer people are oppressed in a heteronormative society in a variety of ways and that some gay men deal with this oppression by tapping into their male privilege. Granted, gay and queer men are probably not sexually assaulting women, but this does not mean that they are incapable of holding some of the very same sexist views of women that are held by their heterosexual and cis-gender counterparts.

Writer-blogger Jamie Tabberer claims that he awoke to the fact that many gay men, like himself, are sexist after reading quotes by actress Rose McGowanin:[100]

> [Gay men are] as misogynistic as straight men, if not more so. You want to talk about the fact that I have heard nobody in the gay community, no gay males, standing up for women on any level?[101]

McGowan later apologized for what she termed an overgeneralization,[102] but some gay men supported much of her criticism of gay, male culture. Writing for *The Guardian*, Patrick Strudwick notes:

> Many gay men individuate their identity from straight men by exaggerating their sexual lack of interest in women. It pours out with misogyny...As a movement we have ignored women, individually and structurally. Along with the many gay rights organisations headed by men over the decades (thankfully Stonewall now has a second woman in charge),there is no more poignant example of this than in the fight against HIV/Aids, where the tender altruism of hordes of lesbian volunteers who tended to dying men in the 1980s has been forgotten.[103]

At the same time, Strudwick notes that the crux of the problem lies in the fact that we live in a sexist world, whether we are heterosexual or gay.[104] When we are raised in a sexist culture, where women's sexualized bodies are placed on display, scrutinized, and objectified, along with the steady stream of messages that women are inferior to men in a host of ways, what would make us think that gay men are immune from being bros?

On the other hand, those who are gender non-conforming or non-binary might be immune from membership in bro culture by virtue of the fact that they reject the socially constructed duality of gender in the first place. Bro culture operates on the principle that gender is starkly binary in nature with one gender possessing power and superiority over the other, which creates a basis of rationalization that often comes in the wake of an episode of physical, sexual, verbal, or emotional bullying, misconduct, or abuse from men. Those gay men who accept gender in binary terms are able to enlist in bro culture by tapping into their male privilege when they find it beneficial to do so. Therefore, the non-binary challenge may be seen as a challenge to bro culture itself, since it dismantles the theoretical structure on which bro culture is founded.

POSTSCRIPT

Being a member of bro culture is to consume and then embody much of the messaging of popular culture. Bros come in many forms and are not simply the stereotype of an upper-middle-class, white, heterosexual fraternity guy who obsesses about sex. And regardless of race, ethnicity, age, occupation, socioeconomic class, and even sexual orientation, bros tend to believe that women are less competent and of less value than men. Many of these men graduate to positions of authority where they are placed in charge of making hiring decisions and determining who receives advancement into positions of greater authority. It should not, therefore, be surprising when men in positions of power and authority are discovered to have sexually harassed and objectified women, some even engaging in sexual assault and rape.

This is not an American problem; it is a world problem. We find similar stories and statistics around the world.[105] Studies have shown that approximately 2 billion women worldwide have experienced sexual harassment, sexual assault, or rape at some point in their lives.[106] The vast majority of these cases of harassment and assault are perpetrated by men, which makes sense when we understand that sexual abuse is about power.[107] But boys are not born with sexism ingrained in their genes. Sexist instruction, like racist instruction, is taught and learned through years of socialization. Understanding how men are turned into bros may help us discover how to raise boys to be better men, who could then lead healthier, more productive lives, which, by extension, would benefit everyone: women, children, and men.

Notes

1. Much of this chapter is designed to be an introduction to the many influences that help shape boys' and men's lives in becoming what we are calling 'bros'; many of these influences will be investigated in much more depth throughout the book.
2. The World Health Organization, *Sexual Violence: Prevalence, Dynamics and Consequences*, Report on Sexual Violence, pp. 1–11. https://www.who.int/violence_injury_prevention/resources/publications/en/guidelines_chap2.pdf
3. Anne Manne, "The Age of Enlightenment: How Wealth Breeds Narcissism," *The Guardian*, July 7, 2014.https://www.theguardian.com/commentisfree/2014/jul/08/the-age-of-entitlement-how-wealth-breeds-narcissism
4. Paul K. Piff, "Wealth and the Inflated Self: Class, Entitlement, and Narcissism," *Personality and Social Psychology*, Vol. 40, Issue 1, 2014, pp. 34–43.
5. Paul K. Piff, Ted Talk, "Does Money Make You Mean?" December 2013. https://www.ted.com/talks/paul_piff_does_money_make_you_mean
6. Jane Hamsher, "Study Shows Being Rich Makes You an Asshole," *Shadow Proof*, June 2014. https://shadowproof.com/2014/07/08/study-shows-being-rich-makes-you-an-asshole/
7. Eric Reed, "Having More Money Might Actually Make You a Jerk," *Business Insider*, July 2014. http://www.businessinsider.com/money-can-make-you-a-jerk-2014-7
8. Paul K. Piff, "Wealth and the Inflated Self: Class, Entitlement, and Narcissism," *Personality and Social Psychology*, Vol. 40, Issue 1, 2014, pp. 34–43.
9. Claire Cain Miller, Kevin Quely, Margarot Singer-Katz, "The Top Jobs Where Women Are Outnumbered by Men Named John," *New York Times*, April 24, 2018. https://www.nytimes.com/interactive/2018/04/24/upshot/women-and-men-named-john.html
10. Ibid.
11. National Center on Parent, Family, and Community Engagement, "Healthy Gender Development and Young Children," Washington, DC. https://depts.washington.edu/dbpeds/healthy-gender-development.pdf

Chapter 1

12. Michael Beschloss, "How an Experiment with Dolls Helped Lead to School Integration," *New York Times*, May 6, 2014. https://www.nytimes.com/2014/05/07/upshot/how-an-experiment-with-dolls-helped-lead-to-school-integration.html
13. NCAAP Legal Defense and Educational Fund, "The Significance of the Doll Test," LDF, 2020. http://www.naacpldf.org/brown-at-60-the-doll-test
14. Natasha Ashby, "Kiri Davis: Filmmaker and Activist," *New York Amsterdam News*, July 2, 2015.
15. Ibid.
16. Thomas Keith, *the Empathy Gap: Masculinity and the Courage to Change*, Media Education Foundation, Northampton, MA. 2015. https://www.worldcat.org/title/empathy-gap-masculinity-and-the-courage-to-change/oclc/973342593
17. William Little, *Introduction to Sociology*, 1st Canadian Ed., BC Open Textbook Project, 2015. Chapter 5.
18. Renae Merle, "Women, Minorities Are Still Nearly Shut Out of This $71 Trillion Industry," *The Washington Post*, May 3, 2017. https://www.washingtonpost.com/news/business/wp/2017/05/03/women-minorities-are-still-nearly-shut-out-of-this-7-trillion-industry/?utm_term=.0735cf6f3e34
19. Business Wire, "U.S. Women and Minority Scientists Discouraged from Pursuing STEM Careers, National Survey Shows," March 22, 2010. https://www.businesswire.com/news/home/20100322006410/en/U.S.-Women-Minority-Scientists-Discouraged-Pursuing-STEM
20. American Society of Civil Engineers, "Discouraging Women from STEM Careers Would Violate ASCE's Code of Ethics," July 1, 2019. https://www.asce.org/question-of-ethics-articles/jul-2019/
21. Public Broadcasting Services, "Why the STEM Gender Gap Is Overblown," April 17, 2015. https://www.pbs.org/newshour/nation/truth-women-stem-careers
22. Kristin J. Anderson and Campbell Leaper, "Meta-Analysis of Gender Effects on Conversational Interruption: Who, What, When, Where, and How?" *Sex Roles*, August 1998.
23. Sally D. Farley, "Nonverbal Reactions to Conversational Interruption: A Test of Complementarity Theory and the Status/Gender Parallel," *Journal of Nonverbal Behavior*, December, 2010.
24. Elizabeth Aura McClintock, "The Psychology of Mansplaining," *Psychology Today*, March 31, 2016. https://www.psychologytoday.com/us/blog/it-s-man-s-and-woman-s-world/201603/the-psychology-mansplaining
25. Ibid.
26. Phil Baker, "Mansplaining Is Something Men and Women Are Guilty of Doing," *Executive Style*, April 16, 2018. http://www.executivestyle.com.au/mansplaining-is-something-men-and-women-are-guilty-of-doing-h0yszg
27. Caroline Turner, "Mansplaining and Womansplaining: When Women Talk Down to Men," *Huffington Post*, December 6, 2017. https://www.huffingtonpost.com/caroline-turner/mansplaining-and-womanspl_b_9995262.html
28. Jillian Kramer, "Female Leaders Who Behave Like Men Are Seen as Bossy," *Glamour*, December 6, 2016. https://www.glamour.com/story/female-leaders-who-behave-like-men-are-seen-as-bossy
29. Rebecca Solnit, "Men Explain Tings to Me," *Guernica*, August 20, 2012. https://www.guernicamag.com/rebecca-solnit-men-explain-things-to-me/
30. Sady Doyle, "10 Years Ago, the Internet Gave Us 'Mansplain.' Let Me, a Woman, Explain Why It Still Matters," *Elle*, March 2, 2018. https://www.elle.com/culture/a19057864/mansplain-10-years-old-internet/

31. Liz Cookman, "Allow Me to Explain Why We Don't Need Words like 'Mansplain'," *The Guardian*, February 12, 2015. https://www.theguardian.com/media/mind-your-language/2015/feb/12/allow-me-to-explain-why-we-dont-need-words-like-mansplain
32. Ibid.
33. Annie-Rose Strasser, "Why We Need to Stop Mansplaining." *Think Progress*, March 3, 2013. https://thinkprogress.org/viewpoint-why-we-need-to-stop-mansplaining-773e26d533a0/
34. William Pollack, *Real Boys: Rescuing Our Sons from the Myths of Boyhood*. Owl Books, Harrisburg, PA, 1999.
35. Ibid., p. 11.
36. Ibid., pp. 23–25.
37. Whether gay men can be bros will be explored in the final section of this chapter and then again in the chapter on politics and bros.
38. Ilene Prusher, "Trump Judges Women By Their Bodies. Do You?" *CNN*, November 5, 2016. https://www.cnn.com/2016/11/04/opinions/trumps-1-to-10-scale-is-nothing-new-for-women-prusher/index.html
39. Don W. Stacks et al., *International Encyclopedia of the Social & Behavioral Sciences*, second edition, *Science Direct*, 2015.
40. G. Gerbner, L. Gross, M. Morgan, N. Signorielli, "Living with Television: The Dynamics of the Cultivation Process". In J. Bryant, D. Zillman (Eds.), *Perspectives on Media Effects*. Lawrence Erlbaum Associates, Hilldale, NJ, 1986, pp. 17–40.
41. Jan Van den Bulck, "Is the Mainstreaming Effect of Cultivation an Artifact of Regression to the Mean?" *Journal of Broadcasting & Electronic Media*, Vol. 47, 2003, pp. 289–295.
42. Sacraparental, Blog site for parents, "The Maisy Test: 4 Questions to Expose Sexism in Kids' TV Shows and Movies," July 15, 2015. http://sacraparental.com/2015/07/14/sexism-in-kids-tv-shows-and-movies-what-to-look-for-and-what-to-do-about-it/
43. Jill O'Rourke, "This Blogger Created a Test to Help Parents Spot Sexism in Kids' Programming," *A Plus*, April 13, 2017.
44. Ibid.
45. M. Gotz, O. Hoffmann, et al., "Gender in Children's Television Worldwide," A Media Analysis in 24 Countries," *Televizion*, 2008.
46. Ibid.
47. Laura K. Zimmerman, "Preschoolers' Perception of Gendered Toy Commercials in the U.S.," *Journal of Children and Media*, Vol. 11, March 2, 2017, pp. 119–131.
48. Caroline Knorr, "Gender Stereotypes Are Messing with Your Kid," *Common Sense Media*, June 19, 2017. https://www.commonsensemedia.org/blog/gender-stereotypes-are-messing-with-your-kid
49. Common Sense Media, "Watching Gender: How Stereotypes in Movies and on TV Impact Kids' Development," June 19, 2017. https://www.commonsensemedia.org/research/watching-gender
50. Rachel Siegel, "Tweens, Teens, and Screens: The Average Time Kids Spend Watching Online Videos Has Doubled in 4 Years," *The Washington Post*, October 29, 2019.
51. The American Academy of Pediatrics, "Media Use in School-Aged Children and Adolescents," November 2016. https://pediatrics.aappublications.org/content/138/5/e20162592

52. Ibid.
53. Maggie A. Brennan, Christopher E. Lalonde, Jody L. Bain, "Body Image Perceptions: Do Gender Differences Exist?" *The International Honor Society in Psychology*, Vol. 15, Issue 3, Fall 2010. https://web.uvic.ca/~lalonde/manuscripts/2010-Body%20Image.pdf
54. A. Feingold, R. Mazzella, "Gender Differences in Body Language," *Psychological Science*, Vol. 9, July 1998, pp. 190–195. http://web.psych.ualberta.ca/~varn/bc/Feingold.htm
55. National Institute of Mental Health report on Eating Disorders, November, 2017. https://www.nimh.nih.gov/health/statistics/eating-disorders.shtml
56. Katharine A. Phillips, David J. Castle, "Body Dysmorphic Disorder in Men," *BMJ*, 2001 November 3; 323(7320).1016, November 3, 2001.
57. Rani Molla, "Poor Kids Spend Nearly 2 Hours More on Screens Each Day than Rich Kids," *Vox*, October 29, 2019. https://www.vox.com/recode/2019/10/29/20937870/kids-screentime-rich-poor-common-sense-media
58. Belinda Luscombe, "Kids Believe Gender Stereotypes by Age 10, Global Study Finds," *Time Magazine*, September 20, 2017.
59. Robert Blum, Kristin Mmari, Caroline Moreau, "It Begins at 10: How Gender Expectations Shape Early Adolescence Around the World," *Journal of Adolescent Health*, Vol. 10, Issue 4, Supplement, S3–S4, October, 2017.
60. The intersection of music and sexism will be the focus of a later chapter where more depth will be given to the influence of music in boys' and men's lives.
61. 2 Chains, Lyrics to "No Lie," 2012. https://genius.com/2-chainz-no-lie-lyrics
62. Cardi B, 21 Savage, "Bartier Cardi," 2017. https://genius.com/Cardi-b-bartier-cardi-lyrics
63. Dorian Lynskey, "Blurred Lines: The Most Controversial Song of the Decade," *The Guardian*, November 13, 2013. https://www.theguardian.com/music/2013/nov/13/blurred-lines-most-controversial-song-decade
64. Ibid.
65. Ibid.
66. World Health Organization, 6C51, Gaming Disorder. https://icd.who.int/dev11/l-m/en#/http%3a%2f%2fid.who.int%2ficd%2fentity%2f1448597234
67. Christina Gough, "Distribution of Computer and Video Gamers in the United Sates from 2006 to 2019," *Statistica*, July 3, 2019. https://www.statista.com/statistics/232383/gender-split-of-us-computer-and-video-gamers/
68. Jessamy Gleeson, Vitriolic Abuse of Anita Sarkeesian: Why the Games Industry Needs Her," *The Conversation*, September, 2014. http://theconversation.com/vitriolic-abuse-of-anita-sarkeesian-why-the-games-industry-needs-her-31826
69. Katharine Schulten, "How Sexist Is the Gaming World?" *The New York Times*, October 17, 2014. https://learning.blogs.nytimes.com/2014/10/17/how-sexist-is-the-gaming-world/
70. Emily Todd VenDerWerff, "#Gamergate: Here's Why Everybody in the Video Game World Is Fighting," *Vox*, October 13, 2014. https://www.vox.com/2014/9/6/6111065/gamergate-explained-everybody-fighting
71. K. Driesmans, L. Vandenbosch, S. Eggermont, "Playing a Videogame with a Sexualized Female Character Increases Adolescents' Rape Myth Acceptance and Tolerance Toward Sexual Harassment," *Games Health Journal*, April, 2015.
72. Alessandro Gabbiadini, Paolo Riva, Luca Andrighetto, Chiara Volpata, Brad J. Bushman, "Acting Like a Tough Guy: Violent-Sexist Video Game Characters, Masculine Beliefs, & Empathy for Female Violence Victims," April 13, 2016. http://journals.plos.org/plosone/article?id=10.1371/journal.pone.0152121

73. Alexandra Sifferlin, "Here's What Sexist Video Games Do to Boys' Brains," *Time Magazine*, April 13, 2016. http://time.com/4290455/heres-what-sexist-video-games-do-to-boys-brains/
74. Ibid.
75. Again, like other categories in this chapter, the influence of pornography in boys' and men's lives will be taken up in detail in a later chapter.
76. American Psychological Association, "Age of First Exposure to Pornography Shapes Men's Attitudes toward Women," August 3, 2017. http://www.apa.org/news/press/releases/2017/08/pornography-exposure.aspx
77. Ibid.
78. American College of Pediatrics, "The Impact of Pornography on Children," June, 2016. https://www.acpeds.org/the-college-speaks/position-statements/the-impact-of-pornography-on-children
79. Ibid.
80. Ibid.
81. Alexandra Katehakis, "Effects of Porn on Adolescent Boys," July 28, 2011. https://www.psychologytoday.com/us/blog/sex-lies-trauma/201107/effects-porn-adolescent-boys
82. Stuart Jeffries, Interview: "Psychologist Philip Zimbardo: 'Boys Risk Becoming Addicted to Porn, Video Games, and Ritalin'," *The Guardian*, May 9, 2015. https://www.theguardian.com/lifeandstyle/2015/may/09/philip-zimbardo-boys-are-a-mess
83. Ibid.
84. Southern Poverty Law Center. https://www.splcenter.org/fighting-hate/extremist-files/group/proud-boys
85. Jane Coaston, "The Proud Boys, the Bizarre Far-Right Street Fighters Behind Violence in New York Explained," *Vox*, October 15, 2018. https://www.vox.com/2018/10/15/17978358/proud-boys-gavin-mcinnes-manhattan-gop-violence
86. Southern Poverty Law Center. https://www.splcenter.org/fighting-hate/extremist-files/group/proud-boys
87. Gavin McInnes, "Everything I Learned in College Was a Lie," *Taki's Magazine*, July 19, 2013. http://archive.is/bKK5u
88. Alexandra Hall, "The Proud Boys: Drinking Club or Misogynist Movement?" *To the Best of Our Knowledge*. https://www.ttbook.org/interview/proud-boys-drinking-club-or-misogynist-movement
89. Ibid.
90. Ibid.
91. Hailey Branson-Potts, Richard Winton, "How Eliot Rodger Went from Misfit Mass Murderer to 'saint' for Group of Misogynists and Suspected Toronto Killer," *Los Angeles Times*, April 26, 2018. http://www.latimes.com/local/lanow/la-me-ln-elliot-rodger-incel-20180426-story.html
92. Ibid.
93. Ibid.
94. Perrie Samotin, Lilly Dancyger, "Incels: Breaking Down the Disturbing, Thriving Online Community of Celibate Men," *Glamour*, April 26, 2018. https://www.glamour.com/story/what-is-incel-breaking-down-online-community-celibate-men
95. Cortney A. Franklin, "Sorority Affiliation and Sexual Assault Victimization," *Violence Against Women*, November, 2015.
96. Cortney A. Franklin, Pratt, Travis C. Bouffard, Leana Allen, "Sexual Assault on the College Campus, Fraternity Affiliation, Male Peer Support, and Low Self Control," *Criminal Justice and Behavior*, November, 2012.

28 Chapter 1

97. Jeffrey B. Kingree, Martie P. Thompson, "Fraternity Membership and Sexual Aggression: An Examination of Mediators of the Association," *Journal of American College Health*, March 2013.
98. This section will be taken up again in Chapter 9 when covering Milo Yiannopoulos and the phenomenon of gay men joining the alt-right.
99. Amit Taneja, "From Oppressor to Activist: Reflections of a Feminist Journey," In Shira Tarrant (Ed.), *Men Speak Out*, second edition, Routledge, New York, 2013.
100. Jamie Tabberer, "Gay Men Like Me Need to Start Acknowledging Our Misogyny Problem," *Independent*, July 27, 2017. https://www.independent.co.uk/voices/gay-men-lgbt-50th-anniversary-misogyny-rupaul-drag-race-fishy-queen-lesbians-a7862516.html
101. Rose McGowan, "On the Need for More Gay Male Feminists," *Advocate*, November 5, 2014. https://www.advocate.com/commentary/2014/11/05/op-ed-rose-mcgowan-need-more-gay-male-feminists
102. Breeanna Hare, "Rose McGowan Apologizes to Gay Community," *CNN Entertainment*, November 6, 2014. http://www.cnn.com/2014/11/06/showbiz/celebrity-news-gossip/rose-mcgowan-gay-apology/index.html
103. Patrick Strudwick, "Yes, There Is Misogyny among Gay Men – But Our Sexist World Is the Problem," *The Guardian*, November 6, 2014. https://www.theguardian.com/commentisfree/2014/nov/06/misogyny-gay-men-sexist-rose-mcgowan-rights-women
104. Ibid.
105. Joseph Chamie, "Sexual Harassment: At Least 2 Billion Women," *Global Issues*, February 1, 2018. http://www.globalissues.org/news/2018/02/01/23899
106. Ibid.
107. Lyn Yonack, "Sexual Assault Is about Power," *Psychology Today*, November 14, 2017. https://www.psychologytoday.com/us/blog/psychoanalysis-unplugged/201711/sexual-assault-is-about-power

2 BRO CULTURE IN THE AGE OF #METOO

> **Key Points**
> - The Power-Threat Model of Sexual Harassment
> - Quid-Pro-Quo Sexual Harassment
> - Sexual Harassment and Title VII
> - Street Harassment
> - Panic Buttons for Hotel Workers
> - Socioeconomics and Contrapower Sexual Harassment
> - Sexual Harassment as Sexual Drive and Conformity to Sexual Scripts
> - The Dark Triad Personality
> - The Tough Guise
> - Reproductive Competition
> - A Hybrid Model of Sexual Harassment
> - Time's Up and the Emergence of #himtoo
> - Race, Ethnicity, and Socioeconomics
> - LGBTQ Sexual Harassment or Can LGBTQ Individuals Be Bros?
> - Implied Consent v. Explicit Consent
> - "Yes Means Yes" and Affirmative Consent
> - Why Men Get Away with Sexual Harassment for So Long
> - Can Women Be Bros?
> - Men's Roles in the #metoo Movement

If bro culture is based on conformity to sexist beliefs and behaviors, the metoo movement is the long-awaited wake-up call bro culture has needed to challenge itself about the longstanding sexist socialization that informs boys and men that it is permissible to sexually harass women. Founded by civil rights activist Tarana Burke, the #metoo hashtag has become synonymous with women reclaiming the right of autonomy over their bodies from the sexual harassment and sexual assault perpetrated by men. In October of 2017, in a span of 24 hours, 4.7 million people used the #metoo hashtag on social media.[1] Unfortunately, bro culture is the antithesis of this wake-up call. Boys are taught, sometimes from very young ages, that their needs and desires should come first, and this precedent has a direct bearing on how boys begin to view and treat girls. A second instruction adolescent boys have been getting for generations is that they need to be assertive and even aggressive in their sexual pursuit of adolescent girls since they are told that there is a cultural protocol when it comes to sex: *boys should pursue girls; girls should not pursue boys*. The conflation of these two basic instructions creates a recipe for sexual harassment such that boys and men view it as *normal, flirtatious behavior* to utter sexually charged comments toward women, or to touch women without consent. One obvious problem is that a man's advances or harassing words and behaviors may not have been requested or welcomed, yet men expect their words and behaviors to be accepted as compliments, flirtation, or humor. Another problem with these behaviors is that when a woman does not respond as a man expects, bros will commonly aim sexist and homophobic slurs at her. This is perhaps the most conspicuous evidence that men who harass women believe they are entitled to women's bodies. A further problem is that men will often interpret a woman's silence after sexual comments as implicit consent. But there is nothing in silence that suggests a woman approved or enjoyed the sexual banter. If anything, silence often suggests an uncomfortable displeasure with the content and direction of a sexually charged advance, but again, too many men are conditioned to believe that chatting up women in a sexual way is part of a normal exchange between men and women.

This chapter will examine two things: why do men sexually harass women and why have men been able to get away with sexually harassing women for so long? There are two basic answers to the first question, which have been traditionally positioned as being competing answers: (1) that sexual harassment is about power, or, (2) that sexual harassment is about sexual desire. It is possible, of course, that sexual harassment involves both a power motive and sexual desire. Yet, many men believe that their sexually charged banter is innocent in nature. They come to this notion because, again, they have been instructed by older boys and men that what they view as flirtatious behavior is part of a normal verbal exchange with women, that "no harm was done," because no ill intent was present. In addition, this chapter will explore the intersectional nuances of sexual misconduct by examining whether members of LGBTQ communities and women can sometimes also practice the bro behaviors of sexual exploitation and how consent has been a muddled and contentious concept in bro communities throughout time. Ultimately, a challenge against sexual harassment, sexual assault, and rape is a challenge against patriarchy, whether the perpetrator of the sexual abuse is a man, woman, or a non-conforming individual.

THE POWER-THREAT MODEL OF SEXUAL HARASSMENT

In the wake of the #metoo movement, a multitude of articles and opinion pieces have been published that try to understand men's sexual harassment of women.[2,3] One of the most common explanations is that sexual harassment is about power. The argument goes that men will exert power over women by placing women in positions of sexual subordination because they feel they can. The most distilled form of sexual harassment as power is ***quid-pro-quo sexual harassment*** where a person in a position of power offers benefits to a subordinate in exchange for sexual favors. This form of sexual harassment is found most often between boss and employer, educator and student, coach and athlete, and other relationships where power-hierarchies are involved. A paradigm example of quid-pro-quo harassment was found in the sexual abuse of women perpetrated by film producer Harvey Weinstein, who not only used his power to make career promises to actresses who would permit his sexual advances, but also used threats of career death to those who refused his unwanted sexual behaviors.[4,5] In 2017, actresses Alyssa Milano and Mira Sorvino were the first to expose Weinstein's behaviors, while producer Peter Jackson confirmed that Sorvino was black-listed by Weinstein when she refused to cave-in to his sexual advances.[6,7]

The first thing to note is that the majority of sexual harassment, like other versions of sexual misconduct, is perpetrated by men, whether the victim is male or female.[8] This is not to say that female perpetrators do not exist, but that the majority of sexual violators are men. In fact, up to 57% of men report having perpetrated a sexually aggressive behavior against a woman in their lifetime.[9,10] Some of these men commit forcible rape and sexual assault while others admit to verbal intimidation, attempts to get a woman intoxicated for the purpose of sex, attempts to get a woman away from her friends and alone in an attempt to get sex, and attempts to coerce a woman in a variety of ways into giving them sex.[11]

Many who argue that sexual harassment is about power claim that men who enjoy and pursue power develop empathy –deficits toward others and are more apt to behave in impulsive ways. Writing for the *Harvard Business Review*, U.C. Berkeley psychologist Dacher Keltner points to studies that have documented how powerful men possess tendencies to sexually harass women.[12] Keltner describes these tendencies as manifesting in two ways: (1) overestimating the sexual interest of others toward them, and (2) sexualizing their work, meaning that they,

> ...[look] for opportunities for sexual trysts and affairs, leer inappropriately, stand too close, and touch for too long a period of time on a daily basis.[13]

Many of these behaviors constitute "testing the water" to see how women respond. But the main point is that they are using their power to get a desired response. Citing Milgram's famous obedience to authority studies, Keltner asserts that men of power often wield their authority knowing that the subject is in a precarious situation: submit or face consequences.

A predictive factor in power theories of sexual harassment is that the greater the gender disparity of the occupation or environment, the higher the rate of sexual harassment. For instance, since the film industry in Hollywood employs far more men than women in positions of authority, the power theory would predict higher rates of sexual harassment. In fact, here are the percentages of women who occupy executive positions in Hollywood:[14]

- 8% of directors
- 10% of writers
- 2% of cinematographers
- 24% of producers
- 14% of editors

With such disparities, the film and television industries are ripe for the consequences predicted by those who argue that sexual harassment is about power, while the #metoo movement has documented that filmmaker Harvey Weinstein's sexual abuse of women was only the tip of an iceberg.[15]

Sociologists Heather McLaughlin, Christopher Uggen, and Amy Blackstone note that while the stereotype of sexual harassment is of a male supervisor harassing a female subordinate, it is sometimes women in positions of authority who are targets of abuse.[16] The theory is that sexual harassment is seen by some men as an equalizer, motivated by control more than by sexual desire.[17] Sexually harassing women who possess power can serve as a humiliation that in the minds of these men, "put her in her place." This theory works well with bro culture, since bros bond around the idiom "bros before hoes." It is part of bro ideology that women primarily exist to look good and satisfy the sexual desires of men. But a woman who enjoys executive power is a threat to this model.

Writing for *The Wall Street Journal*, columnist Elizabeth Bernstein notes that the men who sexually harass women simply "amplify proclivities they already have."[18] Since there are plenty of men who do not sexually harass women, Bernstein's observation fits well with the idea that bro culture helps shape boys and young men into being sexual predators, since many boys are able to avoid bro culture and the toxic consequences that go with it. At the same time, a series of studies document that some of the men who abuse power by sexually harassing women are men who felt powerless in the past, but who now feel a sense of power by engaging in workplace sexual harassment.[19] The studies found that,[20]

- Low-power men placed in a high-power role showed the most hostility in response to a denied opportunity with a woman.
- Chronically low-power men and women given acute power were the most likely to say they would inappropriately pursue an unrequited workplace attraction.
- Having power over women increased harassment behaviors among men with chronic low power.

These findings support **the power-threat model of sexual harassment**, whereby men who feel they have little power compensate by sexually harassing women. This may also account for high rates of intimate-partner violence in the home. If men feel they have been denied power in other areas of their lives, these studies suggest that some will lash out toward victims who are more easily manipulated and abused in an attempt to acquire the power that eluded them so far in life.

One thing that makes sexual harassment so difficult to stop is that men of power use their power to intimidate the women being harassed. This intimidation may manifest as the threat of job loss, which has a silencing effect on victims and gives the harasser the assurance that his behaviors can continue unabated. If men who harass women lose confidence in their ability to harass women with impunity, we should expect to see less work-place sexual harassment, or at least more cautious versions of harassment that shy away from the more visceral forms. For this to happen, men in positions of authority must feel that there is a high likelihood for them to be outed, but this result can come about only if victims and bystanders feel comfortable reporting their unwanted encounters. Currently, for many victims, this is not the case.[21]

Yet another way that sexual harassment can be viewed through the lens of the power-threat model is when sexual harassment is classified as a form of bullying. From street harassment to work-place sexual harassment, many of the behaviors witnessed of men who harass women resemble bullying behaviors. There is, however, a legal distinction between sexual harassment and bullying, which is that sexual harassment is considered to be a form of discrimination that violates **Title VII of the Civil Rights Act of 1964**, while bullying is not.[22] Yet, if sexual harassment is about power, then its connection to bullying is more than a superficial resemblance. Writing for *The Guardian*, author Claire Potter notes that victims of both sexual harassment and bullying report intense fear in the presence of the abuser.[23] The uncertainty of knowing whether the abuser will escalate the abuse places the victim in a state of constant anxiety. Writing for the *Los Angeles Times*, David Lieberman adds that figures such as Harvey Weinstein and *Fox News* Chairman Roger Ailes were known for their cruelty and bullying long before they were exposed as sexual harassers of women.[24] Weinstein's brother "Bob" told the *Hollywood Reporter* that his brother's arrogance and cruelty led to name-calling that brought employees at *Miramax* to tears, while Ailes was famous for his verbal and emotional abuse of employees at *FOX*.[25] Injecting a sexual charge into their bullying, these men infamously harassed dozens of women, while using their power to escape justice for years.

Sheryl Sandberg, COO of Facebook and author of the best-selling book *Lean-in: Women, Work, and the Will to Lead*, reports that she has been the victim of workplace sexual harassment for years, but that the harassment receded as she attained higher positions of power.[26] Yet while serving as one of the most powerful women in corporate America, Sandberg remarks that she is still occasionally met with sexually harassing behaviors, but notes, "only by men who feel that they have more power than I do."[27]

Another common form of sexual harassment is **street harassment**, which women around the world report as a common experience they are forced to deal with, sometimes on a daily basis. Street harassment is the public, unwanted sexual advance usually, but not always, by a man toward a woman. In a study conducted by the international research organization *Promundo* on men from Egypt, Lebanon, Morocco, and Palestine, it was discovered that 31% of men from Lebanon and 64% of men from Egypt admit to having sexually harassed girls and women in public.[28] Other studies have documented that the vast majority of women across cities in Brazil, India, Thailand, and the U.K. have been subjected to street harassment.[29] In the U.S., 65% of women report having experienced street harassment.[30] What this shows is that bro culture is an international phenomenon and not simply an aberrant anomaly of middle-class, white men who pledge college fraternities. All over the world, men have demonstrated a profound lack of respect for women by treating women as sexual objects. With respect to objects, one does not have to consider its feelings or wellbeing, and one cannot feel empathy toward an object. That street harassment is about power can be shown by noting that men who street-harass women will lash out in anger when rejected by using gender and sexual slurs designed to demean a woman's humanity, while attempting to reclaim the man's damaged masculinity. The slur is used to state, "how dare you reject someone who is your superior!"

University of Michigan professor of human sexuality studies Betsy Crane remarks that men are taught throughout their lives that they are entitled to women's bodies and that,

> Challenging a man in particular—we'll just use the heterosexual model—a woman challenging a man around anything is problematic to some degree. She can get called a bitch and she can get diminished in various ways.[31]

Male entitlement to women's bodies is one of the prime lessons of bro culture and a sense of entitlement is embedded in power hierarchies. Rejection is therefore viewed by men who have adopted this training as a subordinate individual being impudent to a superior, which explains the name-calling and threats. This abusive reaction by men also explains many incidents of intimate-partner violence. If a man has been taught that his opinions are more valuable than his partner's opinions, just the mere suggestion of disagreement by a woman in his life could be enough to set off an episode of abuse. Unsurprisingly, intimate-partner violence is a gender-unequal crime with women making up the vast majority of victims and men making up the vast majority of perpetrators worldwide.[32]

SOCIOECONOMICS AND CONTRAPOWER SEXUAL HARASSMENT

A point about sexual harassment not covered in most research is the fact that those who are living close to the poverty line or in blue-collar jobs are victimized at greater rates than those from higher socioeconomic categories.[33] This fact about victimology and low-socioeconomic backgrounds fits perfectly with the power model of sexual harassment. In 2017, the Bureau of Justice Statistics conducted annual household surveys to determine how many individuals experienced sexual assault and rape over the previous six months. The Bureau's report is considered more comprehensive than crime statistics because victims often refrain from reporting incidences out of fear of reprisal. Based on their findings, out of every 100 incidences:[34,35]

84 are women
16 are men
66 are white
13 are black
15 are Latinx
44 are from household incomes of less than $25K per year
41 are from household incomes of more than $25K per year
59 are from self-reported urban areas
28 are from self-reported suburban areas
13 are from self-reported rural areas
77 are not reported to the police
23 are reported to the police

One study reported that rape-blame is more readily assigned to victims who come from low socioeconomic backgrounds than those who come from moderate-to-high economic backgrounds.[36] A common assumption among participants who responded to surveys was that those in lower socioeconomic classes were more culpable for their victimization because they were believed to be more promiscuous, as though somehow making less money makes one more sexually promiscuous.[37]

A report issued from the *U.S. Restaurants Opportunities Centers United* noted of restaurant servers that 80% of women and 70% of men report having been sexually harassed by coworkers, while 80% of women and 58% of men report being sexually harassed by customers.[38] Waiters and waitresses receive much of their income from customer tips in an industry where speaking up may cost a person money. Hospitality workers who clean hotel rooms are also routinely subjected to sexual harassment with 49% reporting that a hotel guest answered the door naked or otherwise exposed himself.[39] Sixty-five percent of cocktail servers at casinos report that a guest touched them without permission.[40] These occupations are overwhelmingly staffed by women who do not enjoy wealth or workplace power. The great preponderance of perpetrators in these cases are men. Harassment has become so commonplace that hotel workers have lobbied for **panic buttons** they can press to alert security that they are being harassed or are in danger of some sort.[41,42]

The Equal Employment Opportunity Commission (EEOC) conducted studies to determine the factors that place workers at risk for sexual harassment and noted that these factors create high-risk environments:[43]

- Language differences between perpetrators and victims
- Significant power disparities between employees and management
- Workplaces where women are a numerical minority in relation to men

- Reliance on customer satisfaction
- Isolated workspaces such as hotel housekeepers
- Alcohol consumption

Employers are responsible for securing harassment-free work environments, but service workers do not garner the same attention as Hollywood stars when their bodies are violated and workspaces are hostile. A revealing point about men who subscribe to bro behaviors, as we have defined them here, is that many prey upon service industry workers in the belief that they are easy targets who will not report abuse.

None of this is to say that those who enjoy power never experience sexual harassment aimed at them. In fact, in some cases, *contrapower sexual harassment* (sexual harassment perpetrated by someone with less power upon someone with more power) can be a fairly common occurrence. In a series of studies, researchers Eros DeSouza and A. Gigi Fansler found that almost one-third of students surveyed admitted to having sexually harassed at least one of their professors, although male students were much more likely to be perpetrators than were female students.[44] In these cases, there are multiple power-dynamics at work, since white male students may feel more entitled to pursue sexual advances of female professors than female students of color might feel pursuing sexual advances with a white, male professor. If power is the central motivation of sexual harassment and other forms of sexual misconduct, then an individual's intersectional identities would be expected to inform who perpetrates and who is victimized.

SEXUAL HARASSMENT AS SEXUAL DRIVE AND CONFORMITY TO SEXUAL SCRIPTS

Writing for *Psychology Today*, psychologist Noam Shpancer notes that there are three factors that contribute to men's sexual harassment of women:[45]

1. Men have the physical ability to do so because, on average, they have greater size and physical strength.
2. Sex drive is linked to testosterone.
3. Acts of dominance and violence are ways that males attract and protect their mates.

Shpancer is not arguing the antiquated view that might makes right, but rather that there are biological factors that influence men's sexual behaviors. The argument is fairly straight-forward: men on average have greater muscle mass allowing them to more effectively coerce women, that men have a higher sex drive than women, and that physical strength and aggression have been markers for sexual attraction for millennia. When you put these factors together, you have a recipe for greater rates of sexual harassment by men toward women than the other way around.

Testosterone has long been considered to be the biological marker for sexual desire, which may be a bit of an exaggeration. Sex drive has been linked to levels of testosterone as one of several factors that influence sexual desire and sexual satisfaction.[46,47] Men produce approximately 20 times the level of serum testosterone than do women.[48] This is not to say that all men have higher sex drives than all women, or that testosterone is the only factor determining sex drive. Factors including stress, work, family, sleep, diet, medical condition, age, and relationship issues can influence one's sex drive.[49] But research tends to agree that men, on average, experience higher sex drives than women.[50]

The third factor that dominant and aggressive men attract women is an archaic remnant of the trope, *nice guys finish last*. As men, it is common to hear, whether true or not, that women want *bad boys*. Traditionally, *bad boys* are men who appear to be dangerous, rebellious, and highly sexual. Clinical psychologist Vinita Mehta argues that the **dark triad personality** is found in men more than it is found in women and subsists of narcissism, psychopathy, and Machiavellianism, which is typified by a cynical disregard for morality and an overarching focus on self-interest.[51,52] Mehta notes that men who are Machiavellian in nature tend to be manipulative, coercive, and sexually promiscuous, the archetype of bro training.[53]

Studies conducted by Gregory Louis Carter of the University of Durham were undertaken to discover whether more women found this dark triad personality more attractive than the control group.[54] Carter presented 128 female undergraduates with descriptions of two men, one possessing the dark triad personality and the other a control personality with the dark personality traits omitted.[55] Factors such as wealth and education were left out of the description to guard against bias. The study found that women were, in fact, more attracted to the dark triad personality man than they were the control man. Carter and his team theorize that women may be more attracted to the dark triad personality due to the fact that men of this kind are manipulative while at the same time effectively charming.[56]

Another study conducted by Ghent University professor Eveline Vincke found that young men who smoke tobacco and drink alcohol create short-term attractiveness benefits in mating contexts.[57] Vincke explains that men will often attune their courtship behaviors to what they believe to be female desires. This finding is consistent with what anti-violence educator Jackson Katz terms **the tough guise,** a performance some men will adopt to appear tough, cool, dangerous, and aloof to attract women and to receive validation from their peers.[58] If boys and young men believe girls and women are attracted to tough, apparently dangerous men, it makes sense that they would assume this persona, whether this persona conforms to who they actually are or not.

In fact, several studies have shown that risk-taking behaviors by men often result in short-term attractiveness to women.[59,60,61] The needle men of this kind attempt to thread with these behaviors is to appear to be cool, tough, and somewhat dangerous, while also trying not to appear too dangerous. One study noted that men will take more risks specifically when they are around women as though it is part of their courting ritual to seem impervious to danger.[62] Evolutionary psychologists view these behaviors as part of **reproductive** *competition*, a notion that extends to animal courting rituals often used by males of a species to ward off competing males. The goal is to appear sexually attractive to females and dangerous to other males.

> **Thought Box**
>
> Think about or list the number of male protagonists in movies who fit the dark triad personality model. Although fictional, a paradigm dichotomy may be found in the character of Captain
> Jack Sparrow of the *Pirates of the Caribbean* series of films when positioned against the more empathic and romantic character Will Turner played by Orlando Bloom. Gregory Louis Carter's research suggests that more women will be attracted to Sparrow than to Turner. Do you believe this to be so or is this simply a stereotype? Explain.

But this dark triad personality is also commonly found in the bro playbook, which is a social script that has long been part of bro culture: the normative view that men *should* aggressively pursue sex with women, while periodically shifting between charm, elusiveness, the appearance of danger, and sexual dominance. For some bros, this amounts to a game of trying to keep women guessing in the hope that the intrigue coupled with the dangerous bad-boy persona is enough to get women to submit sexually. On the flip side of the dark triad personality are boys and men who do not conform to this persona and who sometimes feel that they possess a disadvantage when it comes to attracting mates. But those who zealously pursue sex with women have been instructed by broader culture that this is how men should behave, which is why some men seem surprised when there is pushback to their sexual harassment. One of the more common responses in the face of pushback is that the harassing behaviors were meant as a compliment or that they were simply trying to be funny and should not be taken seriously. But this is the same retort that bullies use when their boorish behavior is challenged. The strategy is to make the critic feel that he or she is the problem by not getting the joke.

University of Texas research scholar Beth A. Quinn adds that the trope "women tend to see harassment where men see harmless fun or normal gendered interaction" is one of the most common findings in sexual harassment research.[63] Men often refuse to see their behaviors as harassing due to the gendered training of bro culture, where objectification and attenuated empathy toward women is commonplace. The bro instruction about girls and women that begins in boyhood is centered around the notion of sex as acquisition, of sex as *taking something from women*. This mentality reinforces a "battle of the sexes" model of sex and gender relations that not only pits men *against* women, but also reinforces the idea to men that women should be viewed as objects that can and should be used.

A HYBRID MODEL OF SEXUAL HARASSMENT

Another way of viewing the causes of sexual harassment is through a hybrid model whereby men seek power over women, while also submitting to sexual desire. A series of studies beginning in 2004 led by psychologist Pamela Smith sought to understand the relationship between power and brain functioning.[64] The impetus for the studies came through conversations with friends who were asked about their jobs. The friends reported that as they were promoted, their empathy toward others changed. One individual stated that becoming a supervisor caused her to prioritize giving orders and getting results over concern for the wellbeing of employees even though prior to her promotion she was one of those employees.[65] Smith and her colleagues discovered that feelings of power are mainly subconscious with one of the side effects being that a person can perceive sexual interest by others that simply isn't there.[66] According to Smith and her research team, this false-positive perception may help explain many cases of workplace sexual harassment. Since the 1960s, sociologists have noted that people with less-power are more concerned about the mindset of those with more power rather than the other way around, since those with less power are economically dependent on decisions made by those who are more powerful.[67] Conversely, those with more power do not feel a dependence on less-powerful people and so empathy toward less-powerful people erodes.

In 2013, a group of scholars headed up by Jennifer Whitson and Joe Magee found that people in positions of power and authority are more goal-oriented and more likely to act on their goals "because the constraints that normally inhibit action are less psychologically present for them."[68] Magee notes that power leads people to objectify other people, to see them in instrumental terms.[69] When men are given power, the objectification of others leads to the sexual objectification of women and pursuing the goal of sexual satisfaction. Using Whitson's and Magee's wording, men in power conceptualize a goal – having sex with women – and act upon that goal by sexually harassing women who are employed in subordinate positions to themselves. This account means that sexual desire coupled with a decreased sense of empathy that comes with power-acquisition work together to create a sexual-harasser. Having power also lowers one's inhibitions that might otherwise prevent that person from acting in ways detrimental to others. The male harasser views women as sexual opportunities, while women are too often placed in the position of having to defend themselves, report the harassing behavior, and brace for the all-too-common backlash of being blamed or being called liars.

Another factor in a hybrid account of sexual harassment is that many men have been taught to conflate sex with power and aggression. One of the more common myths some men have adopted is the view that women find coercive or aggressive sex to be a turn-on. This result was discovered by a team of scholars led by Rush University professor of psychiatry, Ashton Lofgreen.[70] The study found that many men continue to believe that resistance to sex by women is part of a flirtatious game.[71] Belief in these sorts of myths can explain why so many men are astonished when accusations of sexual harassment are leveled against them. There is an assumption by these men that women expect men to be sexually assertive and that flirting and peppering their banter with sexual innuendo is something women want.

TIME'S UP AND THE EMERGENCE OF #HIMTOO

The splash page of the website for the organization *Time's Up* states, "The clock has run out on sexual assault, harassment and inequality in the workplace. It's time to do something about it."[72] Like #metoo, *Time's Up* is a movement grounded in solidarity with survivors of sexual assault and sexual harassment, as well as with those women who are expected to put up with indignities and offensive behaviors toward them by men in order to make a living. What makes *Time's Up* different than #metoo, according to filmmaker Christy Haubegger, is that it's about taking the next step, finding solutions to ending sexual harassment and creating workplace environments where,

> every human being deserves a right to earn a living, to take care of themselves, to take care of their families, free of the impediments of harassment and sexual assault and discrimination.[73]

The focus for *Time's Up* is on workplace equality, since these are spaces where women struggle to receive equal pay and where many single moms work to feed their families and pay their monthly bills. Without workplace protections, women, and especially low-income women, can be subjected to sexual abuse with little-to-no recourse, while living with the fear of losing their jobs if they report wrongdoing.

As with #metoo, *Time's Up* is viewed by many bros as an attack upon men instead of as an opportunity to rethink masculine norms and thereby improve relationships between men and women. Predictably and unfortunately, a backlash to #metoo and *Time's Up* has gained momentum under the banner **#himtoo**, which is to gender what "all lives matter" is to race-relations.[74] Since many bros victim-blame in the wake of reports of men's sexual harassment, assault, and rape, it may have been inevitable that a #himtoo movement would come about. Essentially, the #himtoo movement has materialized as the tagline of the men's rights movement, particularly in the wake of the allegations of sexual assault made by Christine Blasey Ford against then SCOTUS nominee Brett Kavanaugh.[75,76] Kavanaugh went on to be confirmed by the Senate and is now a Supreme Court Justice for life, while Christine Blasey Ford continues to live with death threats.[77] But at the time, Kavanaugh became the poster boy for alleged falsely accused men. The concern is that women can report allegations of misconduct against a man without evidence that serve to damage the man's career and livelihood. The #himtoo movement picked up even more momentum when an Oklahoma woman tweeted that her son would not go on solo dates out of the fear that he would be falsely accused of sexual misconduct "by radical feminists with an axe to grind."[78] In an interesting twist, her son, Navy veteran Pieter Hanson, responded that he was a "feminist ally" and would never support #himtoo.[79]

The #himtoo movement is consistent with the Trumpian strategy of labeling women who report sexual assault and rape as liars. When successful, this label can have the effect of silencing victims who realize that a report of rape or sexual assault can bring a torrent of scrutiny upon them, which can include intimidation, coercion, and actual threats.[80] This is the reason why so many cases of rape and sexual assault go unreported, which is precisely what rapists desire.

LGBTQ SEXUAL HARASSMENT OR "CAN LGBTQ INDIVIDUALS BE BROS?"

Sexual harassment is commonly aimed at members of LGBTQ communities and their stories of abuse against them have been coming out now for years. Surveys have shown that more than half of all individuals who identify as LGBTQ experience sexual harassment.[81] A University of Michigan survey found that LGBTQ students are nearly twice as likely to be sexually assaulted as their non-LGBTQ counterparts+.[82] According to the Centers for Disease Control, members of LGBTQ communities are at higher risk for sexual violence even though they make up a numerical minority when compared to non-LGBTQ individuals.[83] For instance, 37% of bisexual men experience rape, physical violence, or stalking by a partner compared to 29% of heterosexual men.[84]

A point made by many within LGBTQ communities is that while the #metoo movement has been empowering for many, it has focused mainly on white, wealthy, heterosexual, cis-gender women.[85] Other than the allegations brought against actor Kevin Spacey, reports of sexual harassment and sexual assault against high-profile LGBTQ individuals have not received the same visibility as the allegations against powerful, heterosexual men in the entertainment industry. This can leave many LGBTQ individuals feeling like their struggles and challenges do not matter in larger society and can also make LGBTQ individuals targets for abuse. Kristen Houser, Chief Public Affairs Officer at the National Sexual Violence Resource Center, states, "Bias and discrimination end up equaling secrecy and alienation, and when you don't have support systems…that often creates risk factors that people who inflict harm on others are seeking out."[86] As with cases of men raping women, same-sex rapists are empowered by the knowledge that victims will remain silent.

The problem becomes somewhat hidden in queer communities, according to one queer woman, "Sam," as part of a piece written about LGBTQ teens who face sexual assault, because sexual harassment, assault, and rape are ingrained in popular culture as a cis-gender-hetero-centered problem.[87] Sam states,

> How do you say to your friends, 'My girlfriend rapes me' when their only mental definition of rape is a man forcing his penis inside

a woman's vagina? How do you say you were assaulted when it comes back to the idea of 'that doesn't count?' Well, it does count.[88]

Bro culture is such a heteronormative culture that it can seem odd to view a bro as being LGBTQ, but nothing prevents this designation.

The question of whether LGBTQ individuals can be bros is obvious. Anyone can be a "bro" if we define bro behavior as involving a desire to sexually exploit others. Identifying as non-binary or as LGBTQ may serve as a challenge to traditional bro culture, but it does not automatically create people who care deeply about consent or the sexual autonomy of others. But because so much attention has been placed on the sexual harassment of women by cisgender, heterosexual men, a void exists in the research of sexual harassment, sexual coercion, sexual assault, and other forms of sexual violence against, and sometimes perpetrated by, members of LGBTQ communities.

BROS AND THE CONFUSION ABOUT CONSENT

In the foregoing section, we examined the question of whether members of LGBTQ communities can be bros. An ongoing problem appears to be that far too many bros do not understand or want to understand contemporary models of consent. When women, non-binary identifying individuals, LGBT, or heterosexual, male victims state that they did not consent to certain sexual behaviors, bros will often be skeptical because they have been raised on the notion of ***implied consent***, if they care about consent at all. Unlike **explicit consent**, implied consent is a feeling someone has that another person consents to sex without words being exchanged. The notion that *she wanted sex* is often simply a man interpreting behaviors without taking the necessary steps to ask and receive consent. Given that consent can be ambiguous, the **"yes means yes" campaign** was initiated to eliminate ambiguity and to assure that consent is always given explicitly by all parties. In 2014, California Governor Jerry Brown signed the nation's first affirmative consent standard for colleges and universities to use as guidance in sexual assault cases.[89]

Thought Box

Yes means Yes: In the *Washington Post*, writer Jaclyn Friedman argues that those who oppose "yes means yes" are mainly of another generation, but that young people support it.[90] Supporters claim that a verbal affirmation increases sexual accountability, while non-verbal affirmation opens the door to misinterpretations. Critics argue that "yes means yes" turns silent, implied consent into a potential sexual offense.[91] Others claim that verbal affirmation kills the spontaneity and romance of sex. However, those who criticize bro culture as a culture ripe for sexual assault commend "yes means yes" as a campaign that empowers women and discourages rape.[92] What do you think?

In a study, 145 male university students who identified as heterosexual were given questionnaires about sexual consent.[93] The results, according to Binghamton University psychologist Richard Mattson, showed that "men tended to confuse their perception that the woman was sexually interested with her consent to sexual intercourse."[94] Mattson notes that many men rely on "questionable sexual scripts" to interpret women's sexual intentions.[95] The result is that crossing sexual lines without consent is a problem for many men and not simply one or two bad apples. Mattson concludes, "within certain situations, a good many men may be prone to this kind of behavior."[96] These "situations" are all the more complicated with the use of alcohol, which Oxford University researcher David Robert Grimes terms "the most dangerous date-rape drug of them all."[97] In bro circles, alcohol use has longed been considered the best way to get women into compliance with a bro's desire for sex. The mixture of alcohol and problematic scripts that many young men have adopted about women's agency and sexual consent equals a common recipe for rape.

> **Thought Box**
>
> We have all seen the high-profile cases of sexual misconduct allegations aimed at film producer Harvey Weinstein, who co-founded Miramax Films and was without question one of the most powerful figures in Hollywood. Since the allegations surfaced, we have also learned that many Hollywood insiders knew about Weinstein's reputation and his attempts to harm the careers of women who refused his sexual advances.[98] Before reading the following section, why do you believe men like Weinstein get away with sexual misconduct for so long without anyone trying to stop them?

WHY MEN GET AWAY WITH SEXUAL HARASSMENT FOR SO LONG

Why do men sexually harass women? The quick and simple answer to this question is that men believe they can sexually harass women and get away with it. There are usually no cameras documenting their behaviors and much of the time, there are no witnesses who may object. When there are witnesses to the behaviors and the witnesses are other men, there is an unwritten male rule that states, "men do not rat out other men." In my second film, *The Bro Code: How Contemporary Culture Creates Sexist Men*, I called this phenomenon *the bro code of silence*.[99] From boyhood, men are taught to stick together through thick and thin. If a boy does something wrong, other boys who are witnesses to the action understand that it is an iron-clad rule of bro culture not to "tell on him" and not to "rat him out." In high school and college, the phrase that best captures this gender-alliance is *bros before hoes*, a nod to the notion that male alliances take precedence over male-female alliances.

Writing for *Vox*, Liz Plank notes that sexual harassers often band together under the notion that accusations are false reports by women who are disgruntled over any number of grievances or that they are looking for a payday.[100] In the aftermath of allegations of sexual harassment against FOX News personality Bill O'Reilly, fellow accused sexual harasser Donald Trump stated, "I don't think Bill did anything wrong," going on to call O'Reilly *a good person*.[101] In the adage, "It's not what you know, it's what you can prove," sexual harassers have the advantage if only because empirical proof is difficult to document when harassing behaviors are committed in private spaces. Yet, with the emergence of #metoo, women in larger numbers than ever before are coming forward to report abuse, and the numbers are making a difference. With class-action lawsuits, the number of victims get a jury's attention. In the case of Harvey Weinstein, 90 separate women came forward to report his abuse.[102] It is worth noting, however, that many of these victims are high-profile women in Hollywood and their collective prominence carried weight in dethroning Weinstein from his place of power and control. In the vast majority of cases of sexual misconduct, the women who are victimized do not possess the power to unseat a perpetrator or perpetrators. Institutional or business policies may have procedures for investigating claims of sexual misconduct, but many victims have learned that *proof* can be difficult to document when the behaviors were conducted in private or bystanders refuse to get involved.

Another reason why men have gotten away with sexually harassing women for so long is that victims live in fear of being intimidated, blamed, and shamed for the abuse they suffered. As already covered, in the majority of cases, the abuser, who is typically a man, possesses power and authority over victims. This means that those who sexually harass others are confident that their behaviors will not be challenged or revealed. Sadly, harassers are correct. The EEOC reports that 75% of all workplace sexual harassment goes unreported.[103]

WHEN THE SEXUAL HARASSER IS A WOMAN, OR "CAN WOMEN BE BROS?"

There are two basic reasons why we do not hear about women who sexually harass others. First, it is rare. According to Genie Harrison, an attorney who specializes in workplace sexual harassment, "Men can be victims and women can be abusers, and I've represented victims where a woman was the harasser, but I would say it's at best a 99.9%-to-.01% ratio."[104] A second reason why we hear less about women who sexually harass others is that men are taught to be ashamed to be victims. In a patriarchal culture, men are taught to dominate, but to never allow someone to dominate them. This instruction converts into less reporting, less investigation, and less documentation. The EEOC reports that of the 6,758 complaints filed on sexual harassment, 16% were filed by men, but these reports do not identify the gender of the perpetrator.[105]

Todd Harrison, an attorney who litigates cases of sexual harassment, states that men feel embarrassed to report that they have been sexually harassed.[106] Men have been instructed by our culture that they should approach and pursue women but that a role reversal is viewed as cool. That is, many men will remark that they would love to have women flirting with them, because they do not view it as harassment. In one case where a man filed a complaint that his female boss was sexually harassing him, he reports that he was rebuffed and told to deal with it.[107] We do not know how many cases like this exist since as stated above, the EEOC does not document the gender of perpetrators, but the notion that men should *enjoy* a woman's sexual advance comes right out of the bro code, where men are always supposed to welcome sex. Most men know the bro rules surrounding sex and so feel ashamed and unmanly to report sexual harassment aimed at them. But if sexual harassment is mainly about power rather than sexual desire, there is no reason to assume that women who enjoy power would necessarily refrain from sexually harassing a subordinate simply because of their gender, and regardless of the gender of the victim.

In 2018, NYU found Dr. Avital Ronell responsible for sexually harassing her graduate student Nimrod Reitman.[108] After an 11-month Title IX investigation, Ronell was found to have created a hostile work environment through verbal and physical harassment.[109] A number of high-profile feminists signed a letter defending Ronell, stating,

> We testify to the grace, the keen wit, and the intellectual commitment of Professor Ronell and ask that she be accorded the dignity rightly deserved by someone of her international standing and reputation.[110]

But critics were quick to point out that defenses of these kind echo the sort of defenses offered to powerful men who commit the same violations. There were also concerns that a case of this kind where a woman with power is held responsible for harassing a man would undermine #metoo. Commenting about this case, Diane Davis of the University of Texas stated,

> I am of course very supportive of what Title IX and the #MeToo movement are trying to do, of their efforts to confront and to prevent abuses, for which they also seek some sort of justice. But it's for that very reason that it's so disappointing when this incredible energy for justice is twisted and turned against itself, which is what many of us believe is happening in this case.[111]

In the wake of the charges and the decision made by NYU to suspend Ronell for one-full academic year, some of the very same attacks were aimed at Reitman who leveled the allegations, asking why he took so long to file a complaint and why he reciprocated affection with Ronell if he was suffering?[112] Admittedly, a case where a woman was held responsible for sexually harassing a man is rare, but this case supports a finding that, even though rare, women can certainly be perpetrators of sexual misconduct and can perhaps qualify as bros.

MEN'S ROLES IN THE #METOO MOVEMENT?

A common question is "how should men respond to the #metoo movement?" The unfortunate direction most men have taken has been silence or open antipathy. Some men become defensive by taking the regrettable path of challenging the assumption that sexual predation is almost always committed by men. This is the unfortunate decision to defend men from being attacked, but in fact results in defending bad men who are predators. Another poor defense is reminding people that most men do not engage in sexually predatory behaviors, that most men are "good men." This strategy is unhelpful in creating any change in men's behaviors. That many men do not sexually exploit others does nothing to develop strategies to mitigate the behaviors of those who do. Furthermore, there are many men who do not engage in sexual harassment and other forms of sexual misconduct, but who participate in a culture of sexually objectifying women. Participation can be anything from going along with other men who make sexual comments about women without pushing back against their friends and associates out of the fear of being ostracized by the group, to the purchase and usage of pornography, to the silent participation of enjoying the perks of patriarchy without challenging a system that has permitted the sexual exploitation of women forever.

Jackson Katz, founder of *Mentors in Violence Prevention*, advises men to take a stand against the pervasive misogyny that emboldens sexual misconduct against women and others.[113] Transformative change, Katz argues, can occur only when men take action by speaking up against sexual harassment and other forms of sexual misconduct.[114] Actively standing against the sexual exploitation of others takes courage, since male friends and colleagues may push back against a challenge to change long entrenched behaviors. But it is this fear of backlash from other men that envelops and paralyzes a great number of men from speaking out and taking action. History will record whether the #metoo movement was a milestone moment in history that sparked a change in national and global consciousness on sexual exploitation, but a pervasive shift in consciousness in this area can take place only if bro behaviors are effective challenged by women and men working together to create a new awareness about and revision to predatory and sexually exploitative behaviors, and this revision begins with men being open and receptive to change.

POSTSCRIPT

Bro culture has been effectively called out by the #metoo movement. For millennia, boys have been trained to view girls and women as things that look pretty, hot, or sexy, or that bring them sexual enjoyment, but not as individuals with agency and commensurate value. A media culture of films, TV, games, music lyrics and videos has reinforced this training. As a result, it is with skepticism and cynicism that many men have responded to #metoo, which advises men to unlearn much of the sexist instruction given to them throughout life, and to replace it with the progressive view that women are autonomous agents who should be respected as authentic equals. At a minimum, #metoo asks men to simply stop sexually harassing and coercing women into actions that are unwelcomed and unwarranted. Some men are rising to this challenge, while other men are retreating into the regressive enclaves of pornography, misogynistic games and music, or other venues of patriarchal reinforcement that allow them to remain in a state of arrested development from a time in the past when misogyny was normalized and expected. But young women, in particular, are not clones of their mothers and grandmothers. There are indications that the future will not simply be a retread of the past. If young women expect more out of men, it will be incumbent upon young men to adapt, grow, and mature into men who view women as equals and not simply as sexual opportunities and subordinates. This change is all the more urgent given the fact that women are graduating college at higher rates than men and will be in positions of executive management and authority at levels never before witnessed. Men have serious choices ahead of them whether to remain in the adolescent patriarchy of bro culture that revels in physically and sexually oppressing women or to abandon bro culture for an adult world of genuine gender equality where men and women live together as partners.

Notes

1. Cassandra Santiago, Doug Criss, "An Activist, a Little Girl and the Heartbreaking Origin of Me Too," *CNN*, October 17, 2017. https://www.cnn.com/2017/10/17/us/me-too-tarana-burke-origin-trnd/index.html
2. Grant Hilary Brenner, "Why Do Certain Men Resort to Sexual Harassment?" *Psychology Today*, July 16, 2018. https://www.psychologytoday.com/us/blog/experimentations/201807/why-do-certain-men-resort-sexual-harassment
3. Olga Khazan, "Why Men Sexually Harass Women," *The Atlantic*, October 5, 2018. https://www.theatlantic.com/science/archive/2018/10/why-do-more-men-women-sexually-harass/572221/
4. Ronan Farrow, "From Aggressive Overtures to Sexual Assault: Harvey Weinstein's Accuser Tell Their Stories," *The New Yorker*, October 10, 2017. https://www.newyorker.com/news/news-desk/from-aggressive-overtures-to-sexual-assault-harvey-weinsteins-accusers-tell-their-stories
5. BBC Timeline of Weinstein Scandal, *BBC News*, February 24, 2020. https://www.bbc.com/news/entertainment-arts-41594672
6. Daniel Arkin, "Peter Jackson Seems to Confirm Weinstein Blacklisted Mira Sorvino, Ashley Judd," *NBC News*, December 15, 2017. https://www.nbcnews.com/storyline/sexual-misconduct/peter-jackson-seems-confirm-harvey-weinstein-blacklisted-mira-sorvino-ashley-n830166
7. Mira Sorvino, "Why I Spoke Out against Harvey Weinstein," *Time Magazine*, October 11, 2017. http://time.com/4978659/mira-sorvino-harvey-weinstein-sexual-harassment/
8. Office of Justice Programs, Office of Victims of Crime, "Gender of Perpetrator," June, 2014. https://www.ovc.gov/pubs/forge/tips_gender.html

9. A. Abbey, A.J. Jacques-Tiura, J.M. LeBeBreton, "Risk Factors for Sexual Aggression in Young Men: An Expansion of the Confluence Model," *Aggressive Behavior*, Vol. 37, 2011, pp. 450–464.
10. J.W. White, P.H. Smith, "Sexual Assault Perpetration and Reperpetration: From Adolescence to Young Adulthood," *Criminal Justice and Behavior*, Vol. 31, 2004, pp. 182–202.
11. Ibid.
12. Dacher Keltner, "Sex, Power, and the Systems that Enable Men like Harvey Weinstein," *Harvard Business Review*, October 13, 2017. https://hbr.org/2017/10/sex-power-and-the-systems-that-enable-men-like-harvey-weinstein
13. Ibid.
14. Martha M. Lauzen, "Boxed in 2017–18: Women on Screen and Behind the Scenes in Television," *Center for the Study of Women in Television and Film*, September 2018. https://womenintvfilm.sdsu.edu/wp-content/uploads/2018/09/2017-18_Boxed_In_Report.pdf
15. Glamour, "Post-Weinstein, These Are the Powerful Men Facing Sexual Harassment Allegations," *Glamour*, May 18, 2019. https://www.glamour.com/gallery/post-weinstein-these-are-the-powerful-men-facing-sexual-harassment-allegations
16. Heather McLaughlin, Christopher Uggen, Amy Blackstone, "Sexual Harassment, Workplace Authority, and the Paradox of Power," *American Sociological Review*, July 2, 2012. http://journals.sagepub.com/doi/abs/10.1177/0003122412451728
17. Ibid.
18. Elizabeth Sernstein, "Power's Role in Sexual Harassment," *The Wall Street Journal*, February 5, 2018. https://www.wsj.com/articles/powers-role-in-sexual-harassment-1517844769
19. Melissa J. Williams, Deborah H. Gruenfeld, Lucia E. Guillory, "Sexual Aggression When Power Is New: Effects of Acute High Power of Chronically Low-Power Individuals," *Journal of Personality and Social Psychology*, Vol. 112, Issue 2, 2017, pp. 210–223. http://psycnet.apa.org/doiLanding?doi=10.1037%2Fpspi0000068
20. Ibid.
21. Elyse Shaw, Ariane Hegewisch, Cynthia Hess, "Sexual Harassment and Assault at Work: Understanding the Costs," *Institute for Women's Policy Research*, October 15, 2018. https://iwpr.org/publications/sexual-harassment-work-cost/
22. Susan Strauss, "Bullying Vs. Sexual Harassment – Do You Know the Difference?" *Ms. Magazine*, November 15, 2011. http://msmagazine.com/blog/2011/11/15/bullying-vs-sexual-harassmentdo-you-know-the-difference/
23. Claire Potter, "Sexual Harassment Is about Power. Why Not Fight It as We Do Bullying?" *The Guardian*, February 10, 2018. https://www.theguardian.com/commentisfree/2018/feb/10/sexual-harassment-power-bullying-metoo
24. David Lieberman, "To End Sexual Harassment on the Job, End Workplace Bullying," *Los Angeles Times*, November 16, 2017. http://www.latimes.com/opinion/op-ed/la-oe-lieberman-bullying-bosses-20171116-story.html
25. Ibid.
26. Stav Ziv, "Sheryl Sandberg: Sexual Abuse Culture Us about Power, Would Change If Women Had More," *Newsweek*, December 7, 2017. https://www.newsweek.com/sheryl-sandberg-sexual-abuse-culture-about-power-would-change-if-women-had-741756
27. Ibid.
28. Malaka Gharib, "Why Do Men Harass Women? New Study Sheds Light on Motivations," *NPR*, June 15, 2017. https://www.npr.org/sections/goatsandsoda/

2017/06/15/532977361/why-do-men-harass-women-new-study-sheds-light-on-motivations
29. Ibid.
30. Ibid.
31. Coraline Pettine, "Rejected Men Lash Out Because of Threatened Masculinity, Entitlement," *Loquitor, Cabrini University*, February 23, 2018. http://www.theloquitur.com/rejected-men-lash-out-because-of-threatened-masculinity-entitlement/
32. World Health Organization, "Understanding and Addressing Violence against Women," 2012 Report: http://apps.who.int/iris/bitstream/handle/10665/77432/who_rhr_12.36_eng.pdf;jsessionid=A32A1DD3F212D948015E1C3266DBF081?sequence=1
33. Kathryn Casteel, Julia Wolfe, Mai Nguyen, "What We Know about Victims of Sexual Assault in America," *Five Thirty Eight*, September 21, 2018. https://projects.fivethirtyeight.com/sexual-assault-victims/
34. Ibid.
35. The numbers added together do not equal 100% in some cases due to some individuals not reporting their demographic classifications.
36. Bettina Spencer, "The Impact of Class and Sexuality-Based Stereotyping on Rape Blame," *Sexualization, Media, & Society*, April–June, 2016, pp. 1–8. http://journals.sagepub.com/doi/pdf/10.1177/2374623816643282
37. Ibid.
38. Stefanie K. Johnson, Juan M. Madera, "Sexual Harassment Is Pervasive in the Restaurant Industry. Here's What Needs to Change," *Harvard Business Review*, January 18, 2018. https://hbr.org/2018/01/sexual-harassment-is-pervasive-in-the-restaurant-industry-heres-what-needs-to-change
39. Dave Jamieson, "He Was Masturbating…I Felt Like Crying: What Housekeepers Endure to Clean Hotel Rooms," *Huff-Post*, November 20, 2017. https://www.huffingtonpost.com/entry/housekeeper-hotel-sexual-harassment_us_5a0f438ce4b0e97dffed3443
40. Ibid.
41. Keturah Gray, Lauren Effron, "Hotel Housekeepers Use Panic Buttons to Feel Safe on the Job," *ABC News*, April 20, 2018. https://abcnews.go.com/US/hotel-housekeepers-panic-buttons-feel-safe-job/story?id=54503215
42. Josh Eidelson, "Hotels Add 'Panic Buttons' to Protect Housekeepers from Guests," *Bloomberg*, December 13, 2017. https://www.bloomberg.com/news/articles/2017-12-13/hotels-add-panic-buttons-to-protect-housekeepers-from-guests
43. U.S. Equal Employment Opportunity Commission, "Select Task Force on the Study of Harassment in the Workplace," June 2016. https://www.eeoc.gov/eeoc/task_force/harassment/report.cfm#_Toc453686305
44. Eros DeSouza, A. Gigi Fansler, "Contrapower Sexual Harassment: A Survey of Students and Faculty Members," *Sex Roles*, Vol. 48 (June 2003), pp. 529–542. https://link.springer.com/article/10.1023/A:1023527329364
45. Noam Shpancer, "Why Do Men Sexually Assault? Sexual Violence against Women Manifests, rather than Violates, Society's Norms," *Psychology Today*, November 3, 2014. https://www.psychologytoday.com/us/blog/insight-therapy/201411/why-do-men-sexually-assault-women
46. Paul J. Rizk, Taylor P. Kohn, Alexander W. Pastuszak, Mohit Khera, "Testosterone Therapy Improves Function and Libido in Hypogonadal Men," *Current Opinion in Urology*. 27(6) November 2017, pp. 511–515. doi: 10.1097/MOU.0000000000000442

47. S.M. van Anders, "Testosterone and Sexual Desire in Healthy Women and Men," *Archives of Sexual Behavior*, December 2012, pp. 1471–1484. https://www.ncbi.nlm.nih.gov/pubmed/22552705
48. *Psychology Today* report on Testosterone. https://www.psychologytoday.com/us/basics/testosterone
49. Daniel Murrell, "Low Sex Drive: Common Causes and Treatment," *Healthline*, November 9, 2018. https://www.healthline.com/health/low-testosterone/conditions-that-cause-low-libido
50. Ibid.
51. Vinita Mehta, "Why Do Women Fall for Bad Boys?" *Psychology Today*, October 21, 2013. https://www.psychologytoday.com/us/blog/head-games/201310/why-do-women-fall-bad-boys
52. Ben Taylor, "Machiavellianism, Cognition, and Emotion: Understanding How the Machiavellian Thinks, Feels, and Thrives," *Psych Central*, October 8, 2018. https://psychcentral.com/lib/machiavellianism-cognition-and-emotion-understanding-how-the-machiavellian-thinks-feels-and-thrives/
53. Ibid.
54. Gregory Louis Carter, Anne C. Campbell, Steven Muncer, "The Dark Triad Personality: Attractiveness to Women," *Personality and Individual Differences*, June 2013.
55. Ibid.
56. Ibid.
57. Eveline Vincke, "The Young Male Cigarette and Alcohol Syndrome: Smoking and Drinking as a Short-Term Mating Strategy," *Evolutionary Psychology*, February 26, 2016. http://journals.sagepub.com/doi/full/10.1177/1474704916631615#sec-27
58. Will Conley, "Tough Guise: Violence, Media, and Masculinity's Crisis," *The Good Men Project*, November 8, 2011. https://goodmenproject.com/arts/tough-guise-violence-media-and-masculinitys-crisis/
59. J. Bassett, B Moss, "Men and Women Prefer Risk Takers as Romantic and Nonromantic Partners," *Current Research in Social Psychology*, Vol. 9, 2012, pp. 135–145.
60. S. Kelly, R. Dunbar, "Who Dares, Wins. Heroism versus Altruism in Women's Mate Choice," *Human Nature*, Vol. 12, 2007, pp. 89–105.
61. K. Sylwester, B. Pawłowski, "Daring to be Darling: Attractiveness of Risk Takers as Partners in Long- and Short-term Sexual Relationships," *Sex Roles*, Vol. 64, 2010, pp. 695–706. http://doi.org/10.1007/s11199-010-9790-6
62. M. Baker, J. Maner, "Risk-taking as a Situationally Sensitive male Mating Strategy," *Evolution and Human Behavior*, Vol. 29, 2016, pp. 391–395. Retrieved from http://doi.org/10.1016/j.evolhumbehav.2008.06.001
63. Beth A. Quinn, "Sexual Harassment and Masculinity: The Power and Meaning of Girl Watching," *Gender and Society*, Vol. 16, No. 3, June 2002, pp. 386–402. https://www.jstor.org/stable/3081785?seq=1#page_scan_tab_contents
64. Mary Slaughter, Khalil Smith, David Rock, "The Brain Science that Could Help Explain Sexual Harassment," *Quartz*, January 24, 2018. https://work.qz.com/1188071/powers-effects-on-the-brain-help-explain-sexual-harassment/
65. Ibid.
66. Ibid.
67. Ibid.
68. Jennifer A. Whitson, Katie A. Lijenquist, Adam D. Galinsky, Joe C. Magee, Deborah H. Gruefeld, Brian Cadena, "The Blind Leading: Power Reduces Awareness of Constraints," *Journal of Experimental Social Psychology*, Vol. 49,

Issue 3, May 2013, pp. 579–582. https://www.sciencedirect.com/science/article/pii/S0022103112002132
69. Ibid.
70. Sydney Pereira, "Why Do Men Think Women Want to Have Sex When They Don't? A New Study Explains Why," *Newsweek*, December 1, 2017. https://www.newsweek.com/rape-myths-prevail-causing-confusion-some-men-between-sexual-interest-and-727833
71. Ibid.
72. *Time's Up*, Official Website: https://www.timesupnow.com/
73. Alix Langone, "Difference between the 2 Movements – And How They're Alike," *Time Magazine*, March 22, 2018. http://time.com/5189945/whats-the-difference-between-the-metoo-and-times-up-movements/
74. #himtoo will be taken up again in Chapter 4 when covering the experience of men's silence and hostility to women's incremental increases of power.
75. Emma Grey Ellis, "How #HimToo Became the Anti #MeToo of the Kavanaugh Hearings," *Wired*, September 27, 2018. https://www.wired.com/story/brett-kavanaugh-hearings-himtoo-metoo-christine-blasey-ford/
76. The Kavanaugh hearing will be covered more thoroughly in the chapter on bros and politics.
77. Tim Mak, "Kavanaugh Accuser Christine Blasey Ford Continues Receiving Threats, Lawyers Say," *NPR*, November 8, 2018. https://www.npr.org/2018/11/08/665407589/kavanaugh-accuser-christine-blasey-ford-continues-receiving-threats-lawyers-say
78. Aja Romano, "How a Mom's "This Is My Son" Anti-Feminist Brag Went Viral – And Completely Backfired," *Vox*, October 9, 2018. https://www.vox.com/2018/10/9/17955402/this-is-my-son-meme-himtoo-metoo-pieter-hanson
79. Ibid.
80. Elizabeth Renzetti, "Why Women Who Are Sexually Assaulted Remain Silent," *The Globe and Mail*, October 31, 2014. https://www.theglobeandmail.com/news/national/why-women-who-are-sexually-assaulted-remain-silent/article21414605/
81. Julie Moreau, "Most LGBTQ Americans Experience Harassment, Discrimination, Harvard Study Finds," *NBC News*, November 26, 2017. https://www.nbcnews.com/feature/nbc-out/most-lgbtq-americans-experience-harassment-discrimination-harvard-study-finds-n823876
82. University of Michigan, Survey on Sexual Misconduct, 2015. https://publicaffairs.vpcomm.umich.edu/wp-content/uploads/sites/19/2015/04/Complete-survey-results.pdf
83. Centers for Disease Control, The National Intimate Partner and Sexual Violence Survey, "An Overview of 2010 Findings on Victimization by Sexual Orientation." https://www.cdc.gov/violenceprevention/pdf/cdc_nisvs_victimization_final-a.pdf
84. Ibid.
85. Alia E. Dastagir, "She Was Sexually Assaulted within Months of Coming Out. She Isn't Alone," *USA Today*, June 13, 2018. https://www.usatoday.com/story/news/2018/06/13/sarah-mcbride-gay-survivors-helped-launch-me-too-but-rates-lgbt-abuse-largely-overlooked/692094002/
86. Ibid.
87. Ana Valens, "LGBTQ Teens Face Sexual Assault at Higher Rates than Most," *Daily Dot*, October 30, 2017. https://www.dailydot.com/irl/sexual-assault-harassment-lgbtq/

88. Ibid.
89. End Rape on Campus declaration page. http://endrapeoncampus.org/yes-means-yes/
90. Jaclyn Friedman, "Adults Hate 'Yes Means Yes' Laws. The College Students I Meet Love Them," *The Washington Post*, October 14, 2015. https://www.washingtonpost.com/posteverything/wp/2015/10/14/adults-hate-affirmative-consent-laws-the-college-students-i-meet-love-them/?utm_term=.92802ac96b2a
91. Ibid.
92. Jaclyn Friedman, Jessica Valenti, *Yes Means Yes: Visions of Female Sexual Power and A World Without Rape*. Da Capo Press, New York, 2008.
93. Ashton M. Lofgreen, Richard E. Mattson, Samantha A. Wagner, Edwin G. Ortiz, Matthew D. Johnson, "Situational and Dispositional Determinants of College Men's Perception of Women's Sexual Desire and Consent to Sex: A Factorial Vignette Analysis," *Journal of Interpersonal Violence*, November 2, 2017.
94. Ashton M. Lofgreen, Richard E. Mattson, Samantha A. Wagner, "Situational and Dispositional Determinants of College Men's Perception of Women's Sexual Desire and Consent to Sex: A Factorial Vignette Analysis," *Journal of Interpersonal Violence*, November 2, 2017. https://journals.sagepub.com/doi/pdf/10.1177/0886260517738777
95. Ibid.
96. Ibid.
97. David Robert Grimes, "Alcohol Is By Far the Most Dangerous Date Rape Drug," *The Guardian*, September, 22, 2014. https://www.theguardian.com/science/blog/2014/sep/22/alcohol-date-rape-drug-facilitated-sexual-assault-dfsa
98. Josh Barro, "What 'Everybody Knew' about Harvey Weinstein Should Have Been Enough for Him to Face Consequences," *Business Insider*, October 10, 2017. https://www.businessinsider.com/harvey-weinstein-scandal-analysis-2017-10
99. The concept of a bro-code-of-silence will be the focus of Chapter 4.
100. Liz Plank, "The Bro Code that Makes Men Stick Together When They're Accused of Sexual Harassment," *Vo*, April 21, 2017. https://www.vox.com/identities/2017/4/21/15380146/bro-code-men-stick-together-sexual-harassment
101. Maggie Haberman, Matthew Rosenberg, Glenn Thrush, "Trump, Citing No Evidence, Suggests Susan Rice Committed Crime," *The New York Times*, April 5, 2017. https://www.nytimes.com/2017/04/05/us/politics/trump-interview-susan-rice.html
102. *BBC News*, "Harvey Weinstein Timeline: How the Scandal Unfolded," February 24, 2020. https://www.bbc.com/news/entertainment-arts-41594672
103. U.S. Equal Employment Opportunity Commission, Take Force Report on the Study of Harassment in the Workplace, June 2016. https://www.eeoc.gov/eeoc/task_force/harassment/upload/report.pdf
104. Marla Puente, "Women Are Rarely Accused of Sexual Harassment, and There's a Reason Why," *USA Today*, December 19, 2017. https://www.usatoday.com/story/life/2017/12/18/women-rarely-accused-sexual-harassment-and-theres-reason-why/905288001/
105. U.S. Equal Employment Opportunity Commission, Report on Sex-Based Harassment Allegations, 2010–2019. https://www.eeoc.gov/eeoc/statistics/enforcement/sexual_harassment_new.cfm
106. Peter Balonon-Rosen, Kimberly Adams, "One in 7 Men Say They've Been Sexually Harassed at Work," *Market Place*, March 9, 2018. https://www.marketplace.

org/2018/03/09/business/we-asked-if-youd-been-sexually-harassed-work-one-7-men-said-yes
107. Ibid.
108. Zoe Greenberg, "What Happens to #MeToo When a Feminist Is the Accused," *The New York Times*, August 13, 2018. https://www.nytimes.com/2018/08/13/nyregion/sexual-harassment-nyu-female-professor.html
109. Ibid.
110. Ibid.
111. Ibid.
112. Ibid.
113. Jackson Katz, "Why More Men Don't Stick Up for Women Who Are Being Sexually Harassed," *Time Magazine*, October 24, 2017. http://time.com/4993854/men-roles-sexual-harassment/
114. Ibid.

3
FRAT LIFE: A CONTINUUM FROM HONOR SOCIETIES TO TOXIC BRO-HOOD

> **Key Points**
> - Phi Beta Kappa
> - The Social Fraternities
> - The Divine Nine: Black Fraternities and Sororities
> - Ethnic & Religious Diversity in Greek Life
> - Benefits and Costs
> - Derby Days
> - Pledging
> - Hazing
> - Fraternity Men and Rape
> - Themed Parties & Gender Inequality
> - Frat-PAC
> - The Mitigating Effect of Multiculturalism
> - Theta Pi Sigma: An LGBTQIA, Gender-Inclusive Fraternity
> - Solutions

In a book entitled *The Bro Code*, it may be expected that college fraternities will be scrutinized as being toxic environments for both men and women, and this chapter will not disappoint. But not every fraternity is a haven for hazing, binge drinking, drugging, and sexual assault. A number of fraternities have taken a different approach and established themselves as places for progressive beliefs and behaviors. Delta Lambda Phi, for instance, was founded by gay men for all men.[1] They are joined by Alpha Nu, Kappa Psi Kappa, Nu Phi Zeta, and Sigma Phi Beta in providing fraternal organizations that are open and welcoming to young men of all ethnic backgrounds, cultures, and sexual orientations.[2] At Virginia Wesleyan College, the fraternity Sigma Nu has adopted the slogan "respect and fidelity," openly condemning the actions of those fraternities that prey upon women.[3] On the other hand, brothers from a chapter of Sigma Nu at the University of Central Florida were caught on tape chanting, "Let's rape some bitches."[4] Clearly, it's a mixed bag of attitudes and behaviors even within different chapters of the very same national fraternity.

It is also important to note that many young men never experience fraternity life. Some enter the workforce straight out of high school, while others join the military, and still others enroll at a college or university without pledging a fraternity. It isn't that these young men avoid bro culture altogether, but that they bypass organized fraternity life. They may very well hold some of the same attitudes and behaviors so often found among frat-bros, but the institutional surroundings will be different. But for those who pledge a fraternity, they enter a hierarchy that has been given an exemption to Title IX in order to allow gender exclusivity. The gender exclusivity they experience, coupled with other problematic elements that include copious amounts of alcohol, sexually themed parties, and a pervasive acceptance of rape-myth narratives often create toxic environments for women, but also for many of the young men themselves. There are risks and rewards for being a member of a fraternity and this chapter will examine both.

PHI BETA KAPPA

The very first college fraternity in America, Phi Beta Kappa, was established at the College of William & Mary in 1776.[5] Phi Beta Kappa was created with very different regulations than are found in today's fraternities. For instance, it was made up only of upper classmen and faculty members were actively involved in running the fraternity.[6] By 1875, women were admitted into Phi Beta Kappa and it was then and is today an academic honor society, rather than a social fraternity.[7] The secrecy associated with fraternities also existed with Phi Beta Kappa, but not for the reasons found today. Early Phi Beta Kappa members were interested in discussing all sorts of topics of which university officials disapproved.[8] Influenced by the rituals, symbols, and vows of secrecy of the Freemasons, the early members of Phi Beta Kappa were encouraged to view one another as *unalienable brothers* who were bound together for life.[9] As a result of this influence, initiation rituals and special handshakes were established by Phi Beta Kappa's early members.[10] Today, Phi Beta Kappa continues to be a premiere honors society with member requirements including a minimum 3.75 GPA through 90 units, or to be in the top 10% of a student's class.[11] Given that Phi Beta Kappa is considered to be the premiere academic honor society that rewards top students in 286 colleges and universities throughout America in the liberal arts through the sciences,[12] it is remarkable that the fraternities that became known for socializing and later party-culture began by modeling themselves after Phi Beta Kappa.

It should be noted that even in the case of honors-based fraternities and sororities that reward academic excellence, there has been criticism. In the 1960s and 1970s, many students turned down Phi Beta Kappa's invitation citing elitism.[13] Today, enrollment is down due mainly to students either not seeing the point of joining or students simply not being familiar with Phi Beta Kappa.[14] But the charges of elitism mirror sentiment found in some around the country who view academia as elitist and who openly eschew intellectualism.[15] For these, there are plenty of fraternal options that do not emphasize academics.

THE SOCIAL FRATERNITIES

By the early-to-mid 19th century, fraternities became associated with friendship and brotherhood rather than academics.[16] The first fraternity of this type was **Kappa Alpha Society**, founded in 1825, which is considered to be the forbearer of the modern fraternity where young men pledge into a secret brotherhood.[17] It was mainly a social fraternity, rather than an honors society. Students were attracted to it, while faculty opposed it.[18] This was an opportunity for young men to gather in social settings without the oversight of faculty or university officials.

The first national fraternity was **Sigma Phi**, which began in 1831 at Hamilton College, New York.[19] By 1833, the **Order of Skulls and Bones** was organized at Yale University as a secret society, which exists to this day.[20] As of 1992, members are both men and women, and alumni include former Secretary of State John Kerry, and former presidents George H.W. Bush, George W. Bush, and William Howard Taft.[21] Like most fraternal orders, members are sworn to secrecy for life.[22]

In the early 20th century, fraternities had become associated with social clubs. In fact, many fraternities of this era would meet in pubs or taverns instead of lavish fraternity houses.[23] The one development, therefore, that helped to create the modern social fraternity was off-campus housing. The first frat-house was located at the University of Michigan in 1846.[24] Affiliated with the Alpha Epsilon chapter of Chi Psi, the house was located in the woods, which provided the pledges with the seclusion they desired to undertake their activities in secret.[25] Today, frat-houses are owned by a corporation of alumni, the sponsoring national organization, or in some cases, the host college.[26] Some universities have attempted to initiate rules and regulations on frat-house events such as prohibitions on alcohol, but these attempts have been almost universally unsuccessful or limited to success in some fraternities and not others. As a result of these failures and the surrounding culture that instructs young men that women should be viewed primarily as sexual opportunities, many frat-houses today have become synonymous with sexually themed parties, intoxication, hazing, sexual harassment, sexual assault, and rape.

THE DIVINE NINE: BLACK FRATERNITIES AND SORORITIES

Known as "The Divine Nine," there are nine college fraternities and sororities that are historically Black Greek organizations:[27]

- Alpha Phi Alpha Fraternity, Founded 1906, Cornell University
- Alpha Kappa Alpha Sorority, Founded 1908, Howard University
- Kappa Alpha Psi Fraternity, Founded 1911, Indiana University
- Omega Psi Phi Fraternity, Founded 1911, Howard University
- Delta Sigma Theta Sorority, Founded 1913, Howard University
- Phi Beta Sigma Fraternity, Founded 1914, Howard University
- Zeta Phi Beta Sorority, Founded 1920, Howard University
- Sigma Gamma Rho Sorority, Founded 1922, Butler University
- Iota Phi Theta Fraternity, Founded 1963, Morgan State University

Historically Black fraternities and sororities were designed to help young, Black men and women succeed academically and professionally. Alumni from Black Greek Letter Organizations (BGLO) include writers, social activists, educators, civil rights leaders, and professional athletes.[28] They were created because White fraternity and sorority members did not allow Black students to pledge the already established fraternities and sororities.[29] Today, the goals of academic and professional success are still in place, but many of the pitfalls found in White fraternities have plagued the Divine Nine as well. For instance, hazing has been an ongoing problem for historically Black fraternities.[30] In 2014, at the University of Georgia, 11 Black fraternity men were arrested for physically assaulting recruits.[31] At Youngstown State University, nine men were indicted on charges of hazing after two recruits were beaten so badly, they had to be hospitalized.[32]

A different kind of criticism emerged in a piece written for the London School of Economics' U.S. Centre entitled, "How Black Fraternities Are Actually Harmful to Black Culture," wherein Claflin University scholar Ali D. Chambers argues that Black fraternities have become a vehicle for Black men to assimilate into White culture and have also created a self-perpetuating Black oligarchy.[33] Chambers quotes the famous Black historian and sociologist W.E.B. DuBois,

> Our college man today is, on the average a man untouched by real culture. He deliberately surrenders to selfish and even silly ideals, swarming into semiprofessional athletics and Greek letter societies…we have in our colleges a growing mass of stupidity and indifference.[34]

Chambers uses this quote to argue that BGLOs promote conformity to Western values and social norms, that the intension in creating BGLOs was to help young, Black men assimilate into White culture in order to succeed in a largely white-supremacist nation. Chambers also argues that BGLOs create hierarchies by elevating a Black bourgeois class within greater Black culture.[35] The result, according to Chambers, is a suppression of authentic African characteristics and a conformity to White community's "preoccupations, prejudices, and desires."[36] In Chambers' opinion, Black fraternities have perpetuated White supremacy.

In rebuttal, Dwayne Murray, polemarch of Kappa Alpha Psi and Lawrence Ross, author of *The Divine Nine: The History of African-American Fraternities and Sororities*, note that many Black entrepreneurs have emerged from Black fraternities and sororities including Langston Hughes, Michael Jordan, Shaquille O'Neal, Earl Graves, Phylicia Rashad, Lisa Price, and Flora Hyacinth.[37,38] Murray and Ross also note that Black fraternities have raised millions of dollars to create much-needed African-American boarding schools.[39] But the main defense comes from the notion that Black fraternities and sororities serve as organizations where young Black men and women can form alliances, particularly at colleges and universities where Black students are a numeric minority. This is particularly important in light of research that shows mentoring has had a pronounced measure of success for young, Black men in colleges and universities where White students are in the majority.[40,41,42] Another supporting idea is that if Greek life benefits young, White men and women, particularly in terms of career opportunities, correlate opportunities should be available to young, Black men and women who may not be comfortable with or welcomed into White fraternities. Beyond the assistance provided to young, Black scholars, *The Divine Nine* are also known for their community involvement that extends far beyond careers and self-help.[43]

A footnote to BGLOs is that recently, young, White men have pledged Black fraternities, a practice that is defended by some as promoting social justice that "transcends race" and looks to a multicultural future.[44] The idea has gained traction among some young, college men who view inclusion and diversity as guiding principles in social justice activism. Critics worry, however, that non-Black pledges of BGLOs undo the intention of Black fraternities and sororities, which is to elevate the opportunities for young, Black people in a culture that is still dominated and defined by white privilege.

ETHNIC AND RELIGIOUS DIVERSITY IN GREEK LIFE

In addition to historically Black fraternities, Phi Sigma Nu was established as the first Native American fraternity in 1996 at the University of North Carolina, Pembroke, a fraternity that today boasts 11 chapters.[45] There are also a host of Latino Fraternal Organizations that were founded in the 1980s and 1990s and eventually established under two umbrella organizations: The National Association of Latino Fraternal Organizations (NALFO), which consists of fraternities and sororities in the Midwest and West Coast, and Concllio Nacional de Hermandades Latinas, which is composed of fraternities and sororities on the East Coast.[46] There are, moreover, numerous Asian American fraternities and sororities founded mainly on the West Coast, but that now extend throughout the nation.[47] According to University of Connecticut professor Daisy Verduzco Reyes, fraternities and sororities that identify around ethnicities help students of color integrate into the larger campus community.[48] Beyond integration, these Greek organizations help provide support and advocacy for students who bond around heritage, common backgrounds, and common interests.[49]

In addition to fraternities and sororities that have been established by and for students of color, there are today Christian, Jewish, and Muslim Greek organizations that have been established by and for students of faith.[50] More recently, Delta Beta Tau and Delta Beta Om have been established on principles of Buddhism.[51] Writing about the fraternity Sigma Theta Epsilon, a Christian-based fraternity at Bradley University, one advocacy piece claims that drinking, hazing, and a reputation for sexual misconduct are not elements of fraternities that are based on religious foundations.[52] This is not to say that religiosity eliminates problems associated with sex or more specifically sexual misconduct, but there is a longstanding view, whether true or not, that religious involvement mitigates the more toxic elements of bro culture.[53,54,55]

BENEFITS AND COSTS

The most commonly cited benefits of joining a fraternity while in college are career opportunities and career development. According to Monster.com, a job-search website, there are four main job-related benefits to rushing a fraternity or sorority:

- Learning interviewing skills
- A growing network of contacts
- Learning how to dress for success
- Learning time-management skills

Another commonly listed benefit of joining a fraternity or sorority is the involvement one will experience in philanthropic activities. These activities usually take the shape of fundraising for charities such as the National Bone Marrow Registry, The Starlight Children's Fund, The USO, and The Red Cross.[56] The fraternity that led in fundraising for 2017–2018 school year was Sigma Chi, which raised $1,436,883 for the Huntsman Cancer Institute.[57] However, critics note that fraternities like Sigma Chi will usually host two enormous parties each semester under the pretense of fundraising and then carry on as they wish.[58] Consider "**Derby Days**," which is the signature philanthropic event of Sigma Chi. All 239 chapters of Sigma Chi sponsor Derby Days along with many other fraternities. But as one pledge from Pi Beta Phi notes,

> Ostensibly, Derby Days is the exact kind of thing the Greek community loves to be proud of: an extended charity event, during which one might very well "cultivate leadership skills" and "make lasting connections" and "give back to the community" or whatever it says on all those IFC brochures. But, in essence, Derby Days is an emblem of what the mainstream, white Greek system really teaches its participants, which is how to couch a wide spectrum of unseemly behavior under the twin masks of tradition and philanthropy. And no fraternity does this with such monolithic chutzpah as Sigma Chi.[59]

It is a common rejoinder that fraternities use their charitable fundraisers to excuse or explain away their otherwise sexist and predatory behaviors. One example of this sort of ploy was documented at the College of William & Mary during Derby Days, which involved a strip tease contest.[60] In fact, an internal email from the Sigma Chi chapter at William & Mary read:

> There's beer to be drunk, porn to view, and sluts to fuck. Let me reiterate that last point: sluts are everywhere…Never mind the extremities that surround it, the 99% of horrendously illogical bullshit that makes up the modern woman, consider only the 1%, the snatch.[61]

Another problem, according to one sorority pledge, is that sorority women almost always end up doing the work for the charity events, while the Sigma Chi bros bask in the glory of philanthropic do-gooding.[62] During the actual events, such as lip-sync contests, sorority women, writes sorority pledge Meghan McCarthy, "value, above all else, being seen as sexually desirable to these men, and the men want and encourage the women to perform as objects for their entertainment."[63] Even during fundraising events designed to benefit well-deserving charities, the sexual double standard of women as sexual seductresses and men as whistling boosters plays out a longstanding fraternity-sorority script. McCarthy notes, "These men were popular. And that made them powerful. And if we rocked the boat, we could be shunned."[64] Fraternity men know they have power and are more than willing to wield that power to get women to come to their parties and other events, to display their bodies to the pledges, and to endure the sexual harassment that often comes with being a sorority sister. In fact, throughout the nation, banners have been positioned outside of resident halls for all to see by fraternity men that state things like:

- Rowdy and Fun, Hope your baby girl is ready for a good time.
- Freshmen daughter drop off
- Go ahead and drop mom off too
- She called you daddy for 18 years, now it's our turn...[65]

These particular banners were flown by Sigma Nu bros at Old Dominion University, which led to the suspension of the fraternity.[66] But similar banners have been flown by a variety of fraternities at universities around the nation.

How prevalent the sexist and predatory behaviors at fraternities are is unclear, but in a piece in *Higher Ed* entitled "Bad Apples or the Barrel?" writer Jake New notes that each month, between 20 and 30 fraternities are suspended by their residing university.[67] In 2017, Florida State University, Louisiana State University, and Texas State University suspended all Greek activities after each institution had a pledge die.[68] During the same year, Ohio State University suspended all 11 fraternities on its campus after numerous reports of hazing and alcohol-related disorderly conduct.[69] Kappa Delta Rho at Penn State University was suspended after it was discovered that brothers had posted on Facebook, nude pictures of women sleeping or passed out.[70] Recently, all fraternity activities were suspended at Johns Hopkins University when a 16-year-old girl was raped at a frat party.[71] At San Diego State University, a group of Delta Sigma Phi men shouted obscenities and waved dildos at a *Take Back the Night* event on campus, which are events that bring survivors of rape and sexual assault together in an environment of safety, strength, and solidarity.[72,73]

Hundreds of suspensions are handed out each year to fraternities around the nation. Do frat-brothers learn anything and make changes after being suspended? At Yale University's Delta Kappa Epsilon chapter, which was suspended for five years after pledges walked through campus shouting obscene, misogynistic chants, has found itself back in hot water after dozens of women came forward to report being sexually harassed by the men of the chapter.[74] Nick Altwies, founder of the pro-Greek organization *Society Advocating Fraternal Excellence*, notes that because suspensions are temporary and the suspended fraternity may only force two or three offending brothers to leave the fraternity, it is common that within a couple years, they are back to business as usual.[75] Altwies is skeptical that things are going to change as long as the national offices do not step in with mentoring programs and greater supervision.[76] Gentry McCreary, CEO of Dyad Strategies, a consulting firm that helps universities reshape Greek life, recommends banning alcohol from fraternities and argues that things will not change as long as fraternities are glorified bars, plying pledges and sorority sisters with copious amounts alcohol.[77] But a further problem, states John Hechinger, author of the book *True Gentlemen, The Broken Pledge of America's Fraternities*, is that universities market the social experience of fraternities and sororities to prospective students to draw them to the school.[78] Many alumni-donors are also former frat-bros, making it even more difficult for universities to come down harder on fraternities that practice dangerous behaviors.[79] This conflict of interest creates a conundrum for universities: how do we crack down on fraternities to create a safer environment for students, while not alienating our wealthy alumni-donors who support Greek life? As long as this ambivalence exists, it is unlikely that there will be Greek reform.

PLEDGING

In order to become a member of a fraternity, a recruit must pledge his loyalty and trust to the fraternity. Once the pledge has been taken, the initiate will be privy to publicly undisclosed information about the fraternity and sworn to secrecy.[80] First, however, the initiate must rush the fraternity, which means that the recruit must attend social events and answer questions during interviews which serve as a vetting process. The officers of the fraternity then determine whether to offer the recruit "a bid," and if the recruit accepts the bid, he is considered to have pledged the fraternity.[81]

But a common criticism of fraternities is that it is specifically this pledging aspect that creates many of the problems that have garnered fraternities their reputation for being denizens of rape and sexual assault. The idea is that pledges are strictly forbidden to reveal anything that goes on within the fraternity without approval from the officers. So, if frat-members know about the purchase of the date-rape drug rohypnol, better known as *roofies*, to yield women unconscious for the purposes of raping them, they are forbidden from informing university or police authorities. If they have knowledge of a woman or women having been sexually assaulted, they are supposed to keep that information private to the fraternity. Of course, any pledge, if he wished, could disobey the privacy rule and report what he knows, but the male culture that makes up much of frat-culture is centered around proving one's masculinity to the other pledges. This bro validation requires loyalty. So, just as "ratting someone out" in prison carries consequences, reporting your bros who have committed acts of sexual misconduct is an infraction that carries consequences such as being banned from the fraternity. So, the frat-rule that everyone understands is **the bro code-of-silence**: keep all potentially damaging information about the fraternity to yourself.[82]

HAZING

Hazing rituals are often part of the pledging process. Officially, fraternities oppose hazing. In reality, it's another matter. Hazing rituals run the gamut from embarrassing pranks to deadly cases of alcohol poisoning. In 2018, Penn State University student Timothy Piazza, 19, died after a night of binge drinking during his first night of pledging Beta Theta Pi.[83] His blood-alcohol level was 36 as he stumbled through the frat-house and eventually tumbled down a flight of stairs and lost consciousness.[84] Over the next 12 hours, none of his frat-brothers called 911 or reached out for any help whatsoever.[85] Eight members of the fraternity were charged with involuntary manslaughter and the rest were charged with other infractions that included hazing.[86] Piazza's death is not an isolated case. According to the National Institute on Alcohol Abuse and Alcoholism, approximately 1,825 college students die each year of alcohol-related causes.[87] In 2017, Charles Terreni Jr. of Pi Alpha Kappa died by alcohol poisoning after a night of binge drinking at a fraternity party.[88] Also in 2017, Florida State University student Andrew Coffey of Pi Kappa Pi died of alcohol poisoning after fellow frat brothers delayed in calling for help.[89] His blood-alcohol level was .58, well beyond a lethal amount.[90] At LSU, ten frat-brothers were arrested in connection with the alcohol-related death of Maxwell Gruver, who was given large sums of alcohol during a hazing ritual for Phi Delta Theta.[91] The ritual was described to police officers by frat-brothers after they were arrested:

> The pledges arranged themselves in a single line, and were told to go upstairs. Gott doused them in mustard and hot sauce. Then in the hallway, they were forced to stand with their nose and toes against the wall. The only light in the room came from a flashing strobe light. Loud music blared. The questions began. Wrong answers meant the pledge had to take three-to-five-second "pulls" of Diesel, a 190 proof alcohol.[92]

Alcohol-related hazing rituals are replicated at fraternity events each year around the nation. These rituals are supposed to serve as proof that new recruits are worthy to become full-fledged members. Other instances of hazing rituals have been documented by the University of Massachusetts, which include:

- Verbal abuse
- Threats
- Forcing pledges to wear humiliating attire
- Crude and degrading acts, including eating dog food or fried vomit
- Forcing pledges to not take showers for weeks

- Branding
- Public nudity
- Exposure to cold weather for long periods of time
- Paddling
- Mistreatment of animals
- Forced homophobic or homoerotic behaviors[93]

This is only a partial list of hazing rituals found in frat-houses around the U.S. At Wilmington College, Gamma Phi Gamma forced its new recruits to lie on the floor and engage in swimming motions as Icy-Hot was applied to their genitals while pledges whipped them with towels.[94] One pledge was taken to a hospital where one of his testicles was removed due to damage done during the event.[95] At Tulane University, pledges of Pi Kappa Alpha had their genitals doused with cayenne pepper, wasabi sauce, vinegar, and boiling water, which sent two of them to the hospital due to second and third-degree burns.[96] Since 2000, there have been 62 hazing-related deaths and over 200 since the 19th century.[97]

Those who defend hazing argue that extreme cases like those cited above are rare and that more common hazing rituals are not harmful, but allow the brothers to have fun and blow off steam.[98] An attorney, Michael Coard, defending a fraternity in a case of hazing stated, "no one forces you to subject yourself to it," while also noting that there is no criminal intent on the part of those overseeing the hazing.[99,100] The main problem with the first part of Coard's argument is that fraternities are hierarchies where upperclassmen hold power over underclassmen. There are also longstanding masculine norms reinforced for generations and understood by young pledges that men are never supposed to show fear or weakness. So, while walking away is an option, it's not an option. Turning down the 190-proof alcohol, not eating the vomit omelet, refusing to be humiliated or tortured would be a sign of weakness in bro culture. So, you go along to get along, you take the abuse to show 19, 20, and 21-year old men that you are a *real man* who is afraid of nothing and has what it takes to be a frat-bro.

One final important point about hazing that must be mentioned is the often homophobic nature of many hazing rituals. We sometimes witness this type of hazing with high school and college sports teams as much as we do in college fraternities. Writing for *Outsports*, author Cyd Zeigler documents numerous hazing incidents that involve homophobic behaviors such as the notorious example of the hazing incidents at Mepham High School in New York, where younger players were sodomized with broomsticks.[101] Zeigler writes,

> Both latent homosexuality and homophobia are playing a huge role in the hazing abuse our kids are experiencing, and our societal standards that dictate what a "real man" is are to blame.[102]

Hazing is a ritualized way of subordinating one group of people, the pledges, to another group of people, established members, by forcing the pledges to engage in demeaning behaviors. Whether by instructing pledges to hold each others' genitals and walk in a circle, known as "the elephant walk,"[103] or by forcing pledges to lick each other or wear clothing considered to be feminine in nature, fraternities practice homoerotic – homophobic hazing rituals intended to subordinate the pledge to the fraternity's leadership. In one instance, Syracuse University's Theta Tau members were captured on camera simulating oral sex on one another as part of a hazing ritual, while another frat bro in the background shouts, *I solemnly swear to always have hatred in my heart for niggers, spics, and most importantly, the fucking kikes,* to rousing applause.[104]

Beyond the graphic examples of racism, this kind of hazing places on display one of the most toxic aspects of bro culture, the instruction that all things feminine, or in this case homoerotic, are the most degrading and disgusting things a bro can inflict upon another bro's sense of manhood. In most cases, masculinity, in bro culture, is defined by what it is not. Boys are taught that to be a *real man* is to be the antithesis of anything considered to be feminine. Given this particular paradigm of masculinity, frat culture is often a training ground for misogyny and homophobia, lessons that can extend into a young man's professional and personal life well beyond his college years. Naturally, when challenged, frat-bros will vehemently deny that they are homophobic, while their behavior suggests otherwise.

FRATERNITY MEN AND RAPE

Researchers John Foubert, R. Sean Bannon, and Matthew W. Brosi have shown that sorority women and fraternity men are more likely than other university students to be survivors and perpetrators of sexual assault.[105] In further research, social psychologists E. Timothy Bleecker and Sarah K. Murnen found that fraternity men score significantly higher on a rape supportive attitude scale (RSA) than non-fraternity men and that this increased support of rape attitudes correlate positively to the amount of degrading depictions of women found in men's dorm rooms in the form of images, posters, and pornographic screen-saver materials.[106] In fact, women who belong to sororities are 74% more likely to be raped than college women who do not belong to sororities and this is thought to be due to their increased contact with fraternity men and the party scene that often goes along with it.[107] In fact, Wesleyan University's branch of Beta Theta Pi was branded a "rape factory" in a lawsuit against the university and in 2010, Wesleyan officials warned students to stay away from Beta House because the university could not ensure the safety of students on its premises.[108] In 2014, Georgia Tech University disbanded Phi Kappa Tau after an email was discovered originating from the fraternity entitled "Luring Your Rapebait," which included the following numbered guide to bros as instruction:[109]

1. Encounter (spot a girl or group of girls)
2. Engage (go up and talk to them)
3. Escalate (ask them to dance, or ask them to go up to your room or find a couch)
4. Erection (GET HARD)

5. Excavate (should be self-explanatory)
6. Ejaculate (should also be self explanatory)
7. Expunge (send them out of your room and on their way out when you are finished. IF ANYTHING EVER FAILS, GO GET MORE ALCOHOL.

These sorts of internal e-messages within fraternities are not new. From the Kappa Sigma chapter at USC, an email was circulated and leaked that outlined to pledges how to treat women, which read,

> I will refer to females as 'targets.' They aren't actual people like us men. Consequently, giving them a certain name or distinction is pointless.[110]

The dehumanization of women has always been part of rape culture. The author of this post refers to himself and his Kappa Sigma brothers as "cocksmen" who should target women he terms 'sorostitutes' who "will put out."[111] The author then goes on to classify women ('targets') by race:

> Blackberry: A black target
> Blueberry Pie: half-black/half-white
> Pumpkin Pie: A latin/mexican target
> Pecan Pie: half-white/half-latin
> Strawberry Pie: white target
> Cherry pie: A young white target
> Lemon Meringue: Asian target

Fraternities often attempt to dispute or downplay claims of sexual misconduct by stating that emails of this kind and the many cases of sexual assault and rape in frat-houses do not reflect the values of the fraternity or that these are isolated cases that are rare. Are they? Here is a partial list of recent cases:

> Temple University (2018): Fraternity **Alpha Epsilon Pi** president Ari Goldstein was arrested and charged with attempted rape, indecent assault, and witness intimidation.[112]
>
> Utah State University (2015): **Sigma Chi** frat-member Jason Relopez was charged with attempted rape, forcible sexual abuse, and the sexual assault of six women.[113] The university paid $250,000 in damages for improper handling of the case.[114]
>
> Butler University (2016): **Lambda Chi Alpha** member – football player was accused of the rape of two women.[115] The university is now named as a defendant in a federal lawsuit as failing to protect students from male-students with histories of sexual assault.[116]
>
> Baylor University (2015): former president of **Phi Delta Theta**, Jacob Anderson, was charged with four counts of sexual assault with one victim left outdoors and unconscious.[117]

Cornell University (2016): **Psi Upsilon** former president Wolfgang Ballinger was charged with attempted rape, a criminal sex act on a helpless victim, sexual misconduct, and plead guilty to lesser charges.[118] (He expressed no remorse and received six years probation.)

University of Central Florida (2018): **Alpha Tau Omega,** two fraternity men, David Anthony Kirk and Jack Ryan Smith, were charged with sexual battery and rape.[119] The victim was unconscious. This same fraternity had members accused of rape and false imprisonment three months earlier.[120]

Georgia Tech University (2014): **Kappa Sigma,** former fraternity president Christian Kahf was charged with rape.[121] He was convicted and sentenced to 20 years in prison.[122]

Stockton University (2017): **Pi Kappa Phi,** frat-member Zachary Madle was charged with raping four women.[123] The fraternity continues to operate at the university.

University of Alabama (2015): **Delta Sigma Phi** member Taylor Force was charged with raping a 19-year-old woman at a party.[124]

At Yale University, fraternity members from **Delta Kappa Epsilon** marched through campus chanting in unison, "No means Yes, Yes means anal!"[125] The fraternity was suspended after this stunt, but is now back in business with two women in 2017 claiming that they were the victims of sexual assault by the brothers of Delta Kappa Epsilon.[126] Their harrowing stories are recounted in a *Business Insider* piece where one woman shares her account of being held down and raped on a sofa by a much stronger DKE brother who she was unable to fight off.[127,128] More than a dozen women reported to *Business Insider* that they witnessed or experienced instances of nonconsensual sexual contact since 2014 by the brothers of DKE.[129]

At Northwestern University in Illinois, three women reported sexual assault at the hands of members of **Sigma Alpha Epsilon** after being plied with date-rape drugs.[130] In the film *The Hunting Ground*, which documents the epidemic of rape and sexual assault by fraternity men, interviewees claimed that Sigma Alpha Epsilon's reputation was so infamous, students referred to SAE as "Sexual Assault Expected."[131] In 2014, Stanford University suspended Sigma Alpha Epsilon for two years for creating a "hostile environment for female students."[132] Stanford investigators determined that more than 30 women were subjected to graphic sexual images and offensive comments toward women.[133] This is the same fraternity whose chapter members at the University of Oklahoma chanted racist slogans on a bus, singing in unison,

> There will never be a nigger in SAE; there will never be a nigger in SAE; you can hang him from a tree, but he can never sign with me; there will never be a nigger at SAE. [134]

The cases listed above represent a small fraction of the reports of sexual assault and rape emanating from fraternity brothers at frat-houses around the country. A study conducted by the *Center for Public Integrity* reports that 95% of cases of sexual assault and rape on college campuses or off-campus apartments and fraternity houses go unreported.[135] According to different surveys, only 10–40% of cases of sexual assault and rape are reported nationally.[136] Differences in rates are often chalked up to varying definitions of rape in surveys and to definitions found in state law or victims themselves not identifying with the terminology used in surveys such as 'rape' or sexual assault'. Still, reports of sexual abuse are low and there are good reasons why victims of sexual assault rarely report their attack to authorities. Writing for *Psychology Today*, psychologist Beverly Engel lists the following common reasons:[137]

- **Shame**: Victims feel violated in the most personal and intimate way possible. This violation leads to feelings of humiliation and dehumanization.
- **Denial and Minimization**: It is common for victims to blame themselves and for peers and larger society to downplay sexual misconduct and the harms of sexual harassment and sexual assault.
- **Fear**: Victims fear of losing their jobs, fear of being branded as liars, fear of reprisal and further victimization.
- **Low Self-Esteem**: Victims will often already suffer from low self-esteem, which can lead to feelings that they should not cause trouble. These feelings can convert into the victim themselves downplaying the incident to avoid the attention that reporting will bring.
- **Feeling Hopeless and Helpless**: It is common for victims to believe, "What's the use in reporting?" Victims will witness the ways other victims are negatively treated and this negativity creates a deterrent effect for others to step forward to report. Victims also witness little-to-no consequences to the perpetrators, which leaves them feeling that nothing will come of a report even if they file one.

Together, these traumatic feelings often paralyze victims of sexual abuse and explain why victims hesitate to report or decide not to report at all.

Consider the case of Brock Turner. In 2015, Turner was a student at Stanford University who sexually assaulted a young, unconscious woman behind a dumpster outside of a Kappa Alpha fraternity house.[138] Although Turner was not himself a member of a fraternity, he attended the Kappa Alpha party.[139] Two international students caught Turner assaulting the woman and held him until police took him into custody.[140] He was subsequently indicted on five charges and convicted on three counts of felony sexual assault.[141] Upon conviction, Turner was facing up to 14 years in prison. However, Superior Court Judge Aaron Pesky sentenced Turner to six months in jail and to be registered as a sex offender.[142] Criticism of this light sentence was swift and fierce. Judge Pesky was subsequently reassigned to the Civil Division of the California Court system.[143] Cases like that of Brock Turner are precisely why victims worry that reporting will lead to very little to no consequences to the perpetrator. Writing for *Slate Magazine*, writer Christina Cauterucci notes that Turner's father, Dan Turner, lamented in a letter how the conviction had thrown his son's life off track from the trajectory he was on before the rape.[144] To add insult to injury, Brock Turner used his notoriety to attempt to profit by scheduling a speaking tour where he blamed binge drinking for his crime instead of taking responsibility for his actions.[145]

Yet with all of these harrowing stories and double standards, under the Trump administration, Education Secretary Betsy DeVos claims that those accused of rape are treated unfairly, and she proposes to raise the legal standard for culpability higher than current Title IX standards.[146,147] The concern for DeVos is that innocent men may be accused and prosecuted without appropriate due process.[148] Under DeVos' new guidelines,[149]

- Complaints of sexual misconduct can no longer be reported to a resident advisor, but must be reported to official institutional personnel.
- Sexual harassment would now be defined as conduct "so severe" that it denies a person access to the school's education program or activities.
- Colleges and universities would be responsible only for sexual misconduct that occurs on school grounds, but no longer responsible for off-campus locations such as fraternity houses.
- The standard for culpability can now be raised from "a preponderance of the evidence" to "clear and convincing evidence."
- The Office for Civil Rights would now use a higher legal standard to determine whether an institution violated Title IX.

DeVos' argument hinges on the concern that college men may be unjustly accused of sexual misconduct and that the legal authorities are too quick to prosecute and convict. But according to a ten-year study conducted by researcher and clinical psychologist David Lisak and others, the rate of false reporting of sexual assault and rape sits at 5.9%.[150] DeVos, as well as men's rights activists, like to hold out the rare cases of false reporting as evidence that men are allegedly being targeted by disgruntled women who are looking for ways to harm men. A case in point is the 2015 allegation brought against a fraternity at the University of Virginia and published in Rolling Stone magazine as a gang rape.[151] The allegations were eventually determined to be unfounded after an investigation was unable to produce credible evidence.[152] The other well-publicized case of false reporting came in 2006, when three members of Duke University's lacrosse team were accused of rape.[153] Duke University suspended the lacrosse team for two games, the head coach was forced to resign, and the three players were arrested. In 2007, all charges were dropped and North Carolina Attorney General, Roy Cooper, declared the players innocent. The case drew national attention and eventually led to lead prosecutor and Durham County District Attorney Mike Nifong's resignation.[154]

Writing for *The Atlantic*, Caitlin Flanagan argues that as a result of the high rates of sexual assault and rape, fraternities in America should be permanently shut down.[155] The sentiment is understandable, but the recommendation is

Thought Box

In your opinion, are the regulations governing the reporting and adjudicating of sexual **assault** on college campuses too strict or too lenient? Defend your answer. What changes, if any, would you like to see?

unsound. Shutting down fraternities would not end off-campus parties nor the rape culture to which many bros subscribe: the notion that rape is rare, that many cases of rape were consensual but that the victim is exaggerating or reacting to not receiving the relationship he or she was hopeful would take place. Bro culture is a culture that is based on victim blaming, a culture that finds reasons to blame women, while searching for reasons to exculpate men. Many bros buy into the "boys will be boys" ethos, which provides an instant explanation and excuse for bad behaviors. Yet this phrase is the pinnacle of male bashing, since it attributes by nature some of the most abhorrent traits possible: that men are selfish, violent, sexually aggressive, and, in the case we have been examining here, rapists. The phrase "boys will be boys" is also deterministic, as it provides an explanation that is both fatalistic and vacuous. It pretends that there is nothing we can do about men's predatory behaviors, while not providing any evidence that these claims are true. At the same time, the phrase ignores the fact that many men are not sexually predatory in nature, but on the contrary, are compassionate and caring. Take the young men who tackled Brock Turner and made sure he was turned over to the police. They did not view the circumstance as an opportunity to join in the sexual assault, but rather they saw the occasion as an opportunity to be responsible and assist a young woman who was being attacked by a predator.

Still, the gender inequality between fraternity men and sorority women and the predictably high rates of sexual assault at frat-houses are summed up in a piece by the online magazine *Odyssey*:

> The Greek system is set up in a way that expects women to impress men. The most direct example of this is that the parties happen at fraternity houses. This blatantly states that fraternities hold the power and are therefore higher in the social hierarchy. Girls are expected to flock to the houses IF they're lucky enough to be put on a list. This sometimes involves texting your friends and begging to be put on said list, which is extremely degrading. This list system also often results in unequal proportions of men and women at the parties, guaranteeing that there will be more prospects for the men. Again, it puts more power in their hands. This is a problem that could be very easily solved by letting sororities host parties; however, many sororities have national regulations that don't allow them to have alcohol in their houses. Although I understand the reasoning behind this rule, I believe that it is unfair for fraternities to not enforce the same rule.[156]

As noted, sororities across the nation abide by the rule that alcohol is prohibited at sorority houses, while this rule is not enforced at fraternity houses. It is a recipe for rape, sexual assault, and other forms of sexual misconduct.

> **Thought Box**
>
> One idea that has been tossed around for years to decrease the rates of sexual assault and rape at college parties is to only allow sororities to host parties, where alcohol is banned, and to eliminate frat-parties altogether. This would place women in charge of parties, and would also assure that isolated rooms could be locked and secured so that men cannot trap women in upstairs bedrooms or basements. What do you think?

THEMED PARTIES & GENDER INEQUALITY

In the magazine *Men's Health,* young frat-men are given advice on how to throw themed parties that give the men the best chance of receiving sex.[157] There are a number of these themed parties, but those that place women in the most vulnerable state to men's unwanted advances are centered around the following themes:

- Lingerie Night
- Anything But Clothes
- Bros and Hoes (several versions of this including CEOs and Office Hoes)
- XXX-mas Party
- Seven Deadly Sins
- Rubik's Cube (Party-goers exchange clothes)

As *Men's Health* puts it,

> Invite every hottie you can find on campus to show off their sexiest lingerie while you proudly don skivvies of your own. Girls get a free shot for wearing high heels. The point of the party is to get a bunch of drunk, half-naked people together and see what happens.[158]

Note that with a number of these parties, the theme itself expressly promotes gender inequality with different versions of Bro and Ho in the title, while other themes implicitly promote gender inequality where women are expected to dress in sexually revealing clothes, while the men are not. With the bro-ho-themed party, Men's Health notes,

> No costumes for the guys, very little clothes for the girls. Get a keg, some condoms, and you're pretty much good to go.[159]

Each of the themes is designed to feature women as sexual seductresses for men, while the alcohol and drugs work as intoxicants to turn a 'no' into a 'yes'

Figure 3.1 "Pimps and Hoes" Party[160] © David McHugh/Shutterstock.

or a 'maybe', or oftentimes, turn a 'no' into silence. When transportation is also under the supervision of the men at the party, and there is no university oversight, the themed frat-parties are a perfect storm of circumstances where men sexually prey upon women and then call it "consensual" later by pointing out that the women dressed for sex, which is the hackneyed trope that "the women were asking for it." (Figure 3.1)

The titles of the themes themselves represent a clear power imbalance with men as "CEOs, Pimps, and Bros" and women as "hoes." Frat-men will often attempt to avoid culpability by noting that women themselves help organize the parties and want to participate in themed parties where they are referred to as 'hoes." But these parties must be viewed against the background of the patriarchal culture in which they are thrown. Men hold a distinct power advantage over women throughout the world in terms of economic, political, academic, and judicial power. Reinforcing this gendered imbalance is a training ground for the patriarchal world that awaits most women, and frat-bros are only too happy to exploit that imbalance. Within much of Greek life, those women who do not agree to help with organizing and participating in the "bro-ho"-themed parties are relegated to the category of persona non grata, and are shunned from social events and parties where one's status is codified.

FRAT-PAC

College fraternities and sororities, it turns out, have their own political action committee often called Frat-PAC.[161] Wealthy fraternity and sorority members and alumni pay politicians to "support our brothers and sisters in Congress and those who champion Greek issues."[162] So-called "Greek issues" include building new chapters around the country, but also ensure that fraternity brothers and sorority sisters are politically connected to powerful politicians who may be able to help them in their careers.

Beyond these self-serving purposes, Frat-PAC also lobbies Congress to block efforts by colleges and universities from properly investigating cases of rape and sexual assault by disallowing any university investigation until a police investigation has been concluded.[163] One of many criticisms of this policy is the concern that rape survivors are often uncomfortable reporting to police officers who sometimes have a reputation for not handling victims of sexual assault well.[164] But Frat-PAC has also come to the aid of sexual assault suspects, claiming that the due process rights of male suspects are violated by allowing universities to investigate before or during police investigations. One sorority sister, critical of Frat-PAC argues, "This is almost as if Frat-PAC is giving the survivors an ultimatum: Choose to prosecute your rapist in court, or feel threatened and unsafe on campus."[165] As we have seen previously in this chapter, rape and sexual assault victims are often hesitant to come forward out of the fear of being blamed, shamed, or threatened, and the Frat-PAC "ultimatum" assures that more rape survivors will remain silent rather than putting themselves through this ordeal.

Frat-PAC has also donated over $1 million to block a bill that would revoke federal financial aid from anyone found guilty of hazing other students.[166,167] It is clear that Frat-PAC is concerned mainly with covering up sexual misconduct and hazing, but often at the expense of victims who could place fraternities at risk through legal actions that include class-action lawsuits and the shuttering of some fraternities.

THE MITIGATING EFFECTS OF MULTICULTURALISM

As mentioned at the beginning of the chapter, new or somewhat new to many campuses, is the emergence of multicultural fraternities and sororities that offer support to students who have been traditionally excluded from Greek affiliation.[168] Whether Latinx, Asian, Native, Pacific Islanders, or simply "multicultural fraternities and sororities," the appearance of Greek organizations that allow young people to explore and celebrate their heritage in a nation that has not been welcoming to people of different cultures and subcultures has been appreciated by the many college students in American universities who do not identify as Black or White. In fact, in 2013 at the University of Texas, Austin, the first Muslim fraternity, Alpha Lambda Mu was formed, soon to be followed by the first Muslim sorority Mu Delta Alpha.[169]

Multicultural fraternities represent a change to traditional fraternities in a beneficial and unexpected way by not garnering a reputation for hazing because, as one pledge states, "most of our groups do not participate in Rush."[170] Rushing a fraternity involves participation in social events over a period of time that allows members to better know the recruits. However, it is during this time when hazing often takes place. By eliminating Rush, along with rejecting a culture of violence and alcohol, multicultural fraternities have so far been able to avoid the unacceptable behaviors that have been associated with fraternities that practice forced binge drinking and other forms of hazing. Rafael Ramirez, of Columbia University's multicultural Eta chapter of Alpha Phi Alpha, explains,

> Brothers will check each other to make sure that everyone is respecting each other and it's a safe community. We want to create an environment where, however you identify, you feel comfortable enough to want to be around us and participate in whatever is going on.[171]

Of caring about a rally in Manhattan to protest police violence, Ramirez adds,

> Who else was actually going to support something I cared so much about? I realized it's the group of men of color who understand those kinds of struggles.[172]

Jen Recher, president of the National Multicultural Greek Council agrees and states, "Multicultural organizations create a safe space where people of all colors, religions, sexualities and gender expressions feel at home."[173]

For multicultural Greek organizations, there is an importance placed on not being like party-frats that have established bad reputations for themselves. Being someone who is considered "other" in a xenophobic nation is challenging so that multicultural fraternities and sororities create safe spaces and mutual support. These fraternities and sororities also show that treating all Greek organizations as being the same is a stereotype. In fact, multicultural Greek life may turn out to be the role model for all Greek life, where destructive party culture can be converted into diversity-affirming centers of acceptance, and where women are finally treated as authentic equals instead of "targets" for bros who view women as nothing more than sexual opportunities.

THETA PI SIGMA: AN LGBTQIA, GENDER-INCLUSIVE FRATERNITY

One obvious problem for fraternities and sororities is their gender-exclusivity at a time when transgender people are fighting for equal rights. When fraternities use insulting slurs and phrases like "no homo" or "that's so gay," they are clearly not welcoming environments for members of LGBTQ communities. Furthermore, given the fact that fraternities and sororities are granted certain exemptions from Title IX to exist as gender-exclusive organizations, the emergence of gender-inclusive Greek-letter organizations were born in 2005 with the creation of Theta Pi Sigma at UC Santa Cruz.[174] Formerly known as Delta Lambda Psi, Theta Pi Sigma is a queer-focused, gender-neutral fraternity that

74   Chapter 3

is hoping to branch out nationally and internationally.[175] The stated purpose of Theta Pi Sigma is to provide a vehicle for:

> ...positive leadership, change, and growth in the queer, transsexual, transgender, questioning, pansexual, lesbian, intersex, gender-queer, gay, bisexual, asexual, and ally communities.[176,177]

There is a "Greek spirit" of learning and solidarity that is attractive to TPS and many fraternities, but gender-exclusivity in tandem with the infamous sexism, homophobia, transphobia, and xenophobia that has typified some fraternities left LGBTQIA individuals out of Greek life. The inclusive nature of Theta Pi Sigma hopes to change that and to create a welcoming environment for those who want the benefits of Greek life without the many detractions that are often come with exclusivity.

POSTSCRIPT

Earlier in the chapter, writer Caitlin Flanagan suggested that universities shudder fraternities in order to keep women safe from the predatory behaviors that have become synonymous with far too many frat-bros. Oklahoma State University professor John Foubert suggests that fraternities should lose their Title IX exemption so that Title IX complaints can be filed against the fraternities that continue to abuse women.[178] Foubert notes that in research conducted on the high rates of sexual harassment and assault of women by fraternity men, it is the fraternity experience itself that contributes to these high rates.[179] The reason for this is that fraternities, being gender-exclusive organizations, breed and reinforce rape myth narratives such as the view that women who go to parties want sex regardless of whether they do not explicitly express consent. Another common rape-myth trope is the view that women "like to be forced" or enjoy so-called "rough sex," which plays into the "Blurred Lines" song lyric that states, "I know you want it," whether the woman wants it or not. Foubert also notes that fraternity men infamously immerse themselves in pornography, which promotes the view that women *always* want sex. Essentially, the word 'no' does not exist in pornography unless it is part of so-called "rape fantasy," where the woman's objections are ignored.

In a study conducted by Foubert, Johnathan Newberry, and Jerry Tatum of the College of William and Mary, researchers note that,

> Men who joined fraternities during the year and had seen a rape prevention program at the beginning of the academic year were significantly less likely to commit a sexually coercive

act during the year than control group men who joined fraternities.[180]

The particular program matters, of course, and there are numerous programs that are advertised as programs to prevent rape and sexual assault.[181] Some of them are simply online programs, while others are performance-based or workshop-oriented programs. But integrating rape-prevention programs into fraternity life is certainly one way of addressing the ongoing problem of sexual assault that is infamously associated with fraternity men.

In addition, fraternity-focused workshops that instill respecting women's autonomy and that encourage members to speak up when pledges observe sexually aggressive behaviors in other men is needed. If college fraternities were shut down, off-campus party culture would continue. It would simply exist under a different banner. There is no reason to believe that the shuttering of fraternities would bring about a renaissance in the way men think about women without there also being a revolution in the way boys and men think about masculinity. Foubert, in fact, recommends "a fundamental redesign of Greek life" that does not include living in a house where alcohol is consumed regularly and where parties are held as one of the most important activities of the house.[182] Anti-sexist, antiviolence educator Jackson Katz argues that successful prevention must include frank conversations about gender, since it is men who overwhelmingly carry out sex-based crimes.[183] But simply shutting down fraternities without sex-based violence prevention would not end sex-based abuse or get young men to begin the necessary conversations and self-examinations that could create changes in the way they currently view women, sex, and consent.

Finally, multicultural and gender-inclusive fraternities provide a template for how frat-life could improve fundamentally if men were open to the idea of shedding exclusivity from their identity. The benefits of Greek life would not be hampered, but extended to everyone if notions of privilege and hierarchy were replaced with notions of inclusivity that transcend race, ethnicity, gender, sexual orientation, and the many identities that are used to distinguish between people.

Notes

1. Delta Lambda Phi, Official Website. https://dlp.org/
2. Daniel Funke, University of Georgia, "LGBT Fraternities and Sororities Look to Make Greek Life More Inclusive," *USA Today*, 2015. https://www.usatoday.com/story/college/2015/03/18/lgbt-fraternities-and-sororities-look-to-make-greek-life-more-inclusive/37401389/
3. Sammy Nickalls, "This Fraternity Is Supporting Women and Fighting Sexism, One Sign at a Time," *Hello Giggles*, August 27, 2015. https://hellogiggles.com/news/fraternity-supporting-women-fighting-sexism-one-sign-time/
4. Ibid.
5. Craig L. Torbenson, Gregory Parks, *Brothers and Sisters: Diversity in College Fraternities and Sororities*, Associated University Press, Teaneck, New Jersey, 2009.
6. Ibid.
7. Claremont McKenna College, "History of Phi Beta Kappa," https://www.cmc.edu/registrar/pbk/phi-beta-kappa-history
8. William T. Hastings, "Phi Beta Kappa as a Secret Society with Its Relations to Freemasonry and Antimasonry Some Supplemental Documents," United Chapters of Phi Beta Kappa, Richmond, Virginia.

9. Kurt G. Piehler, "Phi Beta Kappa: The Invention of an Academic Tradition," *History of Education Quarterly*, Vol. 28, No. 2, Summer, 1988, pp. 207–229.
10. William T. Hastings, "Phi Beta Kappa as a Secret Society with Its Relations to Freemasonry and Antimasonry Some Supplemental Documents," United Chapters of Phi Beta Kappa, Richmond, Virginia.
11. University of California, Berkeley, "Eligibility Criteria for Membership," *The Phi Beta Kappa Society*, May, 2018. https://pbk.berkeley.edu/criteria/
12. The Phi Beta Kappa Society Official Website. https://www.pbk.org/About
13. Emily M. Bernstein, "Phi Beta Kappa Key Being Turned Down by Many Honorees," *The New York Times*, May 26, 1996. https://www.nytimes.com/1996/05/26/nyregion/phi-beta-kappa-key-being-turned-down-by-many-honorees.html
14. Ibid.
15. David Niose, "Anti-intellectualism Is Killing America," *Psychology Today*, June 23, 2015. https://www.psychologytoday.com/us/blog/our-humanity-naturally/201506/anti-intellectualism-is-killing-america
16. Craig L. Torbenson, Gregory Parks, *Brothers and Sisters: Diversity in College Fraternities and Sororities*, Associated University Press, Plainsboro Township, NJ, 2009.
17. Official Site of the Kappa Alpha Society. https://www.ka.org/
18. Craig L. Torbenson, Gregory Parks, *Brothers and Sisters: Diversity in College Fraternities and Sororities*, Associated University Press, Plainsboro Township, NJ, 2009.
19. Ibid.
20. Buster Brown, "Skull & Bones: It's Not Just for White Dudes Anymore," *The Atlantic*, February 25, 2013. https://www.theatlantic.com/national/archive/2013/02/skull-and-bones-its-not-just-for-white-dudes-anymore/273463/
21. Ibid.
22. Ibid.
23. Thomas S. Harding, *College Literary Societies: Their Contribution to Higher Education in the United States, 1815–1876*, Pageant Press International, New York, Privately Published.
24. Clarence Frank Birdseye, *Individual Training in Our Colleges*, The MacMillan Company, New York, 1907, retrieved, 2008.
25. Ibid.
26. Ibid.
27. A listing of the nine traditionally Black fraternities and sororities in America, "The Divine Nine and the National Pan-Hellenic Council." http://www.blackgreek.com/divinenine/
28. Ali D. Chambers, "How Black Fraternities Are Actually Harmful to Black Culture in the U.S.," *LSE United States Politics and Policy*. http://blogs.lse.ac.uk/usappblog/2017/09/15/how-black-fraternities-are-actually-harmful-to-black-culture-in-the-us/
29. Michel Marriott, "Black Fraternities and Sororities End a Tradition," *The New York Times*, October 3, 1990. https://www.nytimes.com/1990/10/03/us/education-black-fraternities-and-sororities-end-a-tradition.html
30. Dustin J. Seibert, "Why Is Hazing Still a Thing in Many Black Greek Organizations?" *The Root*, April 26, 2016. https://www.theroot.com/why-is-hazing-still-a-thing-in-many-black-greek-organiz-1790855126
31. Walter M. Kimbrough, "The Hazing Problem at Black Fraternities," *The Atlantic*, March 17, 2014. https://www.theatlantic.com/education/archive/2014/03/the-hazing-problem-at-black-fraternities/284452/

32. Associated Press, "Men Indicted in Ohio Fraternity Hazing Case," *FOX News*, March 17, 2012. https://www.foxnews.com/us/9-men-indicted-in-ohio-fraternity-hazing-case
33. Ibid.
34. Ibid.
35. Ibid.
36. Ibid.
37. Michel Martin, "After 100 Years, Why Black Frats Still Matter: An Interview with Dwayne Murray and Lawrence Ross," *NPR*, July 7, 2011. https://www.npr.org/2011/07/07/137672103/after-100-years-why-black-frats-still-matter
38. Janell Hazelwood, "10 Celebrity Power Women Who Pledged the Divine Nine," *Black Enterprise*, July 18, 2017. https://www.blackenterprise.com/10-celebrity-power-women-who-pledged-the-divine-nine-black-sororities-celebrities/
39. Ibid.
40. Yolanda B. Gibson, "The Impact of Mentoring Programs for African American Male Community College Students," *Journal of Mason Graduate Research*, Vol. 1, Issue 2, 2014, pp. 70–82. https://journals.gmu.edu/index.php/jmgr/article/view/216
41. Taurean M. Douglas, "African American Males, Mentorship, and University Success: A Qualitative Study," Eastern Kentucky University, January 2017. https://encompass.eku.edu/cgi/viewcontent.cgi?article=1481&context=etd
42. Derrick R. Brooms, "Building Us Up: Supporting Black Make College Students in a Black Male Initiative Program," *Critical Sociology*, August 4, 2016. https://journals.sagepub.com/doi/10.1177/0896920516658940
43. Taylor Epps, "How Black Greek Organizations Are Helping Our Community," *ABC News-Buffalo*, February 7, 2020. https://www.wkbw.com/news/local-news/how-black-greek-organizations-are-helping-our-community
44. Kourtney Gray, "Why Would a White Person Join a Black Fraternity?" *Blavity*, April 28, 2016. https://blavity.com/white-person-join-a-black-fraternity
45. Corey M. Still, Breanna R. Faris, "Understanding and Supporting Historically Native American Fraternities and Sororities," Special Issue: *Critical Considerations of Race, Ethnicity, and Culture in Fraternity & Sorority Life*, pp. 51–59, Spring, 2019.
46. Official Site of NALFO: Latino Greeks United: https://nalfo.org/
47. Mariah Bohanon, "Multicultural Fraternities, Sororities Offer Communities of Support for Students Traditionally Excluded from Greek Life," *Insight Into Diversity*, February 26, 2018. http://www.insightintodiversity.com/multicultural-fraternities-sororities-offer-communities-of-support-for-students-traditionally-excluded-from-greek-life/
48. Marissa Armas, "Stepping, Strolling and Community: Latino Fraternities, Sororities Grow in Popularity," *NBC News*, August 23, 2017. https://www.nbcnews.com/news/latino/stepping-strolling-community-latino-sororities-fraternities-grow-popularity-n794696
49. Mariah Bohanon, "Multicultural Fraternities, Sororities Offer Communities of Support for Students Traditionally Excluded from Greek Life," *Insight*, February 26, 2018. https://www.insightintodiversity.com/multicultural-fraternities-sororities-offer-communities-of-support-for-students-traditionally-excluded-from-greek-life/
50. Ibid.

78 Chapter 3

51. Claire Trageser, "Delta Beta Om: Buddha Comes to San Diego's Greek System," *NPR*, September 26, 2015. https://www.npr.org/2015/09/26/443718282/delta-beta-ohm-buddha-comes-to-san-diegos-greek-system
52. Michael Miller, "Rise of the Christian Fraternity," *The Register-Mail*, September 24, 2007. https://www.galesburg.com/x775331022
53. Dena M. Abbott, Jeff E. Harris, Debra Mollen, "The Impact of Religious Commitment on Women's Sexual Self-Esteem," *Sexuality & Culture*, Vol. 20, 2016, pp. 1063–1082. https://link.springer.com/article/10.1007/s12119-016-9374-x
54. Joshua Pease, "The Sin of Silence: The Epidemic of Denial about Sexual Abuse in the Evangelical Church," *The Washington Post*, May 31, 2018. https://www.washingtonpost.com/news/posteverything/wp/2018/05/31/feature/the-epidemic-of-denial-about-sexual-abuse-in-the-evangelical-church/
55. This final point will be taken up in greater detail in the final chapter of this book.
56. Kaeli Nieves-Whitmore, "13 Fraternities and Sororities Taking Philanthropy to the Next Level," *College Raptor*, November 7, 2019. https://www.collegeraptor.com/find-colleges/articles/student-life/13-fraternities-and-sororities-taking-philanthropy-to-the-next-level/
57. Ibid.
58. Jia Tolentino, "Welcome to Derby Days, the Most Spectacular Con in All of Frat Philanthropy," *Jezebel*, September 30, 2015. https://jezebel.com/welcome-to-derby-days-the-most-spectacular-con-in-all-1733644115
59. Ibid.
60. Meghan McCarthy, "I Fought Back against My College's Sexist Fraternity," *The Atlantic*, February 24, 2014. https://www.theatlantic.com/education/archive/2014/02/i-fought-back-against-my-colleges-sexist-fraternity/284040/
61. Veronica Ruckh, "William & Mary Sigma Chi Sends out Most Bizarre and Disgusting Email about Vaginas Ever Written," *TMS*. https://totalsororitymove.com/william-mary-sigma-chi-sends-out-most-bizarre-and-disgusting-email-about-vaginas-ever-written/
62. Jia Tolentino, "Welcome to Derby Days, the Most Spectacular Con in All of Frat Philanthropy," *Jezebel*, September 30, 2015. https://jezebel.com/welcome-to-derby-days-the-most-spectacular-con-in-all-1733644115
63. Meghan McCarthy, "I Fought Back against My College's Sexist Fraternity," *The Atlantic*, February 24, 2014. https://www.theatlantic.com/education/archive/2014/02/i-fought-back-against-my-colleges-sexist-fraternity/284040/
64. Ibid.
65. Associated Press, "Fraternity Suspended over Banners Hung near Old Dominion Campus," *FOX 2 Now*, August 25, 2015. https://fox2now.com/2015/08/25/fraternity-suspended-over-banners-hung-near-old-dominion-campus/
66. Ibid.
67. Jake New, "Bad Apples or the Barrel?" *Inside Higher Ed*, April 15, 2015. https://www.insidehighered.com/news/2015/04/15/how-widespread-are-issues-facing-fraternities
68. Kalhan Rosenblatt, "Colleges Are Suspending Greek Life. Don't Expect the Ban to Last," *NBC News*, November 19, 2017. https://www.nbcnews.com/storyline/hazing-in-america/colleges-are-suspending-greek-life-don-t-expect-ban-last-n821351
69. Nick Clarkson, "Ohio State Suspends Fraternity Activity Indefinitely," *The Lantern*, November 16, 2107. https://www.thelantern.com/2017/11/ohio-state-interfraternity-council-chapters-suspended/

70. Jake New, "Bad Apples or the Barrel?" *Inside Higher Ed*, April 15, 2015. https://www.insidehighered.com/news/2015/04/15/how-widespread-are-issues-facing-fraternities
71. Ibid.
72. Tyler Kingkade, "Fraternity Booted Off San Diego State Campus Denies Harassing Anti-Rape Activities," *Huff Post*, January 15, 2015. https://www.huffingtonpost.com/2015/01/15/fraternity-sdsu_n_6458150.html
73. Official Site for Take Back the Night Foundation. https://takebackthenight.org/
74. Anny Jackson, "The Frat Barred from Yale for 5 Years Is Back – and Women Are Saying They Warn One Another to Stay Away," *Business Insider*, January 25, 2018. https://www.businessinsider.com/yale-delta-kappa-epsilon-2018-1
75. Jeremy Bauer-Wolf, "Will Greek Crackdown Change Anything?" *Business Insider*, November 20, 2017. https://www.insidehighered.com/news/2017/11/20/experts-punishments-bans-not-effective-changing-greek-culture
76. Ibid.
77. Ibid.
78. Ibid.
79. Ibid.
80. Katie Lambert, "How Fraternities Work," *How Stuff Works*. https://people.howstuffworks.com/fraternity2.htm
81. The Fraternity Advisor, "Rush and Pledging Problems." Retrieved 2 September 2015.
82. The "Bro Code of Silence" will be taken up in detail in the following chapter.
83. Ralph Ellis, "Judge Throws Out Some Charges against Penn State Frat Members in Hazing Death," *CNN*, March 28, 2018. https://www.cnn.com/2018/03/28/us/penn-state-hazing-death/index.html
84. Ibid.
85. Ibid.
86. Caitlin Flanagan, "Death at a Penn State Fraternity," *The Atlantic*, November 2017.
87. National Institute on Alcohol and Alcoholism, "Fall Semester – A Time for Parents to Discuss the Risks of College Drinking," *The National Institute of Health*. https://pubs.niaaa.nih.gov/publications/collegefactsheet/Collegefactsheet.pdf
88. Avital Norman Nathman, "More Stories of College Kids Dying Quietly from Alcohol Poisoning," *Vice*, November 8, 2107. https://tonic.vice.com/en_us/article/ev4vzm/more-stories-of-college-kids-dying-quietly-from-alcohol-poisoning
89. Eric Levenson, "FSU Fraternity Pledge Dies 'Alone in a Room Full of People' at Party," *CNN*, December 21, 2017. https://www.cnn.com/2017/12/20/us/fsu-fraternity-pledge-death-grand-jury/index.html
90. Ibid.
91. Rebekah Allen, Grace Toohey, Emma Discher, "LSU Fraternity Pledge Maxwell Gruver Case: Gut-Wrenching Accounts of Alleged Hazing at Phi Delta Theta House," *The Advocate*, October 11, 2017. https://www.theadvocate.com/baton_rouge/news/crime_police/article_56a5184e-aeb0-11e7-9710-cb2fe0660cfc.html
92. Ibid.
93. University of Massachusetts Report on Three Types of Hazing. https://www.umass.edu/greek/sites/default/files/pdf/examples_of_hazing.pdf
94. Alexandra DiPalma, "Horrible College Hazing Rituals," *Splinter*, March 11, 2014. https://splinternews.com/horrible-college-hazing-rituals-1793840997

95. Ibid.
96. Ibid.
97. Max Cohen, Chris Quintana, "Young Men Have Died in Fraternities Every Year for 2 Decades, buts Frats Are Slow to Change," *USA Today*, September 11, 2019.
98. Snowden Wright, "In Defense of Hazing," *Daily News*, April 12, 2012. http://www.nydailynews.com/opinion/defense-hazing-article-1.1059984
99. Michael Coard, "Can Greek Hazing Be a Good Thing?" *The Philadelphia Tribune*, September 23, 2017. http://www.phillytrib.com/can-greek-hazing-be-a-good-thing/article_dcfe08b4-ec94-526f-8023-d4bd9dd56965.html
100. Ibid.
101. Cyd Zeigler, "The 'Gay' Side of Hazing," *OutSports,* May 24, 2006. https://www.outsports.com/2013/3/3/4061150/the-gay-side-of-hazing
102. Ibid.
103. Jackie Salo, "Frat Accused of Forcing Pledges to do the Elephant Walk," *New York Post*, February 7, 2019. https://nypost.com/2019/02/07/frat-accused-of-forcing-pledges-to-do-the-elephant-walk/
104. Graham Gremore, "Frat Boys Caught on Tape Engaging in Homophobic and Racist Behavior Claim They're the Real Victims," *Queerty*, April 19, 2018. https://www.queerty.com/frat-boys-caught-tape-engaging-homophobic-racist-behavior-claim-theyre-real-victims-20180419
105. R. Sean Bannon, Matthew W. Brosi, John D. Foubert, "Sorority Women's and Fraternity Men's Rape Myth Acceptance and Bystander Intervention Attitudes," *Journal of Student Affairs Research and Practice*, Vol. 50, Issue 1, 2013, pp.72–87.
106. E. Timothy Bleeker, Sarah K. Murnen, "Fraternity Membership, the Display of Degrading Sexual Images of Women, and Rape Myth Acceptance," *Sex Roles*, Vol. 53, October 2005, pp. 487–493.
107. Ibid.
108. Max Reed, "Wesleyan Sued Over 'Rape Factory' Frat House," *Gawker*, October 9, 2012. http://gawker.com/5950277/wesleyan-sued-over-rape-factory-frat-house
109. Erin Gloria Ryan, "Infamous 'Rapebait' Frat Disbanded for Being Entirely Too Rapey," *Jezebel*, April 4, 2014. https://jezebel.com/infamous-rapebait-frat-disbanded-for-being-entirely-t-1558252895
110. Dara Weinraub, "Kappa Sigma Nationals Investigating Viral Email," *Daily Trojan*, March 8, 2011. https://dailytrojan.com/2011/03/08/kappa-sigma-nationals-investigating-viral-e-mail/
111. Margaret Hartmann, "Frat Email Explains Women Are "Targets," Not "Actual People,"" *Jezebel*, Marh 8, 2011. https://jezebel.com/5779905/usc-frat-guys-email-explains-women-are-targets-not-actual-people-like-us-men
112. Sara Shayanian, "Ex-Temple University Frat President Charged with Attempted Rape," *UPI*, May 17, 2018. https://www.upi.com/Ex-Temple-University-frat-president-charged-with-attempted-rape/7461526554155/
113. Courtney Tanner, "She Was Raped at a Utah State University Fraternity. Now the School Will Pay Her $250K and She'll Help Improve its Response to Campus Sexual Assault," *The Salt Lake Tribune*, July 6, 2018. https://www.sltrib.com/news/education/2018/07/05/utah-state-university/
114. Ibid.
115. AP News, "Woman Sues Butler, Fraternity after 2016 Student Rape Report," August 28, 2018. https://apnews.com/68c98cddd8984d0f9260156f3a12896e
116. Ibid.

117. John Carroll, "Ex-BU Fraternity President May Get Plea Deal in Sexual Assault Case," *KWTX News*, Waco, Texas, August 24, 2018. https://www.kwtx.com/content/news/Ex-BU-fraternity-president-may-get-plea-deal-in-sexual-assault-case-491683471.html
118. Susan Svriuga, "Former Cornell Fraternity President Gets Probation in Sex Offense Case," *The Washington Post*, April 12, 2017. https://www.washingtonpost.com/news/grade-point/wp/2017/04/11/former-cornell-fraternity-president-gets-probation-in-sex-offense-case/?noredirect=on&utm_term=.0edd0bcb34c7
119. Annie Martin, "2 UCF Students Charged after Woman Reports Gang Rape," *Orlando Sentinel*, April 25, 2018. https://www.orlandosentinel.com/features/education/school-zone/os-ucf-frat-suspended-20180424-story.html
120. Ibid.
121. Raisa Habersham, "Ex-Georgia Tech Fraternity President Admits Raping Girlfriend, Sentenced to 20 Years," *AJC*, July 20, 2018. https://www.ajc.com/news/crime--law/georgia-tech-frat-president-admits-raping-girlfriend-sentenced-years/3JSSO2EVDCGKewomwcWhvL/
122. Ibid.
123. Rebecca Everett, "Man Accused of 4th Student Rape at Stockton University," NJ.com, *New Jersey*, January 30, 2019. https://www.nj.com/atlantic/index.ssf/2018/07/second_student_accuses_man_of_rape_at_illegal_frat.html
124. Carol Robinson, "UA Student Charged with Rape after Weekend Sex Assault at Fraternity House," *Birmingham Real-Time News*, March 7, 2019. https://www.al.com/news/birmingham/index.ssf/2015/11/ua_student_charged_with_rape_a.html
125. Callum Mason, "Students Outraged as Yale Fraternity Suspended for 'no means yes' Chants Establishes Chapter at Edinburgh," *Independent*, January 29, 2014. https://www.independent.co.uk/student/news/students-outraged-as-yale-fraternity-suspended-for-no-means-yes-chants-establishes-chapter-at-9092845.html
126. Abby Jackson, "The Frat Barred from Yale for 5 Years Is Back – and Women Are Saying They Warn One Another to Stay Away," *Business Insider*, January 25, 2018. https://www.businessinsider.com/yale-delta-kappa-epsilon-2018-1
127. Abby Jackson, "At Yale, Students Found to be Sexual Assailants Return to Campus," *Business Insider*, January 19, 2018. https://www.businessinsider.com/yale-sexual-misconduct-story-2018-1
128. Abby Jackson, "The Frat Barred from Yale for 5 Years Is Back – and Women Are Saying They Warn One Another to Stay Away," *Business Insider*, January 25, 2018. https://www.businessinsider.com/yale-delta-kappa-epsilon-2018-1
129. Ibid.
130. Yaron Steinbuch, "Northwestern Probes Reports of Sex Assault, Drugging at Frat Houses," *New York Post*, February 7, 2017. https://nypost.com/2017/02/07/northwestern-probes-reports-of-sex-assault-drugging-at-frat-houses/
131. Eliana Dockterman, "The Hunting Ground Reignites the Debate Over Campus Rape," *Time Magazine*, March 5, 2015. http://time.com/3722834/the-hunting-ground-provocative-documentary-reignites-campus-rape-debate/
132. Catherine Zaw, "SAE Housing Suspended for Two Years Due to Sexual Harassment Concerns," *The Stanford Daily*, December 13, 2014. https://www.stanforddaily.com/2014/12/12/sae-housing-suspended-for-two-years-due-to-sexual-harassment-concerns/
133. Ibid.

134. Tyler Kingkade, "Oklahoma Frat Boys Caught Singing 'There Will Never Be A N***** In SAE'," *Huff Post*, March 9, 2015. https://www.huffingtonpost.com/2015/03/08/frat-racist-sae-oklahoma_n_6828212.html
135. Suzanne Ito, "New Report Shows 95% of Campus Rapes Go Unreported," *ACLU*, February 25, 2010. https://www.aclu.org/blog/smart-justice/mass-incarceration/new-report-shows-95-campus-rapes-go-unreported?redirect=blog/speakeasy/new-report-shows-95-campus-rapes-go-unreported
136. Michelle Ye Hee Lee, "The Truth about a Viral Graphic on Rape Statistics," *The Washington Post*, December 9, 2014. https://www.washingtonpost.com/news/fact-checker/wp/2014/12/09/the-truth-about-a-viral-graphic-on-rape-statistics/?utm_term=.d50934abc012
137. Beverly Engel, "Why Don't Victims of Sexual Harassment Come Forward Sooner?" *Psychology Today*, November 16, 2017. https://www.psychologytoday.com/us/blog/the-compassion-chronicles/201711/why-dont-victims-sexual-harassment-come-forward-sooner
138. Liam Stack, "In Stanford Rape Case, Brock Turner Blamed Drinking and Promiscuity," *The New York Times*, June 8, 2016.
139. Ibid.
140. Ibid.
141. Ibid.
142. Ibid.
143. Ibid.
144. Christia Cauterucci, "Brock Turner's Father Sums Up Rape Culture in One Brief Statement," *Slate*, June 5, 2016. http://www.slate.com/blogs/xx_factor/2016/06/05/brock_turner_s_dad_s_defense_proves_why_his_victim_had_to_write_her_letter.html
145. Lindsey Ellefson, "Push to Stop Brock Turner Launching Speaking Tour on 'Drinking and Promiscuity' Gains Traction," *Mediaite*, September 8, 2016.
146. David Jesse, "Why Sexual Assault Survivors Are Fuming over Betsy DeVos' Proposed College Guidelines," *USA Today*, September 3, 2018. https://www.usatoday.com/story/news/politics/2018/08/31/devos-sexual-assault-investigation-changes/1157376002/
147. Caleb Parke, "DeVos to Roll Back Obama-era Title IX Regulations Deemed Unfair to the 'Accused'," *FOX Business News*, August 31, 2018. http://www.foxnews.com/us/2018/08/31/devos-to-roll-back-obama-era-title-ix-regulations-deemed-unfair-to-accused.html
148. Sarah Brown, "DeVos's Rules on Sexual Misconduct Long Awaited on Campuses, Reflect Her Interim Policy," *The Chronicle of Higher Education*, August 29, 2018. https://www.chronicle.com/article/DeVos-s-Rules-on-Sexual/244394
149. Ibid.
150. D. Lisak, L. Gardinier, S.C. Nicksa, A.M. Cote, "False Allegations of Sexual Assault: An Analysis of Ten Years of Reported Cases," *Violence against Women*, December 2010.
151. Sheila Coronel, Steve Coll, Derek Karvitz, "'A Rape on Campus, What Went Wrong?" *Rolling Stone*, April 5, 2015. https://www.rollingstone.com/culture/culture-news/rolling-stone-and-uva-the-columbia-university-graduate-school-of-journalism-report-44930/
152. Ibid.
153. William D. Cohan, "Remembering (and misremembering) the Duke Lacrosse Case," *Vanity Fair*, March 10, 2016.

154. Ibid.
155. Caitlyn Flanagan, "The Dark Power of Fraternities," *The Atlantic*, March 2014. https://www.theatlantic.com/magazine/archive/2014/03/the-dark-power-of-fraternities/357580/
156. Lauren Weirich, "4 Things Influencing Gender Inequality in College Greek Life," *Odyssey*, October 4, 2017. https://www.theodysseyonline.com/gender-inequality-greek-system
157. K Aleisha Fetters, "The 10 Sexiest College Party Themes," *Men's Health*, March 9, 2015. https://www.menshealth.com/trending-news/a19532747/sexy-college-parties/
158. Ibid.
159. Ibid.
160. Lucy Sherriff, "Carnage Cardiff's Pimps and Hoes Fancy Dress Theme Sparks Student Petition over Women's Rights," *Huff Post*, September 10, 2012. https://www.huffingtonpost.co.uk/2012/10/08/carnage-cardiffs-pimps-and-hoes-theme-angry-feminist-petition_n_1947599.html?guccounter=1&guce_referrer_us=aHR0cHM6Ly93d3cuZ29vZ2xlLmNvbS8&guce_referrer_cs=70ZFO2QXyKhlM0uWVqQmbA
161. The Fraternity and Sorority Political Action Committee, Official Site: https://fspac.org/
162. Ibid.
163. Tyler KingKade, "Greek Students Denounce FratPAC's Proposal on College Rape Investigation," *Huff Post*, April 1, 2015. https://www.huffingtonpost.com/2015/04/01/fratpac-college-rape_n_6966504.html
164. Ibid.
165. Ibid.
166. John Hechinger, "The Powerful Forces that Fight for American Fraternities," *The Atlantic*, October 6, 2017. https://www.theatlantic.com/education/archive/2017/10/the-powerful-forces-that-fight-for-american-fraternities/542187/
167. Tyler Kingkade, "FratPAC Lobbies Congress for Tax Breaks, To Stop Anti-Hazing Laws," *Huff Post*, July 25, 2013. https://www.huffingtonpost.com/2013/07/25/fratpac-fraternity-lobby_n_3653692.html
168. Mariah Bohanon, "Multicultural Fraternities, Sororities Offer Communities of Support for Students Traditionally Excluded from Greek Life," *Insight Into Diversity*, February 26, 2018. http://www.insightintodiversity.com/multicultural-fraternities-sororities-offer-communities-of-support-for-students-traditionally-excluded-from-greek-life/
169. Ibid.
170. Julie Zeilinger, "Multicultural Fraternities and Sororities Flip the Script on What We Think about Greeks," *MIC*, October 5, 2015. https://mic.com/articles/125195/multicultural-fraternities-and-sororities-flip-the-script-on-what-we-think-about-greeks#.8MFRVcAk3
171. Ibid.
172. Ibid.
173. Ibid.
174. Theta Pi Sigma, Official Site: https://www.thetapisigma.org
175. Ibid.
176. Ibid.
177. Theta Pi Sigma, Official Site: https://www.thetapisigma.org

178. John Foubert, "Why Title IX Is Needed to Rein in Fraternities," *The New York Times*, May 6, 2011. https://www.nytimes.com/roomfordebate/2011/05/05/frat-guys-gone-wild-whats-the-solution/why-title-ix-is-needed-to-rein-in-fraternities
179. Ibid.
180. John Foubert, Johnathan T. Newberry, Jerry Tatum, "Behavioral Differences Seven Months Later: Effects of a Rape Prevention Program," *Journal of Student Affairs Research and Practice*, 2007. https://works.bepress.com/john_foubert/5/
181. NASPA Initiative, "Invest in the Power of Prevention." *Ending Campus Sexual Violence*. https://cultureofrespect.org/colleges-universities/programs/
182. Anna North, "Is College Sexual Assault a Fraternity Problem?" *The New York Times*, January 29, 2015. https://op-talk.blogs.nytimes.com/2015/01/29/is-college-sexual-assault-a-fraternity-problem/
183. T.M. Lindsey, "Jackson Katz: Violence against Women Is a Men's Issue," *Rewire News*, June 3, 2008. https://rewire.news/article/2008/06/03/jackson-katz-violence-against-women-is-a-mens-issue/

4

THE BRO CODE-OF-SILENCE: HOW MEN'S SILENCE HARMS WOMEN AND MEN

> **Key Points**
> - The Bro Code of Silence
> - The Implied Silence of Male Friends
> - The Deafening Silence of Men in the age of #metoo
> - The Bystander Problem
> - The #metoo Backlash
> - Men's Rights Activists
> - When Men Are Sexual Abuse Victims
> - Men as Allies
> - Passive Gender Inclusion v. Active Gender Inclusion
> - Men's Silence is Literally Killing Men
> - Alexithymia

There are two basic ways that men have been instructed to respond to challenge: either through hostile or aggressive behaviors or through silence. The major challenge to men's unacceptable behaviors toward women has come through the #metoo and Time's Up movements.[1,2] We covered these movements in Chapter 2, but need to more thoroughly address men's current responses to these movements, particularly those who are witnesses to other men's sexual misconduct, but fall into bystander roles instead of having the courage to call out these behaviors.

In addition to men's silence in response to #metoo and Time's Up, men have been and continue to be silent and resistant to their own needs for medical and psychological intervention. By avoiding medical checkups and repressing the need for counseling and therapeutic mediation, men's silence is literally killing men. Why men avert medical and emotional intervention that lead to higher rates of psychological affliction, loneliness, debilitated relationships, life-threatening illness, suicide ideation, and suicide itself will be taken up in this chapter with an emphasis on the societally constructed, normative roles for men that are found throughout contemporary culture.

THE BRO CODE OF SILENCE

Building on Chapter 3, Greek life on college campuses begins with rush week, which then turns to the candidate pledging a fraternity or sorority. An integral part of that pledge is making a promise to keep silent in the face of behaviors that could be detrimental to the fraternity such as hazing, drug-use, binge drinking, and sexual assault. But keeping quiet about the behaviors of other men has been part of the bro code for generations. It is common for men to know about the sexual misconduct of other men, because often times, men confide in one another about such things or are present when an episode of sexual misconduct takes place. An unspoken, but tenaciously held male rule is "do not tell anyone else what I just told you, or what you just witnessed." This is **the bro code of silence**. This is one of the central reasons why men like film mogul Harvey Weinstein get away with sexually abusing women for decades. When coupled with the power someone like Weinstein wielded as one of Hollywood's most successful film producers, the bro code of silence assures that other men who may have known about his behaviors, or at least had heard about his behaviors, will remain silent, which ensures that those behaviors will continue. Power assures that victims will also remain silent out of concern for their careers or being called out as 'gold-diggers' or 'liars' or any number of possible slurs or retaliatory accusations.

In addition to the implied silence of male friends, the fact that many men code rape a "women's issue" because women are primarily the targeted victims of men's sexual violence means that men do not view themselves as potential victims of sexual misconduct. Yet, in recent studies, it appears that men are victims of sexual abuse at higher rates than once believed.[3] Where men used to fall between 5 and 14% of reported sexual assault and rape victim-statistics, a recent National Crime Victimization Survey of 40,000 households reported that 38% of incidences of sexual violence were perpetrated against men.[4] But what is most interesting for this chapter are the rates of non-reporting among male victims of sexual violence. It has been known for decades that sexual assault and rape are greatly underreported crimes.[5,6] But the low number of male victims in contrast to female victims was assumed to be the result of men not being targeted for sexual victimhood by heterosexual men, or that men's physical prowess would deter potential assaults. A stigma has therefore been attached to male victims that they are probably gay or physically weak. In either case, a sexist and homophobic culture that reinforces to heterosexual boys and men that being gay or female is synonymous with weakness is a culture where a strong, negative stigma will be assigned to male victims of sexual abuse, which in turn will drive male victims to silence out of fear of being mocked or accused and therefore in some sense complicit in their assault.

What make matters worse is that a number of comedians and comedy media programming have included rape jokes into their repertoire, which stigmatizes rape and sexual assault further by minimizing it as something worthy of laughter. Consider Seth MacFarland's animated comedy show *Family Guy*, which has enjoyed 17 seasons and counting. *Family Guy* has been a huge hit with teens, young adults, and particularly the boys and young men of bro culture. Rape jokes have been sprinkled into the show throughout the years. In fact, one *Family Guy* regular is the character "Quagmire" who is a middle-aged man on constant pursuit of rape if consensual sex is unavailable.[7] In one scene, Quagmire is seen dragging off the body of an unconscious woman and stops only when he realizes he is being filmed.[8] This same scenario returns in a later episode.[9] In another scene, a waiter asks Quagmire if he wants his usual drink with a roofie for his date.[10] In one of the most egregious examples of a joke about violent rape that resulted in murder, the main character "Peter Griffin," who is the father of the Griffin family, watches the news while drinking at a bar with friends. The news anchor reports that the bodies of three young co-eds from a local university were found and that there was evidence they had been raped and murdered, to which Griffin responds, "Everyone's getting laid but me."[11] MacFarlane was once asked by a writer at the New York Times, "Who is your biggest audience?" to which MacFarlane responded, "It's men, 18 to 34."[12]

MacFarland attempts to mitigate the damage by claiming that the audience is not laughing at rape, but rather at Peter's stupidity.[13] But it's unclear how MacFarland or anyone else could know at what his audience is laughing. It's all the more troubling when we realize that, by his own admission, the largest audience demographic is young men who are the very ones who might ridicule another man for having been sexually assaulted, or who will often be those who victim-blame or downplay a case of sexual assault. Not only do these media treatments of rape minimize the trauma to victims of sexual abuse, they also create an environment where men will remain silent rather than endure the mockery and innuendo that often comes with a public acknowledgement of being a male, rape, or sexual assault survivor.

THE IMPLIED SILENCE OF MEN

Girls and boys will often have a collection of friends when growing up that serve as their confidants, their entrusted pals who will keep their most guarded secrets. But beginning in childhood, boys will often bond around the notion that "girls are icky," or "girls are not pals like boys." Like the proverbial treehouse where little boys congregate to discuss their big plans with a sign outside the fortress reading "No Girls Allowed," gender segregation begins, for many boys, in childhood where bonding between same-sex allies takes precedence over developing friendships with girls. At the same time, these early alliances, for most boys, are carefully manicured by parents and others to assure that these friendships are not considered to be homoerotic in any way. Gender is policed by all those of influence around a boy to maintain a binary, heteronormative version of masculinity that allows for boy-only friendships without any hint of sexual interest. It is within these parameters that boys learn to tell and keep one another's secrets. It is considered to be the very essence of betrayal to reveal the secrets of your bros, and understood throughout male culture that your alliances with other boys and men are to be considered primary over your alliances with girls and women.

Of course, as boys get older, the "no girls allowed" rule is disbanded; but for many men, the sentiment does not go away, which is the understanding that we have our bros' backs in the sense that any bad behaviors we know about or suspect may be happening will be kept confidential. In fact, as men begin to widen their circle of friends and associates, far too many men place women into the category of *potential sexual opportunity* rather than as close friends who are respected to the same degree as their male friends. Certainly there are plenty of men who are exceptions to this rule, but to qualify as an exception to the rule, men must unlearn many of the sexist and sexually predatory tropes that flow to them from older men of influence coupled with the mass-media stereotypes that too often one-dimensionalize women as sexual side-kicks in films, video games, or music videos produced strictly for the male gaze.

As the previous chapter noted, you see this sort of male-first thinking with many fraternity "bros before hoes" men who pledge to one another that the actions within the frat-house will be protected as solemn secrets from the outside world, including from any investigative personnel who may be looking into allegations of sexual misconduct. In this way, many frat-houses are incubators for the Harvey Weinsteins of the world who use their power to sexually abuse women, while confident that the men who know what is going on will keep the information to themselves as part of the bro pact, "mind your own business" when another man is abusing his power with women. The silence in these cases is implied because it is usually not the result of actual promises, pledges, or contracts made between men; rather, it is the result of many years of socialization that reinforce a male-understanding that you are always supposed to keep your mouth shut when you're aware of another man's sexual misconduct, and this instruction often extends to men who are coworkers or acquaintances, but not actual friends. For many, this implied silence of men conditions the assurance that misdeeds of a variety of types will be safe from a public reckoning, but it also assures that misdeeds will continue unchecked for protracted periods of time.

THE DEAFENING SILENCE OF MEN IN THE AGE OF #METOO

From the moment that actress Alyssa Milano tweeted the phrase "me too" at noon on October 15th 2017 to document her being the victim of sexual assault, 12 million people within 24 hours responded with me-too tweets.[14] The impact around the world has been nothing less than a global phenomenon of survivors adding their voices to a growing number of women and men who support one another in the reclamation of their right not to be abused. At the same time, a number of feminist writers and scholars have denounced the silent stance many men have taken in the wake of the #metoo movement.[15,16] Anti-violence educator Jackson Katz stated of the male-actors at the Golden Globe Awards in 2018,

The almost total absence of men saying anything (during the ceremony) about the unbelievable present movement and activist energy in the room articulated by women was notable. Men are committing the vast majority of harassment, abuse and violence. Nothing's going to change until both individual men's behavior changes, and institutions that are still largely controlled by men (start) becoming accountable.[17]

Gender scholars have since asked why it is so difficult for men to speak out in support of the women of #metoo. It may be that men in general support the women of #metoo, but because of their persistent silence, it is hard to know. Are men threatened by the allegations of sexual misconduct on the part of so many men? Do they view #metoo as a notification that their own behaviors will no longer be tolerated and perhaps their name could be next on the list of men's names who have sexually harassed women? Is the notion of accountability foreign to men who have enjoyed millennia of unchallenged sexual misconduct? Are men afraid that publicly supporting women would be viewed as courting the enemy and lessening their own standing in the eyes of other men? Katz offers a more sympathetic alternative:

> [Men's silence] doesn't mean that they don't care…it just means that a lot of men don't have the language. Men who do speak out often face pushback from other men who question their manhood or loyalty to the gender. The reason why it's a leadership issue is because it takes some self confidence and strength to do so.[18]

Leadership often involves making tough decisions and taking uncomfortable actions in order to do what is right. In the context of disrupting men's sexual misconduct, this means that men must sometimes confront their male friends who they realize may become defensive and who may also view the intervention as a challenge to their friendship. But taking the step to confront friends knowing that it will not be taken well is the courageous leadership to which Katz refers.

Writing for *Harvard Business Review*, David G. Smith and W. Brad Johnson ask the rhetorical question, "Where are all the Male Allies in U.S. Politics?"[19] Noting that "the problem of the silent man festers at the root of America's ubiquitous workplace sexual harassment and gender exclusion," Smith and Johnson touch upon the longstanding problem of the bystander who knows or suspects sexual misconduct, but says and does nothing.[20] **The bystander problem** is as old as time, but has been refocused today as one of the principle reasons why predators like Weinstein, Cosby, and others are able to get away with sexual harassment, sexual assault, and rape for such long periods of time. A bystander can be a friend, a coworker, a teammate, a family member, or any number of individuals who remain silent, but who have the ability to disrupt the sexual misconduct of their peers, since they already have an established relationship with the person committing the misdeed. Why do so many men remain silent in the wake of a friend's or associate's sexual misconduct? Writing about this issue, Rob Bogosian, founder of RVB Associates, an organization that assists businesses in creating effective leadership strategies argues that there are three basic causes of workplace silence:[21]

- Defense: fear-based silence, whereby employees are afraid to report in a work-environment where they feel their job could be in jeopardy.
- Futility: apathy-based silence, whereby employees may have reported in the past and witnessed inaction on the part of the business. These experiences lead to a growing cynicism that speaking up is a waste of time.
- Social-connections, whereby employees do not want to jeopardize the relationships they have built with coworkers by reporting behaviors they may have witnessed.

At the base of these preventative motives are fear and apathy. If people are afraid, they often seek refuge by withdrawing from activities that draw attention to themselves. Confronting a peer or reporting an act of sexual misconduct takes courage, because there will be consequences, and too often people will look the other way to avoid the possibility of getting involved and being identified as a witness or a snitch. If one either doesn't care what is going on between coworkers or cares but has experienced non-action after taking the risk of reporting to a supervisor, apathy can set in such that future episodes of witnessed misconduct are shrugged off as inevitabilities about which nothing can be done.

Thought Box

For this thought experiment, imagine that you witness what you consider to be sexual harassment, where a friend, teammate, coworker, or family member is the perpetrator. What do you do? (a) confront him immediately about what you witnessed to let him know that his behavior was unacceptable, (b) wait until an appropriate time to speak to him about what you witnessed, (c) bring in other friends or coworkers to create a mini-intervention so that you don't have to act on your own, (d) report to someone else who you believe will do something, (e) do nothing this time and wait to see if it happens again.

We could probably construct a multitude of possible scenarios, but at issue is this: how would you respond if you witnessed or suspected that someone you know is sexually harassing another person?

One of the most comprehensive bystander intervention programs in the nation is *Mentors in Violence Prevention*.[22] Employing workshops, MVP helps students develop strategies of intervention specific to certain situations. Specifically, MVP helps peer groups determine how to best challenge all forms of gender-based violence that may be witnessed or suspected. The program is based on the notion that the best, most credible voices to disrupt gender-based violence and sexual abuse are those who already have relationships of one kind or another with the abuser. Whether friends, family members, coworkers, teammates, classmates, parishioners, or other preexisting relationships, individuals who have the best chance of challenging gender-based violence and misconduct will be those who know the abuser and who can reach out in a supportive way to conduct constructive dialogues aimed at challenging not only the individual behaviors of misconduct, but the cultural norms of masculinity that foster these behaviors in the first place. As long as men view themselves as superior to women, or that girlfriends and wives *belong to them as a form of extended property*, gender-based violence will continue unabated despite whatever criminal punitive measures may be instituted. The courts cannot change men's behaviors and attitudes, but *MVP* works under the assumption that getting men to respect women's agency and autonomy through steady and committed constructive contact with mentors who the perpetrator knows and trusts can be effective.

THE #METOO BACKLASH

One development that many men are embracing is a pushback against the #metoo movement by those who believe that the movement has gone too far, that innocent men may be targeted and convicted in the court of public opinion or lose their jobs without due process. In fact, this has been the ongoing criticism by men like Donald Trump who openly criticizes the #metoo movement as promoting a "guilty until proven innocent" model of justice. On the issue of sexual assault allegations against then Supreme Court nominee Brent Kavanaugh, Trump stated,

> This is beyond the Supreme Court. This is everything to do with our country. When you are guilty until proven innocent, it's just not supposed to be that way. Always, I heard you're innocent until proven guilty. In this case, you're guilty until proven innocent. I think that is a very, very dangerous standard for our country.[23]

Men far and wide have jumped on this bandwagon, knowing that the history of sexual harassment, sexual assault, and rape has been to victim-blame and to place the burden on survivors who are typically called 'liars' and 'women with ulterior motives' as a way to nullify their voices and their credibility. The consequence of calling victims 'liars' and 'opportunists' is that fewer victims will report having been sexually assaulted, which is precisely the hope of sexual predators. Along with threats that are commonly aimed at sexual assault and rape survivors, victims often experience feelings of fear, loss of control, flashbacks, trouble concentrating, guilt, depression, loss of interest in sex, and protracted anxiety.[24]

According to the National Violence against Women Prevention Research Center at the Medical University of South Carolina, there are recognizable and well-documented effects that follow from being victims of sexual assault and rape:

- Post-Traumatic Stress Disorder in approximately one-third of cases, which means that approximately 3.8 million American women have rape-related PTSD.[25]
- Major Depressive Episodes at a rate of three-times that of non-rape-victims.[26]
- Suicide Ideation at four-times that of non-crime victims.[27]
- Suicide Attempts at 13-times that of non-crime victims.[28]
- 13.4 times more likely to have developed alcohol-related problems than non-crime victims.[29]
- 26 times more likely to have drug-abuse problems than non-crime victims.[30]

When rape and sexual assault survivors are belittled, accused of lying, threatened, called names like 'sluts', accused of being opportunists who are looking for a lawsuit, and many other attempts to silence them, the results are predictable: victims will not report.

No one wants a false report to ruin an innocent man's career or place him behind bars, but false reporting is actually quite rare. According to a recent study, approximately 6% of reports of sexual assault were determined to be false.[31] Previous research places the percentages at between 2% and 10%.[32] In fact, The U.S. Department of Justice reports that the vast majority of instances of rape and sexual assault are never reported.[33] The U.S. Institute of Health reports that the most common reason why a girl or woman issues a false report is to conceal adultery or to cover up ditching school.[34] Making matters even murkier is the fact that reports of sexual assault are often determined to be false after a victim recants her report.[35] Cases like these do not necessarily mean that the victim was lying, since victims recant their reports for many reasons that include fear over threats aimed at them by perpetrators or in high profile cases, fans of perpetrators. In the infamous Kobe Bryant rape case of 2003, for instance, the victim began to receive death threats when her identity was released by media personalities.[36,37] In the high-profile case of Dr. Christine Blasey Ford who testified before a Senate committee that Supreme Court nominee Brett Kavanaugh had sexually assaulted her in high school, so many death threats were aimed at her that she and her family moved out of their house.[38] After her testimony concluded, President Donald Trump mocked her publicly at a campaign rally in Mississippi.[39]

Still, the #metoo backlash persists, primarily from men who fear that their behaviors may be called out and made public. A more cynical view would suggest that there are men who recognize and enjoy their privilege so that a movement that places men's abuse in a spotlight with the intent of changing the culture is a threat to those men who would like things to remain just as they are. Some of the more famous men's groups to adopt the approach of attacking the #metoo movement are **men's rights activists**. Like Trump's warning that #metoo advocates a guilty until proven innocent ideology, men's rights groups have adopted the **#himtoo** moniker just as many white people have adopted the 'all lives matter' slogan as an alleged challenge to the Black

Thought Box

Tarana Burke, founder of the #metoo movement states, "Inherently, having privilege isn't bad, but it's how you use it, and you have to use it in service of other people."[40] In the context of gendered violence and sexual abuse, men enjoy privilege in the sense that on average, men are perpetrators and women are targeted victims. Yet, Ms. Burke's quote above suggests that the privilege men have should be used in the service of helping women. This chapter covers the fact that many men have been silent in the wake of #metoo about men's sexual misconduct toward women and reasons have been given for this phenomenon. Why do you think so many men violate Ms. Burke's directive when it comes to women? Do the reasons provided in this chapter exhaust the possible answers to this question, or can you devise other reasons not covered here?

Lives Matter movement. Men's rights activists view feminism as one of the most toxic movements in the world. One of the most noted men's rights activists is Paul Elam, who founded the group "A Voice for Men" and who stated, "feminism is cancer," and adds,

> I find you, as a feminist, to be a loathsome, vile piece of human garbage. I find you so pernicious and repugnant that the idea of fucking your shit up gives me an erection.[41]

Doubling down, Elam notes,

> Should I be called to sit on a jury for a rape trial, I vow publicly to vote not guilty, even in the face of overwhelming evidence that the charges are true.[42]

These are examples of the hostility employed by some men who feel that feminists and #metoo are disrupting the patriarchal power they view as birthrights. It is difficult to know how many men subscribe to these men's rights views since they do not publish a census, but it is safe to say that those who are sympathetic to the men's rights platform live in anonymity and number well if a poll were taken; and though claiming to be apolitical, their views align well with the repeated talking points of conservatives on issues of so-called political correctness, the rebuff of alleged guilty-until-proven-innocent charges, and the general disdain for feminism that is found throughout conservative circles. The outpouring of emotion from victims who took part in bringing the #metoo movement to the forefront of contemporary society can be viewed as the product centuries of silence boiling over into a celebration of solidarity and empowerment. For men like Elam, #metoo represents the nightmare of holding predatory men accountable for their actions for the first time in human history.

WHEN MEN ARE SEXUAL ABUSE VICTIMS

When issues of sexual assault and rape are discussed, they are almost always framed as women's issues even though overwhelmingly it is men who are the perpetrators, and this, as antiviolence educator Jackson Katz has stated on many occasions, makes rape and violence against women men's issues.[43] But we seldom speak about rape as a men's issue. We focus on the victims, who are usually women, and often ignore the perpetrators, who are overwhelmingly men. What is less discussed is men who are themselves victims of rape. Even though one in five women will be raped in their lifetimes, one in seventy-one men will be raped in their lifetimes.[44] This means that about 9% of all rape victims are men, although again, underreporting makes statistics of this kind less reliable. According to the National Institute of Health, because women are victims of rape far more than men, the national discussion tends toward a view of rape as the physically powerful over the physically weak.[45] Therefore, when men are raped, the male victim is viewed as a weak man overpowered by a stronger man and a stigma attaches to the male victim. In the article, "The Sexual Victimization of Men in America," UCLA professors Laura Stemple and Iian Meyer make the point that because men are seldom sexually assaulted in comparison to women, this fact,

> …promotes a counterproductive construct of what it means to be a man…expectations about male invulnerability are constraining for men and boys.[46]

Stemple and Meyer go on to note that even though men are sexually assaulted at lower rates than women, some research has emerged that shows men are victims of sexual assault more frequently than once thought.[47] But one of the main points Stemple and Meyer want to make clear is that assumptions about rape perpetration and victimization feed a common trope that harms men:

> The assumption that men are always perpetrators and never victims reinforces unhealthy ideas about men and their supposed invincibility. These hyper-masculine ideals can reinforce aggressive male attitudes and, at the same time, callously stereotype male victims of sexual abuse as "failed men."[48]

Male victims can be viewed as "failed men" because of a cultural narrative that maintains the sexist dichotomy that *men are and should be strong*, while *women are and should be weak*. Being a male victim of rape is therefore seen through this narrative as a man who is weak, who was unable to defend himself. Men who are victims of rape, therefore, often feel ashamed and this sense of shame causes them to remain silent about their victimization.

Writing for *The Guardian*, David Lisak hits upon one of the most salient reasons why men who are sexually assaulted often remain silent:

> Societal expectations about what it means to be a man may cause a survivor to suppress his trauma. From an early age, men receive

the message that they should never be, or even appear to be, vulnerable or weak; the idea that men cannot be victims is central to gender socialization.[49]

When boys and men *feel* vulnerable, a longstanding rule of the bro code is to never appear to be afraid of, or vulnerable to, anything. Men are supposed to be and appear at all times to be tough and resilient in the face of danger, challenge, and threat. This instruction carries with it the assumption that while men perpetrate violence, including sexual violence, they should never be the victims of sexual violence. Victimhood is almost always framed as being synonymous with fragility, which is coded feminine in bro culture and therefore a sign of weakness.

One of the more encouraging signs that the times may be changing is the fact that some high-profile men have come forward to speak about their sexual victimization. Notably, actor and former NFL player Terry Crews, who is known for being strong, muscular, and in many respects an archetypal alpha male, reported in 2017 that he was sexually victimized by another man.[50] It was actually the many brave women who reported their sexual abuse at the hands of movie mogul Harvey Weinstein who inspired Crews to tell his own story.[51] Initially, Crews did not report the incident out of fear that doing so would ostracize him in the TV and film industries, since the abuser was a powerful industry executive.[52] At the same time, rapper 50 Cent mocked Crews publicly over reporting his story, which is the very thing that men fear when they find the courage to come forward to report their being abused.[53] Men like 50 Cent frame their criticism in humor and sarcasm in the hope that a backlash to their mockery will be viewed as coming from people who simply don't have a sense of humor. This is a common ploy used by men in bro culture who belittle others when they are aware that their public shaming of a victim will be met with criticism. But this also highlights the challenge that comes with trying to change the cultural narrative that paralyzes victims into silence.

MEN AS ALLIES

One of the most important questions for men today is, "what makes a man a good ally to women in the age of #metoo?" University of Victoria professor Wanda Hurren offers this thought:

> A man's legitimacy as an ally to women is only fully expressed when he is an intentional exemplar and fierce watchdog for the behavior of other men. Legitimate male allies consciously engage other men, first demonstrating respect for women and then holding other men accountable for the same.[54]

Hurren notes that what she terms *passive gender inclusion* is cheap and hollow, that it costs men very little to claim to support "women's rights," since this is an abstraction that has little-to-no impact on men's actual lives.[55] By contrast, **active gender inclusion** requires action on the part of men, which includes modifying one's own behaviors, holding other men accountable, and being a role model for others. Some of the men who only practice passive gender inclusion may also practice sexist behaviors by making comments about women's looks or make flirtatious or sexually charged comments aimed at a colleague, or perhaps look the other way when he sees sexually harassing behaviors at work from other men.

> **Thought Box**
>
> As men attempt to be allies to women, there can be missteps along the way. Many men feel unsure about how they can be good allies or could be afraid to say or do the wrong thing. Given that being an ally, whether along lines of race and ethnicity, sexual orientation, or in this case gender, can be tricky, ask women you know or who are classmates, "What makes a man a good ally to women?" and "What should a good male ally never say or do?" Discuss the answers together.

Men can also be strong allies to other men, but not in *the bro code of silence* ways that we have seen in this chapter. Since men are instructed to be emotionally stoic from boyhood through adulthood, along with a go-along-to-get-along attitude with other men when presented with opportunities to abuse their privilege with women, a male ally to other men can support and nurture emotional connectedness with other men who, like themselves, have been socialized to remain silent in the face of pain, fear, insecurity, and self-doubt. Male allies can also help one another overcome the urge to go along with the crowd when it comes to sexist and homophobic words and behaviors. Finally, men can hold other men accountable when they cross the line by threatening or committing physical, sexual, or emotional violence against others. This final measure of being an ally to other men is the most challenging of them all, since those confronted will likely not view the intervention as an action of an ally. In most cases, friends and associates will become defensive and angry when challenged by a peer. This is why programs like *Mentors in Violence Prevention* are so important. They work specifically on effective strategies that men and women can employ to assure that an intervention has the best possible chance of being taken in a constructive and supportive way. But the first step in becoming an effective ally to both women and men is for men to finally abandon the bro code of silence.

MEN'S SILENCE IS LITERALLY KILLING MEN

A different kind of silence that men engage in is silence in the wake of personal problems that could be mitigated through medical intervention or counseling.

Famously, men will avoid going to the doctor for checkups, or in the wake of symptoms that could be indicative of a serious health problem. The procedure that many men avoid is a digital rectal exam to check for the possibility of prostate cancer, which is the second leading cause of cancer death to men each year.[56] Whether men consider this procedure to be homoerotic or somehow inadmissible for men who harbor homophobic beliefs, Dr. Preston Sprenkle of Yale Medical School admits that "some men are exceptionally opposed to it."[57] But beyond specific medical tests and procedures, men are trained from boyhood to be self-sufficient, not to seek out help unless it is an emergency. University of California, Irvine Health Sciences report that 60% of men will not seek out doctor's assistance even if they think they have a serious health problem.[58] In fact, men are three-times more likely than women to admit to foregoing doctor visits altogether within the previous five years.[59] This means that the avoidance of health care is a gendered issue. UCI professor of urology, Faysal A. Yafi reports,

> Men are often embarrassed about health issues that they feel might reflect on their masculinity, and understandably squeamish about the prospect of uncomfortable prostate or rectal exams.[60]

Even Dr. Yafi characterizes this fear as 'understandable'. The excuses most men make is that they are too busy or that they are afraid of finding out something is wrong.[61] The result is avoidance and silence. Drs. Jamin Brahmbhatt and Sijo Parekattil note that these same men will find up to 34 hours per week to play golf or take a trip to Las Vegas, but claim they don't have 60 minutes per year to get a medical check up.[62] The irony here is that men are taught to be tough and fearless, while fear is the driving force that prevents them from scheduling and attending doctor visits. In fact, men are twice as likely as women to admit that they have never seen a doctor even once as adults.[63]

At the same time, predictably, men, on average, die earlier than women by around 4.4 years and there are reasons for this phenomenon,[64,65] of which, Harvard Medical School has listed the most common ones:

- Men take greater risks than women.
- Men, on average, have more dangerous jobs than women.
- Men die of heart disease at greater rates than women.
- Men commit suicide at higher rates than women.
- Men tend to be less socially connected than women.
- Men avoid doctors.[66]

It is also the case that men smoke and drink alcohol in excess in greater numbers than women.[67,68] Men's silence and fear are at the core of much of these problems. Rather than deal with personal issues that can be aided by counseling, men will withdraw and self-medicate with alcohol and other substances.[69] This is part of the male training, beginning in boyhood, that instructs men to be inordinately self-sufficient. Talking about problems, men are taught, is what women do, not men. So, when struggling with feelings of depression, loneliness, fear, and self-doubt, men will retreat into silence, isolation, and alcohol rather than reach out to others for help.

Suicide is a complex subject that involves depression and other forms of mental illness, but of all 45,000 people who commit suicide in the U.S. each year, 77% of them are men.[70] The fact that men complete suicide more than do women has to do with gun culture. In the U.S., six in ten gun owners are men and men commit suicide using a gun more often than do women.[71,72] Using a firearm to take one's own life is a surer means of completion, of course, but there are other things that factor into the decision to take one's life in the first place. Psychologists have long identified one factor among men they term ***alexithymia***, which means having an inability to express and communicate one's emotions.[73] This silence and inability is culturally constructed. Boys are taught to "suck it up," "man up," "get tough," "be strong," and above all else, "never act like a girl." So, when culture labels communication, emotion, seeking help, and expressing fear and doubt *feminine*, boys and men hold inside whatever feelings they are experiencing out of a culturally instituted anxiety that they may be called out for being unmanly. This tough-guy attitude and its association with gun culture must be examined. So much of contemporary masculine imagery in films, TV, games, and music bonds together men and guns as though masculine strength and respect are defined through one's ability to wield violence and intimidation, and nothing does this better than a gun.

The paradigmatic association of guns and masculinity is found in the military, where suicide has been and continues to be a major problem. Troubling statistics on the connection between military service and suicide have been documented for years. Approximately 20 veterans die by suicide in the U.S. each and every day.[74] While male veterans who commit suicide statistically outnumber female veterans who commit suicide, the numbers are much closer than seen in those who never served in the military at 32.1 per 100K (men) to 28.7 per 100K (women).[75,76] This parity suggests that there is something about military service and particularly combat military service that places men and women at greater risk of suicide. Consider the case of Deana Martorella Orellana who served as a Marine and was deployed to Afghanistan in 2010.[77] In 2016, Deana took her own life.[78] Deana's sister Robin retells Deana's feelings when she returned to civilian life:

> She said that she didn't see things the same, and she could handle everything except for the kids. And I don't know what that means. She just didn't talk.[79]

Eventually, a VA officer reported to her family that Deana was suffering from PTSD related to combat, which the family notes Deana had never divulged.[80] The Service Women's Action Network (SWAN) has issued recommendations for stronger social support groups for women and men who are combat veterans or active-duty personnel to help them deal with the potential trauma that often comes with military service.[81] But military culture has not traditionally been an environment where counseling and therapy were encouraged, although this tension is slowly beginning to abate.[82] Even more than what is found in civilian culture, military culture has been historically viewed as a hypermasculine culture where service men and women are expected to handle their own problems rather than reaching out for help from therapists, psychologists, and social workers. The notion of self-sufficiency coupled with concerns about being called out for appearing to be soft, weak, feminine, or gay creates a deadly silencing effect that produces dangers, and sometimes life-threatening dangers, for both women and men.

POSTSCRIPT

Beginning in childhood, boys are instructed by men and peers to remain emotionally stoic except in cases where they are angry. As a result of this conditioning, when confronted with conflict or challenges, men typically take one of two paths: hostility or silence. Hostility can take the forms of verbal, psychological, or physical action. We often witness hostility between men, or between men and their partners in the wake of some sort of conflict. Not seeing a moral high ground to take in defending their actions, many men go silent, while others adopt hostile and violent reactions as the only reactions they have been trained to take when challenged.

Silence is the response men adopt when confronted with circumstances with which they would rather not engage. For instance, even when many men experience physical symptoms of illness, they will resist going to the doctor to assess what is wrong. This medical avoidance literally costs men their lives, since many illnesses are treatable when caught early. Prostate cancer is a good example. More than 230,000 men are diagnosed with prostate cancer each year.[83] Many forms of prostate cancer are slow growing and can be effectively treated through radiation or surgery if caught early.[84] But by the time prostate cancer reaches stage 4, it spreads to areas outside of the prostate such as the bladder, rectum, or nearby organs.[85] In these cases, the chance of remission and cure are very low.[86]

There are a number of theories why men, more than women, avoid medical checkups and psychological interventions, but one common view is that men are taught from childhood to be self-sufficient and never show weakness. Any form of frailty or vulnerability, whether physical or emotional, is considered to be a weakness. Men have also been instructed for centuries that it is their responsibility to be providers and protectors of the family, while ailments inhibit this responsibility. Silence fueled by fears, expectations, and normative rules for being a man is at the heart of these problems.

Notes

1. #Me Too, Official Website. https://metoomvmt.org/
2. Time's Up, Official Website. https://www.timesupnow.com/

Chapter 4

3. Bureau of Justice Statistics, "Data Collection: National Crime Victimization Survey," 2018. https://www.bjs.gov/index.cfm?ty=dcdetail&iid=245
4. Hanna Rosin, "When Men Are Raped," *Slate*, April 29, 2014. https://slate.com/human-interest/2014/04/male-rape-in-america-a-new-study-reveals-that-men-are-sexually-assaulted-almost-as-often-as-women.html
5. Emily Thomas, "Rape Is Grossly Underreported in the U.S., Study Finds," *Huff Post*, November 21, 2013. https://www.huffingtonpost.com/2013/11/21/rape-study-report-america-us_n_4310765.html
6. W. David Allen, "The Reporting and Underreporting of Rape," *Southern Economic Journal*, Vol. 73, No. 3, January 2007, pp. 623–641. https://www.jstor.org/stable/20111915?seq=1#page_scan_tab_contents
7. Alyssa Soren, "Stop Rape Jokes on Family Guy," *Change.org*, 2011. https://www.change.org/p/stop-rape-jokes-on-family-guy
8. Ibid.
9. Ibid.
10. Ibid.
11. Deborah Solomon, "Interview with Seth MacFarlane," *The New York Times*, September 11, 2009. https://www.nytimes.com/2009/09/13/magazine/13FOB-Q4-t.html
12. Ibid.
13. Ibid.
14. Cassandra Santiago and Doug Criss, "An Activist, a Little Girl and the Heartbreaking Origin of 'Me too'". *CNN*. Archived from the original on October 17, 2017. Retrieved October 18, 2017.
15. Tom Pessah, "Men Who Are Silent After #MeToo: It's Time to Speak Up," *The Guardian*, October 20, 2017.
16. Rob Carpenter, "Men Are Appallingly Silent Toward #MeToo," *USC Media Institute for Social Change*, March 21, 2018. http://www.uscmisc.org/articles/2018/3/21/op-ed-men-are-appallingly-silent-toward-metoo
17. Meera Jagannathan, "Why Were Men at the Golden Globes So Quiet on #MeToo?" *Market Watch*, January 8, 2018. https://moneyish.com/ish/why-were-men-at-the-golden-globes-so-quiet-on-metoo/
18. Ibid.
19. David G. Smith, W. Brad Johnson, "Where Are the Male Allies in U.S. Politics?" *Harvard Business Review*, September 26, 2018. https://hbr.org/2018/09/where-are-the-male-allies-in-u-s-politics
20. Ibid.
21. Terri Williams, "Workplace Sexual Harassment and the Culture of Silence," *The Economist*. https://execed.economist.com/blog/industry-trends/workplace-sexual-harassment-and-culture-silence
22. Mentors in Violence Prevention, Official Website, MVP Strategies. https://www.mvpstrat.com/
23. Z. Byron Wolf, "Trump Fine-Tunes His Campaign Attack on the #MeToo Movement," *CNN*, October 3, 2018. https://www.cnn.com/2018/10/03/politics/trump-metoo-movement/index.html
24. Loyola University, Maryland, Typical Responses to Being Victims of Sexual Assault. https://www.loyola.edu/department/counseling-center/students/concerns/sexual-assault/reactions
25. Dean G. Kilpatrick, "The Mental Health Impact of Rape," *National Violence against Women Prevention Research Center*, Medical University of South Carolina. https://mainweb-v.musc.edu/vawprevention/research/mentalimpact.shtml

26. Ibid.
27. Ibid.
28. Ibid.
29. Ibid.
30. Ibid.
31. David Lisak, Lori Gardinier, Sarah C. Nicksa, Ashley M. Cote, "False Allegations of Sexual Assault: An Analysis of Ten Years of Reported Cases," *Symposium on False Allegations of Rape, Violence against Women*, Vol. 16, Issue 12, 2010, pp. 1318–1334. https://web.archive.org/web/20180101025446/https://icdv.idaho.gov/conference/handouts/False-Allegations.pdf
32. Ibid.
33. Lynn Langton, Marcus Berzofsky, Christopher Krebs, Hope Smiley-McDonald, U.S. Department of Justice, Office of Justice Programs, Bureau of Justice Statistics, Special Report, "Victimizations Not Reported to the Police, 2006–2010," August, 2012. https://www.bjs.gov/content/pub/pdf/vnrp0610.pdf
34. AWEA De Zutter, R. Horselenberg, P.J. van Koppen, "Motives for Filing a False Allegation of Rape," *Archives of Sexual Behavior*, Vol. 47, Issue 2, February 17, 2017, pp. 457–464. https://www.ncbi.nlm.nih.gov/pubmed/28213722
35. Katie Heaney, "Almost No One Is Falsely Accused of Rape," *The Cut*, October 5, 2018. https://www.thecut.com/article/false-rape-accusations.html
36. *CNN Law Center*, "Man Accused of Threatening Kobe Bryant Accuser," August 21, 2003. https://www.cnn.com/2003/LAW/08/21/threat.bryant/
37. AP, "Kobe's Accuser Named — Twice," *CBS News*, July 25, 2003. https://www.cbsnews.com/news/kobes-accuser-named-151-twice/
38. Sinead Baker, "Christine Blasey Ford Still Can't Live at Home Because of 'Unending" Death Threats After Her Kavanaugh Testimony, Lawyers Say," *Business Insider*, October 8, 2018. https://www.businessinsider.com/christine-blasey-ford-cant-move-home-kavanaugh-testimony-death-threats-2018-10
39. Bryan Logan, "Days After Calling Christine Blasey Ford a 'Credible Witness', Who Gave 'Compelling Testimony', Trump Mocks Her at a Campaign Rally in Mississippi," *Business Insider*, October 2, 2018. https://www.businessinsider.com/trump-mocks-christine-blasey-ford-at-a-campaign-rally-in-mississippi-2018-10?r=UK&IR=T
40. Emma Brockes, "#MeToo Founder Tarana Burke: 'You Have to Use Your Privilege to Serve Other People,'" *The Guardian*, January 15, 2018. https://www.theguardian.com/world/2018/jan/15/me-too-founder-tarana-burke-women-sexual-assault
41. Paul Elam, Interview, *We Hunted the Mammoth*, October 18, 2013. http://www.wehuntedthemammoth.com/2013/10/18/paul-elam-of-a-voice-for-men-in-his-own-words/
42. Ibid.
43. Jackson Katz, "Violence against Women – It's a Men's Issue," *TEDxFiFiWomen* https://www.ted.com/talks/jackson_katz_violence_against_women_it_s_a_men_s_issue/transcript?language=en
44. National Sexual Violence Resource Center, Info & Stats for Journalists, 2015. https://www.nsvrc.org/sites/default/files/publications_nsvrc_factsheet_media-packet_statistics-about-sexual-violence_0.pdf
45. Lara Stemple, Ilan H. Meyer, "The Sexual Victimization of Men in America: New Data Challenge Old Assumptions," *American Journal of Public Health*, Vol. 104, Issue 6, June 2014. https://www.ncbi.nlm.nih.gov/pmc/articles/PMC4062022/
46. Ibid.

47. Lara Stemple, Ilan H. Meyer, "Sexual Victimization by Women Is More Common Than Previously Known," *Scientific American*, October 10, 2017. https://www.scientificamerican.com/article/sexual-victimization-by-women-is-more-common-than-previously-known/
48. Ibid.
49. David Lisak, "Millions of Men Suffer in Silence after Sexual Abuse. How Can We Help Them Better?" *The Guardian*, November 25, 2017. https://www.theguardian.com/commentisfree/2017/nov/25/men-sexual-abuse-trauma-silence
50. Gwilym Mumford, "Actor Terry Crews: I was Sexually Assaulted by Hollywood Executive," *The Guardian*, October 11, 2017. https://www.theguardian.com/film/2017/oct/11/actor-terry-crews-sexually-assaulted-by-hollywood-executive
51. Ibid.
52. Ibid.
53. Elahe Izadi, "'People Are So Sensitive': 50 Cent Doubles Down After Mocking Terry Crews Over Sexual Assault Claim," *The Washington Post*, June 27, 2018.
54. W. Brad Johnson, David G. Smith, "Too Many Men Are Silent Bystanders to Sexual Harassment," *Harvard Business Review*, March 13, 2017. https://hbr.org/2017/03/too-many-men-are-silent-bystanders-to-sexual-harassment
55. Ibid.
56. Prostate Cancer: Statistics, ASCO.org, Cancer.net https://www.cancer.net/cancer-types/prostate-cancer/statistics
57. Colleen Moriarty, "Do You Really Need a Prostate Check?" *Yale Medicine*, November 13, 2017. https://www.yalemedicine.org/stories/prostate-check/
58. UCI Health, "Why Men Avoid Doctor Visits," November 1, 2016. https://www.ucihealth.org/blog/2016/11/why-men-avoid-doctors
59. Ibid.
60. Ibid.
61. Orlando Health, "Survey Finds Why Most Men Avoid Doctor Visits," *Science Daily*, June 9, 2016. https://www.sciencedaily.com/releases/2016/06/160609064534.htm
62. Ibid.
63. Anna Almendrala, "Here's Why Men Don't Like Going to the Doctor," *Huff Post*, June 13, 2016. https://www.huffpost.com/entry/why-men-dont-go-to-the-doctor_n_5759c267e4b00f97fba7aa3e?guccounter=1&guce_referrer=aHR0cHM6Ly93d3cuZ29vZ2xlLmNvbS8&guce_referrer_sig=AQAAAH74ueGq3K74UKHe4M6M-YV0CzJrEGCUaAJzRPXWGgl6uAEnZQEv3i2rq9j7ZssliBNzzHab3dp35pOWgtMVqd4KPCRW6Qq-ae-2R2rqPQsAiSgNA00hqqeo7GeqoTJqJ4BOyFnGMKWKFssMojFKSzRAdAvW8vvDGE_FUW9lO_7H
64. Robert H. Shmerling, "Why Men Often Die Earlier Than Women," *Harvard Health Publishing, Harvard Medical School*, February 19, 2016. https://www.health.harvard.edu/blog/why-men-often-die-earlier-than-women-201602199137
65. Sebastian Ocklenburg, "Why Men Die Younger Than Women," *Psychology Today*, April 8, 2019. https://www.psychologytoday.com/us/blog/the-asymmetric-brain/201904/why-men-die-younger-women
66. Ibid.
67. Centers for Disease Control and Prevention, "Current Cigarette Smoking Among Adults in the United States," November 18, 2019. https://www.cdc.gov/tobacco/data_statistics/fact_sheets/adult_data/cig_smoking/

68. Centers for Disease Control and Prevention, "Excessive Alcohol Use and Risks to Men's Health," December 30, 2019. https://www.cdc.gov/alcohol/factsheets/mens-health.htm
69. Health Central, "Men's Health: Self-Medicating Depression with Drugs," June 25, 2018. https://healthcentral.nz/mens-health-self-medicating-depression-with-drugs/
70. Centers for Disease Control and Prevention, "Suicide: Facts at a Glance," 2015. https://www.cdc.gov/violenceprevention/pdf/suicide-datasheet-a.pdf
71. Helene Schumacher, "Why More Men than Women Die by Suicide," *BBC Psychology*, March 17, 2019. http://www.bbc.com/future/story/20190313-why-more-men-kill-themselves-than-women
72. D.G. Denning, Y. Conwell, D. King, C. Cox, "Method Choice, Intent, and Gender in Completed Suicide," *Suicide and Life-Threatening Behavior*, Vol. 30, Issue 3, Fall 2000, pp. 282–288. https://www.ncbi.nlm.nih.gov/pubmed/11079640
73. Gary Barker, "Why Do So Many Men Die by Suicide?" *Slate*, June 28, 2018. https://slate.com/human-interest/2018/06/are-we-socializing-men-to-die-by-suicide.html
74. U.S. Department of Veteran Affairs, Office of Suicide Prevention, "Suicide among Veterans and Other Americans 2001–2014" (PDF). Mentalhealth.va.gov. Retrieved 1 June 2019.
75. Alan Zarembo, "Suicide Rate of Female Military Veterans Is called Staggering," *Los Angeles Times*, June 08, 2015. Retrieved 2016 July 18.
76. Claire A. Hoffmire, Ph.D., Janet E. Kemp, R.N., Ph.D., Robert M. Bossarte, Ph.D., Published online: May 01, 2015. *Psychiatric Services*, Vol. 66 Issue 9, September 01, 2015, pp. 959–965. doi:10.1176/appi.ps.201400031. Changes in Suicide Mortality for Veterans and Nonveterans by Gender and History of VHA Service Use, 2000–2010.
77. Jay Price, "Battling Depression and Suicide Among Female Veterans," *NPR*, May 29, 2018. https://www.npr.org/2018/05/29/614011243/battling-depression-and-suicide-among-female-veterans
78. Ibid.
79. Ibid.
80. Ibid.
81. Ibid.
82. Elizabeth A. Prosek, Jessica M. Holm, "Counselors and the Military: When Protocol and Ethics Conflict," *The Professional Counselor*. http://tpcjournal.nbcc.org/counselors-and-the-military-when-protocol-and-ethics-conflict/
83. Daniel Pendick, "Prostate Cancer Lives as it Is Born: Slow-Growing and Benign or Fast-Growing and Dangerous," *Harvard Health Publishing, Harvard Medical School*, August 14, 2013. https://www.health.harvard.edu/blog/prostate-cancer-lives-as-it-is-born-slow-growing-and-benign-or-fast-growing-and-dangerous-201308146604
84. Ibid.
85. Ian Franks, "Stages and Outlook for Prostate Cancer," *Medical News Today*, September 3, 2019. https://www.medicalnewstoday.com/articles/317586.php
86. Ibid.

5 ADVERTISING'S SEXIST CALL TO MEN

> **Key Points**
> - Marketing Sexism to Boys and Men
> - Pornified Ads
> - Sexy or Sexist?
> - Subvertising
> - Training Men that Women Are Consumer Products
> - Self-Objectification
> - Selling Gender-Normality
> - McCracken's Four Consumption Rituals
> - Goffman's Gender Displays
> - Femvertising
> - Selling Heteronormativity
> - Marketing Gay Masculinity
> - Selling Eurocentric Models of Beauty

Sometimes when covering media, advertising escapes scrutiny or is viewed as extraneous to the more visible forms of youth media that include movies, TV shows, games, and internet content. But ads bombard all of us everyday. They can be found on TV of course, but are also found throughout the internet, on billboards and the sides of buses, at sporting events, in magazines and other print media. One thing advertisers have learned over the decades is to target their marketing campaigns to get the best chance of placing their products before consumers they feel will be interested. This is why televised sports often feature ads for pizza, beer, and trucks, while daytime television programming features ads for so-called domestic products, online universities, and a variety of insurance ads aimed at older viewers.

But marketing to youth culture carries its own set of targeted product ads. For years, makers of beer, soft-drinks, sports apparel, fashion and style, gym memberships, computers, game systems and games, movies, affordable car models, and an array of products will team up with music artists, sports stars, and cool, younger actors to sell of host of products considered to be youth-centric. But marketers have also, for years, targeted their marketing campaigns along lines of gender. Whether Hollywood studios creating movie trailers with plenty of violence and action for boys or marketing a new romantic comedy studio heads believe will attract more girls than boys, time is spent constructing ads that agency executives believe will generate the largest possible market share of potential consumers.

Soft-drink makers may feature ads that show NBA stars drinking their sodas or ads for fashion using music stars or cool, young film celebrities wearing their clothing. Cool often drives the train when it comes to marketing to young people. But cool keeps changing and being reinvented. Yet, despite the fact that cool can be elusive and evolving, there are longstanding stereotypes that continue to be used to sell products to boys and young men, and these conventions include featuring sexualized images of women alongside or as an extension to particular products. The old adage "sex sells" is still alive and well in marketing, but could be amended with no change to the content by stating "sexism sells," and sells particularly well to boys and men.

MARKETING SEXISM TO BOYS AND MEN

Over the past decade and a half, starting with the infamous Paris Hilton ad of 2005, Carl's Jr. –Hardee's placed themselves at ground zero in the race to sexually exploit women's bodies to sell product, in this case fast food. But Carl's Jr. – Hardee's is not close to being the first corporation to use sexually exploitative images of and messages about women in the pursuit of profit. For generations, product makers who create products that have nothing to do with sex have routinely placed partially dressed or even nude models into their ads. Many of these ads were specifically designed to appeal to men in male-dominated fields such as automotive repair, or for products thought to be purchased mainly by men such as guns, trucks, and beer, along with shop and power tools. But the Paris Hilton ad launched a marketing campaign that spanned over a decade aimed at a target audience of boys and young men. In fact, in an interview about their ad campaign, Carl's Jr.'s CEO Andy Puzder stated,

> We believe in putting hot models in our commercials, because ugly ones don't sell burgers. We target hungry guys. I like our ads. I like beautiful women eating burgers in bikinis. I think it's very American.[1]

This is perhaps the most bro-friendly quote in the chapter. Not only does Puzder play to the male directive to rate women as "beautiful" or "ugly," he unabashedly admits that his ads are designed to target boys and men, and ends by wrapping his ads around the American flag in a display of fraudulent patriotism. The boast of targeting "young guys" with sexually exploitative ads marked a new chapter in marketing campaigns that openly admit that pornified advertising is specifically aimed at boys and men.[2]

In 2017, Carl's Jr. – Hardee's ended its commercials featuring scantily clad women, claiming that it was time to evolve.[3] As Puzder explained,

> Young, hungry guys aren't as affected by the racy ads with the swimsuit models because you can get a lot of that on the internet now. It's not like it was 10, 12 years ago when we started this.[4]

Beyond the fact that Puzder's ads were heteronormative, Caucasian-normative, sexually exploitative ads, his strategy-reversal was more about the fact that pornography is readily available to boys and young men on the internet such that women in sexual attire isn't enough to hold their interest anymore. Not stated was the fallout of raising boys on sexually exploitative images and narratives about women. Some of the first and most repeated images of women that boys see in their lives are sexual in nature. Advertising is a big part of that repetition.

The depiction of women as mindlessly subordinate and obedient to men goes back ages in advertising. A slew of ads from the 1950s depict women in subservient roles to men with captions that suggest women are incompetent and therefore need men, or that women are both incompetent and hyperemotional such as the 1952 Schlitz beer ad featuring a woman crying while her husband sarcastically blurts, "Don't worry darling, you didn't burn the beer."[5] Or the demeaning ad by Heinz tomato soup that minimizes domestic violence with the caption:

> Most husbands nowadays have stopped beating their wives, yet ladies, there must have been a reason.[6]

Or the humiliating ad by Van Heusen clothing for men that features a woman on her knees serving her husband breakfast in bed, while the caption reads:

> Show her it's a man's world.[7]

As a revealing aside, the late 1940s and throughout 1950s are the timeframe that Trump and his many supporters believe America was great, and the era to which they would like us to return to accomplish the slogan "Make America Great Again."[8]

Ads did not get remarkably better in the 1960s and 1970s with examples as heinous as the Weyenberg shoe ad depicting a woman lying on the ground next to a shoe with the caption:

> Keep her where she belongs.[9]

This particular ad states boldly what most ads of the past had only implied: that women need to know their place, which was assumed to be submissive and subordinate to men. Where women of the past were treated like children in need of discipline or made to understand that they are servants to men, the revised version of women in advertising remained focused on the subordination of women to men, but with the added feature of sexual object. This means that the legacy that informed the sexist Carl's Jr. – Hardee's ads created a clear and consistent narrative about women aimed directly at boys and men: *women are inferior to you in almost every way, but they serve an important function as your sexual playthings.*

> ### Thought Box
>
> Since the Carl's Jr. – Hardee's Paris Hilton ad in 2005, there have been a flood of ads depicting women in sexually provocative attire and positions. Yet some defend these ads as being sexually liberating for women. Examine a number of ads that feature women in sexually provocative positions or in revealing clothing and defend whether you view these ads as liberating from, or conforming to, patriarchy.

In her book *Pornified: How Pornography is Damaging Our Lives, Our Relationships, and Our Families*, author Pamela Paul argues that boys are being raised on pornography through internet use at earlier ages than ever before.[10] But one could argue that pornographic images and messages crept into pop-culture long ago. While not as graphic as hard-core pornography, advertisers have increasingly constructed ads that were once viewed as soft-core pornography or erotica. Los Angeles-based clothing manufacturer American Apparel, for instance, recently released a string of ads that featured women with their legs spread or lying on their stomachs with their rear-ends raised into the air, or in one case, a man standing above a woman holding her legs apart in what is not remarkably different than the poses of soft-core porn of the past. There are hundreds of variations of these ads that a casual perusal of the internet will document, but the theme in these ads is that women are and should be sexually subordinate to men. The normative instruction to men is that women's principal value is found in their looks and sexuality, while the identical message is being normalized to women with the added directive that being sexually attractive and available to men is one of the most important achievements to which women should aspire.

SEXY OR SEXIST?

There is a funny line in the 1984 mockumentary film *This is Spinal Tap* where the band finds out that their album cover has been scrapped by the record company because it is sexist. Lead guitarist Nigel Tufnel, played by Christopher Guest, asks, "What's wrong with being sexy?" 'Tufnel' is so out of touch with the concept of sexism that he conflates 'sexist' with sexy. The band's manager has to explain the difference to him. Yet, how many men and women conflate these two things?

> **Thought Box**
>
> When looking at ads or any form of media representation of women, what is the line between sexy and sexist? That is, what is it, in your opinion, that makes the representation of women either sexy or sexist? Is there a particular way an ad is created whether in the way the model is posed, the clothing she is wearing or lack thereof, the context in which the scene is choreographed, the print content, or a combination of them all that causes an ad to cross the line from being sexy to sexist? Is it especially noticeable when an ad campaign features female and male models in the same ad, perhaps in their pose or attire? Is there a definition, style, or context that causes an ad to cross the line? There is certainly a good deal of subjectivity in what different people find to be sexy, but are there elements of visual or contextual content that cause a piece to qualify as sexist? Here are a few common, but nonexclusive, qualifiers you often find in pieces that judge an ad to be sexist:
>
> - Men wear clothes, and women do not.
> - Men have sexual fantasies, and women occupy those fantasies, while women's fantasies go unaddressed.
> - Men are subjects, and women are objects.
> - The ad uses female bodies or body parts to appeal to heterosexual men.
> - Men in the ad are shown in positions of traditional power, wealth, and status, while women in the ad are posed in positions of traditional subordination.

A power imbalance is key to many of the classic concerns by feminists over the conflation of *sexy* and *sexist*.[11] The women in ads are simply following the cues of a director, which means that the mediated reality we end up seeing in magazines or on television is being manipulated to achieve a particular effect conceived by a marketing agency that is further beholden to a product maker. When the qualifiers listed above appear in ads, someone is consciously making decisions to pose male and female models in certain ways, with certain facial expressions, in a particular context that usually consists of traditional power roles for men and traditional subordinate roles for women. Examples include cases where the male model is standing while looking into the camera as a female model is unclothed or partially clothed while looking up at the man, and there a number of variations on this theme.

A further concern is whether images of female beauty are constructed to represent ideal or normative versions of beauty against which all women are judged. In the book *Woman's Embodied Self: Feminist Perspectives on Identity and Image*, feminist authors Joan C. Chrisler and Ingrid Johnston-Robledo argue that impossible beauty standards are cultural-and-media-constructions that place women in an onerous bind:

> Women are taught that their bodies should be beautiful (but not as a result of too much effort), sexy (but not 'slutty'), pure (but not

prudish), slender (but curvy in the right places), youthful (if they are adults), mature (if they are adolescents), feminine, healthy, and able-bodied.[12]

Advertisers use these normative tropes about feminine beauty to make a profit by encouraging girls and women to be self-conscious about their bodies and overall looks. In effect, product makers assure healthy earnings by undermining women's self-esteem. Author-activist Jean Kilbourne argues that advertisers sell much more than products. They sell "values, images, and concepts of success and worth, love and sexuality, popularity and normalcy."[13] Hoping that they can live up to the culturally constructed templates of beauty found in advertising and other forms of media, girls and women will spend enormous amounts of time and money to reflect the photo-shopped images on display. Similarly, men consume mediated messages and gendered imagery that inform them how *normal* guys should dress and talk, what women's *proper roles* are, and how men should think about and behave toward women.

But a power imbalance is perhaps one of the most salient points that cause an ad to transition from being sexy to sexist. In ads dating back decades, men as subjects pursue women as objects for the purpose of sex. Women in ads, much like in pornography, seem to be perpetually willing and eager to please men. The opposite is seldom true. This double standard creates a power imbalance: *men have sexual desires that must be addressed by women, while women's sexual desires, whatever they may be, are secondary to men's and often ignored.*

Ads are often seen through the eyes of men. That is, ads can be so patriarchal in nature that we can imagine marketing executives asking one another in meetings, "will men like this ad?" One type of ad that is made explicitly to point out the sexism or racism in advertising is found in ads termed **subvertising**. One kind of subvertised ad will feature a male model posed in the typical ways one usually associates with female models. We have seen this in ads that place men in feminized positions of subordination while featuring facial expressions that appear dazed, confused, or sexually seductive. The ads are intended to make audiences laugh, but the underlying didactic lesson is to note that our laughter is a symptom of an upset expectation. That is, when viewers see a man posed as advertisers often pose female models, the laughter is a response to how *silly* the man looks. But this response itself is instructive, since it tells us that advertisers have normalized women as looking silly or hypersexual to the point that we don't laugh when we see women posed like this, but do laugh when men are posed in the very same ways. Another way of putting it is that we don't laugh when we see women posed as though they are silly, foolish, off-balance, in ridiculous contortions, or pouting into the camera in over-the-top displays of sexual desire, because these depictions have been driven into us as *normal* feminine displays. When men are posed like this, the viewer laughs, since men have been normalized in ads and other media as being serious, authoritative, dignified, strong, and even tough or intimidating. Subvertising has done an excellent job of making visible what is hiding in plain sight: that advertisers and many other forms of media carefully sculpt gendered images to us throughout our lives, images that are loaded with the suggestion that women are foolish, irrational, vain, pretentious, childish, frivolous, but given value through their looks and sexual appeal. Bros consume these images just as do girls and women. The constant repetition of consuming imagery and messaging like this is a training ground for bros as they travel through boyhood, adolescence, and adulthood. These gendered messages color the way many men view women in their careers and relationships.

TRAINING MEN THAT WOMEN ARE CONSUMER PRODUCTS

Beyond the effects that advertising has on women, the sense of normalcy constructed by advertising and other media has a profound effect on men. Since advertisers sharply gender-divide power in terms of male-power (commonly defined by wealth, status, and physical strength) versus female-power (commonly defined by beauty and sexual appeal), women and men are habituated to judge themselves and others against these templates. For instance, President Donald Trump, then simply real estate mogul Trump, was asked by radio-show personality Howard Stern to rate actress Halle Barry, to which he stated:

> From the midsection to the shoulders – she's a 10. The face is a solid 8. And the legs are maybe a bit less than that.[14]

The ranking of women by numeric value has been something we have witnessed men do across racial-cultural and socioeconomic divides, but assigning numeric value has also been used by consumer groups throughout time to rank products. Take *Consumer Reports*, a nonprofit organization that is famous for consumer advocacy, but also for investigating product lines for quality where reviews are posted. Items are listed best-to-worst, given numeric value, and reviewed with a brief description.[15,16] Here, we see the clearest analogy of ranking products to men ranking women by numeric value. Products like cars, trucks, refrigerators, televisions, and computers are ranked and judged just as women's faces and bodies are judged by men like Trump. From boyhood, men are instructed to view women as products, things, and gadgets that can be assessed on measurable criteria: face, body, breasts, legs, weight, and overall sexual appeal, not unlike an ad that states:

> The BMW X3: best in comfort, design, technology, utility, and overall driver enjoyment.[17]

This ad is not remarkably different than Trump's assessment of Halle Barry. Both are being judged on criteria that consumers determine to be important. But in the case of women, the consumers are men who feel entitled to serve as beauty and sex-appeal judges. Women are products to be carefully scrutinized for imperfections that would lower their overall ranking. Those who do not measure up are often mocked for their perceived imperfections.

Thought Box

In this chapter, we have been investigating the sexual exploitation of women in ads and the ways that sexual objectification can affect women and men. But some argue that men are also sexually exploited in ads. In some cases, men in ads are displayed in sexually provocative poses or are shown shirtless, revealing rippling abs and upper body muscularity. But as Jean Kilbourne emphasizes, the consequences in the world are different for women and men.[18] Kilbourne notes that we live in a world where women are targeted for sexual abuse at much higher rates than men. Therefore, media that sexually objectify women are more dangerous than media that sexually objectify men. What do you think?

It is no accident that the judgments many men make of women are one-dimensional in nature. That is, we don't see men like Trump saying that Halle Barry is a ten on intelligence, a nine on independence, an eight on acting talent, and a nine on overall personality. The ranking of women is always directed toward physicality and sensual appeal. That women are ranked at all is living proof of the sexual objectification of women by mainstream popular culture as constructed by advertising and other media, and as a training ground for boys and men to view and judge women. This phenomenon also shows clearly that boys and men have been raised to feel entitled to judge women in these ways, while these same boys and men would probably feel indignant if they were the ones being judged.

Fallout from being raised on these gendered tropes runs the gamut. On the one hand, men will assume that they are and should be in charge in relationships, more greatly suited for leadership roles, and that they should make more money than women. Of course, many men will feel inadequate if they are not able to achieve these goals or live up to expectations. On the other hand, some women will **self-objectify**, which means that they will view themselves as products for the male gaze rather than as multidimensional human beings. In the piece "Objectification Theory, Self-Objectification, and Body Image," R.M. Calogero argues that women come to view themselves as sexual objects as a result of living in a culture that mass produces women's bodies as objects of desire.[19] Symptomatic of self-objectification is the constant monitoring of one's body and face in mirrors, or what Calogero terms "self-surveillance."[20] It is not that those who self-objectify are narcissists, but that they hope to control how people view them and place stock in the opinions of others. Where women's beauty is commodified, it makes sense that some women would begin to view themselves as commodities and that men would view themselves as consumers of women's bodies.

By commodifying women's bodies, a heteronormative supply-demand economics is created. Women become the supply, while men provide the demand. Under this model, it is easy to understand why some women would self-objectify. They may view their supply as having value in a power-exchange that may appear lopsided toward men. That is, if men, but not women, are viewed as having power that comes with wealth and other forms of status, women may view their sexual appeal as having transactional value. The problem is, of course, that the playing field is not level. If women's value is measured in physical looks and sensual appeal, then a clock is ticking that favors men over women, since we live in a culture that worships youthful beauty. Proof of this is demonstrated in the vast majority of beauty ads, since models are overwhelmingly in their late-teens-to-mid-twenties and ads are famous for selling the idea that you can look more youthful if you use their products. In addition, how many films can you think of where the male protagonist is middle-to-senior in age while his female love interest is 20 or 30 years younger? How many films reverse this rule? The answers to these questions ('many' to question #1, 'almost none' to question #2) paints a picture of patriarchy running rampant in the scripts of many Hollywood films, and films along with other forms of mass-media are a big part of the social construction of normality.

SELLING GENDER-NORMALITY

Anthropologist Grant McCracken has written extensively about the intersection of commerce and culture and in one seminal piece discusses the **four rituals of consumption**.[21] McCracken uses the concept of a ritual to explain "a kind of social action devoted to the manipulation of cultural meaning for purposes of collective and individual communication and categorization."[22] In short, a ritual represents a process whereby meaning is communicated from a consumer good to individual consumers. Here are McCracken's four consumption rituals:

1. Exchange Rituals
Gifting one another often carries meaning. For example, McCracken notes that a dress gifted to a woman carries with it the concept of the kind of woman she is. Gifting, therefore, assigns meaning to the gift-recipient by the gift-giver. For instance, gifting a short skirt to a particular woman may be interpreted as assigning certain qualities to that woman that are culturally defined through advertising and media prescriptions of what constitutes a "short-skirt wearing woman." These prescriptions may include youthfulness, daring, sexual allure, or any number of culturally normalized traits.

2. Possession Rituals
The possessions one is able to place on display are markers for status and can also signify age, class, gender, occupation, and lifestyle. For instance, people often perform behaviors and display personas that they hope make them look cool, powerful, youthful, or sexy to others. As part of these displays, one who wants to look powerful and wealthy will purchase or lease luxury cars and wear expensive watches or other forms of jewelry, while someone who

is concerned with looking young may have tattoos and piercings applied to their bodies.

3. Grooming Rituals
Since many products are perishable, the consumer must be wary to purchase and repurchase items as they continue to gain and lose popularity, or purchase a replacement item if it is better able to communicate an image the consumer desires. For instance, a particular hair style, item of jewelry, or clothing choice will often come and go out of style, leaving the consumer in the position of policing his consumption choices against the prevailing cultural values.

4. Divestment Rituals
Divestment rituals occur when a product is resold or given away. The consumer must attach new significance to the purchased item to divest the item of attachment to the former owner such as when one purchases a used car or house. This ritual is used to christen a product and thereby make it one's own.

Taken together, consumption rituals are used extensively by men and women to gain status, to make personal statements, to assure that one is keeping up with current trends, or to reinforce an image one has of oneself. When looking at gendered advertisement, it is clear that normative ideas about masculinity and femininity are being sold alongside whatever product a manufacturer produces for consumption. Heterosexual men are also sold a particular demeanor that they are supposed to adopt to appear more attractive to women.

Once particular normative gender displays are codified in popular culture, consumption rituals follow. Men who are interested in attracting women and wish to appear to be wealthy, powerful, or youthful will make purchases that they believe reflect these interests and values. Advertising then sells an image of success, youth, beauty, and power and then links a product to these values, knowing that men and women will consume the product for a desired effect. McCracken's *possession* and *grooming* rituals are particularly suited to these goals. The possession ritual informs you how you should look, while the grooming ritual reminds you that you must continue making purchases to replace those that have faded out of style. In this way, concepts like *cool* and *sexy* are constantly constructed and reconstructed with planned-obsolescence built into the design.

Gendering these consumption rituals, women are often displayed kneeling, recumbent, or off-balance, while also shown in sexualized, yet infantilized ways or are subjects of frivolity. Gone are the traditional poses of strength and authority found among male models, replaced by submission, deference, or distraction. Men are commonly posed looking directly into the camera with a wary look of danger, while women are often posed looking away from the camera with expressions of boredom, confusion, longing, or desire. Famed sociologist Erving Goffman first wrote about these visual and stylistic differences in his seminal work *Gender Advertisements*.[23] Goffman termed these stylized differences **gender displays**,[24] making the case that there is nothing natural about these gendered poses and expressions. They are the product of directors, writers, and producers who are pursuing an image of what they believe best captures masculinity or femininity as they view it, or as they believe it should be. We are then bombarded by these images in a relentless stream of advertising intended to drive consumers to purchase products. But as Goffman in the past and Jean Kilbourne today note, these images become normalized as templates that adolescents and eventually adults are supposed to follow:

> *Here is what looks cool or sexy, now go make the following purchases and do your best to conform to the images we have constructed. But beware, the images we construct are going to continually change, so you must be prepared to change as well by purchasing more products.*

There are, in addition to the various gender displays, gendered messaging embedded within these ads such as *men are strong, while women are weak; men protect, while women need protecting; men are serious, while women are frivolous and vain; men are leaders, while women follow*. When reinforced by family members, friends, acquaintances, celebrities, politicians, coaches, and clergy, these tropes burrow into the minds of men and women at young ages as *simple truths* about gender. Because these tropes are common and ingrained at early ages, they can seem natural. That is, the view that men are strong, stoic, and built for leadership, while women are weak, emotional, and built to support and follow will seem to be factual in nature rather than cultural constructions, particularly when reinforced from early childhood. The link to bro culture is obvious. Boys raised on these media constructed tropes learn early that their gender affords them power and privilege that is not extended to girls and women.

Thought Box

As a visual experiment, look at fashion and beauty ads in magazines or online. Are there companies that seem to be changing the script from the past? That is, can you find marketing campaigns that have broken away from the traditional gendered tropes that have dominated ads for generations? If so, ask yourself, who do you believe is the target audience for this ad? Do you feel the marketing agency is taking a risk or do you view the ad as a long overdue change, or perhaps the revised strategy will increase profits for the company? If you can't find ads that are not problematic, what do you believe a positive gendered ad should look like or incorporate? Is it possible for an ad to depict men and women without also constructing normative gendered roles? At early ages, they can seem natural. That is, the view that men are strong, stoic, and built for leadership, while women are weak, emotional, and built to support and follow will seem to be factual in nature rather than cultural constructions, particularly when reinforced from early childhood. The link to bro culture is obvious. Boys raised on these media constructed tropes learn early that their gender affords them power and privilege that is not extended to girls and women.

In fact, gender displays are often about power. A common trope in advertising is that of men in positions of executive power while women decide which laundry soap is better at getting stains out. A back-to-back comparison of ads makes this double standard perspicuous. Mercedes Benz has long created ads that feature highly successful-looking, older men such as George Clooney and other similar older, white men whose visual appearance symbolize male authority, while Dodge, Honda, Kia, Toyota, Nissan, Chrysler, and Chevrolet construct ads for minivans and SUVs that feature a young mom with her children. In fact, Mercedes Benz titled a recent ad with Clooney as the face of the campaign, "Mercedes-Benz Man" and issued a men's cologne of the same name, while Dodge titled their minivan ad "Supermom."[25,26]

The point is not to demean moms, but to note that it would be highly unusual to find a woman in the Mercedes-Benz ad with a caption reading "Mercedes-Benz Woman," while finding a Dodge ad depicting a dad and his daughter with the caption, "Some Superheroes Use a Phone Booth. Dads Have This." There are power assumptions in play for both of these ads along with a normative message about gender roles: men possess authority and autonomous power, while women are supporters and nurturers. Again, the point is not to denigrate people in supporting and nurturing roles; these roles are invaluable and should be held in great esteem, but rather to note that these roles are almost always gendered toward the view that *men are naturally powerful and women are naturally nurturers*. The preceding tropes actually demean both men and women, since they assume that *women are not naturally powerful and men are not naturally nurturing*.

FEMVERTISING

A conglomerated word has emerged that syncretizes the two words 'feminism' and 'advertising' into 'femvertising'. The idea is that marketers are trying to appear to be aware of and sensitive to the fact that girls' and women's empowerment have been placed front-and-center in mainstream culture, particularly with the ascendency of Donald Trump to the office of president. The Women's Marches have been extraordinary and massive in size. Attendance estimates range at around 4 million in 2017 and 2.5 million in 2018 in the U.S. alone.[27] The marches have been multicultural, multigenerational events with messages of solidarity and political action. In 2018, women ran for political office in record numbers.[28] Advertisers have taken note.

Femvertising actually began several years ago with campaigns that offered girl-and-women empowerment messaging. Hashtag feminism has now become mainstream with ads such as CoverGirl's #GirlsCan and Pantene's #ShineStrong campaigns.[29] Then filmmaker Lauren Greenfield produced the video-short "Like a Girl" for product-maker *Always*, which was aired as one of the Super Bowl ads in 2014.[30] The ad was heralded as being groundbreaking in a medium that had exploited women for generations.[31] Procter & Gamble then launched the #Unstoppable campaign, created by Leo Burnett where girls respond to questions about being encouraged to think and behave in certain ways that society expects of them.[32] Other campaigns include #ThisGirlCan and #HeForShe, which tout men standing up as allies with women in the pursuit of gender equality.[33]

There are, however, critics and concerns. In the 1970s, cigarette maker Virginia Slims coopted feminism with the slogan, "You've come a long way, baby!" Critics were quick to point out that smoking cigarettes did not help women gain any substantial equality with men other than causing women to contract lung cancer and die like many men who smoked.[34] Contemporary concerns about femvertising are a bit different. There is a good deal of ambivalence about the ads. Take, for instance, Dove's "Real Beauty" campaign. Dove launched the "real beauty" ads in 2004 and continues to market ads with this theme.[35] The concept is fairly simple: *instead of showing models who are six feet tall, 105 pounds, and overwhelmingly white, we will use "real women" who come in all shapes, sizes, and colors.* On the surface, the message seems to be that you can and should love yourself no matter what kind of body you have. But, according to media analyst Jennifer Pozner, Dove has more interest in selling product than selling feminism.[36] For instance, as the "real beauty" ads were being launched, Dove also released its skin-firming creams.[37] Pozner notes,

> Dove's attempts are profoundly limited by a product line that comes with its own underlying philosophy: cellulite is unsightly, women's natural aging process is shameful, and flabby thighs are flawed and must be fixed.[38]

Product makers and marketing agencies are in the business of selling product and the recipe that has worked for generations in the beauty industry is to undermine women's self-esteem. So, a nod to body positivity and skin-tone plurality is another marketing attempt to profit from a social justice movement about which marketers are privately hostile, since female empowerment of the kind identified by many feminists runs contrary to the longstanding marketing strategies that have garnered huge corporate profits to companies like Unilever, which produces not only Dove, but Axe and Lynx, ads for which have been notoriously exploitative of women's bodies.[39] The real winner here is capitalism and corporate profit, since body-shaming and body-positivity both create huge streams of revenue.[40] In addition, advertising's limited portrayal of female empowerment in terms of physicality offers up the same stereotypes about women we examined earlier in the chapter, that women's value in a patriarchal culture is captured through looks and sensual appeal, while men's value is found in a multitude of traits that usually center around other forms of power.

This is not to say that all forms of femvertising are bad or exploitative, but like the Disney animated films today aimed at a young audience that wants new, more empowering messaging about girls and women, the corporations that employ femvertising are still in the business of generating profits rather than promoting social justice activism. Yet, the connection to bro culture is an interesting one. Many bros may tune out ads that appear to empower women or perhaps even mock them. But corporate motives aside, femvertised ads are

Thought Box

What is your opinion of femvertising? Some believe it is long overdue and helping to empower girls and women. Others argue that it simply exploits feminist ideals and female empowerment to increase profits. Still others argue that rather than promoting different kinds of empowerment for women, femvertising focuses narrowly on women's physical looks as empowerment. There is no doubt that advertisers in the past have promoted very limited body types for women so that body positivity for everyone is new and important, but do you believe these feminized ads are doing more harm than good or more good than harm?

yet another challenge to bro culture. They represent progressive change in America at a time when conservative cultural and political forces are working to regressively take us back in time. Women's empowerment, like LGBTQ empowerment, or the movements that promote equal treatment for people of color are all moving in a direction that is contrary to bro culture. In essence, bro culture is a culture dedicated to a time that is slowly evaporating, a time when men had unchallenged authority in multiple domains.

SELLING HETERONORMATIVITY

Another longstanding theme in advertising is the heteronormativity that pervades most ad campaigns. Yet, it is notable that certain product makers have chosen to create ads featuring gay couples. Among those companies are Ikea, Nordstrom, Calvin Klein, Campbell's, Starbucks, and Lush bath and beauty products.[41] It is all the more notable that some of these ads feature interracial couples as well. But the rule for advertising is same-race, heterosexual-love-sex relationships as *normal*, which is the very meaning of the term 'heteronormativity'.

Heteronormativity in advertising is also found in the gendered roles depicted in ads. It is still common to see men in traditional, male-dominated occupations or activities, while women are shown in traditional female roles and activities. These sorts of ads and media depictions reinforce a narrative that certain roles and activities are natural or normal for men and women. But the more common way ads employ heteronormativity is seen when ads place women and men together in an ad, in some cases showing a clothed man and a nude woman. In many fashion ads, the woman clings to the man, while the man stares vigilantly into the camera with a protective and threatening gaze. The heteronormativity, therefore, of an ad like this goes beyond the common man-woman-sexual-presentation to also reinforce gender-traditional roles of man as protector and woman as in-need-of-protecting. This is one of many ways that bros are trained throughout life to view their roles as dominant to the roles of women. If one group of people are in need of protection by another group of people, the first group can be viewed as survival-dependent upon the second group.

Another way to witness heteronormativity in ads is when considering fashion ads that feature more than one man. Given that we live in a homophobic culture, how do marketing agencies market to heterosexual men who feel uncomfortable or threatened that their interest in fashion may create an impression that they are gay? One heteronormative solution has been for fashion ads to introduce women into the ad to allay the homophobic fears heterosexual men may feel about an ad that may otherwise be viewed as homoerotic in nature. The idea is that conforming to fashion and beauty standards for men, as constructed by the fashion and beauty industries, *will make you more attractive to women rather than gay.*

When lesbians, or what gender scholar Jack Halberstam might term 'media lesbians', are depicted in ads, they are almost always displayed in ways to attract the male gaze. A typical ad of this type will feature "lipstick lesbians" in sexy attire and sexual positions to turn men on sexually, since homophobia is sold to heterosexual men almost exclusively in terms of *the fear of gay men*, not gay women. If anything, the world of pornography eroticizes lesbians as part of a male, sexual fantasy. So, placing women, whether hetero or gay, in men's couture and beauty ads is a no-lose proposition for marketers, while reinforcing heteronormativity.

MARKETING GAY MASCULINITY

In the foregoing segment, we discussed the ongoing heteronormativity so prevalent in advertising, but as mentioned, marketing firms have begun marketing campaigns that feature and target gay men. This development is in some ways antithetical to bro culture, which has traditionally been a homophobic culture. But advertising's integration of gay men in marketing campaigns maps onto the acceptance of LGBTQ individuals in youth culture generally. Therefore, the changes we witness in advertising serve as a compass for the direction society is taking, since marketing firms, like most other corporate entities, care mainly about driving up profit rather than taking a stand on issues of social justice. But another interesting direction that LGBTQ inclusiveness may take is to disrupt the traditional homophobic stance of bro culture itself. If bro culture begins to adopt the inclusive attitudes of larger youth culture, the mainstay of homophobic slurs and put-downs may be challenged within bro culture. The same could be true of sexist and misogynistic slurs and put-downs if larger male culture begins to respond more positively and proactively toward #metoo and other movements designed to empower victims; but so far, we have seen far less affirming sentiments toward those movements by men.

One problem with marketing gay masculinity is that often, very particular versions of gay masculinity emerge as normative or most-valued. Writing for *The Guardian*, Dejan Jotanovic argues that the common imagery of gay masculinity involves "Boys with muscles. No girls. Ever."[42] Jotanovic goes on to note that "skinny boys" are not found to be interesting or cool.[43] Beyond gender exclusivity and the focus on muscular men, there is also little coverage of gay men of color.[44] Even the film *Moonlight*, argues Michael Arceneaux, writing for NBC News, had more to do with the stigma and brutality that can attend gay men of color than it did valuing gay men of color.[45] White men take center stage in the vast majority of media that depicts or features gay men, and this overemphasis on whiteness helps to shape the values of gay, male culture, while also stigmatizing gay men of color as aberrations from the norm. Middlebury College sociologist C. Winter Han has been making these very points for years.[46] Han writes,

> In contemporary gay media, as in mainstream media, gay people of color don't often exist outside of fantasy cruises to Jamaica, Puerto Rico, or the "Orient." Even when they are present, they exist only as flamboyant sidekicks to "straight-acting" gay White men, who have come to represent the "gay community."[47]

Advertising has the ability to shape values about beauty while affecting self-esteem. Normalizing certain forms of white masculinity as the default setting for gay masculinity constructs a hierarchy whereby white men are viewed as more desirable, while men of color are viewed as less desirable. Bro culture has been imbued with problems of racism for decades with many egregious instances of racism being documented on camera.[48,49] If mainstream advertising promotes a form of white, gay masculinity as normative, then marketers contribute to the ongoing racism in and out of bro culture. Beyond this concern is the obvious fact that marketing to one default mode of gay masculinity conforms to bro culture in its perpetuation of hierarchies. Bro culture has been and continues to be about positioning one group of people over another whether on the basis of gender, sex, race, ethnicity, or sexual orientation.

SELLING EUROCENTRIC MODELS OF BEAUTY

If you didn't notice, most ads feature white models, although this convention is slowly being challenged by some ad agencies. But even with this concession, white is still the default setting for the vast majority of fashion and beauty ads around the world. In many nations, skin-lightening creams and products are sold to people of color to help consumers approximate whiteness, which, of course, is racist.[50] Writing for Teen Vogue, Alisha Acquaye states,

> It is mentally and emotionally taxing when people of color have to repeatedly call out brands whenever they commit an offense against our identity, culture, and complexions.[51]

Product makers construct a noticeably Caucasian-normative definition of beauty, which is then marketed across the world. Much like the ads designed to make women feel self-conscious about their bodies and faces in order to increase profit, global marketers have created a beauty industry that attempts to make people of color self-conscious about skin tone, particularly darker skin tones. The makers of the product *Perfect White* skin cream could not create a more white-supremacist title if they tried.[52] Whiteness is thought to extol power and status, but also stands in as normative beauty. Women and men of color around the world are told that if only they were whiter, they could be more attractive. And while skin-whitening products are sold to both women and men with titles such as *Fair and Handsome* for men, the onus of living up to cultural beauty standards continues to fall mainly on women.

The effects of marketing whiteness to people of color on bro culture serve an insidious goal. It reinforces the idea that people of color possess a flaw by nature due to their skin color, which promotes white supremacism. It further reinforces the racist behaviors we have witnessed in the recent past by white fraternity bros.[53,54] At the same time, normalizing whiteness while pathologizing darker skin tones promotes self-loathing in people of color, while creating a hierarchy within communities of color around lighter and darker skin tones. White bros, like many we have seen and will meet in this text, do not need any help promoting the idea that being white is better, and when added to the privileges of being male and heterosexual, ads that endorse whiteness are boosting the overall sense of entitlement that many white bros already feel is their birthright.

POSTSCRIPT

There is no doubt that culture is changing and will continue to change. What is cool or sexy is a transient concept. But it is also difficult to unlearn long-held, culturally reinforced gender stereotypes. Advertising, like other forms of media, is capable of creating images and tropes that transcend the gender essentialism and soft bigotry that currently clogs print and TV ads. Because a new generation of young people are more progressive in their views about sex and gender, it will be interesting to see whether advertisers evolve on these matters. But there may always be a shadow of suspicion surrounding advertising since marketing agencies, like product makers themselves, are driven by profit, not social justice.

A central concern for the future, since this chapter takes up advertising's sexist call to men, will be how advertisers market specifically to men. That is, certain products and advertising campaigns have been tailored around what marketers believe will attract men. You can see this in ads for trucks, beer, and men's fashion and grooming products, but also in ads featuring male sports figures or occupations thought to appeal mainly to men such as construction work. One-dimensional, gender essentialist ads have been the norm when marketing to men and without a greater male presence in support of the women's movement or as allies of the #metoo and other related movements, it is difficult to see why advertisers would change course. The next generation of men will either influence advertisers to change the way they currently market

Advertising's Sexist Call to Men 121

to men or advertisers in tandem with other cultural policing entities will influence the next generation of men to conform to the sexist tropes of the past. Only time will tell.

Notes

1. Kristen Bellstrom, "Trump's Pick for Secretary of Labor: 'Ugly Women Don't Sell Burgers,'" *Fortune*, December 9, 2016. http://fortune.com/2016/12/09/puzder-women-ads-carls-jr/
2. Caleb Silver, "No Apologies for Sexy Paris Hilton Ad," *CNN Money*, June 1, 2005. https://money.cnn.com/2005/05/24/news/newsmakers/carls_ad/
3. Abha Bhattarai, "Carl's Jr.: Sex No Longer Sells," *The Washington Post*, March 30, 2017. https://www.washingtonpost.com/news/business/wp/2017/03/30/carls-jr-sex-no-longer-sells/?noredirect=on&utm_term=.4b8e4e51146d
4. Ibid.
5. Jim Edwards, "26 Sexist Ads that Companies Wish We'd Forget They Ever Made," *Business Insider*, September 28, 2015. https://www.businessinsider.com/sexist-vintage-ads-2015-9
6. Ibid.
7. Ibid.
8. Gregory Krieg, "Donald Trump Reveals When He Thinking America Was Great," *CNN Politics*, March 28, 2016. https://www.cnn.com/2016/03/26/politics/donald-trump-when-america-was-great/index.html
9. Natalie Angley, "Sexist Ads in 'The Seventies'," *CNN*, July 22, 2015. https://www.cnn.com/2015/07/22/living/seventies-sexist-ads/index.html
10. Pamela Paul, *Pornified: How Pornography Is Damaging Our Lives, Our Relationships, and Our Families*, St. Martin's Griffin, New York, 2005.
11. Bell Hooks, "Feminism: A Movement to End Sexist Oppression," *Feminist Theory: From Margin to Center*, Taylor & Francis Group, Hoboken, New Jersey, 2014. http://mcc.osu.edu/posts/documents/sexism-bhooks.pdf
12. Joan C. Chrisler, Ingrid Johnston-Robledo, *Woman's Embodied Self: Feminist Perspectives on Identity and Image*, American Psychological Association, Washington, D.C., 2017.
13. Jean Kilbourne, Official Website. https://www.jeankilbourne.com/lectures/
14. Ilene Prusher, "Trump Judges Women by Their Bodies. Do You?" *CNN Opinion*, November 5, 2016. https://www.cnn.com/2016/11/04/opinions/trumps-1-to-10-scale-is-nothing-new-for-women-prusher/index.html
15. *Consumer Reports*, Official Website https://www.consumerreports.org/cro/index.htm
16. Goran Radanovic, "10 Best Cars of 2018 and 10 That Aren't Worth Buying," *Hotcars*, July 5, 2018. https://www.hotcars.com/10-best-cars-of-2018-and-10-of-the-not-so-great/
17. Ibid.
18. Madeleine Fraley, "Media Critic Jean Kilbourne Speaks on Objectification in TV and Film," *The Daily Tarheel*, April 5, 2017. https://www.dailytarheel.com/article/2017/04/media-critic-jean-kilbourne-speaks-on-objectification-in-tv-and-film
19. RM Calogero, "Objectification Theory, Self-Objectification, and Body Image." In Thomas F. Cash (Ed.), *Encyclopedia of Body Image and Human Appearance*, Vol. 2.

Academic Press, San Diego, 2012, pp. 574–580. http://scalar.usc.edu/works/bodies/rm-calogero-objectification-theory-self-objectification-and-body-image
20. Ibid.
21. Grant McCracken, "Culture and Consumption: A Theoretical Account of the Structure and Movement of the Cultural Meaning of Consumer Goods," *Journal of Consumer Research, University of Chicago Press*, Vol. 13, No. 1, June, 1986, pp. 71–84.
22. Ibid.
23. Erving Goffman, *Gender Advertisement*, Palgrave, 1979, London, UK.
24. Ibid.
25. Mercedes Benz, Official Website. https://www.mercedes-benz-classic-store.com/en/accessories/glasses-cosmetics/1120/mercedes-benz-man-100ml
26. Aaron Foley, "New Chrysler Minivan to Woo 'Supermom,' Designer Says," *Wards Auto*, April 17, 2013. https://www.wardsauto.com/sae-world-congress/new-chrysler-minivan-woo-supermom-designer-says
27. Hannah Golden, "How Big Were the 2018 Women's Marches? The Numbers Are Massive," *Elite Daily*, January 24, 2018. https://www.elitedaily.com/p/how-big-were-the-2018-womens-marches-the-numbers-are-massive-8001200
28. Heather Caygle, "Record-Breaking Number of Women Run for Office," *Politico*, March 8, 2018. https://www.politico.com/story/2018/03/08/women-rule-midterms-443267
29. Hannah Golden, "How Big Were the 2018 Women's Marches? The Numbers Are Massive," *Elite Daily*, January 24, 2018. https://www.elitedaily.com/p/how-big-were-the-2018-womens-marches-the-numbers-are-massive-8001200
30. Jillian Berman, "Why That 'Like a Girl' Super Bowl Ad Was So Groundbreaking," *Huff Post*, February, 2 2015. https://www.huffingtonpost.com/2015/02/02/always-super-bowl-ad_n_6598328.html
31. Ibid.
32. Leo Burnett, "Always "Unstoppable,"" *Campaign*, July 8, 2015. https://www.campaignlive.co.uk/article/always-unstoppable-leo-burnett/1355319
33. He for She, Official Website. https://www.heforshe.org/en
34. Jean Kilbourne, "Making It Conscious: On the Murky World of Advertising," Jena Kilbourne, Official Website. http://www.jeankilbourne.com/jbp/wp-content/uploads/2017/01/Making-It-Conscious-Jean-Kilbourne.pdf
35. Jack Neff, "Ten Years In, Dove's 'Real Beauty' Seems to be Aging Well," *Ad Age*, January 22, 2014.
36. Jennifer L. Pozner, "Dove's "Real Beauty" Backlash," *Women in Meda & News*, Issue 30, Fall 2005. http://www.wimnonline.org/articles/dovebacklash.html
37. https://www.dove.com/uk/skin-care/skin-firming-cream.html
38. Ibid.
39. Cheryl Wischover, "Axe Leaves Behind Its Legacy of Sexism by Tackling Toxic Masculinity," *Racked, Beauty*, https://www.racked.com/2017/6/28/15874802/axe-rebranding-toxic-masculinity
40. Natalie Zmuda, Ann-Chrstine Diaz, "Female Empowerment in Ads: Soft Feminism or Soft Soap," *Ad Age*, September 2, 2014. https://adage.com/article/cmo-strategy/marketers-soft-feminism/294740/
41. Rashaunna Nelson, "Brands That Support Same-Sex Couples in Their Advertising," *Humans & LGBTQ*. https://humans.media/brands-that-support-same-sex-couples-in-their-advertising

42. Dejan Jotanovic, "The Problem When Gay Culture Fetishises Masculinity Above All Else," *The Guardian*, February 1, 2019. https://www.theguardian.com/commentisfree/2019/feb/01/the-problem-when-gay-culture-fetishises-masculinity-above-all-else
43. Ibid.
44. Michael Arceneaux, "There Is No Black 'Love, Simon' because Gay Men of Color Are Portrayed as Our Pathologies," *NBC News*, April 14, 2018. https://www.nbcnews.com/think/opinion/there-no-black-love-simon-because-gay-men-color-are-ncna865731
45. Ibid.
46. C. Winter Han, "The Deliberate Racism Making #Gaymediasowhite," *American Sociological Association*, Vol. 16, Issue 4, pp. 70–71, December 12, 2017. https://journals.sagepub.com/doi/full/10.1177/1536504217742397
47. Ibid.
48. Tyler KingKade, "Oklahoma Frat Boys Caught Singing 'There Will Never Be A N***** In SAE'," *Huff Post*, March 9, 2015. https://www.huffpost.com/entry/frat-racist-sae-oklahoma_n_6828212
49. Associated Press, "Frat Bros Suspended for Racist Video Re-Enroll at University," *New York Post*, August 30, 2018. https://nypost.com/2018/08/30/frat-bros-suspended-for-racist-video-re-enroll-at-university/
50. Alisha Acquaye, "How Beauty Brans Are Profiting Off Racism," *Teen Vogue*, January 26, 2018. https://www.teenvogue.com/story/how-beauty-brands-are-profiting-off-racism
51. Ibid.
52. Helene Cooper, "Where Beauty Means Bleached Skin," *The New York Times*, November 26, 2016. https://www.nytimes.com/2016/11/26/fashion/skin-bleaching-south-africa-women.html
53. Jake New, "Fraternity Caught On Camera Singing Racist Song," *Inside Higher Ed*, March 9, 2015. https://www.insidehighered.com/quicktakes/2015/03/09/fraternity-caught-video-singing racist-song
54. Tribune News Services, "Evanston-Based Fraternity Says 5 Chapters Acknowledged Hearing Racist Chant," *Chicago Tribune*, February 12, 2016. https://www.chicagotribune.com/news/breaking/ct-evanston-fraternity-racist-chant-20160212-story.html

6
A BRO MANUAL TO MOVIES, TV, AND GAMES

> **Key Points**
> - Disney's Awkward Attempts to Create Diversity and Female Empowerment
> - Summer Blockbusters
> - Superheroes and the Cult of Self
> - The Antihero
> - Reality TV: Televised Frat Parties
> - The Love-Sex Dichotomy or "The Rom-Com as 'Chick-Flick' in Bro Culture"
> - Bro Flicks
> - Gender-Flip Movies
> - Gamer Culture

While many films offer the opportunity to escape reality for a couple hours, others are great teaching tools. Points can be made in the storyline of a film that can move people emotionally or enlighten people on topics they may have never considered or experienced, or inspire people to look at things differently than they might otherwise. Audience members can feel empathy toward the protagonist or a sense of anger and injustice toward the antagonist. Films can document moments in human history that cannot be captured in other ways. Movies can also spark discussions that might not otherwise occur. For instance, in my classes, I notice that students are much more willing to engage in discussions on controversial topics when their analysis is aimed at characters in a film, rather than simply stating their views on controversial issues of the day. Films provide students a safe-space within which to deconstruct and discuss topics like racism, sexism, homophobia, politics, religion, and other potentially volatile issues without having to confront directly their own opinions in an environment where controversy becomes personal. If I ask students what they think about the organization *Black Lives Matter*, or the Trump administration's desire to build a wall along the Southern border of the United States, I almost never get the level of input that we get when discussing a film that takes up issues of contemporary racism or xenophobia.

But films can also reinforce stereotypes and prejudices. For decades, Hollywood movies have followed the familiar pattern of men as protagonists who are placed in positions of authority, and who possess power, courage, strength, and wealth, while women are often placed in positions of support, emotional fragility, or as love-interests, seductresses, and desperate for love. Imagine being a boy raised on typical Hollywood film-narratives. You would probably feel that you have a lot to live up to, but you might also feel superior to women or feel that women need you in order to feel whole. This chapter is going to trace the common gendered narratives found in movies, reality TV, and other youth-centered media that craft a very particular, normative account of gender, and in so doing, reinforce longstanding bro beliefs and attitudes.

DISNEY'S AWKWARD ATTEMPTS TO CREATE DIVERSITY AND FEMALE EMPOWERMENT

We begin by examining animated movies aimed mainly at kids, but sometimes adults too. For many children, animated movies are their first foray into sex and gender representation. Boys and girls learn what the normative expectations are for women and men by watching programming designed for children. In much of this programming, men are strong, muscular, heroic, and courageous, while women are pretty, petite, sexual yet innocent, and obsessed with romance. Pixar's *The Incredibles* is one very successful example of an animated superhero movie featuring a family that possesses and use superpowers to combat a host of supervillains.[1] The father of the family, Bob Parr or "Mr. Incredible," is a classic example of the male superhero protagonist with a greatly exaggerated physique that features a gigantic chest, huge arms and shoulders, and the superpower of immense physical strength. Interestingly, he has self-doubts and foibles that set him apart from many superheroes, but the foundation of superhuman strength and violence as a mediator of evil is intact. The mother and daughter also have superpowers, but not in terms of raw muscular strength. The mother, or "Elastigirl," is unbelievably pliable so that her body can stretch great distances in what may be an ironic superpower for women who feel that they are required to multitask between being professional career women, mothers, and homemakers in what has been termed by many gender scholars, "the superwoman complex."[2]

But if we examine the history of animated films for kids, Disney Studios must be front and center in the conversation. Walt Disney established Walt Disney Productions in 1929 and went from creating cartoons to producing animated feature films with *Snow White and the Seven Dwarves* in 1937, which was both a critical and box office success.[3] Other similar Disney animated films include *Cinderella* (1950) and *Sleeping Beauty* (1959).[4] The theme of these movies were basically the same: A thin, white, beautiful, young woman who is living a life of drudgery, but dreams of the day she finds true-love, is eventually rescued by a muscular, white, handsome prince and taken away to a magical castle where they live happily ever after. These movies became known as the Disney princess movies, since the young, beautiful women end up becoming princesses after falling in love with and marrying princes. Today, many of these films are rightfully criticized for their depiction of women as helpless, ambitionless beings who need men and romance to give their lives meaning. Other female characters in these movies play villains who are often portrayed as physically unattractive characters who are angry, vengeful, and devoted to harming the beautiful, young princess. But most importantly, Disney princesses were depicted as being attractive solely on the basis of their physical looks and deferential-to-men personalities, not due to more complex and meaningful traits such as ambition, wisdom, independence, compassion, courage, and determination.

Then came the women's movement, feminism, and a growing realization that American culture was patriarchal and sexist in nature, a recognition that made Disney princesses anachronistic and backward. Over the ensuing years, Disney Studios had a choice to make remain in the past where the value given to women was measured strictly in terms of looks and passivity, or change with the times and begin to create new animated women, who were autonomous, bold, and looking for much more than love. The growing pains of this transformation have been glaring with offerings such as *Beauty and the Beast* (1991) where a young woman named Belle, who is a bookworm, which is certainly dissimilar to former Disney princesses, meets a man, or actually an ox or werewolf or something, who is abusive until she is able to tame him through love and patience. This has to be one of the most dangerous tropes sold to women for generations: that the love of a good (and beautiful) woman will change an abusive scoundrel into a fine, noble man who was in there all along waiting for the right woman to recognize and bring his nobility to life.

From there, Disney introduced *Mulan* (1998) who is a smart, woman-warrior in ancient China who takes her father's place in going to war against the Huns.[5] She must pass as a man to be accepted as a soldier and ultimately defeat the Hun leader to save the emperor. *Mulan* is certainly no *Snow White* or *Sleeping Beauty*. She is one of the most autonomous and courageous female animated characters in Disney animation history. Entering the 21st century, Disney Studios introduced a host of new princesses including 'Tiana' of *The Princess and the Frog* (2009), the sisters of *Frozen* (2013 & 2019 respectively), and *Moana* (2016). Each of these films is considered to represent a foray into narratives and characters that are feminist-friendly, with some reservations, but they have also been commercially profitable. At $1,325,000,000 worldwide box office gross, *Frozen 2* is the second best-selling animated film in the world, eclipsed only by *The Incredibles 2*.[6] Even with several key objections about the sisters' waif, doe-eyed appearance and Anna's obsession with finding love, *Frozen* passes the Bechdel test by having two named female characters talk to one another about something other than men or love, and without men being present. Still, the alleged feminism of *Frozen* boils down to the older sister, Elsa, not caring about romantic love or finding a man, and coming to terms with her power as something she shouldn't feel she must hide from public scrutiny. In *Moana*, a young princess goes on a harrowing journey to save her people from catastrophe without any hint of romantic love, although she is forced to deal with an obnoxious, male demigod whose powers are needed to return the heart of Te Fiti, a goddess who brought life to the ocean.[7] It is also notable that Moana is not white or petite, which makes the film, according to Los Angeles Times film reporter Jen Yamato, "the most progressive film in the studio's 93-year history."[8]

What often goes undiscussed is the representation of men in animated Disney films. The stereotypes abound with oversized, muscular heroes, conniving villains, and awkward oafs. Disney films also possess an assortment of men who are found in the roles of everything from shopkeepers to fathers to royalty, but they are window-dressing for the men who are either love-interests to the princesses or villains. The male love-interests are often men of wealth and power, but also physical specimens of muscularity who are drawn by cartoonists to be quixotically handsome, while possessing a naïve sense of charm. If you're a boy watching these movies, you probably don't relate to the villain, but you also don't relate to the hero, even if you wish you did. Like the photo-shopped images of models found in fashion magazines, the male characters in animated Disney films are caricatures. For every princess in most Disney films, there is a Prince Charming whose life and characteristics are unattainable.

Yet, even though the Disney films are famous for their princesses, it turns out that male characters are given much more dialogue than the female characters.[9] This reality reinforces the notion that women are to be seen and not heard. Additionally, until quite recently, there have been very few characters of color and those that did exist were often stereotypes. So, if you grew up on Disney animation half a century ago and you are a person of color, it is likely that many of your animated role models, like those in real life, came mainly from white characters. In fact, some of the most beloved Disney films of yore feature ridiculous caricatures of people of color such as the "happy slaves" found in Disney's *Song of the South* (1946), which features "Uncle Remus," an ever-smiling, happy-go-lucky Black man adapted and compiled by Joel Chandler Harris who actually claimed that he hoped the book would be "a wonderful defense of slavery as it existed in the South."[10] Or the fetishizing of Indigenous women in the animated feature, *Pocahontas*, who is depicted as a supermodel in form-fitting dresses who falls in love with a white man, or in the Disney film *Peter Pan*, which features a musical number entitled, "What Makes the Red Man Red."[11] In the Disney film *Aladdin*, which has been rebooted by filmmaker Guy Richie, the mythical land of Agrabah is a place where, according to one of the main songs from the film, "They cut off your ear if they don't like your face. It's barbaric, but hey, it's home."[12] At a time when Islamophobia is peaking with the help of the rhetoric of President Donald Trump who pushed through a travel ban on people coming to the U.S. from predominantly Muslim nations, this film should cement the already pitched fervor of racists and xenophobes of all kinds. Being a young man or woman from the Middle East and watching this film must feel similar to young, Black people of the past watching *Song of the South*. But these sorts of films also feed a racist branch of the bro code, which is comprised of white boys and men who attempt to continue a tradition of American racism. As we saw in the chapter on frat-culture, the young men of *Sigma Alpha Epsilon* were caught chanting racist slurs on a bus. These young men are forming their ideas about manhood around the racist identity of white supremacy, while attempting to explain away their racism as simply being a joke.

SUMMER BLOCKBUSTERS

Summer is a season when film studios target kids with animated movies and target teens with films that cover the well-traveled ground of action-adventure superheroes, coming-of-age love and sex romps, teen rebellion, and raunchy comedies. Since many teens are out of school during the summer with disposable cash that they either earn at minimum-wage jobs or that was given to them by their parents, movies become a main source of entertainment and de facto teaching tools.[13] Teens spend most of their money on clothes and food,[14] but PC gaming and movies haul in more than 40% of the average teen's budget.[15] The films that draw teens to theaters feature certain themes that have long been used to attract a high school to college-aged demographic.

One of the most common themes of the Summer blockbuster is the superhero theme that has clogged theaters for decades. Just the titles of the films or the name of the lead character tells the story:

Batman
Superman
Spiderman
Iron Man
Aquaman
X-men

There are a surplus of men and few women. Other male protagonists include Captain America, Wolverine, Thor, and more recently Black Panther, who is notable for being a Black, male superhero. The women who do make superhero status are Wonder Woman, Mystique, Black Widow, and Jennifer Lawrence's character Katniss Everdeen of *The Hunger Games* trilogy, along with Cat Woman and Harley Quinn who are villains. In most superhero movies, men are brave warriors who save the world from evil, while most of the female characters are love-interests or sexualized sidekicks. Some of the more notable love-interests include Lois Lane (Batman), Mary Jane (Spiderman), Mera (Aquaman), Margaret Carter (Captain America), Virginia "Pepper" Potts (Iron Man), and Catwoman – Selina Kyle (antagonist – love interest to Batman). There are no mainstream Latino, Asian, Native American, or LGBTQ superheroes who have had bankable movies produced about them, and it is only recently that Black, male superheroes (Black Panther and vampire-killer, Blade) have been produced and enjoyed commercial success. This last point is notable, since Hollywood producers, most of whom are white, had to be convinced that a Black superhero would convert into box office success.[16]

But when considering the tropes surrounding superheroes, many of the narratives tell us about our culture and our values. Journalist Mark Bowden, writing for the *NY Times*, notes,

> Films reflect the tastes and values of the period in which they are made. We can trace the changing status of women, evolving ideas about masculinity, war, crime, journalism, the C.I.A. or anything else by Hollywood treatments over the decades. So when historians look back at this glut of superhero flicks, what will they say about us?[17]

According to Bowden, the glut of superhero movies today speak to a **cult of self** mentality, which can be captured in the proclamation "I alone can save the world," a Trumpian mantra that is attractive to many, but especially men, since men are instructed since boyhood by larger culture that their principal role is to provide and protect.[18] The superhero is almost always a solitary figure whose life is built on fighting evil against the odds, even though the individual possesses special powers that make him more capable than the average person. This special power can be especially attractive to boys and young men who feel insecure and unsure of themselves, although for boys and young men of color, or LGBTQ youths, the underrepresentation of superheroes of color and LGBTQ identities may reinforce their own marginalization in a media culture that has not been very inclusive. Having special powers also appeals to many boys and young men who want to have the kind of status and attention that they believe girls and women find attractive, since they may currently feel invisible to women, while movie superheroes are often magnetically attractive to the women in the film.

But in fact, the longstanding superhero regulation to fight evil and injustice typical of the superhero genre now competes with the antihero in some of the newer superhero features. For instance, in the recent *Batman* series of movies, Heath Ledger's supervillain "The Joker" has been every bit as popular as Batman, and in the film *Suicide Squad*, villains are the superheroes in a sense, as they are commissioned by the government to pull off a secret mission where The Joker, played by Jared Leto, and female supervillain Harley Quinn, played by Margot Robbie, team up as accomplices and lovers to wreak havoc on Gotham City.[19,20] In what may be a paradigmatic character that goes from tormented underdog to criminal mastermind, *The Joker*, featuring Joaquin Phoenix in the lead role, is a tale that resonates with many boys and young men who feel that their lives are a testament to being unappreciated and bullied. The transition emblematic of *The Joker* or Peter Parker to *Spiderman* is a conversion that could not be more attractive to boys who go from feeling powerless to commanding power and fear through evolving into a menacing antihero.

The emergence of **the antihero** has today become every bit as valued and cherished as the hero so that good over evil tropes have blurred into the allure of power and attention at whatever cost. The impact on bro culture of the emergent popularity of the antihero is yet to be seen, although placing powerful, but dangerous men on pedestals has been witnessed in the rise of street-racing in the wake of the *Fast & Furious* franchise of films.[21,22] The point is that many boys and men will emulate or look up to those male film characters they view as tough, cool, dangerous, and attractive to women, whether those characters are traditional heroes or villains. An example of this can be seen in the almost worship-like adoration to which many young rappers have testified toward the character *Scarface* in Brian De Palma's film of the same name, featuring the character of Cuban drug-lord Tony Montana as played by Al Pacino.[23] Montana is much like Peter Parker who turns into Spiderman in the sense that he goes from a person who no one notices into a powerful man who demands respect from other men, while suddenly becoming attractive to women. This narrative resonates with many of the young men drawn to bro culture. They may begin as ordinary guys invisible to others, but through frat-affiliation, gang affiliation, or simply presenting themselves as *bad boys*, they shed their skin of unremarkable mediocrity to become notable bros impervious to danger and irresistible to women.

In most superhero movies, the superhero is a man and the woman or women in his life are sexual or romantic assistants. While there may be valiant traits in the man whose secret life is that of superhero (Bruce Wayne – Batman, Tony Stark – Iron Man, Peter Parker – Spiderman), this is not always so. Both Bruce Wayne and Tony Stark are written as playboys or womanizers who use their wealth and power to amass a collection of adoring and sexually available women. The prevailing trope sold to boys and young men is that wealth and power are the ingredients one needs to attract beautiful women who would otherwise be disinterested in *being with someone like you*. Being oneself is to be just another schmuck who is invisible to women, but having an alternate identity as rich, powerful benefactor places men in a desirable-to-women position that is alluring to many pre-bros. This trope insults both men and women, of course. It states to men that who you are is not good enough, and it states of women that women are shallow, opportunists who care only about the gains that come from having a relationship with a wealthy, powerful man.

Thought Box

To what extent do you think movies have an effect on people's thinking? Dating back to Greek dramas, a good versus evil storyline with good triumphing over evil has been the dominant narrative in storytelling, which was long considered to be a healthy, didactic narrative for young people, even if the lesson is simplistic and unrealistic. We may not think that movies have much effect on our thinking, but one study found that viewing certain films had an impact on audience members' views on government.[24,25] University of Dayton professor Michelle C. Pautz argues, "Movies contribute to the political socialization of people (young adults in particular) and so what audiences watch and how certain institutions are portrayed over time can be very significant."[26] Pautz's study is consistent with the work of the famous communications professor George Gerbner, whose *Cultivation Theory* predicted that heavy and long-term media consumption affects a person's worldview.[27] When you think about the emergence of the anti-hero as a pop-cultural phenomenon, might the glamorization of this figure affect the aspirational choices of young people? Or, with men, might the hero-womanizer trope affect the aspirations of boys and young men with respect to their thinking about and treatment of women?

Because so many men are taught that their primary role is to protect and provide, the inability to protect and provide can produce men who feel inadequate and unnecessary. However, the role of provider and protector is part and parcel of patriarchy, since it places women in positions of subordination to men, but also sets the stage for millions of men feeling lost and deficient. The superhero is a fantasy where men can retreat to reclaim their damaged sense of masculinity, but it is the superhero persona itself that can drive the insecurity, since the powerful superhero is a constant reminder to many men of what they are not. The superhero stands as a hegemonic template of masculinity in an age when an increasing number of men are searching for meaning and purpose.

REALITY TV

Starting in the 1990s, television producers realized that they could make TV programming much more cheaply if they stopped using famous actors and instead used young, unknown aspiring actors to perform in the roles usually reserved for name-actors. For the price of one Charlie Sheen or Ashton Kutcher you could get a dozen guys who would happily perform in a reality TV show to get exposure and an entrance into show business. But reality TV does not sell reality; it sells highly scripted and choreographed stereotypes of men and women. In the worst of these stereotypes, women compete for the love-interest of a man in shows like ABC's *The Bachelor*, where a bevy of young, beautiful women battle one another for the right to marry a young, handsome, eligible bachelor.[28] One element of *The Bachelor* that should be noted is that both the bachelor and the many women who compete for his affection are overwhelmingly White. To date, no bachelor has been Black and this overrepresentation of White bachelors and White female contestants feeds a longstanding racist narrative about Black men and White women.[29] Dating back to D.W. Griffith's 1915 film *Birth of a Nation*, Black men have been stereotyped as sexually aggressive and dangerous to White women.[30] This stereotype has long been labeled *The Brute* in racist lore, a caricature that promotes a white-supremacist notion that Black men are innately savage, criminal, and dangerous, particularly toward White women.[31]

The plot of *The Bachelor* does not change much from season to season. Women are shown trying to undermine one another to get the man's attention. The ugly trope underlying this show is that *women cannot be trusted and should view one another as natural enemies*, while also reinforcing an alarming form of misogyny where women are reduced to sexual appliances paraded about for a man to judge. As the show progresses, the bachelor eliminates prospective love-interests until one woman remains as *the lucky woman* who may turn out to be his wife.[32]

In her book, *Reality Bites Back: The Troubling Truth about Guilty Pleasure TV*, author and media critic Jennifer Pozner exposes the four most common tropes about women found in reality TV shows:[33]

- Women are catty, bitchy, manipulative, and not to be trusted, especially by other women.
- Women are stupid.
- Women are incompetent and home and at work.
- Women are gold-diggers.

Reality shows that employ these tropes are essentially an instruction manual for a vicious form of sexism. The man in the show becomes a portrait of power, control, and desirability, while the women are cast as scheming harpies that will say and do anything to undercut their rivals for the prize of being the bachelor's chosen one. In fact, *The Bachelor* is a good example of a bro's dream existence: dozens of women competing for his romantic and sexual attention. It actually flips reality on its head. In real life, very few bros are living lives like the guy in *The Bachelor*, but in the upside-down world of *The Bachelor*, the men are playboy – womanizer Bruce Wayne riding through town in his Batmobile as women swoon. In terms of reviews, *The Bachelor* pulls an underwhelming 3.1 out of 10 on IMDB.[34] Yet, each week over 5 million viewers tune in to witness the sexist eyesore that is indicative of most reality television programming.[35]

You would have to go back to the 1950s and 1960s to see this many young women surrounding one man in the hope of being the one he chooses, and in those days that man was pornographer Hugh Hefner, who boasted of having sex with over one thousand women over the course of his life.[36] The bro code can be described as an updated lifestyle of what was once termed "the playboy philosophy," whereby men viewed women primarily as sexual opportunities who are judged by men on the basis of their physical looks and sex appeal. The playboy philosophy, according to Hugh Hefner and his supporters, was a repudiation of religious repression and an affirmation of sexual liberty.[37] However, Sady Doyle, writing for *Elle*, notes:

> In the new, "radical" Playboy philosophy, women were sour, scolding mommies to be rebelled against or hot commodities to be acquired. This split between conservative misogyny and hip, "liberal" misogyny is still with us, and still expressed in much the same terms. But Hefner never challenged the sexism at the heart of the

social order — he just wanted to remove any responsibility men might bear to the women they slept with, and make sure men's experience of sex was consequence-free.[38]

The entrenched patriarchy at the heart of Hefner's 'playboy philosophy' continued the 1950s tradition of placing women in positions of being sexually objectified accessories to powerful men. After all, in the Playboy Clubs that sprung up around the world in the 1960s through the 1990s, it was not men who were wearing the sexually revealing bunny costumes, lighting women's cigarettes, and feigning amusement and interest when a woman made a sexually suggestive comment.[39]

The Playboy Clubs may have seen their time come and go, but the philosophy embedded in them is still very much alive today. Bro culture, in fact, functions around the view that women are and should be considered first and foremost sexual opportunities. The sexually themed frat parties around the nation are good examples of this mindset, where women are expected to wear sexually revealing outfits, while no dress code exists for the men. Much of reality TV is simply a televised frat-party, starting with MTV's *Jersey Shore* in 2009 and continuing in shows such as *Rock of Love* starring 80s rock-anachronism Bret Michaels and *Flavor of Love*, starring rap-star-curiosity Flavor Flav.[40, 41] So, who could really be surprised that ABC would launch a show like *The Bachelor* where a couple dozen young women compete for the attention and affection of one man?

Even though much of reality TV is scripted and manipulated by directors and producers, transparently scripted TV comedies often depict men as stupid, clumsy, and oafish. From *The Simpsons* to *Family Guy* to *The Office* to *The Big Bang Theory* to the *Dumb & Dumber* duo of films, men are generally dimwitted or at least socially awkward. This stereotype has been around for a very long time, dating back to the slapstick days of CBS's *Gilligan's Island* and of course, *The Three Stooges* and *Laurel and Hardy* even further in the past. But this comedy trope is founded on the normative idea that men should be serious, intelligent, authoritarian, commanding, and in complete control so that the reduction of these traits sets up humor at the expense of those men who do not measure up. The comedic trope of *men as dumb* can also be found at the root of some forms of bullying, where a boy who is socially awkward or not considered to be strong and athletic is targeted for abuse. But bullying aside, this particular trope does men no favors and reinforces an age-old convention that authentic masculinity is smart, quick, powerful, and intelligent in nature; those who do not adequately satisfy this requirement are subject to ridicule and shame.

This trope also contributes to the old-fashioned gender essentialist notion that intelligence is a masculine trait, while emotionalism is a feminine trait, that ambition, independence, and confidence are masculine traits, while deference, dependence, and insecurity are feminine traits. Furthermore, traits like kindness, empathy, and compassion are often portrayed as feminine traits that boys and men *should not* possess or outwardly demonstrate, which is to strip men of holding and displaying some of the most important human traits we possess as human beings. This dichotomizing of human traits creates a predictable gendered binary script in some TV shows and films that allegedly appeal to either men or women, but not both.

THE ROM-COM AND DRAM-COM AS 'CHICK-FLICK' IN BRO CULTURE

The disunion of love and sex in bro culture is stark. Bros have to continually repudiate love to their fellow bros by assuring them that their latest sexual interest is "a hot piece of ass," instead of being someone they care about as a person. One of the longstanding jokes in bro culture when discussing women is that "she has a great personality." Translated in bro vernacular, this means, "she is sexually unattractive." Validation in bro culture comes when one is considered to be "a player," a "ladies man," "has game." Love is antithetical to this position and designates weakness in bro culture. Men get this message through many sources, but films are one of the more pervasive places where sex is positioned as a normative pursuit for men, while love is depicted as a normative pursuit for women. Film after film portray women as looking for love, as searching for the perfect fit that will complete her, while men are repeatedly displayed as trolling for sex and doing what is needed to avoid commitment. Bro culture has adopted these tropes by reinforcing in men that love and commitment are feminine traits, while the never-ending pursuit of sex with as many different partners as possible is a masculine trait.

According to Deborah Barker and Kathryn McKee of the University of Mississippi, the birth of the 'chick-flick' moniker came in the late 1980s with the film *Steel Magnolias* and later *Thelma and Louise,* starring Susan Sarandon and Geena Davis as two women who forge a friendship and determine to take their own lives rather than submit to patriarchal authority.[42,43] *Thelma and Louise* became an anthem for feminism with its theme of autonomy and resistance to male dominance.[44] But to many men, the "chick flick" nickname represented a way to marginalize and demean films like *Thelma and Louise* where women are protagonists who demonstrate strength and independence.

As more films featured women in the role of protagonist, fewer titles followed the feminist anthem of Thelma and Louise, instead opting for regressively sexist themes found in romantic comedies and romantic dramas such as *Twilight, How to Lose a Guy in 10 Days, Love Actually, He's Just Not That Into You,* and *Pretty Woman*. The themes found in movies of this kind are finding love, winning back love, beating the odds for love, and powerful men protecting fragile women. For instance, writing for *The Guardian*, David Cox states of the protagonist Bella in the *Twilight* trilogy,

> Instead of sorting herself out, she opts for escape to a parallel universe. There, she'll be able to join a coterie who'll be guaranteed to accept her. She'll have to be undead, but you can't have everything.

The rescuer who'll whisk her away from the challenges of reality will, of course, be a man. Actually, Edward's a vampire, but no matter, he's incredibly good-looking. He may be a dangerous dude, but a woman's love can tame him.[45]

The stereotype of women looking for and doing anything to get love in *Twilight* rival the Disney cartoons of the past, with the handsome prince sweeping the maiden away from her dreary life to the happily ever after.

In another romantic comedy, *Think Like a Man*, starring Kevin Hart, Michael Ealy, Regina Hall, and Taraji Henson, there is a schema for the film that writer Athene Donald describes as

Look like a girl,
Act like a lady,
Think like a man,
Work like a boss.[46]

Donald notes, "if our poor little mushed-up brains were merely themselves we'd never get anywhere in the workplace, so we have to aspire to think like men."[47] This "lean-in" philosophy for women makes at least two mistakes. It assumes that women and men are metaphysically distinct such that men are rational and emotionally stoic, success machines with a sufficient amount of ambition to get the job done no matter what, while women are talkers and feelers who never quite reach success without the help of men or at least without emulating men. This trope also ignores the fact that much of corporate America continues to be top-heavy with men at the executive level of management so that women are still dependent on men to hire or advance them.[48,49] When the directive becomes "think like a man," the culpability is placed on women to change in order to be successful instead of requiring men to change by checking their male privilege and questioning their own sexism when it comes to their making hiring and advancement decisions. But the directive also validates to boys and men that men are natural-born leaders and decision-makers, while girls and women can only aspire to leadership and success by mimicking men.

One of the main problems with movies today is that the Hollywood assemblage of power is overwhelmingly male. Consider the power brokers who write, direct, produce, and have creative input in making feature films and TV shows. Of the top 100 grossing films of 2018, women were greatly underrepresented:

- 4% of directors
- 15% of writers
- 3% of cinematographers
- 18% of producers
- 18% of executive producers
- 14% of editors

With so few women in positions of executive authority over creative content, it cannot be surprising that the majority of films and TV shows produced each year carry bro-friendly themes and sexist misrepresentations of both women and men.

One of the more famous titles that has been labeled "chick flick" is *Mean Girls* starring Lindsay Lohan and written by Tina Fey. One interpretation of *Mean Girls* is that striving to compete for popularity and prettiness undermines female alliances and ultimately defeats the goal of women's empowerment. But the bro interpretation of such films is that women in positions of protagonist who are also powerful and autonomous are a threat to masculine power and therefore quickly marginalized and dismissed as "chick flicks." The moniker "chick flick" is a way for men to ignore and demean women's authority in order to return women to the stereotypes found in bro-friendly films like *Hot Tub Time Machine* and *Hot Tub Time Machine 2*, where women are reduced to sex props and jokes are exercises in prepubescent gross-out scenes, where homophobia also runs rampant.

Bro comedies from *Superbad* to *American Pie* to *Wedding Crashers* feature an exhausted narrative that stretches back decades: that the goal for men is to get sex by any means necessary, which includes lying, spying, scheming with your bros, plying women with alcohol, or in *The 40-Year-Old Virgin*, bros trying to get their bro, Andy Stitzer, to have his first sexual encounter. These themes are in stark contrast to those found in comedies designed to appeal to women. As stated earlier, the films that bros label "chick flicks" are typically about finding love, love lost, love reborn, balancing work and love, having children, starting over, romantic betrayal, romantic forgiveness, and in some cases, competition between women for status, love, or career. Some films try to walk the line between bro and chick flick like *Jerry Maguire*, which follows the life of a sports agent who is surrounded by testosterone-filled clients and rivals, but who learns that love is more important than being the most successful agent in the business.

It should also be said that many men enjoy films regarded as "chick flicks," but bros are a particular segment of male culture that defines itself by repudiating the feminine and assuring other bros that they are heterosexual, which often means that they join in the revelry of demeaning women and gay people as part of bro validation. This repudiation of the feminine does great damage to men, since it robs men of the opportunity to be emotionally whole, of being able to embrace sides of the human condition that bro culture instructs should bring shame such as feeling and expressing love.

Why are so many men turned off by films about love? Some have written about the phenomenon of men fearing intimacy as the basis for steering clear of films that revolve around romance and love. Writing for *Psychology Today*, therapist Seth Meyers notes that in 15 years of practice, he has noticed that more men than women are uncomfortable with discussing intimacy and emotional vulnerability.[50] According to Meyers, the main reason why men are uncomfortable discussing emotional vulnerability is having experience with former relationship trauma whether romantic in nature or due to neglect by or loss of parents.[51] But this explanation ignores the fact that many women also experience relationship trauma without mocking and avoiding films with plots about love and intimacy. The reason why so many men avoid what they term "chick flicks" is because they have been raised in a culture where masculinity is defined by renouncing the feminine in favor of an emotionally debilitated version of manhood that practices juvenile masculinity, the kind masculinity that thinks girls are icky and dumb when they were six years old, but who today retain the judgment that women are "dumb" while adding the notion that women are important for being sexually attractive and available to men. When bros categorize women in this painfully limited and regressive way, they not only demean women, they demean the value and power of love and intimacy over the immediate gratification of sex, and then codify this latter quest as authentically masculine. Men who value love are then marginalized in bro culture through a host of sexist and homophobic slurs and putdowns that include "soft, wimp, weak, wussies, pussies, and fags." The damage done is done to both women and men, as the men of bro culture are setting themselves up for lives of solitude and loneliness, devoid of the emotional intimacy and connection that comes with love.

BRO FLICKS

If there are films labeled "chick flicks" by some, "bro-flicks" would be a mixture of *Hot Tub Time Machine*, actions films like *Scarface*, superhero films like *Iron Man*, and perhaps *Sharknado*. There are themes to bro-friendly films that can be witnessed across genres. To begin, one filmmaker who has a long, distinguished career producing and directing films that guys tend to love is Martin Scorsese whose catalog includes gangster classics *Goodfellas*, *Casino*, *The Departed*, and *The Irishman*. The men of Scorsese films are violent men who demand respect from those around them, while never showing any form of weakness. They are tough, powerful, often violent men who command respect through fear and intimidation. Interestingly, Scorsese didn't always produce such bro-friendly films; his 1974 film *Alice Doesn't Live Here Anymore* followed the life of a single mother who is trying to earn enough money to care for her son. But Scorsese's career took off when he began making pictures that featured a cadre of tough, violent male characters who stop at nothing to achieve respect and fortune.

As covered earlier, the Oliver Stone film *Scarface* is one of the foundational bro films in the bro catalog of movies. In fact, *Scarface* previewed writer-director Quentin Tarantino's body of work, which has been described as "rock & roll spaghetti Westerns,"[52] the themes of which are revenge narratives where certain forms of violent masculinity are on display in the service of getting even for an unresolved grievance. In *Reservoir Dogs*, Tarantino's debut film, some have seen a feminist subtext to the film,[53] even though the film features an all-male cast of killers, sadists, and psychopaths. But with *Reservoir Dogs*, Tarantino introduced a certain type of masculinity that permeates many of his films, a template that centers around emotional stoicism, gratuitous violence, demanding respect, and getting revenge if one feels wronged. *Pulp Fiction* continues this foray into masculine stereotypes with hit men, an organized crime boss, a bygone boxer looking for his last big score, and a rape scene involving men raping another man.[54] The women of *Pulp Fiction* are a confluence of wives and girlfriends of various criminals and tough guys whose roles are generally supportive in nature. With the *Kill Bill* films, Tarantino offers his first female protagonist, but in a typical masculine role as revenge-seeking assassin who will stop at nothing to fulfill her goal of complete annihilation of those who attempted to kill her on her wedding day.[55]

The guy-friendly aspect of Tarantino's body of work no doubt involves his recurrent theme of violent, tough-guy masculinity, but with the twist of revenge that appeals to many men who feel disrespected, bullied, and overlooked. The tonic that restores one's masculine pride, in Tarantino films, is the testosterone-fueled reclamation of power and control one has had stripped away by other, more powerful bullies and persecutors. This plot-turn attracts men from various ends of the male spectrum. From the jockocracy of men who already view their physical strength as a means to acquire or maintain respect to the techie-nerdocracy of men who may feel that they have been disrespected throughout their lives without recourse. Tarantino films provide masculine resuscitation in a culture that measures masculinity in terms of pride, respect, power, and control. When women display power in Tarantino films, it is a very masculine definition of power, whereby violence is the antidote to redress feelings of being wronged.

In the last section, the film *Hot Tub Time Machine* was spotlighted as one of many bro-friendly comedies. But if one is paying attention, there are themes or rules to bro comedies and bro dramas that have been around for decades.

RULE #1: BRO COMEDIES OR DRAMAS ARE NOT ABOUT ROMANCE AND LOVE; RATHER, THEY ARE ABOUT SEX

Since many young men are instructed that love is weakness, while sex is power, it makes sense that the films produced for boys and men would follow this basic rule. From *Superbad* to the *American Pie* franchise to older films such as *Revenge of the Nerds* and *Porkies*, the repetitive story line in these films is the quest by boys and young men to get women in a place where they will give the men consensual or nonconsensual sex, whether that means getting them drunk, which would then be a case of rape, or spying on them while they are getting dressed or taking showers. These kinds of films are sometimes called "coming of age" movies, but since the entire modus operandi of the male protagonists is finding ways, including unscrupulous ways, of getting girls and women to have sex with them, the expression "coming of age" literally becomes an expression that means coerced sex as a rite of passage into manhood. With this pretext in place, it is unsurprising that an "incel" group of young men have emerged who possess an aggrieved sense of entitlement over women's bodies.[56]

RULE #2: BRO COMEDIES FEATURE HOMOPHOBIC CONTENT

Because boys and men are taught to repudiate the feminine, this instruction extends to gay men. So, it is not uncommon for the protagonists in bro-friendly films to utter homophobic remarks or demonstrate homophobic behaviors to assure his bros that he is not gay or does not possess any feminine characteristics. *Hot Tub Time Machine* is a classic example, where a man makes a wager with another man, whereby the loser of the wager has to give another man a blowjob. This is viewed in the movie as the most unmanly and demeaning thing a man can do, which by extension demeans gay men as not being *real* men.

RULE #3: BRO COMEDIES FEATURE GROSS-OUT HUMOR AND RISK-TAKING BEHAVIORS

Particularly since the rise of MTV's *Jackass* TV show and film franchise, guy-humor has been defined by gross-out humor that includes farting and other body noises or otherwise embarrassing behaviors and circumstances that leave the protagonist in a position of awkwardness and humiliation. The best two examples come from the actor who has perfected embarrassing, self-deprecation: Ben Stiller. In *There's Something About Mary*, Stiller joins a list of actors who appear in a scene of getting caught masturbating, while in *Along Came Polly*, Stiller clogs the toilet at his hope-to-be girlfriend's apartment, and of course, gets caught doing it. With respect to the show *Jackass*, the point is for young men to prove to other young men how dangerously irresponsible they can be as a surrogate for tough-guy masculinity. That is, since the men of *Jackass* are not muscular athletes or prototypical tough guys, their masculinity is proven by undertaking extremely risky stunts that place their lives and health in jeopardy for the sake of showing that they actually are tough guys, but couched in the guise of humor. It should also be noted that Rule #2 comes into play with the men of *Jackass* since it is common for the stunts they practice to have a homoerotic overtone, but again, in an effort to be funny and therefore ultimately homophobic in intention.

RULE #4: BRO COMEDIES ALMOST ALWAYS FEATURE MEN WHO LIVE IN A STATE OF ARRESTED DEVELOPMENT

The best illustration of this rule is found in *The Hangover* film franchise, where men in their 30s behave as adolescents, indulging in the kind of irresponsible behaviors that lead to regrettable outcomes that are supposed to be funny. This rule features a bachelor-party that leads to booze-induced memory loss, run-ins with law enforcement, missing teeth, and bewildering face tattoos. The boys-will-be-boys ethos is on display throughout these kinds of movies with the *Jackass*-laced question lingering in the air: How much trouble can a group of men get into and survive? *The 40-Year-Old Virgin* is another good example of a middle-aged man in arrested development who gets bro tips on how to become a womanizing bro like them. The overwhelming theme of movies of this kind is that men should be worldly and experienced in their abilities to seduce women into having sex with them. A man who is not experienced in this way is delegated once again in bro culture to *not a real man* status.

RULE #5: THE PROTAGONISTS ARE ALWAYS MEN

This rule may go without saying, but it should be said. Bro-friendly films are about the lives of men, not women. But notice that films designed to attract female audiences will often feature men in the role of protagonist such as the films *Jerry Maguire* and *Silver Linings Playbook,* but bro films never feature women in the role of protagonist even in those cases when the woman is an action hero such as *Laura Cross* or *Wonder Woman*.

RULE #6: WHEN BRO FILMS ARE DRAMA OR ACTION IN NATURE, VIOLENCE IS USUALLY AT THE CENTER OF THE PLOT

As seen in the Tarantino catalog or any number of action-adventure films, the male protagonists settle their differences with violence. This rule reinforces the old-fashioned trope that men do not solve conflicts with mature discussion, negotiation, and compromise, but with physical force. There are too many examples of this trope to come close to listing them all, but it is generally considered in bro culture to be properly masculine for men to resort to physical confrontation, intimidation, and violence when met with conflict. Films repetitively document this instruction as a statute. Talk is then replaced with action as a mantra of bro culture, a directive that is interestingly found throughout political discourse, particularly when a male politician attacks a rival male politician. The idea is that men-of-action do not waste their time talking about things; they simply get things done as though thinking and negotiating are feminine traits that should be replaced with action in the heat of the moment.

RULE #7: WHEN BRO DRAMAS FEATURE WOMEN, THE WOMEN ARE EITHER IN THE ROLE OF SEXUAL OR ROMANTIC PARTNER, OR THEY ARE FOUND IN ROLES OF FRAGILITY IN NEED OF PROTECTING BY THE MALE PROTAGONIST.

This rule applies to the majority of superhero movies, but also applies to most dramas that feature men in positions of authority. Women are sex props in most bro movies, while in others they are in dependent roles to men. Films that break this rule such as *The Devil Wears Prada* or *G.I. Jane* or *The Hunger Games* trilogy are notable for exactly that reason.

RULE #8: WHEN BRO DRAMAS FEATURE WOMEN, THE WOMEN ARE OFTEN HIGHLY EMOTIONAL IN CONTRAST TO THE MALE PROTAGONISTS WHO ARE CALM, RATIONAL, AND DELIBERATE, OR AS NOTED EARLIER, VIOLENT.

Like rule #6, this rule applies to the majority of superhero movies and action films that portray tough, invulnerable, male lead characters. But it also applies to films where men assume positions of leadership, whether in business, politics, military, or any other field where it is assumed that men have power. The women in these movies, by contrast, are often hyper-emotional, unsure, frightened, insecure, and in need of male guidance and assistance. Interestingly, violence and rage are not viewed by bros as being hyper-emotional, but rather as a necessary and highly masculine response to conflict. Emotionalism of the kind bros reject and bemoan as feminine tends to be crying, showing fear, appearing to be unsure, or any sort of behavior that they interpret as being unmanly. Unsurprisingly, when men scream and yell, bros interpret these behaviors as being forceful, while women who do the very same thing are interpreted in bro culture as being shrill and whiney. This double-standard flows from the most elemental rule of bro culture, which is *men are superior to women*. So, men screaming is a sign of strength and conviction, while women screaming is a sign of emotionalism and therefore weakness.

Thought Box

Identify and engage in discussions on films that you believe qualify as bro-friendly films. What, in your opinion, qualifies them for bro-film status? Do the qualities change depending on whether the men in the scene are of different races and ethnicities? How are women characterized in these films? How is homosexuality treated in the film, if it comes into the plot? What is the overall take-away in these films? That is, what gendered messages do you believe the film is trying to convey?

Taken together, these bro rules are found in the majority of Hollywood movies. From the earliest ages, boys are raised on the notion that they are superior to girls in most ways and that girls are and should be subordinate to boys. This instruction remains firmly in place throughout adolescence and into adulthood. The boys and men who reject these rules are often castigated by bros and learn to avoid bro spaces where they may be subject to ridicule and bullying. Bro spaces can be open to boys and men who do not conform to traditional hypermasculine body types, but it is assumed that these boys and men conform to the *Jackass-Hot-Tub-Time-Machine* model that promotes the sexual objectification of women, the scorning of feminized masculinities, the willingness to demonstrate immature masculinities through unnecessary and sometimes dangerous risk-taking behaviors, and homophobic and sexist words and behaviors when in contact with other bros. In essence, movies are teaching tools that are more than capable of reinforcing all of the bro traits we have noted here. Bro culture is not caused by movies or TV shows, but validation is given by media to millions of bros around the world who are looking for confirmation that their regressive views about gender, sex, women, and gay people are correct.

GENDER-FLIP MOVIES

For decades, it has been made clear by a multitude of women in the film industry that there has been and continues to be a poverty of diverse and complex roles for women. What some film studios have done more recently is reinvent the male-centric films of the past with women in the roles that men once occupied. These are called **gender-flip movies** such as *Ocean's 8, Hunger Games, Divergent, Gravity, Maleficent*, and the remakes of *Ghostbusters* and *Mad Max: Fury Road*, which have found their way into movie theaters across the nation.[57] Gender-flip movies are films with female protagonists that are usually found taking on traditional male roles of action-centered rescuer.[58] These films represent a dramatic shift from the past. However, according to Catherine Paura, chairperson and CEO of Capstone Global Marketing and Research Group, "Women will go to a male-oriented movie, but men have to be dragged to a female-oriented one."[59] The idea that women will go to male-centered movies, but men will not go to women-centered movies has been an abiding mantra of Hollywood film studios for decades. One theory for why this is so is offered by Kate Cuthbert, managing editor of Escape Publishing:

> [Men] have no practice in relating to characters that act as windows rather than mirrors. It's uncomfortable and requires empathy and patience, and men, so very often reflected in the culture around them, do not know how to enter into a fictional (or otherwise) world where they do not hold the place of power.[60]

The idea that men have an empathy gap can be taken in a nature or nurture direction and arguments have been made to support each.[61, 62] However, studies have found that any gendered empathy gap that may exist is not the result of genetics alone.[63] Some maintain that empathy is higher in women than men because of alleged differences in their brains, but this view has been largely either overstated or debunked.[64] One area of the brain that is thought to be responsible for social cognition (the *straight gyrus* or SG) is actually larger in the brains of boys than girls.[65] What researchers found is that the size of one's SG is not correlated to one's biological sex, but rather to one's adoption of femininity or masculinity.[66] That is, how one views oneself in masculine or feminine terms has been shown to correlate to the size of the area of the brain considered to be responsible for social cognition, or in simpler terms, empathy.[67] This does not mean that biology does not contribute to one's capacity for empathy, but that it is much more complicated than to reduce the capacity for empathy or compassion to biological sex.

What we do know is that historically, boys and girls have been socialized in very different ways. In the past, what were considered to be traits of masculinity or traits of femininity were usually reinforced in boys and girls at early ages. Many boys were taught to be competitive, while many girls were taught to be cooperative. This dichotomized gender training can still be seen in the parenting styles of many parents today. However, we cannot overgeneralize, since many boys and girls depart from their normative upbringings, and in fact, increasingly, many young parents are raising their children differently than they were raised, with less emphasis on instilling predetermined gender roles.[68,69]

Still, it is common for Hollywood producers and heads of film studios to create and market films with a targeted gender in mind. At the same time, older moviegoers are not used to seeing women in role of the protagonist, particularly in cases where the protagonist is behaving in ways or taking on roles traditionally reserved for male characters. So, with respect to films that feature strong women in leadership roles or roles of rescuer, there has been a backlash.[70] Those men who adopt and defend a traditional masculine status quo often feel both threatened and bewildered by strong women taking on strong roles. In one example, men's rights activists, which are a group of angry men who blame feminism for virtually every social ill they can imagine, blame Hollywood filmmakers for pushing what they see as feminist-themed movies. Writing about the film *Mad Max: Fury Road* and one of its lead characters portrayed by Charlize Theron, men's rights vlogger Aaron Clarey declares:

> I'm angry about the extents Hollywood and the director of Fury Road went to trick me and other men into seeing this movie. Everything VISUALLY looks amazing. It looks like that action guy flick we've desperately been waiting for where it is one man with principles, standing against many with none.[71]

Clarey goes on to complain,

> [F]eminism has infiltrated and co-opted Hollywood, ruining nearly every potentially-good action flick with a forced female character or an unnecessary romance sub-plot to eek [sic] out that extra 3 million in female attendees...[72]

The men who, like Clarey, want to return to the 1950s, or perhaps the 1850s, when men ruled with unquestioned authority, are frightened by the prospect that their superhero fantasy world might not be as appropriately masculine, and therefore badass, without the protagonist being a man. It may be that male critics of these kind feel that they are losing power in a world where they define their power as being in control over women, or that they feel a loss of purpose if they view their purpose as being in the position of being provider and protector.

One criticism of so-called gender-flip movies is that the notion of power that the protagonist enjoys is a traditionally masculine notion of power. That is, a common trope in movies that involve male power is men as physically dominant or violent. Saving the world from space aliens or evil villains almost always involves a male protagonist employing physical strength and violence to achieve his goals. He is also commonly much more intelligent than many of those around him. This trope, no doubt, plays well with men and particularly bros who already view themselves as strong and smart. The rescuer trope is also a longstanding male allegory that boys have been raised on for generations. Some men might feel lost or stripped of what they believe to be their proper role if women are suddenly placed in the roles they believe are rightly reserved for men. Movies that depict strong women in positions of authority strike at the heart of this patriarchal norm and by extension, bro culture.

> **Thought Box**
>
> Why do you think some men are threatened by strong, female protagonists in movies? Are men insecure about their roles in a changing society? Are they angry that they may be losing power and authority to women? Are they anxious that a feminist-friendly world would call them out for their sexism and misogyny, while they enjoy their sexism and misogyny? What do you believe is going on in the minds of men who pushback against strong, female characters in movies?

GAMER CULTURE

One of the more toxic environments for women where bro culture is robustly celebrated is gamer culture. Exposed by feminist media critic Anita Sarkeesian as a cesspool of toxic bro behaviors in what was eventually termed *gamergate*, gamer culture has garnered a reputation for noxious sexism and homophobia.[73] The gamergate controversy began in 2014 when a harassment campaigned was launched at Anita Sarkeesian who posted on her YouTube channel critical commentaries about the toxic masculinity on display within gamer culture.[74] The response from members of gamer culture was swift and savage, as death and rape threats were posted against Sarkeesian, while her home address was leaked online.[75] Sarkeesian fled her home and canceled speaking engagement out of fear for her life and safety.[76] Other women who criticized gamer culture were also targeted by members of the gamer community, including game developer Zoe Quinn, with similar threats.[77]

Many young women who play multiplayer, interactive games have encountered hostile and highly sexist comments upon other members learning they are not men. Gamer Leena Van Deventer describes a typical set of comments women in gamer culture are forced to endure:

> We got a girl in here, boys! What are you wearing? Have you got any pics? Have you got any nude pics? Do you fuck guys who like games?[78]

She continues by noting that she can sometimes hear them masturbating, while other male gamers find it hilarious.[79] What many gamers who are women do is identify as men so they don't get harassed, or simply exit out of the game when the comments begin to get too hostile and threatening. A main point here is that the bros who engage in these misogynistic behaviors feel a sense of entitlement, as though the game environment is their personal porn-site where they can say anything they want, while the women are left to either endure it, exit out, or fight back.

Research psychologist Rachel Kowert and social scientist Johannes Breuer have examined gamer culture to understand why the culture is so bitterly sexist, and what they found is that while gamer culture has always been a male-dominated space, it has been the emergence of many more girls and women that has brought out the especially toxic responses by some men.[80] Like locker rooms, gamer environments are viewed by many of the men of gamer culture as *male-only-safe-spaces* where men can let their sexism fly without repercussion. Part of this attitude is no doubt similar to that found in the environments of some forms of social media where the contributor feels protected by the anonymity of computer-generated comments and the pseudonym he is using as an avatar.

But Kowert and Breuer believe that the main problem of sexism within gamer culture is due to the male-centricity of the gamer industry, the content of the games themselves, the entrenched feelings that gamer culture is and should be a male-dominant environment by members of the gamer community in tandem with the overall socialization process of childhood and adolescence that reinforce sexism throughout society.[81] On the other hand, as gamer culture continues to diversify, including the addition of many more women, it remains to be seen whether gamer culture will adapt and modify or dig in against what they view as an intrusion into a bro sanctuary where they can say anything with impunity no matter how sexist, intrusive, or threatening.

POSTSCRIPT

As stated in the opening of the chapter, movies are teaching tools. The lessons begin in childhood and continue throughout our lives. While broadcast media that include movies and TV-shows continue to undergo change, many of the same gendered tropes that occupied films and TV-shows in the past continue to proliferate today. As contributing factors in the socialization of girls and boys, media can help or harm the construction of bro culture. In particular, as long as movies and TV shows depict characters in starkly gendered ways with male characters written as leaders, authorities, and womanizers as something to be revered and emulated, while female characters are written as supporters and sexual sidekicks, bro culture will flourish. Media are normalizers. Collectively, media sanctify certain behaviors and condemn others. And lest we forget, the film and television industries are fields where dozens of powerful men have now been called out for their sexual harassment and in some cases, sexual assault of women. For real transformative change, there will in all likelihood need to be top-down innovations that involve far greater promotion of women and women of color in decision-making roles that guide script-writing, casting, producing, directing, and executive production. In the meantime, audiences will probably have to endure more bro-friendly themes and characters in the movies, TV-shows, and games people consume.

Notes

1. *IMDB* Website, The Incredibles, box office and other statistics. https://www.imdb.com/title/tt0317705/
2. Bailey Williams, "If This Sounds Familiar, You May Have It Too," *Odyssey*, September 29, 2014. https://www.theodysseyonline.com/superwoman-complex
3. Walt Disney Studios, "The History of Animation," https://www.disneyanimation.com/studio/our-films
4. Inkoo Kang, "We Need a Disney Princess to Explain How We Got So Hung Up on Disney Princesses," *Slate*, April 2, 2018.
5. Janet Maslin, "A Warrior, She Takes on Huns and Stereotypes," *The New York Times*, June 19, 1998.
6. Beatrice Verhoeven, Cassidy Robinson, "30 Highest Grossing Animated Movies of All Time Worldwide," *The Wrap*, November 22, 2019.
7. Sandie Angulo Chen, "Moana," *Common Sense Media*, 2016.
8. Jen Yamoto, "The Revolutionary 'Moana': Disney's Most Unapologetically Feminist Princess Yet," *Daily Beast*, April 13, 2017. https://www.thedailybeast.com/the-revolutionary-moana-disneys-most-unapologetically-feminist-princess-yet
9. Carolyn L. Todd, "You Won't Ever Watch Disney Movies The Same Way After Reading This," *Refinery 29*, April 8, 2016. https://www.refinery29.com/en-us/2016/04/107983/disney-movies-male-characters-more-lines
10. https://en.wikipedia.org/wiki/Uncle_Remus
11. Nerdy POC, "Examining Racist Tropes in Disney Animated Films," April 22, 2017. https://medium.com/@nerdypoc/examining-racist-tropes-in-disney-animated-films-562279a9565a
12. John Evan Frook, "'Aladdin' Lyrics Altered," July 12, 1993. https://variety.com/1993/film/news/aladdin-lyrics-altered-108628/
13. Driscoll, Catherine. Teen Film: *A Critical Introduction*, Berg Publishers, 2011, Oxford, UK.
14. Piper Jaffray, Data Source, *Share of Teen' Spending by Category*, Marketing Charts, October, 2017. https://www.marketingcharts.com/demographics-and-audiences-80708
15. Stuart Sopp, "Where Teens Spent their Gaming Money this Summer," *Venture Beat*, September 14, 2017. https://venturebeat.com/2017/09/14/where-teens-spent-their-gaming-money-this-summer/
16. Samantha Cooney, "The Number of Women Who Direct Hollywood Movies Is Still Embarrassingly Small," *Time Magazine*, January 4, 2018. http://time.com/5087673/film-directors-diversity-report/
17. Mark Bowden, "Why Are We Obsessed with Superhero Movies?" *The New York Times*, July 6, 2018. https://www.nytimes.com/2018/07/06/opinion/sunday/ant-man-wasp-movies-superheroes.html
18. Ibid.

19. Michael Cavna, "The One Aspect of 'Suicide Squad' that Saved It from Becoming a Flop," *The Washington Post*, August 9, 2016.
20. Jane Bordeaux, "The Very Misunderstood Harley Quinn," *Medium*, March 9, 2017.
21. *The Guardian*, Movies Section, "Fast and Furious Fuels Increase in Street Racing," June 26, 2001. https://www.theguardian.com/film/2001/jun/26/news
22. Emily Price, "The Fast and the Furious' Films Might Have Caused an Increase in Speeding," *Fortune*, January 31, 2018. https://fortune.com/2018/01/31/fast-and-furious-speeding/
23. Hardeep Phull, "People Hated 'Scarface' Until Hip-Hop Have It Cred," *New York Post*, April 12, 2018. https://nypost.com/2018/04/12/people-hated-scarface-until-hip-hop-gave-it-cred/
24. Michelle C. Pautz, "Films Can Have a Major Influence on How People View Government," *LSE USCenter*. https://blogs.lse.ac.uk/usappblog/2015/03/12/films-can-have-a-major-influence-on-how-people-view-government/
25. John Guida, "How Movies Can Change Our Minds," *The New York Times*, Op-Talk, February 4, 2015. https://op-talk.blogs.nytimes.com/2015/02/04/how-movies-can-change-our-minds/
26. Michelle C. Pautz, "Argo and Zero Dark Thirty: Film, Government, and Audiences," *Cambridge University Press*, Vol. 48, Issue 1, January 2015, pp. 120–128. https://www.cambridge.org/core/journals/ps-political-science-and-politics/article/argo-and-zero-dark-thirty-film-government-and-audiences/889B13ED0B53B2DF7C09372D4ACCECE5
27. Mass Communications, "From Theory to Practical Application," *Mass Communication Theory*, An Overview of Cultivation Theory. https://masscommtheory.com/theory-overviews/cultivation-theory/
28. Samantha Conney, "Why People Are So Obsessed with The Bachelor, According to the Woman Who Wrote a Book On It," *Time Magazine*, March 4, 2018.
29. Whitney Friedlander, "Finally a Black 'Bachelor'? ABC's President Weighs In," *CNN Entertainment*, August 5, 2019. https://www.cnn.com/2019/08/05/entertainment/bachelor-black-lead-bachelorette-jed/index.html
30. Richard Brody, "The Worst Thing about "Birth of a Nation" Is How Good It Is," *The New Yorker*, February 1, 2013.
31. David Pilgrim, Ferris State University, "The Brute Caricature," *Jim Crow Museum of Racist Memorabilia*, November, 2000. https://www.ferris.edu/jimcrow/brute/
32. Bachelor, The Synopsis, *Ace Show Biz*. https://www.aceshowbiz.com/tv/bachelor_the/summary.html
33. Pozner, Jennifer. *Reality Bites Back: The Troubling Truth about Reality TV*. Seal Press, 2010.
34. IMDB.com, Page for *The Bachelor*. https://www.imdb.com/title/tt0313038/
35. Rick Kissell, "Ratings: 'The Bachelor' Finale Strong, Notches ABC's Top Monday in Two Years," *Variety*, March 15, 2016. https://variety.com/2016/tv/news/ratings-abc-the-bachelor-finale-strong-up-vs-last-year-1201730354/
36. Kimberley Dadds, "Well, He Is the Head of Playboy: Hugh Hefner Reveals He's Slept with 'Over a Thousand' Women," *Daily Mail*. March 26, 2013. https://www.dailymail.co.uk/tvshowbiz/article-2299324/Hugh-Hefner-reveals-hes-slept-thousand-women.html
37. Carrie Pitzulo, "The Playboy Philosophy," *Politico*, September 30, 2017. https://www.politico.eu/article/the-playboy-philosophy-hugh-hefner-politics-womens-rights/

148   Chapter 6

38. Sady Doyle, "Exactly What Kind of Sexual Revolution Did Hugh Hefner Inspire?" *Elle*, September 29. 2017. https://www.elle.com/culture/a12638096/exactly-what-kind-of-sexual-revolution-did-hugh-hefner-inspire/
39. Bruce Handy, "A Bunny Thing Happened: An Oral History of the Playboy Clubs," *Vanity Fair*, April 22, 2011.
40. Kelsey Wallace, "Shot through the Vagina, and Rock of Love Is to Blame," *Bitch Media*, January 20, 2009.
41. LaToya Jefferson-James, "This Is How 'Flavor of Love' Exploited the Worst Stereotypes of Black Women," *Vice*, December 18, 2015.
42. Deborah Barker, Kathryn McKee, *American Cinema and the Southern Imagery*. University of Georgia Press, Athens, Georgia, 2011.
43. Elyce Rae Helford, "How Does "Thelma & Louise" Display a Connection to Feminist Film Theory?" *The Take*, April 7, 2018. http://screenprism.com/insights/article/how-does-the-movie-thelma-louise-display-a-connection-to-feminist-film-theo
44. Ibid.
45. David Cox, "Twilight: The Franchise That Ate Feminism," *The Guardian*, July 12, 2010. https://www.theguardian.com/film/filmblog/2010/jul/12/twilight-eclipse-feminism
46. Athene Donald, "Why I Refuse to 'Think Like a Man'," *The World University Rankings*, August 14, 2015. https://www.timeshighereducation.com/blog/why-i-refuse-think-man#survey-answer
47. Ibid.
48. Coco Brown, "Why Men Still Dominate Corporate Boardrooms," *Fortune*, June 7, 2017. http://fortune.com/2017/06/07/most-powerful-women-career-advice-corporate-boardroom-diversity-workplace-inequality-favoritism/
49. Quentin Fottrell, "In Corporate America, a Shockingly Low Number of Women Make It to the C-suite," *Market Watch*, April 30, 2018. https://www.marketwatch.com/story/in-corporate-america-a-shockingly-low-number-of-women-make-it-to-the-c-suite-2018-04-30
50. Seth Meyers, "Fear of Intimacy in Men: Cause, Relationship Problems, Tips," *Psychology Today*, April 15, 2013. https://www.psychologytoday.com/us/blog/insight-is-2020/201304/fear-intimacy-in-men-cause-relationship-problems-tips
51. Ibid.
52. Charles McGrath, "Quentin's World," *The New York Times*, December 19, 2012. https://www.nytimes.com/2012/12/23/movies/how-quentin-tarantino-concocted-a-genre-of-his-own.html
53. Leigh Kolb, "Twenty Years Latre: 'Reservoir Dogs,' Masculinity and Feminism," *Bitch Flicks*, December 19, 2012. http://www.btchflcks.com/2012/12/twenty-years-later-reservoir-dogs-masculinity-and-feminism.html
54. IMDB.com, Pulp Fiction, Plot Summary. https://www.imdb.com/title/tt0110912/plotsummary
55. IMDB.com, Kill Bill: Vol. 1, Plot Summary. https://www.imdb.com/title/tt0266697/plotsummary
56. Terri Coles, "How Men Get to the Point Where They Identify as 'Incel'," *Huff Post*, June 5, 2018. https://www.huffingtonpost.ca/2018/06/05/incel_a_23451320/
57. Tim Grierson, "Roundtable: What Do Women Think of Hollywood's New Gender-Flip Movies?" *Mel Magazine*. https://melmagazine.com/en-us/story/roundtable-what-do-women-think-of-hollywoods-new-gender-flip-movies

58. Brooks Barnes, "From Now On, Women Save the World," *The New York Times*, September 3, 2014. https://www.nytimes.com/2014/09/07/movies/fall-arts-preview-hollywood-has-realized-that-movies-starring-women-can-make-money.html
59. Ibid.
60. Karen Pickering, "Why Can't Men Love Chick Flicks?" *The Sydney Morning Herald*, October 30, 2018. https://www.smh.com.au/lifestyle/life-and-relationships/why-can-t-men-love-chick-flicks-20181029-p50cm8.html
61. Philip Zimbardo, "Young Men and the Empathy Gap," *Psychology Today*, August 15, 2017. https://www.psychologytoday.com/us/blog/hero/201708/young-men-and-the-empathy-gap
62. Rico Fischer, Jordan Holbrook, John Barry, "How Wide if the Gender Empathy Gap?" *Male Psychology*, 2016. https://www.malepsychology.org.uk/wp-content/uploads/2017/07/john_barry.pdf
63. Tereza Pultarova, "Genes Can't Explain Why Men Are Less Empathetic Than Women," *Live Science*, March 12, 2018. https://www.livescience.com/61987-empathy-women-men.html
64. Lise Eliot, "Girl Brain, Boy Brain?" *Scientific American*, September 8, 2009. https://www.scientificamerican.com/article/girl-brain-boy-brain/
65. Jessica L. Wood, Dwayne Heitmiller, Nancy C. Andreason, Peg Nopoulos, "Morphology of the Ventral Frontal Cortex: Relationship to Femininity and Social Cognition," *Cerebral Cortex*, Vol. 18, Issue 3, March 2008, pp. 534–540. https://academic.oup.com/cercor/article/18/3/534/284575
66. Ibid.
67. Ibid.
68. Katie Herzog, "Hipster Parent Reject Gender Norms by Raising Kids without Problems," *The Stranger*, April 4, 2018. https://www.thestranger.com/slog/2018/04/04/26001767/hipster-parent-rejects-gender-norms-by-raising-kids-without-pronouns
69. Joyce J. Endendijk, Marleen G. Groenveld, Marian J. Bakermans-Kranenburg, Judi Mesman, "Gender-Differentiated Parenting Revisited: Meta-Analysis Reveals Very Few Differences in Parental Control of Boys and Girls," *PloS ONE*, Vol. 11, Issue 7, July 14, 2016, e0159193. https://journals.plos.org/plosone/article?id=10.1371/journal.pone.0159193
70. Courtney Kirchoff, "Dear Feminist Hollywood: Stop Trying to Make Female Action Heroes a Thing..." *Louder with Crowder*, May 7, 2016. https://www.louderwithcrowder.com/dear-feminist-hollywood-stop-trying-to-make-female-superheroes-a-thing/
71. Aja Romano, "'Mad Max: Fury Road' Draws the Ire of Men's Rights Activists," *Daily Dot*, March 1, 2020. https://www.dailydot.com/parsec/reviewer-reaction-mad-max-sexism/
72. Ibid.
73. Jordan Erica Webber, "Anita Sarkeesian: 'It's Frustrating to be Known as the Woman Who Survived #Gamergate'," *The Guardian*, October 16, 2017.
74. Caitlin Dewey, "The Only Guide to Gamergate You Will Ever Need to Read," *The Washington Post*, October 14, 2014.
75. Ibid.
76. Ibid.
77. Ibid.

78. Kate O'Halloran, "'Hey Dude, Do This': The Last Resort of Female Gamers Escaping Online Abuse," *The Guardian*, October 23, 2017. https://www.theguardian.com/culture/2017/oct/24/hey-dude-do-this-the-last-resort-for-female-gamers-escaping-online-abuse
79. Ibid.
80. Research Gate Interview with Scientists Rachel Kowert and Johannes Breuer, "Another Look at Sexism in the Gamers Industry," *Science Connected*, November 11, 2015. https://magazine.scienceconnected.org/2015/11/another-look-at-sexism-in-the-games-industry/
81. Ibid.

7

MUSICAL MISOGYNISTS: THE BEAT OF BRO CULTURE

> **Key Points**
>
> - The Spillover Effect
> - The Wonton Sexism in Pop Music
> - The Classical and Operant Conditioning of Boys and Men
> - Conflicted Artists and an Injustice about Critiques of Rap
> - Socially Conscious Rap
> - Cultural Appropriation
> - The Fallout to Women of Color
> - Intersectional Feminism
> - Bro-Country
> - The Misogyny of Metal
> - The Male-centricity of the Music Industry
> - Postscript

Bro-culture has a soundtrack and that soundtrack includes music that judges, denigrates, threatens, and sexually objectifies women, while insulting both women and those in LGBTQ communities. Music of this kind spans almost all genres including rock, R&B, country, hip-hop, rap, and metal. Fans of bro music transcend race and ethnicity, socioeconomic class, and sometimes sex and gender, as many women are fans of artists who sexually exploit and demean women. Music, like film, is one of many sources of instruction, where messaging about sex, gender, romance, wealth, all things considered cool, and many other topics interesting to youth culture are marketed to young consumers. But central to much of popular music for generations has been a pervasive sexism that portrays women in exceedingly one-dimensional, demeaning, and sexually objectified ways.

Of course, there are many music artists and groups that do not frame their lyrics around sexist themes. There are, in fact, music artists who construct lyrics that promote women's empowerment and equality, but the majority of artists who do this are female artists. It is rare for male artists to construct lyrics that advocate for the empowerment of women, but it does happen. Artists that include REM in the 1980s to Eddie Vedder of Pearl Jam in the 1990s to John

Legend, Keith Urban, Macklemore, and controversially Drake today have created music that is feminist-friendly, while hip-hop-rock hybrid group Beastie Boys transformed over the years from a party band into more progressive, gender-positive artists.[1] But the overwhelming rule has been and continues to be that male music artists employ women in their songs as sexual commodities or romantic partners more than anything else. When women are sexually objectified in music, boys and men are raised on the idea that women are primarily objects of lust, here to fulfill their sexual fantasies, and have little-to-no value beyond this function. Given a steady stream of sexist tropes in music as part of an overall media saturation of chauvinist messaging, many men will come to devalue women as possessing importance beyond sexual utility. This entails that men will deprecate women's aspirations, accomplishments, and opinions as insignificant in comparison to men's accomplishments and opinions. Psychologist Nathan A. Heflick terms this **"the spillover effect."**[2] When women are perceived primarily as sexual seductresses, research has shown that men who view women this way rate them as being less intelligent and less competent than men.[3]

This marginalization of women's competency contributes to men's violence against women, since men who sexually objectify women do not believe women have the ability or right to challenge their authority. When disagreement occurs within relationships, men of this kind will feel disrespected, leading to heightened states of aggression and violence, and intimate partner violence is the number-one cause of injury to women, aged 15–44, in the world.[4] Music lyrics and videos are part of this steady diet of sexist media that include sexualized, but passive women coupled with aggressive men in positions of power. This dichotomy sets the stage for creating insecure men who feel threatened by smart, successful women.

THE WANTON SEXISM IN POP MUSIC

In the foregoing chapter, we examined movies as being powerful teaching tools and templates for behavior, but popular music is also a teaching tool that speaks mainly to the young. From the earliest moments of music that featured singers, young people have gravitated toward music as a guide for everything from teen style to teen angst, while most of the singers who had chart-topping songs became heartthrobs for some and inspirations for others. In fact, record companies have long marketed music stars as romantic or sexual icons in addition to their role as singers and songwriters.

Turning to some of the more notable singing stars of the past, Frank Sinatra was one of those singers labeled a "crooner," which denoted a vocalist who made teenagers swoon with romantic or lustful desire.[5] Notably, "crooner" was a designation attached almost entirely to male vocalists.[6] While the designation fell out of fashion by the mid-1960s,[7] the concept did not. That is, the singer as a romantic or sexual symbol only escalated from the 1960s to what we witness in the marketing of singing stars today. Yesterday's crooner became today's rock star, rap star, pop star, or country star.

The marketing of a singer's image is today every bit as important as the marketing of their music. In fact, some artists have consciously crafted their image around sexuality and sensuality. Artists like The Beatles, The Rolling Stones, Led Zeppelin, David Bowie, Marvin Gaye, and many others in the 1960s and 1970s were as famous for their sexual appeal as their music. By the 1980s, the artist Prince took the subjects of sex and sensuality, both in his music and live show, to an entirely new level.[8] In fact, Prince and before him, David Bowie, were two of the first artists to empower gender non-conforming people and their legacies live on in many artists today. This is not to say that their lyrics and body of work are free from complications and problems, but it is worth noting over the past 50 years, there have been music artists who stood against the tide of tradition, including those traditions found in gender and sexuality.

Yet underneath the gender and sexual liberation found in the work of some artists has been a steady and constant deluge of sexism and misogyny. Going back to the 1960s, singing star Jack Jones performed the Burt Bacharach song "Wives and Lovers," which won Jones a Grammy in 1963 for best vocal performance.[9] The song's lyrics warn married women to keep themselves physically and sexually attractive or else their husbands will leave them for more attractive women.[10] The sexism of exhorting women to worry and obsess about their looks has been an ongoing harangue for generations. The beauty industry itself leads the charge of attempting to undermine women's self-esteem by pointing out the alleged flaws and blemishes in their appearance in order to convert insecurity into profit. So, music certainly holds no monopoly on sexist instruction.

But the sexism of the Bacharach hit of the past is tepid when compared to the misogyny found in hundreds of songs since the 1960s. What is also notable is that sexism and outright misogyny can be found in songs of artists of all of the major genres of popular music, whether rock, R&B, pop, rap, or country. Some examples from the 1970s include:

Rock: From The Rolling Stones' "Under My Thumb," where Mick Jagger explains that the woman in the song will do whatever she is instructed to do.
R&B: From The Ojay's "Ain't No Woman Like the One I Got," where a woman's value is linked to her obeying the singer's desires and orders.
Pop: From Mac Davis' "Baby Don't Get Hooked on Me," where a woman is warned that she will be used and discarded.

As time passed, the treatment and depiction of women in music continued to slide down the road of sexism and misogyny in some cases with far more contempt and degrading messaging than ever before. From the 1980s, we get:

Rock: From AC/DC, a sampling of their titles, *Go Down, Big Balls, Let Me Put My Love Into You,* preview *sexual conquests* with little reference to consent.

R&B: From Rick James, "Cop and Blow," which is an urban expression that captures the practice of pimps recruiting women to be prostitutes when one of the women in their *stable* leaves.[11]

HARD ROCK-METAL: From Guns N' Roses, "It's So Easy" is a song where singer Axl Rose instructs "a bitch" to turn around, because he has a use for her.

HIP HOP: From 2 Live Crew's "Dick Almighty," or almost anything from their song catalog, where women are reduced to sex props who should obey the power of the man's penis.

Motley Crüe bass player Nikki Sixx boasts, "I sport a cave-man mentality. A woman should be a lady on your arm and whore behind the door."[12] These artists and their representative songs, along with thousands more, serve as a generational instructional manual for boys and men. Writing for *The Guardian*, singer Hayden Thorpe notes that when you ask teen boys what they want to be when they grow up, music star is always in the top ten. Thorpe writes, "Being a guy in a band is a huge projection of masculinity."[13] The attraction to being a music star for boys makes sense in a music culture that mass produces hypermasculine models of manhood where men possess unfettered sexual availability to women regardless of the gender politics in contemporary society. In fact, a common message found in the lyrics of song after song is that if you are a music star, women will do anything you want them to do.

A much more sinister set of lyrics involve the trope that women can be and should be sexually abused. In the song "ROCKO," rap artist Rick Ross admits to drugging and raping a woman, while artist Kool G Rap, in his rhyme "Hey Mister Mister" boasts of beating women up.[14,15] These are merely a couple examples out of thousands of songs that feature men bragging about physically and sexually abusing women. The boys and young men who consume these songs are classically conditioned to view women with contempt. In brief, **classical conditioning** involves subjecting an individual to repetitive stimuli with the goal of achieving a conditioned response. Pavlov's famous experiment with dogs that salivated at the sound of a buzzer is a classic example of a conditioned response.[16] Behavioral psychologist John Watson was able to show through a series of experiments with children that classical conditioning also works on human beings.[17] Psychologist B.F. Skinner continued this line of research focusing on **operant conditioning**, whereby an individual is subjected to positive or negative reinforcement with the goal of shaping the individual's behavior in a particular direction.[18]

The way these two types of conditioning work in bro culture extend beyond music. While the lyrics of hundreds of songs classically condition men through repetition to view women solely as sexual androids, bros police one another's behaviors, which is where much of the operant conditioning comes into play. Even the terminology bros will use when referring to women will be policed. A bro who admits to having romantic interest in a woman may be quickly cajoled into terming her a bitch or piece of ass. The consequences for appearing to be too kind, sensitive, or loving can come in the form of being called a *pussy* or *fag*. Most men have experienced these kinds of attacks and putdowns at some point in their lives, and usually at a young age. Since no one wants to be singled out for bullying and abuse, boys and men learn to quickly comply with the language of the bro code.

With respect to boys and men who consume music with violent content aimed at women, the results are not as predictable as the conditioned responses of rats or dogs to organized stimuli, but according to the American Academy of Pediatrics,

> As with popular music, the perception and the effect of music-video messages are important, because research has reported that exposure to violence, sexual messages, sexual stereotypes, and use of substances of abuse in music videos might produce significant changes in behaviors and attitudes of young viewers.[19]

There are, of course, neurological and environmental differences between individual boys and men that contribute to whether a particular boy or man acts out violently against a girl or woman. Men's violence against women is not produced as an algorithm that creates a necessary outcome given a circumstantial stimulus. But again, the steady influence of music that promotes violence against women works in tandem with the many other pop-cultural influences that are documented in this book that advance the idea that women are inferior to men or as having at most sexual utility for men, but certainly not to be viewed as authentic equals to men. The point is that boys who consume a steady stream of music that degrades women are inculcating a constant stream of narratives about the proper roles for men and women that include viewing women as less important than men, believing that controlling women is an appropriate role for men, infantilizing women as being in need of protection and supervision, viewing women as having value primarily in terms of their looks and sexual availability, or in some cases, justifying the mistreatment of women.

Consider the case of music star Chris Brown who very publicly physically assaulted singing and acting star Rihanna and later stated that she caused the violence.[20] Brown pled guilty and accepted a plea deal that included five years of probation and 180 days in jail or 1,800 hours of labor-oriented service.[21] Since this event, Brown has been accused of physically assaulting a woman at a San Diego nightclub, was cited for hit-and-run, was arrested and charged with felony physical assault in Washington D.C., acted out aggressively and violently while undergoing rehabilitation treatment, was sentenced to one-year in jail after violating the terms of his parole, was accused of battery in Las Vegas, was arrested and charged with assault with a deadly weapon in California, was ordered to stay away from former girlfriend Karrueche Tran after Tran obtained a restraining order based on her claim that Brown tried to kill her, was accused of sexual assault at his own home, and accused of rape in Paris.[22,23] In fact, Brown himself posted on his Instagram page,

> Ladies, y'all be complaining about niggas as being stalkers and in love with y'all, kinda crazy and shit and you get tired of it. Well, guess what? I'm one of them niggas! If I love you, bitch, ain't nobody gonna have you. I'm gonna make you miserable.[24]

Yet despite these high-profile acts of violence and intimidation, Brown continues to enjoy the support of millions of fans.[25] Author Karen Post notes:

> It's all about connecting with your audience. If his fans don't mind or admire his bad boy behavior, the circumstantial publicity keeps you on the pop culture radar.[26]

The behaviors that would end careers in many walks of life has not substantially harmed Brown's career, and if Post is correct, may have even helped his career by maintaining a "bad boy" image that has been cultivated by some music stars and their management.

Consider the average male fan of Chris Brown. He cannot be oblivious to the charges and behaviors, but chooses to support Brown through record and concert sales. The fact that Brown continues to thrive speaks to the support many fans have toward an artist who has been attached to the physical and sexual assault of women for over a decade. Of course, fans could be in denial about Brown's many violent episodes, or they may be apathetic to the violence "because they like the music," or they may think Brown is cool for having a bad reputation. Whatever the case may be, Brown's many male fans reinforce the notion that steady contact with music or artists who promote violence toward women, in a culture that rewards artists who demean women in their songs, desensitizes boys and men to actual violence against women. According to the National Institute of Health, research has shown that repeated exposure to violent media creates low anxious arousal, as measured by skin conductance levels and a lexical decision task.[27] This means that repetitive contact with violent media, in this case media that describes or advocates violence toward women, conditions a desensitized response from the men who consume it.

Thought Box: Blurred Lines

The biggest hit of 2013 was "Blurred Lines" by Robin Thicke, featuring T.I. and Pharrell. Two videos for the song were produced and released, one featuring scantily clad women dancing around while the male singers performed and interacted with the models and a second version where the female models were completely nude while the male performers sang and leered at the models. The title of the song is taken from national conversations about sex and consent. During the women's marches, women carried signs that proclaimed, "There are no blurred lines." In the song, the male protagonist repeatedly claims, "I know you want it," even though she's a "good girl." Critics point out that the lyrics were a case of classic victim blaming in the wake of sexual assault.[28] When women are raped, it is common for rapists to claim that it was a consensual sexual encounter, even though the victim insists that no consent was given. Hence, the line of consent is "blurred." In the video, male power and female submissiveness are on display. Why do you think a song and video of this nature can become so popular and supported by both men and women? Is the "rapey" nature of the song misunderstood? Do people excuse the content because they simply like the beat or the way the song sounds? Evaluate why a song of this nature can become a huge hit despite its content and potential consequences to women and rape survivors.

Brown is not an isolated case. A casual glance at music over the past few decades makes the point that we live in a culture that glamorizes and rewards music artists who perform songs that degrade women while boasting about it:

> The song "One Less Bitch" by rap icons N.W.A is a saga that reinforces the view that women are worth nothing other than providing sex to men on demand, a theme echoed by hundreds of artists. In this particular rhyme, some of the women are murdered.[29]
>
> Rap icons Snoop Dogg and Dr. Dre made a career around the "Bitches ain't shit" directive, where a constant stream of vulgar and violent epithets is directed toward women.[30]
>
> In the song "Amityville," rappers Eminem and Bizarre boast that they had 10 of their boys take away his little sister's virginity after killing his own mother.[31]
>
> In the song, "You," rap artist Chief Keef warns a woman that he will kill her if she doesn't perform oral sex on him.[32]
>
> In his song "Kill You" and many other of his songs, Eminem warns a woman that he will choke her to death, and repeats in the chorus that he is going to kill her.[33]

Writing directly to Snoop Dogg, but by extension all music artists who denigrate, threaten, and boast about harming women, Editorial Director of Colorlines, Angela Helms asks,

> Where were your aunties and grandmas when you were spitting "Bitches ain't shit but hos and tricks"? Where were they when you low-key warbled about gang rape in "It Ain't No Fun"? Or how about in 2003, when you showed up to the MTV Awards with two women on leashes, or when you rolled around with an old pimp like that shit was cute?[34]

Music videos are another place to find violent misogyny as witnessed in the video for the song "Animal" by Maroon 5, where a sociopathic killer is stalking a woman, while singer Adam Levine cautions that she will be his prey.[35] The video then features the stalker having sex with the woman, leading RAINN's Katherine Hull Fliflet to warn,

> no one should ever confuse the criminal act of stalking with romance. The trivialization of these serious crimes, like stalking, should have no place in the entertainment industry.[36]

The trope that violence is simply part of sex normalizes abuse at a time when the FBI reports that 1,500 women each year are killed by their husbands or boyfriends, while approximately 2 million men beat their partners each year.[37]

Imagine if these songs were racist in nature instead of sexist and misogynistic in nature. Imagine further white artists singing or rhyming incredibly demeaning or violent lyrics aimed at Black people. How quickly would their careers come to an end and their work condemned as racist propaganda? Yet we live in a culture where men can demean and violently threaten women through lyrics and videos, while profiting enormously. All of this is so at the same time that the number one cause of injury to women around the world, as mentioned earlier, is domestic violence.[38]

Thought Box

For fans of artists like those spotlighted above, would you support white artists who performed lyrics that demean and threaten people of color with violence because the music sounded good or had a good beat? If you would not, how do you justify supporting male artists who demean and threaten women with violence? Is your support for one but not the other evidence of holding a double standard? In general, how do you justify your support for misogynistic music?

Notable is the fact that what is called *gangsta rap*, past and present, is supported by many female fans as well as male fans. Eminem, for instance, has millions of loyal fans who are women, some going as far as claiming that feminist women can join misogynists in loving Eminem's work.[39] What happens in these cases is that misogynistic bros point to the fact that women defend Eminem to defend their own consumption and proliferation of misogyny. The argument goes, "if women defend and enjoy Eminem's work, then his music cannot be condemned for being misogynistic." This is like saying, "if some Black people support Trump, then Trump is not racist." The measuring tool for racism or sexism becomes whether some of those in subordinated groups approve or defend the views, policies, and in this case lyrics of misogynists.

The argument is framed, "if the artist has female fans, then by definition the artist is not misogynistic."

One of several concerns for this strategy is that artists like Eminem have been marketed by their record labels as more than simply music artists, but as sexual icons as well. This means that in addition to viewing artists like Eminem as talented musical artists, girls and young women are groomed to view men like Eminem as being sexually and romantically attractive. In these cases, a potentially violent man who makes incredibly demeaning and brutal comments about women can be reinterpreted as a "bad boy" who is misunderstood, who is actually a good guy and ally to women "deep down." This same spin can be used to explain away Eminem's homophobia as well. What this strategy does for bros is to allow young men to adopt the Eminem style of demeaning women and gay people, while ironically maintaining that they are allies to women and gay people, then using this irony to position themselves as bad boys who women love. A parallel strategy is to state that Eminem's robust criticism of Donald Trump, while supporting Colin Kaepernick, apparently means that he is progressive and *woke* about what is going on in America.[40] But nothing stops a person from being politically left and a misogynist homophobe at the same time. Writing for *Musiqology*, John Vilanova notes,

Thought Box

Consider the artist Eminem, or similar artists who lyrically demean women and gay people. Does the fact that these artists have female fans or gay fans mean that the artists are not misogynists or homophobes? Can someone be a fan of an artist like Eminem who spits rhymes about raping women maintain that she or he is feminist?

> How do we appreciate the critique while still condemning much of its substance? Eminem's critiques are part of a noxious world where the most resonant way for a man to diss another man is to attack his manhood. Eminem doesn't only suggest that Trump "lacks nuts;" he suggests that that is a bad thing. More than half the nation's population similarly "lacks nuts" and it is most certainly not a bad thing. This type of attack furthers the second-class status of women in the American hierarchy, where they are paid less, assaulted more, and the negative against which norms emerge. What's the worst insult to call a man? A woman.[41]

Vilanova highlights a tension within progressive circles. There is a desire to embrace those who are fighting against misogyny and racism, but using misogyny to fight misogyny is not successfully defended simply by claiming that the critique is ironic; it is to admit that the individual leveling the criticism is committing the very same troubling misogyny as the person he is criticizing, and ultimately, that is neither progressive nor helpful in changing the culture. But a further problem is that bros can glom onto and imitate artists like Eminem in an effort to vindicate themselves as "good guys" who are using irony or humor to make a progressive point. As the great poet Audre Lorde warned, "the master's tools will never dismantle the master's house."[42] Using misogyny will not eliminate misogyny.

CONFLICTED ARTISTS AND AN INJUSTICE ABOUT CRITIQUES OF RAP MUSIC

Whenever media critics begin to focus on music, it doesn't take long for many of them to gravitate to rap music, and from there it doesn't take long for them to begin critiquing people of color, and particularly Black people, as though the lyrics expressed in gangsta rap represent the views of Black people in general. First, the misogynistic and violent lyrics found in gangsta rap in no way represent the work of all rappers let alone the views of Black people in general. There are a multitude of hip-hop and rap artists who do not simply rhyme about money, drugs, spreading violence, and the mistreatment of women. In fact, many artists past and present have gained fame as being *socially conscious* rappers. The most prominent rappers considered to be socially conscious and who have been around a long time include Chuck D and Public Enemy, Black Star, Talib Kweli, Mos Def, Immortal Technique, Common, Dead Prez, Nas, KRS-One, and DMX, among many others.

At the same time, many rappers, including some just mentioned, have forged a complicated body of work, weaving socially conscious rhymes within a larger song catalogue that has been repudiated as misogynistic and promotional of violence. These artists include Tupac Shakur, The Notorious B.I.G. (Biggie Smalls), Jay-Z, Kanye West, N.W.A, Lupe Fiasco, and controversially, Eminem. There have also been rappers and groups considered purely exploitative of women such as 2 Live Crew, Rick Ross, Snoop Dogg, Dr. Dre, 50 Cent, Lil Wayne, and others. Today, it is not uncommon to find complicated rappers who are socially conscious like J Cole, but who also blur the line between socially conscious and problematic lyrics such as Kendrick Lamar. In his song, "Alright," Lamar inspires and encourages communities of color that "We gon' be alright," which was taken up by Black Lives Matter marchers with some claiming that the song became a unifying theme of the movement.[43] Still, others have called out what they view as Lamar's sexism in songs like "Humble" that appear to be progressive, but that arguably miss the mark. In the publication, *Afropunk*, writer Sesali Bowen argues,

> Men like Kendrick Lamar have built their careers on the pretense of social consciousness. But the reach of that consciousness never seems to go the distance when it comes to gender. Their vision of empowerment for Black women is usually just a different version of sexism and misogyny.[44]

Similarly, writing for *The Atlantic*, Mychal Denzel Smith notes,

> Lupe Fiasco's "Bitch Bad" is only the latest example of a male hip-hop star trying to empower women but actually demeaning them.[45]

There is a hip-hop legacy at play here where male rappers presume to speak for women's rights and empowerment, while creating more controversy. Tupac Shakur's "Brenda's Got a Baby" is a classic example of a story about a pregnant 12-year-old with absentee parents who makes poor decisions, causing some to interpret the rhyme as blaming the young girl for her present circumstances.[46] Even rapper Drake, who has sometimes been identified as a feminist rapper,[47] has created more controversy for his alleged desire to police and control women's sexuality in songs like "Nice for What," about which writer Shannon Lee argues,

> While listening to "Nice for What," we are exposed to an inevitable utterance of "ho," and history suggests Drake will be back to spitting lyrics that degrade and objectify women in no time.[48]

In the #metoo era, when some men are trying to understand their roles or wonder how they can support women as allies, male music artists can be and have been detriments by trying to spin their own versions of being allies without the express input of women themselves. This solipsistic approach to becoming an ally creates further tensions between men and women, as young men adopt a Drake or Lamar version of alliance that is not what many women endorse as authentic allyship, leaving some men feeling bewildered or resentful.

At the same time, a resurgence of socially conscious themes in hip-hop and rap has energized a youth-culture that seems to be looking for causes to support, whether Black Lives Matter, the Women's Marches and movement, or being allies to LGBTQ communities. Rappers such as Young M.A, Chance the Rapper, Angel Haze, and Little Simz, just to name a few, are forging a new legacy and without surprise, many of these new artists are women LGBTQ artists.

Thought Box

Consider artists such as Tupac Shakur in the past or Drake and Kendrick Lamar today. What are your opinions about male artists who seem to be conflicted when it comes to the representations of and opinions about women? Are they simply old-fashioned examples of men trying to police women's sexual choices or do you see it differently? Do you have a problem with rappers blurring the line between socially conscious and potentially exploitative rhymes?

But many critics of rap music often reduce hip-hop and rap to the violent and misogynistic rhymes that oftentimes create the most attention, which promotes a cultural stereotype of epic proportions. It usually doesn't take these critics long to use these criticisms to take aim at people of color. An art form is converted into a social commentary about communities of color and the alleged problems and faults of those trapped in low socioeconomic neighborhoods. These criticisms take a predictable and well-trodden path: view people of color as being irresponsible, as being hyper-violent and hypersexual, as being preoccupied with wealth and self-promotion, as glamorizing drug taking and the use of violence as a means to settle scores, as being openly misogynistic and homophobic, and many other negative stereotypes that are usually found in the literature of the Ku Klux Klan.[49]

So, why do many rappers continue to proliferate negative stereotypes that include the denigration of women? In the film *Beyond Beats & Rhymes*, filmmaker Byron Hurt exposes the fact that much of the gangsta rap that took over the tracks played at clubs and on radio stations in the early to mid-1990s and that continues in certain forms today, was promoted by record executives in an effort to draw white kids into the folds of hip-hop culture in order to expand the fan base and increase record sales.[50] While rap artists before the emergence of gangsta rap were selling records in respectable numbers, the major record labels wanted to create much higher sales numbers and doing so entailed getting white kids to buy the records. So, an emphasis was placed on signing and promoting artists who were not rhyming about issues of social justice, but instead creating and performing music that celebrated "sexual conquest" and the sexual objectification of women, while boasting about violence, invulnerability, drugs, party-culture, and an overall street-reputation of hypermasculine toughness. Record label executives viewed these themes as more commercially profitable and better able to lure white, suburban kids into hip-hop culture than themes that documented the harshness of living in the city where police abuse was rampant.[51] Chuck D, of Public Enemy, states in *Beyond Beats & Rhymes* that once the major labels bought up the indie-labels that produced most of the rap and hip-hop music of the 1990s, a transition took place that converted songs like "Fight the Power" into Snoop Dogg's "Gin and Juice."[52] The examination and condemnation of systematic and institutionalized racism gave way to the sexual exploitation of women and partying, themes considered by record company executives to have mass-male appeal.

As a side-by-side comparison, the iconic rap group Public Enemy sold a very respectable two million copies of their 1990 Def Jam-release, *Fear of a Black Planet*, which has been described as an Afrocentric, political album that challenged the status quo in America on issues of institutional racism and the changing face of power around the world.[53] By 2000, the major labels had jumped into the fray of signing hip-hop and rap artists, who had previously found label support only through independent labels such as Def Jam and Death Row Records. With Eminem's Interscope release *The Marshall Mathers LP* selling over 35 million copies worldwide with themes of violence, drug use, homophobia, and the sexual objectification and exploitation of women, the major labels had struck gold, or in this case "diamond," which is a measurement of selling more than 10 million copies.[54,55] White kids and especially young, white boys and men could now get behind the tropes fed to them by the first white artist who was crowned by the ruling Black rappers of the time as being the real thing.[56] The major record labels were giddy, making more money than they could imagine by selling messages of hatred toward women, gay bashing, and wanton violence and intimidation toward other men. It should be noted that the major record labels of Interscope, Sony, EMI, Universal, Warner, BMG, Virgin, and Atlantic are overwhelmingly run by white men who are not making decisions based on a commitment to social justice.[57] It did not take long for white kids living in the suburbs to begin emulating what was being sold to them as Black, street culture and all of the stereotypes that went with it.

CULTURAL APPROPRIATION

The pop-cultural designation "bro" is itself an example of cultural appropriation, as young, white men have adopted the expression and mannerisms from their interpretations of Black, male culture. "Bro" is shorthand for "brother" and has found its place in the greetings and conversations of young, white men throughout the nation. In the article, "How the Bro Became White," writer Alexander Abad-Santos notes that the "bro" derivation of "brother" has been used to refer to African-American men for generations.[58] The appropriation of "bro" began in the early 1990s with the film *Encino Man* starring Sean Astin and Pauley Shore as two young, white party-guys living in the San Fernando Valley who bring a caveman, Brendan Fraser, back to life.[59] The script direction literally reads, "Stoney and Hank have been bros since grammar school."[60] Today, "bros" are predominantly white, but continue to take cues from hip-hop culture on how to dress and talk. Backward baseball caps and baggy shorts are today's standard-issue uniform of nonconformity against what is believed to be stiff, white, middle-class cultural norms, but have ironically become the fashion templates of suburban, white, masculine conformity.

In his book, *Why White Kids Love Hip Hop: Wangstas, Wiggers, Wannabes and the New Reality of Race in America,* author Bakari Kitwana discusses why white kids are drawn to rap music.[61] Kitwana explains the terminology he employs:

> Wangsta: made popular by rapper 50 Cent, a wangsta is a white kid who is a fake gangsta. These are white youths who take on the "personifications of hip hop."[62]
>
> Wigger: a term used as a white stand-in for the n-word. These are white kids, once again, who adopt clothing styles and street terminology to approximate what they believe to be an urban, Black persona.
>
> Wannabee: this term is used in many contexts, but simply means a person who aspires to be someone he or she is not.

Cultural appropriation by some white and Asian American boys and girls of what they consider to be Black culture remains popular among those who think that being part of hip-hop culture makes them cool or attractive. One of many harms done when white kids attempt to appear "Black," as they view "Black," is that stereotypes are reinforced through caricatures. These caricatures become stand-ins for reality such that white people in numbers begin to view Black people as the caricatures being performed by white imitators. Bridget Minamore, writing for *Grazia*, states,

> ...myself and many other black women don't like it when white people – men or women, gay or straight – use their voices and mannerisms to act 'like we do', usually for comic effect...When a white person puts on that tone of voice (you know which one I mean), snaps their fingers and twists their head proclaiming 'ain't nobody got time for dat', they erase the nuances of actual black women's lives and further simplistic and hurtful generalisations.[63]

In essence, white people who adopt these caricatures are doing what blackface minstrel performers did years ago: reinforcing hurtful and vicious stereotypes that contribute to an already existing racism that permeates American culture. In bro culture, white bros will adopt certain mannerisms that they view as "Black" and cool to relate to one another without considering the way that these mannerisms feed an ugly and mean-spirited stereotype that has been hawked by white supremacists for generations. At this point, white imitators may believe that their performance is authentic in the sense that it reflects "who they really are," but the legacy of cultural appropriation by white imitators belies this authenticity. It is simply another attempt by white men, much like the white musical artists of the past who appropriated the blues and R & B, to profit from a performance that is not their own.

THE FALLOUT TO WOMEN OF COLOR

A study published by researchers at the University of Illinois reported that white men who consume misogynistic rap music and music videos consistently claim that Black women are more promiscuous than White women.[64] The racist views of white rap-music consumers found in these reports are consistent with the claim made in Hurt's film *Beyond Beats & Rhymes*, where antiviolence educator Jackson Katz astutely quips, "If the KKK were smart enough, they would have invented Gangsta rap, since it is such a caricature of Black masculinity."[65] Much like the 1915, D.W. Griffith film *Birth of a Nation*, misogynistic rap reinforces stereotypes about Black men, including the racist trope that Black men are hypersexual, that Black men are dangerous and violent, and that Black men are hyper-materialistic. But beyond these crude stereotypes, the videos produced by sexist and misogynistic artists are replete with images of women of color who appear to be content with their secondary status as sexual things who are always ready and willing to comply with men's sexual desires. In actuality, of course, many of these women are models being paid to play a role, but male consumers of these videos seem not to understand or care that these are performances scripted for the women by a writer and director who are crafting mediated images for male artists who wish to project a hypermasculine, street-hard persona to fans who have bought in to a particular version of masculine power.

Georgetown University professor of sociology, Michael Eric Dyson, writing for the *NY Times*, reflects that while there is much that is edifying about and empowering to men and women of color in hip-hop,

> There's no doubt that gangster rap is often sexist and that it reflects a vicious misogyny that has seized our nation with frightening intensity. How painful it must be for black women, many of whom have fought valiantly for black pride, to hear the dissonant chord of disdain carried in the angry epithet "bitch."[66]

Dyson goes on to note that the sexism and misogyny found in the lyrics of some artists' work find origins that long preview gangsta rap, so that misogynistic rap and hip-hop is but a symptom of larger social paradigms that have embraced sexism and misogyny for generations.[67] But as Dyson notes, the fallout to women of color has not been discussed or documented nearly as much as has the criticism of the music artists themselves. The fact that women of color must contend with both racism and sexism from outside and inside communities of color speaks to what scholar and social activist bell hooks notes as a leading issue within ***intersectional feminism***, which is a form of feminism that activist-scholars such as Columbia University's Kimberly Crenshaw have championed as a response to middle-class, white feminism.[68,69] Scholar and activist Angela Davis in her seminal work, "Women, Race, and Class," powerfully addresses the experiences of Black women as outside the purview of many white women, and often ignored by mainstream analyses of the treatment of women in America.[70] The combination of being a woman of color and coming from lower socioeconomic classes has been treated as a recipe for invisibility by many who examine and evaluate the challenges that women face today. But with Black women and Latinas being called everything from "hoes" to "bitches" to "gold-diggers" in contemporary music that is consumed by a largely male fan base, the problems are both compounded and marginalized at the same time.

Some of the fallout of stereotyping women of color in hip-hop lyrics and music videos is, according to writer Byron Mason II, [that]

> adolescent boys who see these videos [can] grow up with unrealistic expectations for their sexual partners. Worse, adolescent girls, primarily adolescent girls of color, could grow up thinking that they are only worth what their bodies have to offer.[71]

Furthermore, according to Carolyn West of the University of Washington, "Black girls are not seeing positive images of what they can be."[72] In the article,

"Women of Color in Hip Hop: The Pornographic Gaze," professor Margaret Hunter of Mills Colleges notes that there are three tropes found in hip-hop of women of color that are repeated throughout lyrics and videos:

- Consistent with pornography, women of color are commonly characterized as sex workers, strippers, and prostitutes.
- Women's voices are used to sell particular images of women and gender ideologies.
- Women are valorized for their loyalty to male partners despite dangers to themselves.[73]

To this last trope, online magazine *Black-Feminisms* notes that women in rap music are reduced to two roles: loyal girlfriend or video hoe.[74] In *Hip Hop: Beyond Beats & Rhymes*, this dichotomy is termed "Sisters and Bitches," with men arbitrating the distinction based on the clothes women choose to wear.[75] Women are compartmentalized into those who can be respected and those who should not, the latter being a category of women who can be treated in any way the male protagonist sees fit, including in any sexually degrading and even violent manner the man views appropriate.

A final observation from Black-Feminisms is that some artists in rap and hip-hop who employ sexist and misogynistic imagery to their songs and videos have created what they term "modern day minstrelsy," whereby "the 'gangsta and the jezebel" communicate Black and Brown gender relations to consumers who are largely white and middle class."[76] The caricature of women of color as "bitches and hoes" to be sexually objectified and abused plays to a parallel narrative that can be found in 18th- and 19th-century white slave owners' views of slaves. Commodifying Black women and Latinas to a male fan base teaches young men to devalue women of color and pornifies women's bodies, while contributing to the ongoing problem of men's violence against women. Repeatedly degrading women through lyrics and visual imagery normalizes the mistreatment of women to young, male audiences who are at an age when they are attempting to figure out their relation to and relationships with women. Writing for *The Huffington Post*, Shanita Hubbard concludes that while men's violence against women is not simply a problem for hip-hop culture,

> What if we showed how much we value black women by refusing to support artists who create music that normalizes abuse? What if we stopped supporting artists who are so casual with their abuse that they tell us about it in their lyrics?[77]

Hubbard levels a daunting challenge toward those who support music that celebrates men's violence toward women. Some may contend that the challenge will be ignored, but at a time when the empowerment of women is emerging into the mainstream of popular culture with the success of the women's marches and the historical rise of women in politics, it may be possible to find the misogyny embedded in the music of certain artists to be regarded as a relic of unchallenged male power just as the Ku Klux Klan and Alt-right politics are viewed as a desperate attempt to retain white power at a time of increasing multiculturalism.

BRO-COUNTRY

Over the past several years, country music has witnessed the emergence of a sub-genre termed 'bro-country' for its fusion of country with hip-hop and rock-themed lyrics.[78] Artists including Florida Rosen, Luke Bryan, Jason Aldean, and Jake Owen have carved out a niche in country music by focusing on themes of alcohol consumption, women, partying, and trucks.[79] Actually, Trace Adkins previewed "bro-country" with his song "Honky Tonk Badonkadonk," which obsesses about women's bottoms.[80] Much like many rock music artists whose music celebrates the degradation and sexual objectification of women, bro-country artists are white, heterosexual men who have profited enormously from their chauvinism. Yet, white music stars have seldom received the kind of searing criticism for their sexism that music stars of color have experienced and this is true of bro-country artists as well.

The emergence of bro country coincided with the recession of classic rock, and not coincidentally. When classic rock artists were delegated to oldies radio programming, musicians and song writers who made their livings in the classic rock world of excesses that included alcohol and drug indulgence and the sexualizing of women were largely out of work, unless one happened to be a member of a successful classic rock band of the past that could continue to play its oldie-hits to an aging fan base not interested in younger artists and new forms of music. Many of these musicians and song writers moved to Nashville to seek revived careers in the burgeoning sounds of neo-country music that was a hybrid of country and pop. But the lyrical themes of rock music came along for the ride. Writing for Mic Magazine, Elena Sheppard reports,

> Country music has changed, and traded in its gravitas and story songs for a new archetype of hard partying, tattoo covered, baseball-cap wearing white guys, looking for late night lovin', and a perfect patch of tailgate grass. These are the country bros.[81]

The frat-friendly themes of bro country would have fit nicely into the Mötley Crüe or AC/DC song catalogs, where women are "fast machines" that "keep their motors clean."[82] In bro country, Friday and Saturday nights are the only nights worth mentioning, when women are converted into "girls" in songs like Billy Currington's "Hey Girl," Luke Bryan's "Country Girl (Shake it for Me)," or Tim McGraw's "Southern Girl." There is plenty of alcohol consumption as a precursor for sex as in the song "Night Train" by Jason Aldean or Luke Bryant's "My Kind of Night," where women as girls get the distinction of becoming "side-rides" and given the task of looking hot. Women as 'girls' and alcohol as sexual persuader have been themes in songs for decades across many genres of music. But the sexism in these lines repeatedly flow into the minds of boys and young men who consume bro country, while forming their views about girls and women. Country music has always appealed more to a white, conservative fan base, which adheres to a notion of Southern culture that includes the Confederate flag and a traditional notion of gender essentialism. But according to the FBI, if you look at the states where women are most likely to be murdered by men, per capita, it reads like a tour schedule for bro-country artists:

> South Carolina, Louisiana, Alabama, Nevada, Tennessee, Texas, Oklahoma, North Carolina, Missouri, Alaska, New Mexico, Texas, (Florida did not submit a report).[83]

The FBI report noted that guns were the most common means men use to kill women, and unsurprisingly, the states listed have some of the most easy-to-access gun laws in the nation.[84] When women are portrayed as sexual and romantic opportunities, but not equals to men, as a trope that begins in boyhood, the stage is set for mistreating women when disagreements arise, and the results can be deadly. Bro are the recipients of this dangerous and deadly message, which helps explain the incredibly high rates of intimate partner violence in America and around the world.[85]

THE MISOGYNY OF METAL

One form of music that draws an almost entirely white, male audience and overwhelmingly composed of white, male musicians is metal. There are many subgenres of metal that include heavy metal, thrash metal, glam metal, black metal, death metal, industrial metal, goth metal, and even Christian metal, but one commonality is the attraction to white, male audiences. It is not that people of color and women are never found among metal fans, but the predominance of white males is palpable. One of metal's biggest bands is Cannibal Corpse, a band that sings about rape, murder, torture, infanticide, and necrophilia.[86] In their song, "Stripped, Raped, and Strangled," Cannibal Corpse boasts about the violent rape and murder of young women.[87] In the song, "Fucked to Death" by metal stars Devourment, singer Ruben Rosas declares, "I need a cunt around my dick," and goes on state that he needs to fulfill his sexual desires and then stab a woman to death.[88]

Many fans of metal respond to lyrics like these by claiming that they are only intended to be taken as fantasy, like the content of horror films. But writing for Noisey Magazine, Jill Mikkelson notes,

> Culture does not exist nor is it created in a vacuum. The social context of any work of art matters. In this case, it's the fact that the World Health Organization says that "over a third of women globally have suffered violence from a partner or sexual violence from another man."[89]

Mikkelson also asks, if content of this sort is meant to be fantasy, why it is that so many young men have *this particular fantasy?*[90] One can fantasize about anything. But notice that a genre of music that fantasized about child molestation or lynching people of color would be roundly rejected, while fantasies about raping and murdering women are profitable. The double-standard inherent in music, also found in video games and some films, is defended as fantasy, but those fantasies that are excused and defended possess content that *fantasize* about harming women.

> ### Thought Box: On Fantasy
>
> In the foregoing section, we find that violent misogyny is defended as fantasy when it appears in the lyrics of songs or found in video games. But few of these apologists would approve fantasy-content of molesting children or hanging Black people from trees. The concern for fantasies of these kinds would be that one who is interested in the fantasy of molesting children are probably pedophiles, while those interested in the fantasy of lynching Black people are racists. So, what does it say of a person that their fantasy is raping, torturing, and murdering women? What do you make of the defense that it is simply fantasy?

You will probably not get bros to admit that their music and gaming choices are fed, in part, by their contempt for women, but we cannot escape the question of why bros who are attracted to art forms that celebrate violent misogyny are attracted to those particular art forms in the first place. We often see similar forms of misogyny in the pornography that many bros consume. These vicious forms of misogyny also feed the anger found in the Incel-rebellion bros discussed in Chapter 1, where young men feel entitled to women's bodies and become filled with rage toward women who do not allow them access to their bodies. The misogyny found in metal becomes the narrative soundtrack to these young men who can fantasize about, if not actually brutalize women who do not conform to the pornified image they have of women, an image that invokes compliant or forced-to-be compliant women.

Interestingly, there are female metal bands or metal bands with female-fronted singers such as Nightwish, Xandria, Halestorm, Theatre of Tragedy, and Arch Enemy, but predictably, they are rarely booked on national tours and all but ignored by mainstream metal-music media.[91] Writing for the Houston Press, music critic Kristy Love states,

> Being a fan is an act of submission. Lower-ranked males despise the disruption in hierarchy represented by a successful female. They're jealous, and don't want to give up power.[92]

Hard-core punk band War on Women's singer Shawna Potter adds,

> I can't speak about all genres of music, but many [rock] bands started out as protest music; music meant to call out those in power

and challenge the status quo. Well, there's nothing more status quo than sexism, so if they really wanted to be punk...they'd fight those ideals by championing equality and justice, putting victims of gender-based violence first.[93]

Like those hip-hop and rap artists who continue to keep alive the celebration of abuse toward women, metal music may be facing its own reckoning with misogyny. But since metal music has become a somewhat marginalized genre of music, particularly in America, there may be less interest by those who produce and promote the music to change, particularly when we consider that the majority of artists and fans are boys and men.

THE MALE-CENTRICITY OF THE MUSIC INDUSTRY

One reason why music has been so unapologetically sexist in nature is that the industry has been and continues to be top-heavy with men at the helm of power, and until recently it has overwhelmingly been white men who have called the shots.[94] Each year, Billboard Magazine publishes its list of "Power 100" people in the music industry.[95] That list is currently made up of 83 men and 17 women.[96] Writing for *Billboard Magazine*, Melinda Newman notes one reason why there are so few women producing records, stating, "There are myriad reasons, including a lack of role models."[97] Like so many professions, young women who may be interested in pursuing a career in the music industry do not have many women to look up to who have served as producers. Alex Hope, one of only a small handful of female music producers, states,

> There have definitely been times you'll [suggest] an idea and the artist will pass over it and the guy in the room will say the same idea and they'll say, 'I love it,' and you're like, 'Oh, my Lord.'[98]

Much like the film industry, there is an assumption based on tradition that men are better producers and directors, which is itself part of a larger sexist assumption that men are better at activities and professions that require technical knowledge. Since producers make executive decisions over the available recording options when making a record, the lack of women in the role of producer also speaks to a longstanding sexist assumption that men make better leaders than women. We see this assumption in politics, business, policing, and many other areas of human endeavor where leadership is required.

A lack of representation is also found among songwriters and artists themselves. Of all artists, whether solo artists, duos, or groups that charted songs on Billboard, only 22% were women.[99] Dr. Stacy Smith of USC's Annenberg School of Communication notes,

> The voices of women are missing from popular music. This is another example of what we see across the ecosystem of entertainment:

Women are pushed to the margins or excluded from the creative process.[100]

Over the past six years, women wrote only 12% of the songs that charted on Billboard's charts, while women made up only 2% of the producers of songs that charted.[101] Of five of the top categories for Grammy nominations, less than 10% were women and less than one-third of this 10% of women were women of color.[102]

Carla Marie Williams, who has written songs for singing star Beyoncé, states bluntly, "Equality in the music industry definitely still doesn't exist; it's male-dominated through and through."[103] Like the film industry, women in the music industry have also experienced a range of sexually harassing behaviors from men.[104] It is against this background that we find male artists who produce sexist and sometimes violently misogynistic songs. Women within the music industry have spoken out against the sexism and misogyny they have experienced, but rarely are their voices heard and acknowledged by the men in the industry. For instance, in response to the complaints of an underrepresentation of women within the music industry, Neil Portnow, president of the Recording Academy, stated that women need to "step up" if they want to reside in positions of influence, leading music star Pink to retort, "Women in music don't need to 'step up'—women have been stepping up since the beginning of time. Stepping up and stepping aside."[105]

Speaking about those who have the power to decide who wins Grammys and who do not, singer-songwriter Mary Lambert, sharing her experience of looking around the room of Grammy personnel, declares, "It's just all straight cis white dudes. And maybe three women? Maybe three people of color? In the whole room! And those people are picked by the Recording Academy, by the executives. That accountability needs to be there!"[106] The result of a male-dominated music industry, Lambert notes, is that,

> What we hear on the radio and mainstream music is all through a filter of the male gaze.[107]

This is why much of the music released by male artists continues to be bro-friendly tributes to women as sexual or romantic trifles, relegated to roles of "babe," "girl," "chick" or "hottie" when not denigrated as "bitch," "ho," "slut," "skank," or "pussy." What is missing in almost all music produced by male artists is the notion of women as partners or equals, as having value for more than what they can offer men. Of course, as long as sexist and misogynistic music continues to create enormous profits for the men who produce it, there is little reason to think that music of this kind is on its way out.

POSTSCRIPT

Music, like many forms of art and entertainment, has trained generations of boys and men that women's roles are primarily to please men in subordinate positions of sexual plaything or romantic partner. While there is nothing inherently wrong with so-called love songs, there is a problem when male music stars one-dimensionalize women as nothing other than love or sex interests or reduce women to body parts by fetishizing women's breasts or derrieres, and it is certainly a huge problem to depict women as "whores," "sluts," "bitches" and other vicious terms of degradation. But as the world witnesses the increasing power of women in many areas of life, bro culture itself will be challenged. The swagger of the young male who loudly attests his entitlement to women's bodies, his insistence of demeaning and degrading women, his wanton use of sexist slurs to denigrate women and other men, his reductionist desire to fetishize parts of women's bodies, and his ambition to maintain his privilege and power over women and men he views as weak or soft may finally be facing its most ardent reckoning.

Notes

1. Jenni Miller, "8 Feminist Male Musicians We Love," *Refinery29*, December, 2014. https://www.refinery29.com/en-us/feminist-male-musicians#slide-4
2. Nathan A. Heflick, "The Sexual Objectification Spillover Effect," *Psychology Today*, June, 2011. https://www.psychologytoday.com/us/blog/the-big-questions/201106/the-sexual-objectification-spillover-effect
3. Ibid.
4. *AMA*, "Domestic Violence Is the Leading Cause of Injury to Women Aged 15–44," *Canadian Family Physician*, Vol. 56(3), October, 1999, pp. 2317–2322. https://www.ncbi.nlm.nih.gov/pmc/articles/PMC2328613/
5. Madeleine Gannon, "To Sing Forevermore: How the Microphone, Radio and the Crooners Changed the Music Industry," *The Michigan Daily*, October 18, 2018. https://www.michigandaily.com/section/arts/sing-ever-more-how-microphone-radio-and-crooners-changed-music-industry
6. Ibid.
7. Martha Bayles, "The Greatest Generation of Crooners," *The Wall Street Journal*, May 2001.
8. Tim Grierson, "Prince Wanted 2 Sex U Up," *MEL*. https://melmagazine.com/en-us/story/prince-wanted-2-sex-u-up
9. Brie Dyas, "Jack Jones' 'Wives & Lovers' Could Be One of the Most Offensive Songs, Ever," *Huff Post*, December 6, 2017.
10. "Flash Lyrics, the Lyrics to 'Wives and Lovers'," https://www.flashlyrics.com/lyrics/jack-jones/wives-and-lovers-59
11. *Urban Dictionary*, providing definitions of terms used on the streets that do not appear in traditional dictionaries and thesauruses. https://www.urbandictionary.com/define.php?term=Cop%20%26%20Blow
12. Deborah Wilker, "Crue: No Apologies for Sexist Attitudes," *South Florida Sun Sentinel*, January 1990. https://www.sun-sentinel.com/news/fl-xpm-1990-01-19-9001190965-story.html
13. Olly Alexander, Hayden Thorpe, Gaika, "Modern Masculinity and Music: 2016, the Year of the Ambiguous Male," *The Guardian*, August 2016. https://

www.theguardian.com/music/2016/aug/01/modern-masculinity-and-music-2016-the-year-of-the-ambiguous-male
14. Genius Lyric Site, the lyrics to 'U.O.E.N.O,' https://genius.com/Rocko-uoeno-lyrics
15. Genius Lyric Site, the lyrics to Hey Mister Mister, https://genius.com/Kool-g-rap-hey-mister-mister-lyrics
16. Jason G. Goldman, "What Is Classical Conditioning (And Why Does It Matter?)," *Scientific American*, January 2012.
17. Kendra Cherry, "The Little Albert Psychology Experiment," *Very Well Mind*, December 2019. https://www.verywellmind.com/the-little-albert-experiment-2794994
18. Harvard University, Department of Psychology, B.F. Skinner. https://psychology.fas.harvard.edu/people/b-f-skinner
19. American Academy of Pediatrics, "Impact of Music, Music Lyrics, and Music Videos on Children and Youth," *Pediatrics*, Vol. 124, Issue 5, November 2009, pp. 1488–1494. http://pediatrics.aappublications.org/content/124/5/1488
20. Louise Donovan, "Chris Brown's Response to the Night He Assaulted Rihanna Is Unconscionable," *Elle*, August 2017. https://www.elle.com/uk/life-and-culture/culture/news/a37820/chris-brown-rihanna-domestic-violence/
21. Alan Duke, Ted Rowlands, "Chris Brown Pleads Guilty in Rihanna Assault Case," *CNN*, June 2009. http://www.cnn.com/2009/SHOWBIZ/Music/06/22/chris.brown.hearing/index.html
22. Corinne Heller, "A Timeline of All of Chris Brown's Arrests and Legal Troubles," *E-News*. July 2018. https://www.eonline.com/news/949860/a-timeline-of-all-of-chris-brown-s-arrests-and-legal-troubles
23. Samuel Petrequin, Associated Press, "Chris Brown Accuser Alleges Multiple Rapes and Forced Cocaine, Lawyer Says," *USA Today*, January 2019. https://www.usatoday.com/story/life/2019/01/24/chris-brown-accuser-alleges-multiple-rapes-paris-lawyer-says/2667108002/
24. Evan Real, "Chris Brown Warns Future Lovers that He's a Stalker in Disturbing Video," *Us Weekly*, February 1, 2017. https://www.usmagazine.com/celebrity-news/news/chris-brown-warns-lovers-that-hes-a-stalker-in-disturbing-video-w464333/
25. Adam Howard, "Chris Brown's 'Bad Boy' Image Has Helped Him – Will That Change?" *NBC News*, September 1, 2016. https://www.nbcnews.com/news/nbcblk/analysis-can-chris-brown-s-bad-boy-brand-survive-latest-n640621
26. Ibid.
27. Barbara Krahe, Ingrid Moller, L. Rowell Huesmann, Lucyna Kirwil, Juliana Felber, Anja Berger, "Desensitization to Media Violence: Links With Habitual Media Violence Exposure, Aggressive Cognitions, and Aggressive Behavior," *Journal of Personal Social Psychology*, Vol. 100, Issue 4, April 2011, pp. 630–646. https://www.ncbi.nlm.nih.gov/pmc/articles/PMC4522002/
28. Melinda Hughes, "Robin Thicke's "Blurred Lines" Gets the Feminist Response It Deserves," *Mic*, July 27, 2013. https://mic.com/articles/56585/robin-thicke-s-blurred-lines-gets-the-feminist-response-it-deserves#.CydT8ZdcA
29. Genius Lyric Site, the lyrics for "One Less Bitch," https://genius.com/Nwa-one-less-bitch-lyrics
30. Angela Helm, "Snoop, Please Space Us Your Rage about Trump, Mr. 'Bitches Ain't Shit'," *The Root*, May 21, 2018.
31. Genius Lyric Site, the lyrics to 'Amityville.' https://genius.com/Eminem-amityville-lyrics

Chapter 7

32. Genius Lyric Site, the lyrics to 'You.' https://genius.com/Chief-keef-you-lyrics
33. Candace Amos, "Eminem Still Hasn't Changed His Misogynistic Ways – See 5 of His Most Brutal Lyrics against Women," *New York Daily News*, August 7, 2015.
34. Angela Helm, "Snoop, Please Space Us Your Rage about Trump, Mr. 'Bitches Ain't Shit'," *The Root*, May 21, 2018.
35. Suzan Clarke, "Maroon 5's Video for 'Animals' Sparks Outrage Over Depiction of Stalking," *ABC News*, October 3, 2014. https://abcnews.go.com/Entertainment/maroon-5s-video-animals-sparks-outrage-depiction-stalking/story?id=25932577
36. Ibid.
37. PBS Information on domestic violence, based on the work of Dr. Susan Hicks, Director of the Family and Violence Institute. https://www.pbs.org/kued/nosafeplace/studyg/domestic.html
38. *AMA*, "Domestic Violence Is the Leading Cause of Injury to Women Aged 15–44," *Canadian Family Physician*, October, 1999, pp. 2317–2322.
39. Marcia Dawkins, "Can Feminist Women Love Eminem? Absolutely," *Huff Post*, November 6, 2013. https://www.huffingtonpost.com/marcia-alesan-dawkins/eminem-feminist_b_3880974.html
40. Kay Wicker, "Eminem Wasn't Just Calling Out President Trump. He Was Talking to His Fans," *Think Progress*, October 11, 2017. https://thinkprogress.org/eminem-trump-supporters-bet-f1038948beac/
41. John Vilanova, "Yes, We Still Need to Talk about Eminem's Misogyny," *Musiqology*, October 16, 2017. http://musiqology.com/blog/2017/10/16/yes-we-still-need-to-talk-about-eminems-misogyny/
42. Audre Lorde, "The Master's Tools Will Never Dismantle the Master's House," *Sister Outsider, The Crossin Press Feminist Series*, 1984. https://www.goodreads.com/quotes/291810-for-the-master-s-tools-will-never-dismantle-the-master-s-house
43. Walter Ray Watson, Andee Tagle, Daoud Tyler-Ameen, "Both Party and Protest, 'Alright' Is the Sound of Black Life's Duality," *NPR*, August 26, 2019.
44. Gender Bent, "Even "Conscious" Rappers Have Problematic Lyrics about Women: It's Time We Addressed this Pervasive Misogynoir," *Afropunk*, May 1, 2018. https://afropunk.com/2018/05/even-conscious-rappers-have-problematic-lyrics-about-women-its-time-we-addressed-this-pervasive-misogynoir/
45. Mychal Denzel Smith, "Rap's Long History of 'Conscious' Condescension to Women," *The Atlantic*, August 28, 2012. https://www.theatlantic.com/entertainment/archive/2012/08/raps-long-history-of-conscious-condescension-to-women/261651/
46. Ibid.
47. Jenessa Williams, "Does 'Nice For What' Mark a New Era for Feminist Drake?" *Gal-Dem*, April 15, 2018. http://gal-dem.com/nice-for-what-feminist-drake/
48. Shanon Lee, "I Don't Need Drake's Feminist Anthem, 'Nice for What.' It Won't Fix Hip-hop's Misogyny Problem," *The Lily*. https://www.thelily.com/i-dont-need-drakes-feminist-anthem-nice-for-what-it-wont-fix-hip-hops-misogyny-problem/
49. Laura Green, "Negative Racial Stereotypes and Their Effect on Attitudes Toward African-Americans," *Jim Crow Museum of Racist Memorabilia*, Ferris State University,
50. Byron Hurt, "Beyond Beats & Rhymes," *Independent Lens*, 2017. http://www.pbs.org/independentlens/hiphop/

51. Bossip Staff, "Black Music Executives Continue to Promote Death and Negativity for Profit," *Bossip*, July 30, 2014. https://bossip.com/1007490/for-discussion-have-hip-hop-music-executives-sold-black-people-out-to-make-money-43081/
52. Byron Hurt, "Beyond Beats & Rhymes," *Independent Lens*, 2017. http://www.pbs.org/independentlens/hiphop/
53. Ian McCann, "'Fear of a Black Planet': How Public Enemey Hit Back against the World," *U Discover Music*, April 10, 2019.
54. Bryan Rolli, "Eminem Is The Only Artist To Have Seven Albums Reach 1 Billion Streams on Spotify," *Forbes*, January 22, 2019.
55. Lee Vann, "19 Certified Diamond Rap and R&B Albums," *Hip Hop Wired*, March 11, 2015. https://hiphopwired.com/450958/19-certified-diamond-rap-rb-albums/
56. Stereo Williams, "Eminem's White Privilege: How Slim Shady Was Crowned the 'King of Hip-Hop'," *Daily Beast*, December 23, 2018.
57. Paul Resnikoff, "The Music Industry: It's Still a White Boys' Club," *Digital Music News*, January 20, 2014. https://www.digitalmusicnews.com/2014/01/20/whiteboysclub/
58. Alexander Abad-Santos, "How the Bro Became White," *The Atlantic*, October 9, 2013. https://www.theatlantic.com/entertainment/archive/2013/10/how-encino-man-changed-race-bros/310146/
59. IMDB page for *Encino Man*, 1992. https://www.imdb.com/title/tt0104187/
60. Alexander Abad-Santos, "How the Bro Became White," *The Atlantic*, October 9, 2013. https://www.theatlantic.com/entertainment/archive/2013/10/how-encino-man-changed-race-bros/310146/
61. Bakari Kitwana, *Why White Kids Love Hip Hop: Wangstas, Wiggers, and the New Reality of Race in America*. Basic Civitas Books, May, 2006.
62. Bakari Kitwana interviewed by Ed Gordon and Farai Chideya, "Why White Kids Love Hip Hop," *NPR*, July 27, 2005. https://www.npr.org/templates/story/story.php?storyId=4773208
63. Bridget Minamore, "Why White People 'Acting Black' Really Can Hurt," *Grazia*, July 16, 2015. https://graziadaily.co.uk/life/opinion/white-people-acting-black-really-can-hurt/
64. Travis L. Dixon, Yuanyuan Zhang, Kate Conrad, "Self-Esteem, Misogyny and Afrocentricity: An Examination of the Relationship between Rap Music Consumption and African American Perceptions," *Group Processes & Intergroup Relations*, April 17, 2009. https://journals.sagepub.com/doi/pdf/10.1177/1368430209102847
65. Byron Hurt, "Beyond Beats & Rhymes," *Independent Lens*, 2017. http://www.pbs.org/independentlens/hiphop/
66. Michael Eric Dyson, "Bum Rap," *The New York Times*, February 3, 1994. https://www.nytimes.com/1994/02/03/opinion/bum-rap.html
67. Ibid.
68. bell hooks, "Dig Deep: Beyond Lean In," *The Feminist Wire*, October 28, 2013. https://www.thefeministwire.com/2013/10/17973/
69. International Women's Development Agency, "What Does Intersectional Feminism Actually Mean?" May 11, 2018. https://iwda.org.au/what-does-intersectional-feminism-actually-mean/
70. Angela Davis, *Women, Race, and Class*. Vintage Books, New York, 1983.
71. Byron Masson II, "Hip-Hop Misogyny's Effect on Women of Color," *The Prindle Post*, January 18, 2018. https://www.prindlepost.org/2018/01/hip-hop-misogynys-effects-women-color/
72. Ibid.

73. Margaret Hunter, Kathleen Soto, "Women of Color in Hip Hop: The Pornographic Gaze," *Race, Gender & Class*, Vol. 16, Issue 1–2, 2009, pp. 170–191. https://www.jstor.org/stable/41658866?seq=1#page_scan_tab_contents
74. Ibid.
75. Byron Hurt, "Beyond Beats & Rhymes," *Independent Lens*, 2017. http://www.pbs.org/independentlens/hiphop/
76. Black Feminisms, An Examination of Hunter's and Soto's "Women of Color in Hip Hop: The Pornographic Gaze," https://www.blackfeminisms.com/women-color-hip-hop/
77. Shanita Hubbard, "Black Women Love Hip Hop, But Doesn't Love Us Back," *Huffington Post*, January 28, 2018. https://www.huffingtonpost.com/entry/opinion-hubbard-metoo-hiphop_us_5a6b6162e4b0ddb658c60925
78. Jonathan Bernstein, Jon Freeman, Joseph Hudak, Brittney McKenna, Marissa R. Moss, "Baby You a Song: Bro-Country's 30 Biggest Bangers," *Rolling Stone*, December 3, 2019.
79. Ibid.
80. Genius Lyric Site, the lyrics for Honky Tonk Badonkadonk." https://genius.com/Trace-adkins-honky-tonk-badonkadonk-lyrics
81. Sarah Boesveld, "The Appeal and Possible End of Beer-drinking, Hip-shaking, Woman-ogling Bro-country," *National Post*, 2020.
82. Genius Lyric Site, the lyrics for "You Shook Me All Night Long," https://genius.com/Ac-dc-you-shook-me-all-night-long-lyrics
83. Melissa Jeltsen, "The States Where Women Are Most Likely to be Murdered by Men," *Huffington Post*, September 17, 2015. https://www.huffingtonpost.com/entry/murder-women-report_us_55f85315e4b0c2077efc3713
84. Jacquelyn C. Campbell et al., "Risk Factors for Femicide in Abusive Relationships: Results from a Multisite Case Control Study," *American Journal of Public Health*, Vol. 93, Issue 7, pp. 1089–1097, July 2003. https://www.ncbi.nlm.nih.gov/pmc/articles/PMC1447915/
85. Terri Hamrick, "Domestic Violence Awareness Month: What a Week Without Domestic Abuse Would Look Like," *USA Today*, October 26, 2019.
86. Bill Thompson, Kirk N. Olsen, "Death Metal Is Often Violent and Misogynist Yet It Brings Joy and Empowerment to Fans," *The Conversation*, February 21, 2018. http://theconversation.com/death-metal-is-often-violent-and-misogynist-yet-it-brings-joy-and-empowerment-to-fans-91909
87. Genius Lyric Site, the lyrics for "Stripped, Raped and Strangled," https://genius.com/Cannibal-corpse-stripped-raped-and-strangled-lyrics
88. Metro Lyric Site, the lyrics for "Fucked to Death," http://www.metrolyrics.com/fucked-to-death-lyrics-devourment.html
89. Jill Mikkelson, "It's Time to Stop Making Excuses for Extreme Metal's Violent Misogynist Fantasies," *Vice*, January 21, 2016. https://noisey.vice.com/en_us/article/rb8bnd/death-metal-misogyny
90. Ibid.
91. Kristy Love, "Metal's Problem with Women Is Not Going Away Anytime Soon," *Houston Press*, November 11, 2015. https://www.houstonpress.com/music/metals-problem-with-women-is-not-going-away-anytime-soon-7858411
92. Ibid.
93. Ibid.
94. Hannah Ellis-Petersen, "Upper Reaches of Music Industry 'a man's world', Diversity Study Finds," *The Guardian*, January 9, 2017. https://www.theguardian.

com/business/2017/jan/09/upper-reaches-of-music-industry-a-mans-world-diversity-study-finds
95. Billboard Staff, "The Power 100: Billboard's 2018 Power 100 List Revealed," *Billboard*, January 25, 2018. https://www.billboard.com/articles/business/8096144/billboard-2018-power-100-list
96. Bonnie Marcus, "The Music Industry Remains a Boy's Club: How Do Women Break In?" *Forbes*, April 3, 2018. https://www.forbes.com/sites/bonniemarcus/2018/04/03/the-music-industry-remains-a-boys-club-how-do-women-break-in/#1da63ef5d3f7
97. Melinda Newman, "Where Are All the Female Music Producers?" *Billboard*, January 19, 2018. https://www.billboard.com/articles/business/8095107/female-music-producers-industry-grammy-awards
98. Ibid.
99. USC Annenberg Staff, "In Music Industry, Female Songwriters and Producers Are Outnumbered by Men," *USC News*, January 25, 2018. https://news.usc.edu/135288/in-music-industry-female-songwriters-and-producesr-are-outnumbered-by-men/
100. Ibid.
101. Ibid.
102. Ibid.
103. Nadia Khomami, "Music Industry Is Still a Boy's Club, Says Beyonce Songwriter," *The Guardian*, March 8, 2018. https://www.theguardian.com/music/2018/mar/08/music-industry-still-boys-club-beyonce-songwriter-carla-marie-williams
104. Ibid.
105. Amy Zimmerman, "Female Artists Speak Out against Music Industry Sexism at SXSW," *Daily Beast*, March 15, 2018. https://www.thedailybeast.com/female-artists-speak-out-against-music-industry-sexism-at-sxsw
106. Ibid.
107. Ibid.

8
PORNOGRAPHY: SEX-ED FOR BROS

> **Key Points**
> - The Playboy Philosophy
> - Porn Goes Viral
> - Power-Imbalance Porn
> - Sexting
> - Gentlemen's Clubs as Bro Academies
> - The Gendered Porn Gap
> - The Orgasm Gap
> - The Pornification of Pop Culture
> - Fetishizing Lesbians
> - Porn and Erectile Dysfunction
> - Porn and Racism
> - When Porn is Politicized

As discussed throughout this book, bro culture is a segment of male culture that views sex as one of the most important things to pursue in life, but not as acts of intimacy. Bros are trained to view sex as conquest, as something gained, as something taken. For those bros who are heterosexual, women are sexual opportunities or what the bros of USC's chapter of Kappa Sigma termed, "targets, not actual people."[1] Here is part of the transcript of the actual letter that was sent out to Kappa Sigma bros:

> I will refer to females as "targets". They aren't actual people like us men. Consequently, giving them a certain name or distinction is pointless. A man is possessed with getting his nut off. He exists solely to spread his seed in any pie that will have him.[2]

Kappa Sigma later maintained that the letter was not written or disseminated by anyone in their fraternity and suggested that another fraternity may have written the letter as a prank.[3] But even if it was a prank, it speaks to the mindset of bros who find denigrating women to be funny. A similar tactic is used when fraternities engage in homophobic slurs and behaviors. All of the toxicity is supposed to evaporate because the bros were "just joking." This is a longstanding strategy of bros: make wildly sexist, homophobic, and racist statements and then attempt to slither off the hook of culpability by insisting that it was all a big joke, and that critics need to develop a better sense of humor. This ploy makes critics appear as though they are the ones who have a problem, rather than the bros who utter the sexist or homophobic comments.

Boys are not born bros; they are made bros. The construction of the bro comes about through any number of influences in a boy's life, but one of those influences is pornography, which most boys begin viewing between ages 8 and 11.[4,5] Writing for *Psychology Today*, Alexandra Katehakis notes that the brains of children have great plasticity in reaction to varying environments such that,

> When an adolescent boy compulsively views pornography, his brain chemistry can become shaped around the attitudes and situations that he is watching."[6,7]

Katehakis adds that porn teaches adolescent boys that sex and love are two separate things, which begins a process of viewing sex as devoid of intimacy and emotional power.[8]

The vast majority of pornography is made by men for men, for the purpose of sexual arousal and masturbation, but most importantly to profit financially. This means that competition drives content and the way this has played out over the past two decades is for content to become more extreme, more demeaning toward women, and less egalitarian. With boys viewing pornography at younger ages than ever before, given screen access at home and through cell phones, pornography can be said without exaggeration to be a form of sex education for those boys who grow up to be bros.

This is not to say that women do not view and enjoy pornography, but from its inception, porn has been made primarily for men and has helped to shape many men's views about women, sex, and consent. This section will, therefore, focus on pornography's impact on heterosexual boys and men, rather than taking up the more nuanced niche domains of porn that cater to women, couples, gay men or lesbians. As one example of these nuances, the issues surrounding pornography that is made for gay men is complicated by the fact that there is no historical precedent of one group of gay men sexually subordinating another group of gay men. A case is also sometimes made that pornography produced for gay men helps validate sexual orientation to those who have been alienated and marginalized in a heteronormative, homophobic culture. This is not to say that there are not problems with pornography made for gay men that are and should be addressed by LGBTQ communities. But the overwhelming majority of pornography is marketed to heterosexual men with an emphasis on men achieving orgasm, sometimes to the detriment of the woman or women in the scene. It is a men's-needs-and-desires-first form of media that uses women as interchangeable sex commodities that are in the scene strictly to aid the man in achieving orgasm. As such, bros routinely use porn as a masturbatory aid and as an instruction manual on how to treat women.

THE PLAYBOY PHILOSOPHY

The porn of yesteryear is tame by contemporary standards and was distributed mainly through magazines, porn theaters, and later VHS and DVD sales. The internet drastically altered the content and availability of pornography. But starting in the 1950s and 1960s, pornographers like Hugh Hefner began featuring images of nude women in magazines. Hefner's *Playboy* magazine was marketed as an alleged form of sexual freedom and rebellion against the sexual repression of organized religion.[9,10] However, what was termed the *Playboy philosophy* was sold alongside the social justice messaging of women's reproductive rights and sexual liberation, but this philosophy was aimed at men:

> Sexual liberation for women means consequence-free sex for men.

Shunned was the idea of marriage and commitment, replaced with a hedonistic lifestyle of "free love" and a scorching double standard for women and men. The women of *Playboy* were "bunnies," literally wearing the trademark bunny ears of Playboy, while dressed in lingerie and high heels, who served as eye-candy for men who would purchase subscriptions to view, lust-over, and masturbate to scantily clad and nude women. No such corollary existed for women until *Playgirl Magazine* was published in the 1970s.[11] In no way were the bunnies of Hefner's fantasy world politically positioned to change the world for the empowerment of women. They were instead lingerie-clad bunnies at the ready to light a man's cigarette, get him a drink, rub his shoulders, giggle at his sexually charged jokes, and pretend to be flattered or interested when men chatted them up with crude sexual suggestions.

The Playboy philosophy boiled down to women's bodies on display for men's consumption as a surrogate for the empowerment of women. Larger culture reinforced this disempowering double standard by assuring that few women enjoyed careers that rivaled the power and authority of men's careers. Hefner's Playboy promise was a promise to men:

> You will be able to live in a man's world with women overwhelmingly placed in roles of domestic and sexual servitude, while sexual freedom will be reserved for men as "swinging singles" who are living lives infinitely better than the poor, henpecked men who were forced to answer to their wives.[12]

Enemies to the Playboy philosophy were branded as sexually repressed conformists who had been browbeaten into a life of marital orthodoxy by the prudish clergy of conservative religion.

Hefner created the illusion of sexual freedom by appealing to men that the women's liberation movement was a sexual opportunity for men. Writing about the harrowing days when she worked for Hefner and at age 22 became one of his many sex partners, Holly Madison reports,

> I knew when I accepted the invitation to go out with him that I was getting into something racy. The only light [in his room] was coming

from two massive televisions that were playing porn. The girlfriends, in various stages of undress, were sitting in a semicircle at the edge of the bed — some kneeling, some standing, some lying down.[13]

Madison goes on to describe the lifestyle as one of sexual servitude to Hefner, while being disallowed by Hefner to seek employment of any kind.[14] If any of the *playmates*, as they were called, left the Playboy mansion to go out for the evening, they had a strict curfew to back to the mansion no later than 9:00 p.m.[15] Madison's memories serve as an apt illustration of the Playboy philosophy: young women serving an older man who has the resources and power to get whatever he wants. In fact, Madison also recounts the memory that the young women were given drugs or what Hefner termed "thigh-openers" to "loosen them up."[16]

Hefner lived the life dreamed of by the typical bro, a carefree existence with many young women attending to his sexual desires. The problem is the only place that any of this makes sense is within the world of pornography, which is why bros are attracted to porn the way that moths are attracted to light. Through porn, bros can be Hugh Hefner for a few minutes with consequence-free, sexual access to many different women who will perform whatever sexual task is required.

PORN GOES VIRAL

Throughout the 1980s pornography flourished, albeit under the scrutiny of the Meese Commission, ordered by then president Ronald Reagan with the task of investigating and making recommendations about the porn industry.[17] During the 1980s, porn theaters were slowly being replaced by video sales, which were produced by a large conglomerate of pornography production companies working largely out of Southern California. The most significant moment for the porn industry was the moment when the internet first launched porn sites. From that instance, the days were numbered for pornographic magazines and DVDs. Today, the internet is the number-one distributor of pornography and that fact has carried consequences. With millions of boys having screen access in their bedrooms, at school, at work, and anywhere they happen to be, porn has been able to creep into their viewing lives at earlier ages than ever before. As noted earlier, most boys are initiated into porn between the ages of 8 and 11.[18] So, instead of the first forays into conversations about sex coming from a parent, teacher, or even personal experience in their teens, most boys are now viewing pornography as their first exposure to sex and doing so at ages when many boys have no understanding of sex, let alone an appreciation of the strong emotions and feelings of intimacy that can accompany sex. At these young ages, boys also have little understanding of or respect for consent, or recognizing that the mediated sex found in the video clips they are viewing is not necessarily a reflection of reality.

At the same time, even though pornography is not and should not be considered on a par with the disciplined sex education courses one receives in middle school or high school, for many boys, porn is de facto sex education. Unmonitored porn viewing places into boys' minds normative messages about sex, which are then codified through repeated exposures. One of the reasons sex education exists in schools is to assure that accurate information is given to young people about sex instead of the misinformation that often accompanies non-academic sources. In one's teens, it is not uncommon to hear falsehoods such as *pregnancy cannot occur the first time one has sex*, or *STDs can only be transmitted through penis-vagina intercourse.* Porn is the equivalent of hearing stories on the street from uninformed sources about sex. But in some ways it is worse, because beyond the fact that condoms are not used in porn, the narratives of porn scenes are carefully constructed by producers and directors to bring about a desired outcome.[19] Porn pretends to be educational by claiming that it exposes people to options, role-playing, and fantasies and then terms their product ***sex-positive education.***[20] By depicting pornography as educational or artistic, the porn industry attempts to get courts to view pornography as deserving of first-amendment protection, which it currently does not possess.[21]

At present, porn websites make up fully 30% of all internet sites.[22] But increased competition has driven content to more extreme forms of pornography. If you own a porn site that features the same thing as millions of other porn sites, and the number of total porn websites increases daily, what can you do to distinguish your site from the others? One pornographer puts it this way:

> It's become rougher. It's become generally more humiliating. Anyone can open the internet and find anything they want, and when you watch this, you go, ok, what's the next step? You're always curious about going deeper and deeper and deeper.[23]

The rougher, more humiliating forms of pornography began some years ago with ***gonzo porn***, which involves the cameraman getting involved sexually with the other performers while continuing to film from a POV perspective. But as competition continued, the race was on for increased membership subscriptions. This led to even more extreme forms of pornography such as those in the following categories that are commonly found on websites today:[24]

- Rape and sexual assault porn, including time-stop and drunken porn
- Coerced Porn, sometimes found in boss – secretary porn
- Bukkake porn (multiple men, one woman, involving humiliation)
- Cheating porn
- Incest porn
- Hentai – cartoon porn
- Teen porn, sometimes called 'barely legal' porn

These categories that once would have taken some searching to find are now mainstream categories of pornography and are in fact some of the most popular search phrases in porn.[25] It isn't necessarily that more aggressive or violent forms of porn are more popular as it is that popular forms of porn feature hyper-subordinated women or content that is widely considered to be unethical or even illegal as though the taboo nature of the act is what attracts the porn consumer. The women or "barely legal" participants in these categories of porn are presented as being willing to do anything the man or men in the scene instruct them to do, sometimes over the threat of losing or gaining a job, needing a ride, or wanting a good grade on a test.

Yet, supporters of porn usually emphasize the fact that popular porn clips today tend to be less aggressive and violent as though the absence of actual violence exonerates porn from the rippling effects of sexist beliefs and abusive behaviors in the world.[26] But one does not have to view violent forms of pornography to believe that women should be subordinate to men at home and in the workplace. Nonviolent forms of porn reinforce this trope quite well, since some of the most popular forms of porn feature much older men sexually engaging with "a teen" and in fact popular scenes often involve the power imbalance of teacher – student, father – babysitter, father – stepdaughter, or secretary – boss. The bros who consume **power-imbalance porn** are many of the same bros who end up in positions of corporate power. They may express their strong loathing of "violence against women" and profess to care about women's empowerment, but then advance a man to a position of authority over an equally qualified woman due to an entrenched implicit or explicit sexism that was produced over years of consuming the porn-directive that women have an important sexual role, but do not and should not compete with men for positions of power.

Additionally, in the world of porn, the word 'no' does not exist, except as part of 'rape-porn' where women in the scene are raped as part of a fantasy or are actually raped, since audiences cannot often tell whether the woman in the scene is acting or actually being raped.[27] The alleged excitement of such forms of porn is that there is lustful elation in engaging in behaviors considered to be socially taboo, but that explanation is vacuous. These same men would not enjoy, we would hope, viewing child-porn, although it is even more socially taboo and in fact, illegal. So, it cannot boil down to some alleged excitement over doing something *because it is taboo*. There must be more to it.

One hypothesis is that some bros find porn of this nature alluring *because the men in the scenes dominate, subdue, and often force themselves on the women in the scenes*. That is, it could well be that men who resent the growing success of women in a variety of professions, including professions once occupied entirely by men, feel that porn "puts women in their place" and therefore restores what they believe to be a natural gendered order to things. These are men who believe *they do not hate women*, so that in surveys they will check the appropriate boxes in favor of women's rights.[28] Hence, a writer like Justin Lehmiller, who authors a piece for *The Huffington Post* entitled, "Does Pornography Cause Men to Hate Women?" draws the predictable position that viewing porn does not cause men to hate women, but that most men who consume porn hold egalitarian views toward women.[29] Lehmiller writes,

> Specifically, porn watchers reported more positive attitudes toward women holding positions of power, toward women in the workplace and toward abortion.[30]

But what does one expect men to say when asked about their views on women? Who is going to respond, "I hate women, and furthermore, my porn usage made me hate women!" The man who denies a woman advancement in a job she is eminently qualified for, and instead gives it to a man because he believes men are better suited for roles of authority than women, might also claim that he believes in gender equality. On the issue of abortion, many sexist men love the fact that abortion is legal because it gets men off of the hook of culpability in the event of an unwanted pregnancy. How many men, in fact, have paid for abortions? This in no way means that they are gender egalitarians.

The misogyny in power-imbalance porn is palpable, yet popular. Writing about the culture that has produced these toxic forms of pornography, *New York Times* columnist Rachel Moran states of Bukkake porn:

> To gather around a woman and cum on her face as a group [was] originally used in Japan as a form of punishment; it is now performed for kinky pleasure. We need to loudly voice a question and more loudly voice its answer — the question being, *whose pleasure?* Why have we allowed ourselves to be sold the lie that women enjoy a degrading form of torture? The degradation *is* the torture — let us be clear about that. Strangers' semen ejaculated over any of us cannot cause us physical harm. The harm is psychological, emotional, and intentional.[31]

When boys search for porn and imagery of this kind greets them, what may begin as curiosity can continue into a lifetime of habitual porn usage with whatever attitudes and beliefs that may create. But even if boys are turned off by porn that features violence and humiliation, the subordination of women to men in porn is inescapable. Stripped of intimacy and emotional power, porn creates a world of women purely as sexual objects who do exactly as the man in a scene dictates.

Thought Box

Why do you think more extreme forms of porn have become so popular? Many of the men who consume porn of this kind would never want to see their daughters treated as the women in the scene are being treated, yet this consideration does not appear to deter men from viewing and masturbating to porn of this kind. Some bros will actually claim that these forms of porn are funny? What exactly is funny about them? Why specifically is porn that humiliates women or depicts women in subordinate positions to men so popular?

SEXTING

One conspicuous measurement of the effect porn has had on young people is the phenomenon of sexting that has swept American schools. Sexting is defined broadly as the sending or receiving of sexual words, images, or videos via technology.[32] Young people who are already immersed in plenty of pornography view sexting as an extension of their porn usage. Writing for the *NY Times*, University of Indiana professor of psychology Michelle Drouin reports that in her research of 745 U.S. college students, sexting is one of the most popular forms of sexual communication between young people today.[33] For those who report being in a committed romantic relationship, 80% admit to having sent and received sexually explicit text messages and 60% admit to have sent or received sexually explicit pictures or videos.[34] A 2017 study by the Kinsey Institute reports that 74% of American adults engage in sexting of one kind or another.[35] Drouin notes that the attraction to sexting is that it is pornography, but personally customized for you.[36]

One of many problems with those who sext is that when sexual images of underage people are electronically sent between people, the transmission qualifies as child pornography.[37] Under the Prosecutorial Remedies and Other Tools to End the Exploitation of Children Today (PROTECT) Act of 2003, it is illegal to produce, distribute, receive, or possess any obscene visual depiction of a minor engaging in sexually explicit conduct.[38] In other words, much of the sexting between middle school or high school aged youths qualifies as child pornography. Young people, however, have not often been deterred because an action is illegal. Law professor Mary Graw Leary terms teen sexting, "self-produced pornography," much of which qualifies as child porn.[39]

The intersection of sexting and pornography is an obvious one. In fact, some porn websites have hacked and stolen sexted images for content.[40] Notable instances have become newsworthy when the sexting images or words hacked come from celebrities.[41] But, of course, when mainstream news covers a story of celebrity sexting, the coverage itself validates sexting to millions of young people following the story. Dr. Zoe Hilton of the University of Toronto reports that celebrity sexting has created a boom among teenage sexting, adding,

> Obviously children and particularly older children are looking at celebrities and are looking at what the adult population are doing. I think we've got to the point with older teenagers where sexting is a normative behaviour.[42]

But Dr. Hilton also notes that sexting can become exploitative as we have seen with revenge porn, where a breakup leads to a jilted partner sharing private messages and images on the internet, or when an individual attempts to extort money or more images from a person under the threat of exposing his or her sexted images.[43] Online predators have engaged in what is now termed *sextortation* by threatening to publicly expose sexted images if the targeted individual does not pay them a price.[44] In 2008, Jessica Logan, a teenager from

Ohio, took her own life after a nude photograph of her was sent by her former boyfriend to everyone at her high school.[45] Out of this incident, Ohio passed the Jessica Logan Act, which extends anti-bullying laws to include cyber-harassment and electronic-based bullying.[46]

In addition to the concerns raised above, researchers at the University of Texas found that teens who sext are more likely to engage in sexual behaviors.[47] They also found that girls are asked to send an explicit sext (68%) more often than boys (42%).[48] In an article published in *Frontiers in Psychology*, researchers Rosario Del Rey, Monica Ojeda, and others report that sexting affects boys and girls differently.[49] While boys and girls do not appear to be negatively affected short-term, girls were found to experience depression and annoyance long-term.[50] Other studies report that while girls and boys can feel pressured to sext, it is more common for girls to feel pressure by a boyfriend to send sexually charged words and images across electronic text.[51] These findings fit well within the pornified world of bro culture, where sexually themed frat parties place the burden on women to wear sexually revealing clothes, but not the men. The reverse of this, which is utterly consistent with men intruding on women's autonomy, are the penis photos men will send to women, often without consent.

Sexting has become yet another way for bros to conduct their sexual trolling for girls and women, while dictating the rules of the game. Scandals from around the nation have been reported at middle schools and high schools.[52] Bros who work in professional capacities, and particularly those in positions of authority, have been caught in sexting scandals that have ended careers. Former congressman Anthony Weiner was infamously caught in a sexting scandal involving six women, which ultimately ended his marriage and caused him to spend 15 months in prison when it was revealed that one of the women he was sexting was in actuality a 15-year-old girl.[53,54] It can be debated whether those who get caught in such scandals have sexual disorders or addictions, but it has certainly become part of the bro palate to use electronic devices, including cell phones, to extend their reach of porn-influenced behaviors to girls and women who may not want or consent to receiving images of men's penises or other sexually explicit content.

In fact, given the popularity of sexting as part of 21st-century pornography, it cannot be surprising to find that porn apps are now available for cell phones, the most famous of which is Mikandi, which markets animated Hentai porn, allowing anyone of any age to download hardcore content onto their phones.[55,56] Many other companies have now joined the rush to create porn apps for a growing market of porn consumers.[57] This is great for the bro, since he can now take his porn anywhere he goes. One potential downside, however, is that one's porn use can be more easily made public, as smartphones are more vulnerable to being hacked than PCs.[58] Almost one-quarter of all malware on mobile phones comes from porn sites.[59] In addition, showing porn content on your phone to others at work is yet another way that a bro can commit workplace sexual harassment.[60,61] The options for porn-abuse are endless in bro culture, but going forward, we can expect technology to be on the forefront of that abuse.

GENTLEMEN'S CLUBS AS BRO ACADEMIES

Because sex creates vulnerability and requires trust, there have always been interconnections between sex and power. One can see this power imbalance on display at so-called strip clubs or more euphemistically, *gentlemen's clubs*, which are bro sanctums. The typical strip club is based on the capitalistic platitude of supply and demand. Women possess the supply and men possess the demand. A naïve view of this relationship is found in the notion that the sexual exchange between the strippers and the customers is, like that of prostitute and 'john', one of equals who are willingly exchanging capital for commodities. But the truth is more complex.

Clubs market themselves as glamorous venues where beautiful women dance for sophisticated gentlemen. Writing for CSUN's paper, *The Sundial*, Luis Rivas notes of his time as a manager at a strip club:

> The owners gave me simple advice: treat the women like shit; don't show empathy or compassion; it's a weakness and they will eventually take advantage of you.[62]

In most strip clubs, the dancers are independent contractors who must give between 20% and 50% of what they earn each night to the club.[63] Dancers must compete for clients on nights when customers are few. This means, for many dancers, their take-home pay can be as little as $50 per night. Without unions or labor negotiators, the dancers are forced to battle club owners and managers for pay. It is also the case that many dancers perform sexual acts for money in the VIP rooms, which are closed off from the rest of the club, even though these acts are illegal and clubs deny they occur. Sex acts at clubs have been documented in many porn clips and anonymous employee confessions even though strip clubs are famous for having "no-touch" policies.[64]

Another truth about some strip clubs, and porn for that matter, is that there are performers who have been brought into the sex business through sex trafficking. Research has shown that approximately 70% of women who work in strip clubs, massage parlors, and pornography are trafficked into the sex industry.[65] Because sex trafficking is an illegal, shadow industry, numbers can be difficult to document, but Homeland Security recently claims to have 60 active investigations in the Los Angeles area alone.[66] Erotic dancers themselves have discussed the problem of sex trafficking in their industry, claiming to know other dancers who were sex trafficked into the business, but worry that cooperating with authorities might cost them their jobs.[67]

Journalist Susannah Breslin spent ten years reporting on the sex industry and notes that many of the men who frequent strip clubs are lonely and looking for human connection.[68] Notably, however, Breslin also insists that many of the men who patronize clubs feel powerless in their everyday lives, while having women pursue them, albeit for money, makes them feel powerful.[69] If you are a man who was raised in bro culture, you were told from an early age that *you* should be in charge, that *you* are more important than women, that *you should* control relationships. But for those men who feel that they are trapped in a mundane job where their opinions do not matter, coupled with a feeling that they *are not* important, particularly to women, the strip club allows them to escape into a world where they can be bros again, where they can transport themselves into an environment where they have power, where they can feel desired, and where the bro promise of unfettered access to women's bodies is fulfilled.

One final thing to say about the connection between strip clubs and bro culture is that because strippers are routinely denigrated in society as being cheap and valueless, the strip club represents a brick-and-mortar business that reinforces the Freudian "Madonna-whore complex" that instructs bros that there are two kinds of women: the women you can and should respect and the women you can and should disrespect.[70] When men compartmentalize women into categories, the justification for mistreating certain women is built into the definitions. Gentlemen's clubs feature few gentlemen, but many bros who live out the instructions bro culture offers them, which is the lesson that women are here for their sexual enjoyment.

THE GENDERED PORN GAP

With respect to pornography usage, perhaps unsurprisingly, there is a gendered porn gap that finds men consuming pornography at much higher rates than women.[71] Given findings of there being a sexual double standard of who is giving the orders and who is taking the orders in the vast majority of pornography, it is not surprising that men consume porn at much higher rates than women. One of the most notable studies on pornography found that among heterosexual couples, there has been significant conflict about porn usage.[72] Couples therapist Daniel Dashnaw notes that many of his clients suffer from a lack of sexual intimacy, which is not the same as simply having sex.[73] *Sexual intimacy* is the emotional response that follows from sexual activities between partners or what family therapist Lisa Thomas identifies as being open and connected with another person.[74] Dashnaw reports that many couples who come to him for counseling do so at the request of the female partner who believes their male partner's use of pornography has stripped their relationship of affection, intimacy, and emotional power.[75]

Dashnaw argues that porn allows consumers to construct scenarios that best fit their masturbatory desires.[76] For male consumers, this means that they can change partners, scenarios, sets, positions, and particular sex acts at will. Inevitably missing from these choices are any feelings of romance, love, or intimacy. The typical porn clip today runs five to ten minutes in length and involves anywhere from one to three sexual positions, ending in the man or men in the scene achieving orgasm. The most common scene in porn involves oral sex, changed briefly to vaginal or anal sex, with the man finishing by ejaculating on the woman's face or in her mouth.[77]

This formatting of sex to specific sexual scripts allows men to tailor their porn experience, but also creates the ability for men to avoid entirely any emotional connection between themselves and their sexual partners. Since porn-based sex is virtual and anonymous, men can construct a ritual of masturbation that is not dependent on romance, love, intimacy, or emotion. Instead, men appear to value what pornographers refer to as "the money shot," which involves actually seeing the men in the scene releasing their sperm onto the woman.[78] One of the most notorious pornographers in history is John Stagliano, who states of the money shot:

> When you do a cum-shot, you should do it on the most beautiful part of a woman's body. If a girl has a pretty face, cumming on that emphasizes it. The face is the most communicative thing we have.[79]

For Stagliano and other male pornographers, the sexual rush is found in humiliating women, and ejaculating on a woman's face is one of the best ways to accomplish that goal. A person's face is one of the most physically unique things about them, and the women of porn often wear a good deal of makeup to emphasize their faces. Pornographers use this fact to soil the most defining physical feature of women. In this way, the women of porn are interchangeable things not worthy of kissing, but eligible for a facial cum-shot to strip them of their dignity and blur their identities. For many bros, sex is an opportunity to use a woman's body for self-gratification. But connecting the act of ejaculation with humiliation provides many bros with a sense of power. Author and sex advice columnist Dan Savage notes that "facials are degrading, and that's why they're so hot."[80] Others have argued that ejaculating on a woman's face is a desire for validation.[81]

But for those who view porn as validating or as "sex-positive," it is difficult to square with the narratives actually created by pornographers themselves. Writing for the *Huffington Post*, author and professor of sociology, Gail Dines, shares an actual porn scene as described by the pornographers who filmed the scene:

> Big Tits. Check. Airhead. Check. Daddy Issues. Check. Brook Ultra has all the makings of being the next big deal in big tit porn. I can totally see the LA companies gobbling up this cunt, but we had her first. Today, she was trained to be a submissive little whore, taking cocks in all three holes. Pauly Harker blew her asshole out with his giant knob. We shot some great fucking anal gapes with this pig...so much that you could see what she had for dinner last night. Another well rounded scene with a model who's top shelf. Enjoy this...and when you see her all over the place, remember who taught that cunt the ropes.[82]

The celebration of degradation and humiliation in pornography of this kind belies a narrative that much of porn is designed to support sex-positive, pro-validation messaging. Beyond scenes promoting degradation and even torture, the instruction to bros is that women should be viewed with contempt, and used sexually with no regard to their humanity.

THE ORGASM GAP

When boys are raised on pornography, all of the normative messaging embedded in porn comes along for the ride. This messaging includes the notion that women are and should be subordinate to men, that coerced sex is fun and normal, that women always want sex and in fact want the very same kind of sex that men want, and finally, that consent is unspoken and unnecessary. In the majority of porn clips, women serve men, not the other way around. One of the most conspicuous pieces of evidence for this point is *the orgasm gap* in pornography. In research on porn, it was discovered that out of Pornhub's 50-most viewed videos, women appear to reach orgasm 13% of the time as compared with men who appear to reach orgasm 78% of the time.[83,84] Unsurprisingly, this orgasm gap is mirrored in actual life. A study of 833 undergraduate students found that 91% of men, as compared to 39% of women, report always or nearly always achieving orgasm during sex.[85]

One abiding notion that appears to have been debunked is the belief that it is more difficult for women to reach orgasm than men.[86] Sexologist Shere Hite, in her book *The Hite Report: A National Study of Female Sexuality*, found that 95% of women are able to achieve orgasm through masturbation within minutes.[87] Yet when with a male partner, women achieve orgasm in far fewer instances.[88] One study concluded that the orgasm gap is the result of a long-standing sexual double standard in society, which places greater emphasis on men's pleasure than on women's pleasure.[89] Nowhere is this sexual double standard more apparent than in pornography. The normative message being sent to adolescent boys and men of all ages is that their pleasure is more important than the pleasure of their female partners. In fact, the majority of porn-clips end with a man achieving orgasm. There is seldom any "cuddle time" or portrayals of emotional intimacy after the man in the scene reaches orgasm. The messaging of porn is clear: sex is not about emotional intimacy; it is purely about sexual release, and more specifically, men's sexual release.

THE PORNIFICATION OF POP CULTURE

Pornification has been defined as adding sexually explicit or sexually implicit content to materials that were not originally pornographic or sexual in nature, such as placing sexually suggestive content into ads for food or fashion.[90] While pornography exhibits some of the most striking examples of the subordination of women by men, imagery and narratives throughout popular culture do much the same thing. We find illustrations of this in music, film, television, advertising, gaming, and internet content. It really is inescapable. In the case of advertising, women have long been used as body-props to sell product. As we saw in a previous chapter, some companies, like Carl's Jr. – Hardee's, spent over a decade using sexually exploitative images of women to sell fast food. But we also see this kind of treatment of women in fashion and beauty ads. In a Duncan Quinn ad, we find a scantily clad woman who has apparently been murdered. Duncan Quinn is a company that sells men's fashion, making it all the more atrocious that a campaign aimed at men uses a woman as a dead, sexualized body-prop to sell clothing. But as we have seen throughout this book, in the bro world, women are things to be used sexually, while their humanity is ignored. They are valued solely for their looks and sexual appeal. When an ad conflates sexual appeal and violence, the message could not be more irresponsible. It reinforces the notion that women are things that are interchangeable and replaceable, while also normalizing violence against women, which is the number one cause of injury to women in the world.[91]

We see pornified pop culture in many other places as well. In gamer culture, for instance, female avatars are typically depicted featuring hypersexualized bodies and outfits, particularly in games designed for male viewers such as the *Grand Theft Auto* series where male gamers can go to strip clubs, solicit prostitutes, and then physically abuse them after having sex with them. In gamer culture, the male avatars often stereotype men of color as violent criminals, while female avatars are sexual sidekicks. The average age of gamers playing GTA has been estimated to be between 10 and 30 years, the prime ages for shaping boys into men.[92] In one article, a father defends allowing his four-year-old son to play Grand Theft Auto, remarking,

> He [the son] didn't beat any hookers with a baseball bat. He didn't deal drugs. He didn't go on a murderous rampage.[93]

The defense many men compose are of this kind. The claim that they or their sons have not committed rape, murder, or other forms of violence is supposed to stand as a defense for enjoying virtual rape, murder, and mayhem that includes violence against women. The common refrain is that playing games of this kind is to indulge only in fantasy, not reality. Yet, how many of these responsible men would play a *fantasy game* where children are seduced and raped? How many would enjoy the fantasy play of lynching Black people in a game? The answer is, not many, outside of pedophiles in the former case and white supremacists and neo-Nazis in the latter case. If playing a game about pedophilia would entail that you may be a pedophile, or enjoying a game about lynching people of color would entail that you are racist, what does it say of a man who enjoys the fantasy play of raping and murdering women? This father believes he is being a responsible father by allowing his four-year-old son to play a game that features these gaming options *because* his son is not carrying these actions out in actual life. But the question should not be whether a four-year-old has committed rape, but how does a childhood soaked in sexism and misogyny play out throughout a man's life? That a man does not commit rape and murder does not mean that he treats women with respect, dignity, and equal competence.

The bro is a construction that begins in childhood. Video games are today's toys on which many boys are raised. Game makers care about the same thing that all product-makers care about: profit. They could not care less about the welfare of boys, nor about the long-term effects their games may have on the beliefs and attitudes men have about women. Almost all of the meta-analyses on games have focused on whether gaming increases levels of aggression and violence without any concern for the way that boy's attitudes about women are shaped by game-play, particularly when factored beside hundreds of pop cultural influences each day that reinforce the view that women have value primarily in terms of their looks and sexual appeal.

> **Thought Box**
>
> Even though there are an increasing number of women who are part of gamer culture, it is still made up primarily of boys and young men. Why, in your opinion, do men dominate gamer culture? Are there intersections between game play and pornography in the ways that women are depicted and treated?

On the connection between game play and sexist attitudes, a study conducted by Douglas Gentile of Iowa State University notes,

> Many different aspects of life can influence sexist attitudes. It was surprising to find a small but significant link between game play and sexism. Video games are not intended to teach sexist views, but most people don't realize how attitudes can shift with practice. Nonetheless, much of our learning is not conscious and we pick up on subtle cues without realizing it.[94]

Boys and girls adopt beliefs and attitudes daily from a number of sources. Sexist content is strewn throughout society, but games, like music, have become a central part of many boys' formative experiences. The repetition of gaming in an environment that has not been friendly to girls and women is a prime source of training and reinforcement of sexist tropes. Borrowing from the work of famed media scholar George Gerbner, Gentile notes, "If you repeatedly 'practice' various decisions and choices in games, this practice can influence your attitudes and behaviors outside of the gaming world."[95] When we factor in research showing that boys, on average, watch three hours of television and engage in two hours of gaming each day, the repetition of practicing sexist choices adds up.[96]

Finally, as witnessed in the chapter on music, pornified lyrics and videos are rampant in the music of many music artists. Both male and female music stars have taken the path of reflecting the tropes found in porn to create lyrical content and video imagery. For many young men, music is an important part of their lives and can influence the way they talk, dress, think, and behave. From Rock to Rap to Country, male music stars, in particular, peddle an old-fashioned sexist narrative about women that comes right from the reels of pornography. One of the more common music tropes for male music stars is the hackneyed impression that the rock star or rap star is irresistible to women, which is driven home by a countless stream of women at his disposal in videos. This pornified missive might also explain why so many female music stars employ hypersexual lyrics and racy videos. However, an important distinction is often made by fans, critics, and others between cases when female stars use their own sexuality than when male stars exploit women's sexuality. In the first case, naked or scantily clad women are viewed by some to be empowering, while in the second case, naked or scantily clad women are considered to be exploited.[97] Women have long struggled to love their own bodies in a culture that judges women's bodies and polices women's sexual choices. Men, on the other hand, have sexually exploited women for millennia. Still, being empowered can be a difficult thing to measure in a patriarchy that rewards treating women as sex objects.

> **Thought Box**
>
> In your opinion, what is the line that determines whether a scene or song or video is empowering or exploitative? While women have fought for generations to own their sexuality without permission or acceptance from men, we live in a patriarchal culture that continues to assess women's value in terms of looks and sex appeal. Women are routinely represented as one-dimensional characters in film, TV, music, and games, and when women gain executive power in business and politics, it is common for criticism to revolve around their looks instead of their ideas. So, do hypersexual music stars, like porn performers, help to empower women or to reinforce the patriarchal notion that women have value mainly as decorative props for the male gaze?

FETISHIZING LESBIANS

According to Pornhub's "year in review" data, there were almost 34 billion visits to Pornhub in 2018 and just under 5 million visits to Pornhub each day.[98] The average viewer of pornography spends 10 minutes, 33 seconds viewing clips, about the time it takes for men to masturbate to orgasm.[99] The form of porn viewed most, according to Pornhub, is lesbian porn, but not because lesbians view porn more than any other group.[100] The majority of porn featuring women-on-women sex is constructed for male viewers. The women in "lesbian porn" may not be lesbians at all, but are positioned, dressed, and made up to appeal to heterosexual men, who have been trained to view lesbianism as sexually arousing, while these same men have been socialized to view gay-male sex as not simply disinteresting, but actually disgusting.[101] In a study chaired by Karen Blair of St. Francis Xavier University, physiological reactions in heterosexual men were basically the same when watching two men display physical affection for one another as when viewing images of maggots.[102] These reactions were measured through levels of salivary alpha-amylase, a digestive enzyme that is associated with stress and is especially responsive to disgust.[103]

But the attraction to lesbians by heterosexual men is a pornified phenomenon reinforced by decades of media that suggest men might be able to join in. The sex offered in much of lesbian porn is wildly unrealistic and presented as fantasy to the male viewer. Writing for *Everyday Feminism*, Melissa A. Fabello notes that actual lesbians are lesbians for one another, not for dudes.[104] Yet in the world of pornography, it is not unusual for a scene to initially involve two women having sex with one another, while ultimately the two women work together to get a man to reach orgasm. The *lesbians*, therefore, serve as prefatory stimulation for what will ultimately be the service of a man. This particular narrative reinforces what USC gender scholar Jack Halberstam has been saying for some time, that media lesbians are constructions for the male gaze.[105] An illustration of this can be seen in mainstream Hollywood movies like *Chasing Amy* starring Ben Affleck and Joey Lauren Adams.[106] In the film, Holden (Affleck) pursues Alyssa (Adams) even though Alyssa maintains that she is a lesbian. They eventually have a brief sexual and romantic affair, which Halberstam notes is a typical script-development in the way Hollywood treats lesbians. One character in the film, in fact, states to Holden, "she just hasn't found the right guy yet."[107]

Homophobia is mainly, but not exclusively, a men's thing. For the bro, homophobia is simply part of bro culture. For many bros, boyhood was a time when using the term 'gay' was routinely used as a synonym for 'stupid' or 'weak' or 'feminine'. The point, of course, was to compare being gay to being unacceptable in some way, even though boys who use the word usually deny that they intend their judgment to apply to gay men. By the time most boys reach young adulthood, the word 'gay' and the negative connotations associated with it have been etched into their brains. In C.J. Pascoe's arresting book *Dude, You're a Fag: Masculinity and Sexuality in High School*, Pascoe heard it put from one boy this way,

> To call someone gay or fag is like the lowest thing you can call someone. Because that's like saying that you're nothing.[108]

The roots of homophobia in bro culture extend far beyond porn, of course, but porn reinforces a false narrative to boys and men about lesbians, which is that lesbians are sexually interested in men. The fetishizing of lesbianism in porn conditions men to once again view women in strictly utilitarian ways. It can also set up homophobic anger and violence if men believe that lesbians secretly want heterosexual sex, but are turned down in real life by actual lesbians.

PORN AND RACISM

An under-examined area of pornography is the level of racism found in many porn features. With titles such as *Black Bitches, Blacks on Blondes, Geisha's Girls,* and *Gang Banged by Blacks*, even some within the porn industry have been calling out the explicit racism.[109] Attorney Dan Gilleon, who represents a porn performer in a lawsuit against a pornography production company, states:

> Racism seems to flourish in the [adult] industry because a large segment of society doesn't care, and that's where these abuses stem from.[110]

When you amalgamate apathy from consumers and industry insiders with the uptick in hate speech and hate crimes in the Trump era,[111] then recognize the longstanding history of racism in America, it cannot be surprising that racism has become an explicit feature of pornography.

The denigration and stereotyping of people of color found in porn is part of what boys experience when traversing the porn universe. Black men are typecast as oversexed beasts who crave white women, a stereotype that draws upon the film *Birth of a Nation*, which was used as a recruitment tool by the Ku Klux Klan.[112] Latinas and Black women, who reportedly earn half to two-thirds what white women earn in the industry,[113] are routinely cast as "ghetto whores" or hypersexual hotel maids.[114] This is all the more dangerous when we recognize that hotel housekeepers are routinely at risk for sexual harassment and sexual assault.[115] Asian women are normalized as sexually subservient seducers who *enjoy* being submissive to men.[116]

Rather than being sexually liberating, as advertised by the porn industry, pornographers package and market racist stereotypes in a world replete with racism, discrimination, and ongoing bigotry-fueled mistreatment. Racist porn titles also have the effect of minimizing and undermining important social movements such as *Black Lives Matter*. One porn film, for instance, is titled *Black Wives Matter*, while another film parodied Eric Garner, the Black man killed on camera by New York police officers, sparking outrage and protests across the nation.[117] No social movement or tragedy is immune from the tentacles of porn, which view these moments as opportunities to make a joke at the expense of others, while profiting from the exploitation. At a time when Sigma Alpha Epsilon bros in Oklahoma were captured on video shouting, "There will never be a nigger at SAE,"[118] much of the porn industry remains entrenched in the past, promoting some of the most disgusting and dangerous racist stereotypes imaginable.

WHEN SEX EDUCATION IS POLITICIZED AS PORN

To end this chapter, it is important to note how pornography is sometimes used as a scare tactic by those on the political right in conversations about sex education in public schools. One unfortunate consequence of the polarizing politics in contemporary America is that sound sex education programs, which have empirical results in preventing teen pregnancy and lowering STD rates, are termed *pornographic* in an attempt to eliminate these programs from public schools. The results are predictable.

Consider the organization *Stop Comprehensive Sexuality Education*, a division of *Family Watch International*, which claims to have the goal of preserving children's purity and innocence, while terming comprehensive sex education a "war on children."[119] This organization compares comprehensive sex education [CSE] to pornography by claiming that CSE "normalizes anal and oral sex, promotes homosexual and bisexual behavior, teaches children sexual pleasure, promotes solo or mutual masturbation, eroticizes condom use, promotes gender confusion, violates parental rights, and undermines traditional values," among other alleged wrongs.[120]

According to *The American College of Obstetricians and Gynecologists*, which examined the efficacy of sex education programs using empirical studies, comprehensive sex education has been shown to "reduce sexual activity including sexual risk behaviors, STDs, and teen pregnancy."[121] In addition, despite the fact that politically conservative organizations continue to portray comprehensive sex education as being opposed to abstinence education, comprehensive sex education promotes abstinence as the best way to avoid pregnancy and STDs.[122] But CSE also provides the important information young people need to protect themselves if they choose to engage in sexual behaviors. According to studies, 42% of high-school age girls and 44% of high school age boys have had sex.[123] In surveys of teenagers, 80% of teens who engage in sex report using condoms with a whopping 99% of girls claiming to use some form of contraception when having sex.[124] These numbers seem to be borne out by drops in the rate of teen pregnancies, which are at a 40-year low.[125]

By comparison, abstinence-only programs, which are now termed "sexual risk avoidance programs," have been shown to be ineffective.[126] The Centers for Disease Control found that by contrast, comprehensive sex education reduces the age of first sexual contact, reduces the number of sexual partners, reduces the frequency of unprotected sexual contact, and reduces both STDs and teen pregnancy.[127] Even a casual glance at pornography shows that nothing in pornography educates young people about protecting themselves against any of these dangers. In pornography, condoms are not used, there are no conversations about the dangers of unprotected sex, there are routinely multiple partners, and major outbreaks of STDs including HIV have occurred within the porn community.[128,129] The conservative right uses comparisons between comprehensive sex education and pornography as a scare tactic designed to undermine empirical results in order to promote what they believe to be a Bible-friendly version of sex education. This amounts to telling kids not to have sex, scaring them with horror stories of what can happen to them if they do engage in sex, selling them a heteronormative version of "normal sex," which contributes to the continued discrimination and mistreatment of LGBTQ youths, and then employing blind faith that kids will simply obey the commands and repress one of the most powerful instincts that flow from the amygdala, hippocampus, and limbic system of the brain.

But are abstinence-only programs effective in reducing the number of underage teens who engage in sex or in reducing teen pregnancy? In published studies, students who participate in abstinence-only programs are just as likely to engage in sex as those who participate in comprehensive sex education programs.[130] When looking at students in a side-by-side comparison of sex education programs, those who participate in abstinence only programs are positively correlated to higher rates of teen pregnancy and birth.[131] Furthermore, those teens who take a "virginity pledge" are less likely to use condoms when they engage in sex, which leads to higher rates of HPV.[132] A study undertaken as part of the National Longitudinal Study of Adolescent Health, reports:

> About 18 percent of the girls who had never taken virginity pledges became pregnant within six years after they began having sex. Meanwhile, 30 percent of those who had taken a pledge—and broken it—got pregnant while not married.[133]

Because boys and girls who take virginity pledges rarely participate in comprehensive sex education programs, they are not informed on methods to protect themselves from pregnancy and STDs, unless someone in their family or friend group discusses these issues with them. At the same time, those who take virginity pledges also suffer from recurring problems with sex later in life. As researchers at the University of Washington noted, "men who take virginity pledges may struggle with long-lasting issues with sex, even after they're married," while other studies have reported similar findings in follow-ups with women.[134]

Yet, $90 million in tax funds are spent annually on abstinence-only sex education programs.[135] Abstinence-only programs are heteronormative, marriage-only programs that are unrealistic and leave young people uninformed on how to protect themselves from the dangers that can follow from unprotected sex. In addition, abstinence-only programs promote traditional male-female binary roles of aggression-passivity that contribute to a cycle of men's violence against women.[136] If all this were not enough, as mentioned earlier, the *National Institute of Health* has shown that the implementation of abstinence-only sex education programs is positively correlated to higher rates of teen pregnancy.[137] Abstinence-only sex education simply does not work! The comparison of comprehensive sex education to pornography is a wildly inaccurate analogy that spreads fear and panic in a field that requires calm, accurate information.

POSTSCRIPT

Pornography has, for the most part, won the public relations war against the anti-pornography movement by convincing a majority of young people that porn is fun, educational, and liberating. But pornography is also a central feature of bro culture, a culture that celebrates the sexual subordination of women. In the age of #metoo, bros can retreat into the realm of pornography where it is still 1988 and women are treated as commodities found backstage at a Mötley Crüe concert. Even in porn clips that do not feature violence or humiliation, women follow orders and do what is expected of them, which is to sexually satisfy the man or men in the scene, and this is the point. Bros view women as sexual commodities more than as human beings, which is why bros support pornography and sexually themed college parties where women dress in provocative lingerie for the sexual pleasure of men. There are, of course, bros on the margins of bro culture who are bystanders and hangers-on, but the core of bro culture revolves around the idea that women are sexual opportunities, and like the narratives found in the vast majority of pornography, that women are and more importantly *should be* subordinate to men.

Notes

1. Margaret Hartmann "Frat Email Explains Women Are 'Targets,' Not Actual People," *Jezebel*, March 8, 2011. https://jezebel.com/frat-email-explains-women-are-targets-not-actual-pe-5779905
2. Ibid.
3. Ibid.
4. Alyson Schafer, "Kids Watching Porn: It's Happening Much Earlier than You Think," *The Huffington Post, Canada*, October 28, 2016.
5. Jane Randel, Amy Sanchez, "Parenting in the Digital Age of Pornography," *The Huffington Post*, February 26, 2017. https://www.huffingtonpost.com/jane-randel/parenting-in-the-digital-age-of-pornography_b_9301802.html
6. Harvard University, "In Brief: The Science of Early Childhood Development," *Center of the Developing Child*, 2017. https://developingchild.harvard.edu/resources/inbrief-science-of-ecd/
7. Alexandra Katehakis, "Effects of Porn on Adolescent Boys," *Psychology Today*, July 28, 2011. https://www.psychologytoday.com/us/blog/sex-lies-trauma/201107/effects-porn-adolescent-boys
8. Ibid.
9. Laura Mansnerus, "Hugh Hefner, Who Built the Playboy Empire and Embodied It, Dies at 91," *The New York Times*, September 27, 2017. https://www.nytimes.com/2017/09/27/obituaries/hugh-hefner-dead.html
10. Ibid.
11. Matthew Rettenmund, "A Penis on Every Page: The Rise and Fall of Playgirl," *Esquire*, June 24, 2017. https://www.esquire.com/entertainment/a55592/playgirl-magazine-history/
12. Sady Doyle, "Exactly What Kind of Sexual Revolution Did Hugh Hefner Inspire?" *Elle*, September 29, 2017. https://www.elle.com/culture/a12638096/exactly-what-kind-of-sexual-revolution-did-hugh-hefner-inspire/
13. Amy Odell, "Holly Madison Reveals What It Was Really Like To Be with – and Sleep with – Hugh Hefner," *Cosmopolitan*, June 22, 2015.
14. Ibid.
15. Ibid.
16. Amy Odell, "The 14 Worst Things about Hugh Hefner, as Revealed in Holly Madison's New Book," *Cosmopolitan*, June 22, 2015. https://www.cosmopolitan.com/entertainment/books/news/a42332/holly-madison-book-worst-things-about-hugh-hefner/

17. Robert H. Burger, "The Meese Report on Pornography and Its Respondents: A Review Article," *The Library Quarterly: Information, Community, Policy, The University of Chicago Press*, Vol. 57, No. 4, October, 1987, pp. 436–447.
18. Jane Randel, Amy Sanchez, "Parenting in the Digital Age of Pornography," *The Huffington Post*, February 26, 2017. https://www.huffingtonpost.com/jane-randel/parenting-in-the-digital-age-of-pornography_b_9301802.html
19. Ron Sokol, "Are Porn Actors Now Required to Wear Condoms?" *Daily Breeze*, February 13, 2018. https://www.dailybreeze.com/2018/02/13/ask-the-lawyer-are-porn-actors-now-required-to-wear-condoms/
20. Jamie Duncan, "5 Sex-Positive, Female Friendly Porn Sites," *Ecosalon*, May 3, 2017. http://ecosalon.com/5-sex-positive-female-friendly-porn-sites-nsfw/
21. Alison Frankel, "Why Violence, But Not Sex, Is Protected by the 1st Amendment," *Reuters*, July 23, 2012. http://blogs.reuters.com/alison-frankel/2012/07/23/why-violence-but-not-sex-is-protected-by-the-first-amendment/
22. Michael Castleman, "Dueling Statistics: How Much of the Internet Is Porn?" *Psychology Today*, November 3, 2016. https://www.psychologytoday.com/us/blog/all-about-sex/201611/dueling-statistics-how-much-the-internet-is-porn
23. Marlow Stern, "Why Porn Has Gotten So Rough," *Daily Beast*, August 4, 2019. https://www.thedailybeast.com/why-porn-has-gotten-so-rough
24. Ibid.
25. Eran Shor, Kimberly Seida, "Harder and Harder? Is Mainstream Pornography Becoming Increasingly Violent and Do Viewers Prefer Violent Content?" *The Journal of Sex Research*, April 18, 2018. https://www.mcgill.ca/sociology/files/sociology/2018_-_journal_of_sex_research.pdf
26. Ibid.
27. "5 Porn Fantasies That Are Popular Online But Disturbing in Reality," *Fight The New Drug*, August 8, 2019. https://fightthenewdrug.org/5-popular-porn-categories-that-are-considered-sexy-online-but-are-disturbing-in-reality/
28. Justin Lehmiller, "Does Pornography Cause Men to Hate Women?" *Huff Post*, December 6, 2017.
29. Ibid.
30. Ibid.
31. Rachel Moran, "We Cannot Reject the Toxic Culture Pornography Has Created Without Rejecting Pornography Itself," *Feminist Current* December 12, 2017. https://www.feministcurrent.com/2017/12/12/women-obligation-speak-pornography/
32. Caroline Colvin, "The Psychology behind Sexting Reveals Exactly Why It's So Addicting," *Elite Daily*, April 16, 2019. https://www.elitedaily.com/p/the-psychology-behind-sexting-reveals-exactly-why-its-so-addicting-17025806
33. Michelle Drouin, "Sexting Is More Common than You Think," *The New York Times*, June 9, 2011. https://www.nytimes.com/roomfordebate/2011/06/09/whats-wrong-with-adult-sexting/sexting-is-more-common-than-you-think
34. Ibid.
35. Survey Results, "Technology and Sexuality: Results from Clue and Kinsey's International Sex Survey," *Hello Clue*, August 8, 2017. https://helloclue.com/articles/sex/technology-modern-sexuality-results-from-clue-kinseys-international-sex-survey
36. Caroline Colvin, "The Psychology behind Sexting Reveals Exactly Why It's so Addicting," *Elite Daily*, April 16, 2019. https://www.elitedaily.com/p/the-psychology-behind-sexting-reveals-exactly-why-its-so-addicting-17025806

37. Mark Theoharis, "Teen Sexting," *Criminal Defense Lawyer*. https://www.criminaldefenselawyer.com/crime-penalties/juvenile/sexting.htm
38. Ibid.
39. Mary Graw Leary, "Sexting or Self-Produced Child Pornography – The Dialogue Continues – Structures Prosecutorial Discretion within a Multidisciplinary Response," *The Catholic University of America, CUA Law Scholarship Repository*, 2010. https://scholarship.law.edu/cgi/viewcontent.cgi?article=1234&context=scholar
40. Romona McNeal, Susan Kunkle, Mary Schmeida, *Cyber Harassment and Policy Reform in the Digital Age: Emerging Research and Opportunities*. IGI Global, Hershey, Pennsylvania, 2018.
41. Evann Gastaldo, "44 Celebrity Sexting Scandals," *Newser*, July 27, 2013. https://www.newser.com/story/171561/44-celebrity-sexting-scandals.html
42. Amanda Williams, "Celebrities Causing Boom in Sexting Among Teenagers: Child Protection Chief Says Young Are Attempting to Imitate Adults and Famous People," *Daily Mail*, November 20, 2014. https://www.dailymail.co.uk/news/article-2841976/Celebrities-causing-boom-sexting-teenagers-Child-protection-chief-says-young-attempting-imitate-adults-famous-people.html
43. Ibid.
44. Linda Childers, "The Rising Threat of Sextortion – And What To Do If It Happens To You," *Allure*, October 16, 2017. https://www.allure.com/story/online-predators-blackmail-sextortion-victims-explicit-images
45. Kashmir Hill, "After Teen 'Sexting' Suicide, Parents Sue, Well, Everybody," *Forbes*, December 7, 2009. https://www.forbes.com/sites/kashmirhill/2009/12/07/after-teen-sexting-suicide-parents-sue-well-everybody/
46. Jennifer Stump, "The Jessica Logan Act," *Ohio Legislative Service Commission Final Analysis*, May 4, 2012. https://www.lsc.ohio.gov/documents/gaDocuments/analyses129/12-hb116-129.pdf
47. Raychelle Cassada, "Teen Sexting – The Real Issue," *Psychology Today*, April 7, 2013. https://www.psychologytoday.com/us/blog/teen-angst/201304/teen-sexting-the-real-issue
48. Ibid.
49. Rosario Del Rey, Monica Ojeda, Jose Casas, Joaquin Mora-Merchan, Paz Elipe, "Sexting Among Adolescents: The Emotional Impact and Influence of the Need for Popularity," *Frontiers in Psychology*, Vol. 10, August, 2019. doi: 10.3389/fpsyg.2019.01828
50. Ibid.
51. Nancy Bazilchuk, "Girls Experience Sexting More Negatively Than Boys," *Science Nordic*, July 30, 2018. https://sciencenordic.com/children-and-teenagers-communication-forskningno/girls-experience-sexting-more-negatively-than-boys/1457490
52. Kelly McLaughlin, "Nearly 50 Student Were Caught in a Sexting Scandal at a Georgia High School," *Business Insider*, March 15, 2019. https://www.businessinsider.com/union-county-high-school-sexting-scandal-2019-3
53. Susan Donaldson James, "Anthony Weiner: Frat Boy Behavior or Deeper Problems?" *ABC News*, June 7, 2011. https://abcnews.go.com/Health/anthony-weiner-showed-poor-impulse-control-potential-sign/story?id=13783977
54. Matthew S. Schwartz, "Ex-Congressman Anthony Weiner Finishes Prison Term," *NPR*, February 18, 2019. https://www.npr.org/2019/02/18/695640275/ex-congressman-anthony-weiner-finishes-prison-term

55. Cade Metz, "The Porn Business Isn't Anything Like You Think It Is," *Wired*, October 15, 2015. https://www.wired.com/2015/10/the-porn-business-isnt-anything-like-you-think-it-is/
56. Cosmo Frank, "Why Do Millennials Love Cartoon Porn So Much"? *Cosmopolitan*, July 13, 2015.
57. Joe Hindy, "10 Best Adult Apps and Porn Apps for Android!" *Android Authority*, March 21, 2020. https://www.androidauthority.com/best-porn-apps-for-android-686789/
58. Margi Murphy, "Your Cellphone Porn Habit Isn't As Secret As You Think," *New York Post*, September 7, 2017. https://nypost.com/2017/09/07/your-cell-phone-porn-habit-isnt-as-secret-as-you-think/
59. Zeynep Yenisey, "Here's Why You Should Never Watch Porn on Your Phone," *Maxim*, November 1, 2017. https://www.maxim.com/maxim-man/why-you-shouldnt-watch-porn-on-your-phone-2017-10
60. Ibid.
61. Stav Ziv, "Here's What You Can Do If You're Sexually Harassed at Work," *The Muse*. https://www.themuse.com/advice/how-to-deal-with-sexual-harassment-at-work
62. Luis Rivas, "Confessions of a Former Strip Club Manager," *The Sundial*, April 28, 2013. https://sundial.csun.edu/2013/04/confessions-of-a-former-strip-club-manager/
63. Ibid.
64. Brian Gates, "13 Dancers and Employees Explain Just How Dirty Strip Clubs Are," *Thought Catalog*, March 2, 2015. https://thoughtcatalog.com/brian-n-gates/2015/03/13-dancers-and-employees-explain-just-how-dirty-strip-clubs-are/
65. Stephanie Sandoval, "The Connection between Adult Entertainment and Sex Trafficking," *Two Wings*, March 27, 2017. https://withtwowings.org/adult-entertainment-sex-trafficking/
66. Los Angeles Daily News, "How Strip Clubs Are Helping to Fight Sex Trafficking," *Huff Post*, December 6, 2017. https://www.huffingtonpost.com/2014/01/16/strip-clubs-sex-trafficking_n_4609906.html
67. Ibid.
68. Nisha Lilia Diu, "Why Men Really Go To Strip Clubs," *The Telegraph*, April 8, 2012. https://www.telegraph.co.uk/journalists/nisha-lilia-diu/9181569/Why-Men-Really-Go-to-Strip-Clubs.html
69. Ibid.
70. Meera Jagnnathan, "Men Who Buy Into The 'Madonna-Whore Dichotomy' Have Less Satisfying Relationships," *Market Watch*, February 5, 2018.
71. Jason S. Carroll, Dean M. Busby, Brian J. Willoughby, Cameron C. Brown, "The Porn Gap: Women's Pornography Patterns in Couple Relationships," *Journal of Couple & Relationship Therapy*, Vol. 16, Issue 2, pp. 146-163, November 14, 2016. https://www.tandfonline.com/doi/abs/10.1080/15332691.2016.1238796?journalCode=wcrt20
72. Ibid.
73. Daniel Dashnaw, "Pornography and Marital Conflict," *Couples Therapy, Inc.*, February 10, 2017. https://couplestherapyinc.com/porn-and-marital-conflict/
74. Lisa Thomas, "Why Intimate Sex Is the Key to a Successful Relationship," *Psychology Today*, August 10, 2016.
75. Daniel Dashnaw, "Pornography and Marital Conflict," *Couples Therapy, Inc.*, February 10, 2017. https://couplestherapyinc.com/porn-and-marital-conflict/

76. Ibid.
77. Mark Hay, "The Oral History of the Money Shot," *Vice*, December 11, 2016. https://www.vice.com/en_us/article/qkbwd5/an-oral-history-of-the-moneyshot
78. Ibid.
79. Ibid.
80. Hugo Schwyzer, "He Wants to Jizz on Your Face, But Not Why You Think," *Jezebel*, January 11, 2012. https://jezebel.com/he-wants-to-jizz-on-your-face-but-not-why-you-think-5875217
81. Ibid.
82. Gail Dines, "UCSB, Feminism and Porn," *HuffPost*, February 8, 2014. https://www.huffingtonpost.co.uk/gail-dines/porn-industry-and-misogyny_b_5427951.html?guccounter=1&guce_referrer=aHR0cHM6Ly93d3cuZ29vZ2xlLmNvbS8 &guce_referrer_sig=AQAAABtM5VW1uPSCAbf5qeSikXe_CPgU2bgjIQWUf 5M083awtgJ8aqoDWikuytteiX-pAESVI8KkgSaVO3wA8BhLrks3eK_L54a O2KDyZh2QPTXtQL3YG6oJSVsn1y7cwJU1MIvr58kWfigrdSA7v56BxUCj TUYF28K48wDktoX9Owb9
83. Ellen Scott, "Women Are Less Likely than Men to be Shown Reaching Orgasm in Porn," *Metro*, June 27, 2017. https://metro.co.uk/2017/06/27/women-are-less-likely-than-men-to-be-shown-reaching-orgasm-in-porn-6737749/
84. Launched in 2007, Pornhub is one of the largest pornographic video sharing sites on the internet.
85. L.D. Wade, E.C. Kermer. J. Brown, "The Incidental Orgasm: The Presence of Clitoral Knowledge and the Absence of Orgasm for Women," *Women Health*, Vol. 42, Issue 1, 2005, pp. 117–138. https://www.ncbi.nlm.nih.gov/pubmed/16418125
86. Laurie Mintz, "Orgasm Gap: Picking Up Where the Sex Revolution Left Off," *Psychology Today*, May 20, 2018. https://www.psychologytoday.com/us/blog/stress-and-sex/201805/orgasm-gap-picking-where-the-sex-revolution-left
87. Shere Hite, *The Hite Report: A National Study of Female Sexuality*, Seven Stories Press, New York, 1976, Reprinted November, 2003.
88. Laurie Mintz, "Orgasm Gap: Picking Up Where the Sex Revolution Left Off," *Psychology Today*, May 20, 2018. https://www.psychologytoday.com/us/blog/stress-and-sex/201805/orgasm-gap-picking-where-the-sex-revolution-left
89. Barbara J. Risman, Elizabeth Seale, "Betwixt and Be Tween: Gender Contradictions among Middle Schoolers," *Families as they Really Are*, W.W. Norton, January 2009. https://sites.lsa.umich.edu/elizabetharmstrong/wp-content/uploads/sites/218/2015/01/Armstrong-England-Fogarty-Norton-Volume.pdf
90. Pamela Paul, *Pornified: How Pornography Is Transforming Our Lives, Our Relationships, and Our Families*, Times Books, New York, April 2007.
91. The College of Family Physicians of Canada, "Domestic Violence Is the Leading Cause of Injury to Women Aged 15–44," *Canadian Family Physician*, October 1999, pp. 2317–2322. https://www.ncbi.nlm.nih.gov/pmc/articles/PMC2328613/
92. Alfred Hermida, "Parents Ignore Game Age Ratings," *BBC News*, June 24, 2005. http://news.bbc.co.uk/2/hi/technology/4118270.stm
93. Matthew Orona, "My 4-Year-Old Son Plays Grand Theft Auto," *Venture Beat*, June 5, 2010. https://venturebeat.com/community/2010/06/05/my-four-year-old-son-plays-grand-theft-auto/
94. Iowa State University, "Video Games Influence Sexist Attitudes," *Science Daily*, March 28, 2017. https://www.sciencedaily.com/releases/2017/03/170328105908.htm
95. Ibid.

96. Ibid.
97. Meredith Levande, "Women, Pop Music, and Pornography," *Duke University Press*, Vol. 8, Issue 1, 2007, pp. 292–321.
98. Sarah Rense, "The Human Race Really Outdid Itself with Porn Searches in 2018," *Esquire*, December 12, 2018. https://www.esquire.com/lifestyle/sex/news/a52061/most-popular-porn-searches/
99. Gavin Evans, "Pornhub Reveals Most Popular Search Term for Every State," *Complex*, January 17, 2018. https://www.complex.com/pop-culture/2018/01/most-popular-pornhub-search-term-every-state
100. Men's Health Staff, "Pornhub Reveals the 10 Most Popular Porn Categories of the Last 10 Years," *Men's Health*, September 11, 2019. https://www.menshealth.com.au/most-viewed-porn-categories-last-10-years
101. Eric W. Dolan, "Straight Men's Physiological Stress Response to Seeing Two Men Kissing Is the Same as Seeing Maggots," *PsyPost*, June 29, 2017. https://www.psypost.org/2017/06/straight-mens-physiological-stress-response-seeing-two-men-kissing-seeing-maggots-49217
102. Breanna Maureen O'Handley, Karen L. Blair, Rhea Ashley Hoskins, "What Do Two Men Kissing and a Bucket of Maggots Have in Common? Heterosexual Men's Indistinguishable Salivary Alpha-amylase Responses to Photos of Two Men Kissing and Disgusting Images," *Journal of Psychology & Sexuality*, Vol. 8, Issue 3, pp. 173–188, May 2017. https://www.tandfonline.com/doi/abs/10.1080/19419899.2017.1328459
103. Ibid.
104. Melissa A. Fabello, "Fantasy vs. Reality: Lesbian Sex in Pornography," *Everyday Feminism*, February 21, 2013. https://everydayfeminism.com/2013/02/fantasy-vs-reality-lesbian-sex-in-pornography/
105. Judith Kegan Gardiner, *Masculinity Studies and Feminist Theory*, Columbia University Press, New York, 2002.
106. Amaris Alexandra Andrade, "Chasing Amy: Slut Shaming, Homophobia, and Bisexual Erasure," *Penn State University*, Queer Representations, August 9, 2016. https://sites.psu.edu/queerrepresentation/2016/08/09/chasing-amy-slut-shaming-homophobia-and-bisexual-erasure/
107. Ibid.
108. C.J. Pascoe, *Dude, You're a Fag: Masculinity and Sexuality in High School.* University of California Press, 2011.
109. Aurora Snow, "The Rise of Racist Porn," *Daily Beast*, June 23, 2018. https://www.thedailybeast.com/the-rise-of-racist-porn
110. Ibid.
111. John Eligon, "Hate Crimes Increase for the Third Consecutive Year, F.B.I. Reports," *The New York Times*, November 13, 2018. https://www.nytimes.com/2018/11/13/us/hate-crimes-fbi-2017.html
112. Alexis Clark, "How 'The Birth of a Nation' Revived the Ku Klux Klan," *History*, July 29, 2019. https://www.history.com/news/kkk-birth-of-a-nation-film
113. Tracy Clark-Flory, "Pornography Has a Big Race Problem," *Business Insider*, September 1, 2015. https://www.businessinsider.com/pornography-has-a-big-race-problem-2015-9
114. G. Lynsey, "Does Mainstream Porn Have a Race Problem?" *Glamour*, July 13, 2017. https://www.glamour.com/story/mainstream-porn-and-race
115. Robin Urevich, "Hotel Housekeepers Call for Panic Buttons amid Sexual Harassment," *The Guardian*, August 3, 2018. https://www.theguardian.

com/us-news/2018/aug/03/california-hotels-housekeepers-panic-buttons-sexual-harassment
116. Amy Sun, "Mainstream Porn Has Taught You a Lot about Asian Female Sexuality – But It's All a Direct Result of Racism," *Everyday Feminism*, April 13, 2015. https://everydayfeminism.com/2015/04/porn-asian-woman-sexuality/
117. Chauntelle Tibbals, "There's a Serious Tacism Problem in the Porn Industry," *MIC*, February 19, 2016. https://mic.com/articles/135555/there-s-a-serious-racism-problem-in-the-porn-industry#.ehx1v9CyQ
118. Tyler Kingkade, "Oklahoma Frat Boys Caught Singing 'There Will Never Be a N***** In SAE,'" *Huff Post*, March 8, 2015.
119. Family Watch International, "The War on Children," https://www.comprehensivesexualityeducation.org/
120. Family Watch International, "Comprehensive Sex Education: The Harmful Effects on Children," Online Handout. https://www.comprehensivesexualityeducation.org/wp-content/uploads/Harmful-Effects-10.17.17.pdf
121. USC Nursing, "America's Sex Education: How We Are Failing Our Students," *USC Department of Nursing*, September 18, 2017.
122. Planned Parenthood, "Why Support Comprehensive Sexuality Education?" *Planned Parenthood, Arizona*. https://www.plannedparenthood.org/files/6914/0080/0572/2013-04UpdatedWhyCompeSexEd_handout.pdf
123. Sara G. Miller, "How Many Teens Are Really Having Sex These Days?" *Live Science*, June 22, 2017. https://www.livescience.com/59573-teen-sexual-activity-report.html
124. Ibid.
125. Planned Parenthood, "Reducing Teen Pregnancy," *Planned Parenthood Federation of America*. https://www.plannedparenthood.org/uploads/filer_public/94/d7/94d748c6-5be0-4765-9d38-b1b90d16a254/reducing_teen_pregnancy.pdf
126. Sarah McCammon, "Abstinence-Only Education Is Ineffective and Unethical," *NPR*, August 23, 2017. https://www.npr.org/sections/health-shots/2017/08/23/545289168/abstinence-education-is-ineffective-and-unethical-report-argues
127. John Santelli, "Abstinence-Only Education Doesn't Work. We're Still Funding It," *The Washington Post*, August 21, 2017. https://www.washingtonpost.com/news/posteverything/wp/2017/08/21/abstinence-only-education-doesnt-work-were-still-funding-it/?utm_term=.2eebdf9b3f58
128. Dennis Romero, "HIV Is Officially a Bedfellow in Porn," *LA Weekly*, February 12, 2016. https://www.laweekly.com/news/hiv-is-officially-a-bedfellow-in-porn-6591475
129. Shaya Tayefe Mohajer, "Syphilis Outbreak in Porn Industry Prompts Calls for Shutdown," *NBC News*, August 21, 2012. https://www.nbcnews.com/health/health-news/syphilis-outbreak-porn-industry-prompts-calls-shutdown-flna1B5494279
130. Patrick Malone, Monica Rodriquez, "Comprehensive Sex Education vs. Abstinence-Only-Until Marriage Programs," *The American Bar Association*, Spring 2011. https://www.americanbar.org/groups/crsj/publications/human_rights_magazine_home/human_rights_vol38_2011/human_rights_spring2011/comprehensive_sex_education_vs_abstinence_only_until_marriage_programs/
131. Kathrin F. Stanger-Hall, David W. Hall, "Abstinence-Only Education and Teen Pregnancy Rates: Why We Need Comprehensive Sex Education in the U.S.," *PLos ONE*, Vol. 6, 2011. https://www.semanticscholar.org/paper/

Abstinence-Only-Education-and-Teen-Pregnancy-Rates%3A-Stanger-Hall-Hall/0c0b60e3d74a6aa4f71292de361bf13d8e52d765

132. Loga Khazan, "The Unintended Consequences of Purity Pledges," *The Atlantic*, May 4, 2016. https://www.theatlantic.com/health/archive/2016/05/the-unintended-consequences-of-purity-pledges/481059/
133. Ibid.
134. Tara Culp-Ressler, "How Virginity Pledges Can End Up Hurting Kids," *Think Progress*, August 20, 2014. https://thinkprogress.org/how-virginity-pledges-can-end-up-hurting-kids-11751562f595/
135. John Santelli, "Abstinence-Only Education Doesn't Work. We're Still Funding It," *The Washington Post*, August 21, 2017. https://www.washingtonpost.com/news/posteverything/wp/2017/08/21/abstinence-only-education-doesnt-work-were-still-funding-it/?utm_term=.3fd3918526f1
136. Sarah McCammon, "Abstinence-Only Education Is Ineffective and Unethical," *NPR*, August 23, 2017. https://www.npr.org/sections/health-shots/2017/08/23/545289168/abstinence-education-is-ineffective-and-unethical-report-argues
137. Kathrin F. Stanger-Hall, David W. Hall, "Abstinence-Only Education and Teen Pregnancy Rates: Why We Need Comprehensive Sex Education in the U.S.," *PLoS ONE*, Vol. 6, 2011. https://www.ncbi.nlm.nih.gov/pmc/articles/PMC3194801/

9

TRUMP AND THE BRO WORLD OF POLITICAL SEXISM

Key Points

- Politics is [Still] a Man's Game
- The Many Media Attacks on Women in Politics
- The Bitch – Ditz Dichotomy
- The Rise of Trumpian Misogyny
- The Conservative Refutation of Political Correctness to Whitewash Bigotry
- Slurs
- No Platforming
- Gay, White Bros and the Alt-Right

Women have fought for generations to achieve the same rights and treatment that men have taken for granted for themselves. The biggest obstacle facing women has been and continues to be those men who do not view women as their authentic equals. Of course, there have been and continues to be some women who also argue against women's full participation in every aspect of public life. Conservative, antifeminist attorney Phyllis Schlafly, for instance, fought her entire life against the Equal Rights Amendment, which proposes to guarantee equal legal rights for all American citizens regardless of sex.[1,2]

The early presidents, themselves, believed it was preposterous to consider giving women the right to vote, let alone the right to run for public office, own land, run a business, get an education, or ascend to positions of leadership. It was believed that women did not possess the same intellectual abilities or emotional stability as men. This sort of thinking is the same sort of reasoning that slave-owners used to justify slavery. They would claim that some people were inferior by nature so that their highest aspirations could only be that of servitude to others.[3] On a parallel track, men have attempted to justify the unequal treatment of women on similar grounds. One favorite stereotype of women is the view that women are too emotional and not sufficiently rational to take up positions of political leadership.

The journeys for slaves and non-slave women are not, of course, a perfect parallel. African women who were enslaved had very different experiences than the European women who came with the men who founded the colonies. Yet there are similarities. The colonists who purchased human beings as property routinely raped, beat, and murdered the African women in their service and saw nothing wrong with these behaviors since they believed they could treat slaves with the same disregard as they would any object of property.[4] But men of the past also felt that their wives were de facto, if not legal, property. Women had almost no rights and so very little recourse in the face of physical and sexual abuse at the hands on their husbands.

Politics, as a paradigmatic career-path of power, has long been dominated by men. Many of these men carried the bro beliefs and attitudes of their youths right into their careers, and to this day, women in politics often struggle under the yoke of mistreatment and double standards that result from men who were raised believing that women are of less value than men. This chapter documents the mistreatment and double standards that we have come to expect when bros dominate political office.

POLITICS IS [STILL] A MAN'S GAME

From the earliest moments of American colonization, men have dominated fields of power. From business to science to education to the military to government, men have staked a claim to power as a *natural right* over women for millennia.[5,6] We see this throughout the long journey to the 19th amendment that gave women the right to vote in 1920 to today's businesses that are top-heavy with men in positions of authority. The exclusion of women from executive positions has been a calculated practice. From men-only universities that included all Ivy League universities until the 1960s and 1970s to Wall Street traders,[7] the halls of power were not open to women until very recently. In fact, the only reason why Ivy League universities eventually accepted women was not due to some high-minded desire to create equal rights, but because admission numbers were down and there was a concern about being underfunded.[8] One Princeton University grad in 1936 worried that Ivy League universities might dilute the brilliance of their student body by admitting women and thereby upsetting,

> Princeton's sturdy masculinity with disconcerting, mini-skirted young things cavorting on its playing fields.[9]

Today, the pool of candidates that reach Congressional seats are drawn almost entirely from those who have college degrees.[10] Out of a total of 535 members of the Senate and House combined, 507 have college degrees.[11] In fact, Harvard University has produced the most Congresspersons of any university in America, followed by Stanford and Yale.[12] What is interesting about this list is that beyond the fact that graduating from one of these universities usually requires that one has resources, nationwide the ratio of women to men in colleges and universities is 56% women to 44% men, but at Harvard, Stanford, and Yale, the ratio is 52% men to 48% women.[13] These numbers can be viewed as progress for women, since the history of gender diversity at colleges in general and Ivy League universities specifically has been dominated by men.[14] But these numbers tell us that the so-called *elite universities* are not reflecting the documented gender gap found in most other colleges and universities. Today, an unprecedented gender gap favoring women has been witnessed across higher education, and not just in America, but throughout the world.[15] Going on two decades, women are now entering and graduating from colleges and universities at much higher rates than men.[16]

However, these higher numbers of women graduating from universities has not yet translated into gender parity in politics. Like education, the history of politics has decidedly been a man's game. All elected governors before 1975 were men other than those women who were the wife or widow of a former governor.[17] As late as 1973, no member of the U.S. Senate was a woman.[18] Today, 25 out of 100 Senators are women.[19] In that same year of 1973, there were 16 out of 435 or 3% of House of Representatives were women.[20] Today, that number sits at 127 out of 435 or 23%.[21] So, while the numbers have increased, women are still woefully underrepresented in positions of government. Today, of President Trump's 20 Cabinet members, only four are women.[22] Rutgers University recently published statistical research exposing the male-dominance in politics today by showing the percentage of women in government positions even after a 2018 midterm election that witnessed a record number of women winning seats in Congress.[23]

- 23% of Congress
- 25% of the Senate
- 9% of governors
- 34% of Lt. governors
- 28% of state legislators
- 20% of mayors[24]

According to American University professor of government Jennifer Lawless and Loyola Marymount University political science professor Richard Fox, there are a number of reasons why women are severely underrepresented in government offices, among them being:[25]

- Women are more likely than men to perceive the electoral environment as highly competitive and biased against female candidates.
- Women witnessed the sexism aimed at Hillary Clinton and Sarah Palin in previous elections.
- Women are less likely than men to think they are qualified to run for public office.
- Female candidates are more risk averse than their male counterparts.
- Women do not like the negative campaigning often associated with modern campaigns.
- Women are not encouraged by others to run for office as compared to men.
- Women are still expected by society, and often their male partners, to assume the majority of childcare and household tasks.

The domination of men in politics may explain why many women understandably view it as a profession hostile to women. Unsurprisingly, and in large part due to the success of the #metoo movement, numerous members of Congress have been found to have engaged in sexual harassment.[26] This has also been true at state and local levels, with the vast majority of harassers being men.[27] In fact, to date, 23 different women have leveled allegations against Donald Trump for an assortment of sexual misdeeds including rape and sexual assault.[28]

Add to this the many regressive statements made by male politicians and judiciary in recent years, and you have a recipe for a system that is riddled with sexist thinking. For instance, here is a sampling of quotes made by male politicians about women:[29,30,31]

- "Doctors should make sure a lady who reports a rape isn't making it up in her scheming lady-mind." ~ Idaho Senator Chuck Winder
- "If a woman has the right to an abortion, why shouldn't a man be free to use his superior strength to force himself on a woman?" ~ Conservative lobbyist, former Maine House of Representatives Lawrence Lockman
- "I'm not sure we need half a billion dollars for women's health issues." ~ Former Florida Governor Jeb Bush
- "Statutory rape isn't rape when a girl seems older than her chronological age." ~ Montana District Judge G. Todd Baugh
- "Having sex with an unconscious woman is fine as long as she's your wife." ~ Utah State Representative Brian Green
- "You know, it doesn't really matter what the media write as long as you've got a young and beautiful piece of ass." ~ 45th President of the United States, Donald Trump

When you include male political media pundits, we witness a steady stream of sexism and misogyny aimed at women with the effect of reinforcing in men the view that women are inferior in almost every way. These two quotes illustrate well what women have had to deal with from men, and mainly white men, who feel empowered and entitled to judge women, in this case radio personality Rush Limbaugh, who was given the Medal of Freedom at the State of the Union address by President Donald Trump in 2020:[32]

- [Women] are out there protesting what they actually wish would happen to them sometimes.[33]
- Feminism was established so as to allow unattractive women access to the mainstream of society.[34]

By giving Limbaugh the Medal of Freedom by the most powerful individual in the nation, the President of the United States, Trump validated everything that Limbaugh stands for, including his mind-numbing misogyny, racism, homophobia, and xenophobia. But it is important to note the bro-cultural influence found in these statements. Bros often position remarkably sexist, homophobic, and racist statements as being jokes so that they can plead no responsibility when called on their bigotry. For the bro, including these older, political bros, the hint of humor alleviates, in their minds, any stain of culpability. They can trash women, gay people, and people of color, while insisting that it was all meant to be a joke. It's an old strategy for the bro that dates back generations. But lying beneath the alleged humor are viciously sexist sentiments that reveal a deep-seated contempt for women. That elected officials who wield the power to create public policy and determine the fate over people's lives indulge in sexist bigotry is especially troublesome, since their collective words shape not only legislation and decrees that affect us all, they serve as role models to young people, many of whom will turn into the next generation of lawmakers and judges.

THE MANY MEDIA ATTACKS ON WOMEN IN POLITICS

Beyond all the slurs against women made by male politicians, male members of the media are also fond of trashing women as witnessed in the following quotes starting again with Medal of Freedom recipient Rush Limbaugh:[35]

- "I love the women's movement, especially when walking behind it." ~ radio personality Rush Limbaugh
- "Didn't men give you the kitchen?" ~ Fox News personality Brian Kilmeade in response to Gretchen Carlson's question about sanctuary spaces in the home.
- "extremely cunty" and "two of the biggest white whores in America." ~ Fox News host Tucker Carlson describing Alexis Stewart and Britney Spears, after which he defiantly refused to issue an apology.[36]
- "When you look at biology, the roles of a male and a female in society, and other animals, the male typically is the dominant role." ~ Fox News contributor Erick Erickson
- "Would that be considered boobs on the ground?" ~ former Fox News host Eric Bolling referring to the first female fighter pilot for the United Arab Emirates. Bolling was later fired by Fox News after sending photos of his penis to women at his office.[37,38]
- "I guess you could argue that Bill Cosby probably helped women in their careers." Fox News host Sean Hannity quipping about Cosby's rape charges[39]
- "I don't hate women; they're very convenient to have around. They just shouldn't be voting." ~ Conservative talk host Glenn Beck[40]
- "If we get a woman into the Oval Office, the most powerful person in the world, what's the downside?" former FOX News talk-host Bill O'Reilly, "You mean besides the PMS and mood swings?" FOX contributor and author of *A Man's No Nonsense Guide to Women*, Marc Rudov[41]

It should be noted that many of these men have also been accused of sexual harassment[42,43], while the former head of FOX News, Roger Ailes, was fired for sexual harassment. To add to this pattern, Fox News co-president Bill Shine resigned among allegations that he fostered a work environment where sexual harassment and racism went unchecked[44], while the longstanding face of Fox News talk, Bill O'Reilly, was forced out after multiple allegations of sexual harassment.[45] It cannot be surprising that men who possess power and who employ such cavalier sexism are often the same figures under investigation for sexual harassment. It should be noted, however, that if these men were hurling similar attacks toward Black people instead of women, we would assume they are Ku Klux Klan-sympathizers and their careers would likely come to an abrupt end. But women continue to be public targets of sexist bigots with much less repercussion to the bigot.

Other instances of media sexism can be seen in the descriptions of female politicians by journalists. When Senator Kristin Gillibrand of New York addressed the ways that the military handle cases of sexual assault, media talking heads described Senator Gillibrand as "beautiful," "petite," "blonde," "perky," and as having "a soft, girly voice."[46] Even as historically high numbers of women sought and attained political office in the 2018 midterms, media sources termed it "a pink wave."[47] We also witness the casual sexism by members of the media who tell female politicians that they should smile.[48] Media pundits cannot seem to stop themselves from trivializing women in politics or focusing on irrelevant aspects that have nothing to do with their jobs as lawmakers, things they would almost never say to men in the same position.

Yet more examples of the sexist treatment women in politics receive is the double-standard of attacking those female politicians with children as being irresponsible mothers for pursuing a career in politics, a charge never leveled against male politicians with children.[49] The shaming of women with children who pursue careers is nothing new. The assumptions underneath the attack are sexist in both directions, meaning that it first assumes that the sole role for women in the world is to raise children, but it also assumes that men are incapable raising children, or that taking care of children is somehow beneath their dignity as men. The further assumption underneath this sexist attack is that women and men are apparently incapable of working as a team to raise children. In today's economy, it is not possible for many families to survive on only one income, making the attack on women all the more egregious. But the attack on women in politics is even worse in some ways, since it represents yet another tactic to shame women into staying out of politics where contributions to policymaking shape our nation and the world.

THE BITCH–DITZ DICHOTOMY

Another way that bro politicians and bro journalists marginalize women who attain political power is to focus on women's looks rather than their views. One noticeable example of this took place with comments aimed at former Senator and Secretary of State Hillary Clinton and former Alaska Governor Sarah Palin. Clinton has been attacked for her physical appearance and tough demeanor throughout her political life. Conservative provocateur Alex Jones once quipped,

> Look at her face! All she needs is green skin![50]

Throughout Trump's presidential campaign, slogans at rallies appeared stating, "Trump that Bitch!" "Life's a Bitch – Don't Vote for One," and ""KFC Hillary Special: 2 Fat Thighs, 2 Small Breasts…Left Wing."[51] The onslaught against Clinton was constant and focused on a combination of her physical appearance and her alleged angry demeanor. When male politicians appear tough, it is often leveraged as strength and proof that he would be a good leader. Trump's base, for instance, seems to revel in his bullying approach to perceived opponents.[52] Male politicians, in fact, are often praised for being tough and criticized if they are perceived as being soft. George H.W. Bush once paid a political price when he was characterized as "a wimp" in a Doonesbury cartoon that depicted him as soft, weak, and ineffectual.[53] This label continued to plague him throughout his political career. On the other hand, the same toughness that is praised in many male politicians is relabeled *bitchiness* in female politicians.

With older women in politics, a focus is almost always placed on whether they have had a facelift or on some other physical feature rather than their political positions.[54] Right-wing talk show host Dennis Miller called House Speaker Nancy Pelosi, "a shrieking harridan magpie," and ultra-conservative talk host Mark Levin stated, "our friends in San Francisco will keep re-electing shrill Pelosi as long as her makeup holds up."[55] Conservative radio-talk fixture Rush Limbaugh uttered, "if Pelosi wants fewer births, she should put pictures of herself in every cheap motel room," adding, "That will keep birthrates down because that picture will keep a lot of things down."[56] Reactionary radio-talk host Michael Savage described Pelosi as, "Mussolini if he came back and wore ugly clothing and put on bad makeup and had too much Botox," while G. Gordon Liddy quipped, "if they stretch Nancy Pelosi's face anymore, she can be used as a drum in the Marine Core (sic) Band."[57] The rule in American politics is, the more political power a woman has attained, the more vicious and personal the attacks.

There was a different sort of backlash to Sarah Palin. Instead of being labeled *a bitch*, she was often referred to as a *ditz* whose value was reduced to her physical appearance. Writing for New York Magazine, Amanda Fortini notes,

> Sarah Palin has been variously described as a diva who engaged in paperwork-throwing tantrums, a shopaholic who spent $150,000 on clothing, a seductress who provocatively welcomed staffers while wearing only a towel, and a "whack-job"—contemporary code for hysteric.[58]

Comic-provocateur Bill Maher stated of Palin during an opening monologue for his show,

> Did you hear this – Sarah Palin finally heard what happened in Japan and she's demanding that we invade 'Tsunami'. I mean she said, 'These 'Tsunamians' will not get away with this.' Oh, speaking of dumb twats, did you hear about…[59]

The common reading of Palin's ascendancy to national prominence was that while she was a ditz, her looks made her a marketable commodity. Media analyst Jennifer Pozner, writing for *NPR*, notes that *MSNBC* contributor Donny Deutsch termed Palin, "the new feminist ideal," because, "women want to be her; men want to mate with her."[60] These sentiments would never be stated of a male politician. The needle that female politicians have to thread for media pundits to take them seriously is to be *properly feminine, but not too feminine* and *properly tough, but not too tough*. It's a no-win situation.

A more contemporary example of media's obsession with the physical appearance of female politicians is the treatment of House Representative newcomer Alexandria Ocasio-Cortez. Washington Examiner writer, Eddie Scarry, tweeted, "Hill staffer sent me this pic of Ocasio-Cortez. I'll tell you something: that jacket and coat don't look like a girl who struggles."[61] Scarry reduces a member of the House of Representatives to being "a girl" and the clothes she wears becomes the story. When a quote misattributed to Ocasio-Cortez made its way through the media, she responded,

> This reinforces lazy tropes about women leaders in media: Older [and] seasoned, but unlikeable; Passionate, but angry; Smart, but crazy; Well-intentioned, but naive; Attractive, but uninformed or gaffe-prone. It's unoriginal, lazy, and men don't get the same either/or coverage.[62]

Ocasio-Cortez nails the dichotomous and reductionist thinking that is commonplace in the way that media pundits tend to treat female politicians. Gaslighting has been a common way for some men to treat women who attain power in an attempt to undermine their competency. Trump, for example, who loves the juvenile practice of name-calling, referred to *MSNBC* personality Mika Brzezinski as "crazy" and claimed that Rep. Maxine Waters has a "low-IQ."[63] These tactics have been around for generations and reflect an insecure masculinity that comes with those who feel threatened by the rising power of women.

While it is true that Donald Trump's physical appearance has been criticized, most notably his weight, orangish complexion, and trade-mark hair, Trump is an exception to the rule, in part because of his flamboyancy and his tendency to center his speeches around himself instead of the topic at hand. In general, it is uncommon for media pundits to focus on the physical appearance or particular physical traits of male politicians. But women in politics have been subjected to this sort of scrutiny forever. Political strategist Celinda Lake notes,

> When women's ideas are threatening or women's power is threatening, you often see them referred to in terms of their appearance. It's a way to distract, to trivialize and to divert attention from the important things women are saying and doing.[64]

Beyond the attention given to the physical appearance of female politicians, there is also "the likeability test" with which many women in politics are forced to contend. Shilpa Phadke, vice-president of the women's initiative at the Center for American Progress, notes,

> The research shows women have to find a sweet spot so they are 'warm enough'. They're expected to conform to certain positive stereotypes and avoid certain negative stereotypes. This double standard doesn't just exist in politics: if the presidency is gendered, so is business, so is the media, so is Hollywood. What's happening with Elizabeth Warren is no different from what is faced by working women every day.[65]

Judging women on the basis of their looks and likeability are bro habits that go back generations. It is an old-fashioned tactic to keep women in a place of subordination to men, who have always granted themselves the authority to be judges of women. Bros will sometimes claim that they are not sexist by saying things like, "I would support a woman for president, just not *that* woman." Since women are given a long list of favorability tests, *and must pass them all* for men to approve, men can arbitrate and ultimately reject any woman by simply noting that she failed to meet this or that standard of perfection. Meanwhile, male politicians do not have to be perfect looking and likeable to win election after election.

THE RISE OF TRUMPIAN MISOGYNY

Donald Trump is a bro, albeit a bro in his mid-70s, which reinforces the point that bro-hood is not a phenomenon reserved for teenage or college-aged men. Moreover, as covered in the last section, misogyny in politics is not a new phenomenon; however, Donald Trump represents a new chapter of unapologetic sexism and misogyny in the modern era. Before Trump, most politicians were cautious not to flirt with public statements that could be viewed as sexist and racist, but those days are over. During the 2016 campaign, a now infamous audio tape was discovered and released to the public of Trump boasting about sexually assaulting women to former radio and television host Billy Bush, a tape that many believed at the time would sink Trump's chances of becoming president.[66] A portion of the transcript reads as follows:

> UNKNOWN: She used to be great. She's still very beautiful.
> TRUMP: I moved on her, actually. You know, she was down on Palm Beach. I moved on her, and I failed. I'll admit it.
> UNKNOWN: Whoa.
> TRUMP: I did try and fuck her. She was married.
> UNKNOWN: That's huge news.
> TRUMP: I moved on her like a bitch. But I couldn't get there. And she was married. Then all of a sudden I see her, she's now got the big phony tits and everything. She's totally changed her look.
> BILLY BUSH: Sheesh, your girl's hot as shit. In the purple. It better not be the publicist. No, it's, it's…

TRUMP: Yeah, that's her. With the gold. I better use some Tic Tacs just in case I start kissing her. You know, I'm automatically attracted to beautiful — I just start kissing them. It's like a magnet. Just kiss. I don't even wait. And when you're a star, they let you do it. You can do anything.
BUSH: Whatever you want.
TRUMP: Grab 'em by the pussy. You can do anything.[67]

At first, Trump denied that it was his voice on the tape, but Billy Bush later confirmed that it was in fact Donald Trump who made these statements.[68] As everyone now knows, the tape had little effect on Trump's popularity with a base of voters who eventually elected him president, and this is the point. The open misogyny heard by everyone in the audio tape was not a deal-breaker, and in fact, cemented his reputation for saying what is on his mind without attenuating his thoughts or language.[69] A rallying cry, in fact, for Trump and his base is that he is not politically correct.[70,71] As a result of Trump's slurs and intolerance, his racist, sexist, and xenophobic statements are now considered by many to be proud refutations of political correctness instead of what they in fact are: expressions of hatred and bigotry.

Thought Box: The N-word and the B-word

The N-word continues to be a paradigm of unacceptable speech due its long history of racist intent, as a word that has been used to strip away the humanity of Black people in America. Even with Trump's animus toward political correctness, he and his supporters are careful not to use the N-word, at least not publicly. Yet, the B-word, C-word, W-word, S-word, (bitch, cunt, whore, slut) and many others are used toward women and men daily, safe in the knowledge that their usage will not draw the kind of fire that using the N-word will draw. Why do you think sexist language is used by both men and women, and often with great bravado, while the N-word is out-of-bounds?

On the other hand, the N-word continues to be a slur that will draw terminal fire and so its avoidance escapes charges of political correctness. Radio and television pundits know better than to let slip the N-word or they will find themselves out of a job. Yet sexist verbiage in political discourse is not only routine, but often celebrated. For example, when asked what the "Trump Doctrine" is, a senior White House official stated,

The Trump Doctrine is 'We're America, Bitch.' That's the Trump Doctrine.[72]

Letting fly a longstanding slur that has been aimed at women and all things considered to be feminine is used by Trump surrogates to stand for weakness as the defining statement of the Trump administration's guiding doctrine. This is the same word used by bros around the world. The B-word has long been a stand-in for weakness and softness, which are then attributed to actual human traits such as kindness, compassion, and empathy. Trumpian strength, by contrast, is viewed as masculine, tough, bold, and brash, while weakness is defined as feminine, kind, compassionate, loving, and soft. But another way of putting all this is that men are strong and built for leadership, while women are soft and built to be supporters.

One of many perspicuous examples of Trumpian misogyny was witnessed in the aftermath of the confirmation proceedings for then nominee Brett Kavanaugh to the Supreme Court. Dr. Christine Blasey Ford accused Brett Kavanaugh of having sexually assaulted her when they were in high school.[73] Dr. Blasey Ford had nothing to win by testifying under oath and a lot to lose. She received death threats throughout her testimony and continues to receive threats to this day.[74,75] She was not and is not looking for a book deal.[76] During testimony, she was riddled with questions by an Arizona sex-crimes prosecutor brought in by Republican Senators to subject her to what amounted to a cross-examination in an effort to destroy her credibility.[77] Still, Blasey Ford was not rattled and claimed to remember the events with "100% certainty" and never wavered from her account.[78] After her testimony, Kavanaugh was also questioned during which several Republican Senators publicly exploded in anger including South Carolina Senator Lindsey Graham who accused Democrat Senators of staging the allegations to delay the confirmation process until after the midterm elections.[79]

But the worst misogyny was reserved for Trump himself who used a campaign rally in Mississippi to publicly mock Blasey Ford, suggesting she was lying and had a faulty memory, while adding that Kavanaugh's "life is shattered."[80] The "shattered" life of Kavanuagh, however, resulted in his being confirmed to the U.S. Supreme Court for life with words of great praise for his character from Congressional Republicans.[81] This is a longstanding strategy of bros to undermine the credibility of sexual assault and rape survivors. When women report sexual misconduct, they are often attacked with charges of lying, or of trying to gain retribution against a man who did not view the sexual encounter as working toward a committed relationship, or arguing that she or he was drinking and may not remember events accurately, or that she is a gold-digger looking for a payout, or simply that the sexual encounter was consensual. The goal is the same: attack the victim. These efforts have the effect of silencing victims who realize that reports of sexual victimization will be met by an onslaught of accusations against them.

In fact, Brett Kavanaugh was a bro. By all accounts, his high school and college days were spent partying and boozing, in Kavanaugh's own words:

> I was not perfect in those days, just as I am not perfect today. I drank beer with my friends, usually on weekends. Sometimes I had too many. In retrospect, I said and did things in high school that make me cringe now.[82]

The purpose of this story is not to rehash the Kavanaugh proceedings, but to note that many men are groomed to be bros in their youth and that grooming includes drugging, binge-drinking, womanizing, and sometimes crossing the line into sexual misconduct of various kinds. Unless these men experience a circumstance-triggered epiphany, many of them end up carrying these attitudes into their professional lives.

Trumpian misogyny, while strongly criticized by many, has created something of a numbing effect on many others. The barrage of sexist name-calling, mocking, and bullying is so prolific and frequent that there is a worry that Trump may have lowered the bar for future politicians. The thinking is that if you can trash women and become the President, then why would others stop from doing the same thing? It teaches boys that bro behaviors yield success, while teaching girls that they will be gaslighted or worse if they attain political power.

THE CONSERVATIVE REFUTATION OF POLITICAL CORRECTNESS TO WHITEWASH BIGOTRY

In both his campaign to become president and throughout his presidency, one constant from Trump that excites his base is Trump's insistence that he despises political correctness.[83] In fact, Trump recently argued,

> I think the big problem this country has is being politically correct. I've been challenged by so many people and I don't, frankly, have time for total political correctness. And to be honest with you, this country doesn't have time, either.[84]

This theme has struck a nerve in America with most Americans claiming that they oppose political correctness.[85] The question is, "what exactly is political correctness?" Conservative organization *The Heritage Foundation* claims that political correctness is "suicide of the intellect," as though something about it dumbs us down.[86] According to *The Heritage Foundation*, universities are mainly to blame for indoctrinating young people with the view that we must aim to never offend others, no matter how slight.[87] This is a wild caricature of the campus climate of most universities.[88] In fact, quite the opposite is the rule as surveys have found that university students are more open to free speech than those in most other environments.[89,90] What many critics of alleged political correctness get wrong is the view that criticizing opinions of those with whom we disagree is somehow a plea for political correctness, when in fact it is more free speech. That some conservative personalities have been booed or shouted down is an example of one group of people exercising free speech to criticize another group of people exercising free speech. But conservative operatives try to persuade people that disagreement with them somehow equals censorship and politically correct activism. Actual censorship would involve audiences being forced to remain silent by some authority when confronted with opinions they do not support.

Writing for *New York Magazine*, journalist Ed Kilgore astutely argues that "'political incorrectness' is just 'political correctness' for conservatives."[91] So, if conservatives view a moratorium on using the b-word or s-word toward women as political correctness, it becomes a point of pride for conservatives to use the b-word or s-word as much as possible. A politician like Trump can then break out any number of slurs at one of his many rallies to robust cheers of support. Denigrating women, immigrants, or people of color becomes a patriotic refutation of something the president claims is ruining the country such that the forces of PC-culture are rebuked as being "the real problem."

Slurs and name-calling have been around for centuries and are designed to harm, marginalize, and silence groups of people. Mihaela Popa-Wyatt and Jeremy Wyatt in their article, "Slurs, Roles and Power," argue that slurs are a form of hate speech that aims at creating a power imbalance.[92] For instance, when one goes from stating the descriptor 'homosexual' to stating the slur 'faggot', one is judging an individual as having less value, less moral standing, and as deserving of denigration and mockery. Similarly, the transition from the word 'woman' to the word 'bitch' is a transition that denigrates an individual as being unworthy of respect and decent treatment. But importantly, the slur also denigrates the category and not simply the individual. When one aims the N-word at a Black person to slur the person, the slur attaches to the individual through their participation in the category *Black people*. It would be unusual and ineffective for the N-word to be aimed at a white person, since the word's history has been attached to identities of race and ethnicity. However, because we live in a patriarchy that exalts the masculine over the feminine, the slur *bitch* can be and often is aimed at men as a way to say that the individual is *beneath the dignity of being a man*. It is to say that a man being compared to a woman is one of the worst possible insults one can aim at a man.

But for Trumpian conservatives, using the B-word toward a woman or man has become a patriotic way of standing up to liberal or progressive insistence that we have become a PC-nation. The reality is that being politically incorrect by using slurs and other demeaning language is a way for the more powerful to keep in place the less powerful. It is a way of saying that my ability to put you in your place through the use of slurs is a sign of my authority and superiority over you. Recently, Donald Trump Jr. called Senator Mitt Romney of Utah "a pussy" because Romney voted to convict his father in the impeachment trail.[93] This is a classic example of shaming a man with a feminized slur to suggest that he is not a real man. In reality, Romney's vote showed a great deal more courage than those who went along to get along. Romney knew full well that his vote would be met with strong disapproval by members of his party, but followed his conscience nonetheless.

Consider how Nazis attempted to control the narrative in pre-World War II Germany by using propaganda aimed at Jewish people. The hope was to instill a visual and narrative spin to manipulate a population into holding anti-Semitic beliefs as being patriotic to the goals of Germany.[94] It is important to note the use of patriotism to motivate hate-speech. This is how one can be successful in getting people to use slurs and hate-speech, while viewing resistance as adherence to political correctness. The *real* problem becomes political correctness itself, instead of those who are proliferating hatred. When effective, "forces of political correctness" become traitors to national goals and national pride.

Today's conservative political paradigm in America is a blueprint for whitewashing bigotry as patriotism. So, a person like Trump can stereotype and demean entire groups of people to the chants of "USA, USA, USA…" by his acolytes with little backlash from conservatives who might feel uncomfortable by what they are witnessing. Trump's propaganda, in fact, has been so persuasive to large blocks of conservatives that to challenge Trump is to challenge America and to risk one's political future. With a wave of his wand or the penning of a tweet, Trump can market bigotry as patriotic and critics as slaves to political correctness.

The political *bro* is someone who uses this sort of reasoning to defend his sexism, racism, or xenophobia. One of many examples is former U.S. House member Todd Akin, who at a campaign stop claimed that women who are victims of "legitimate rape" rarely get pregnant.[95] Unfortunately for Mr. Akin, his political career came before Trumpian attacks on political correctness and he lost the election to Claire McCaskill in 2012.[96] Today, a Trump loyalist can make similar claims and then rebuff critics as being servants to political correctness to the cheers of audiences. Consider all of the denigrating claims Trump has made about women. Throughout his life he has referred to women as "dogs," "pigs," "fat," "ugly," "disgusting," "horse-face," "low-life," "bimbo," "bitch," and once posted a picture of Republican Senator Ted Cruz's wife Heidi Cruz in a split-screen shot that featured his own wife Melania Trump with the attached caption, "Images are worth a thousand words."[97]

This is bro behavior at its most toxic: demean women by attacking their looks and thereby reduce women's value to their physical appearances. What Trump does with these bullying behaviors is enable and empower bros to do likewise. He opens the door to hostility toward women with the built-in response to any who might criticize, "I don't believe in political correctness." Trump's base capitalized on his sexism, in fact, during campaign rallies by selling t-shirts emblazoned with the slogan "Trump that bitch," referring to then candidate Hillary Clinton.[98] That particular shirt is emblematic of Trump's entire campaign and presidency in three easy steps: demean perceived enemies with slurs and bigoted speech, encourage followers to join in the mockery, dismiss criticism as misguided loyalty to political correctness. This same recipe allows Trump and his surrogates to defend the Confederate flag, white nationalism, and neo-Nazis as "very fine people."[99,100]

NO PLATFORMING

No platforming is an expression that was created in the UK as a student boycott against allowing certain individuals to speak on college campuses.[101] This practice was designed to halt what was believed to be hate-speech on college and university campuses, but has been criticized by conservatives as censorship and a threat to free speech.[102] Like the complaint about political correctness, those who criticize no platforming typically argue that conservative speakers are being targeted by those who wish to quash differing opinions. In March of 2019, Trump signed an executive order that threatens to cut federal funding to those colleges that, in his terms, are "hostile to free speech."[103] At the same time, many college and university codes of behavior prohibit hate speech on campus and particularly the use of slurs and messages that incite violence.[104]

Many conservative media pundits have argued that speakers have a right to speak at public college campuses, because as publicly funded institutions, they are considered to be public forums.[105] However, courts have ruled that college campuses are not the same as public parks or streets, and are instead "limited public forums."[106] In the case of *Perry Education Association v. Perry Local Educators' Association*, the Supreme Court ruled,

> The First Amendment does not guarantee access to property simply because it is owned or controlled by the government.[107]

As a result of this ruling, colleges and universities have created codes of behavior that restrict or regulate campus speech.[108] At the same time, courts have ruled that campuses cannot interfere with student groups bringing speakers to campus unless the speaker advocates violent rebellion against the government or advocates violent and disruptive actions on campus.[109] But it can be difficult to determine whether a speaker poses a public safety concern and whether that safety concern flows from the views of the speaker or the backlash to the speaker's appearance. There is also the Title IX requirement that college campuses provide safe, inclusive, and welcoming learning environments.[110] If a speaker comes to campus and proceeds to bash LGBTQ people, women, people of color, or those from minority religions, university officials have the right to interpret the talk as creating a hostile learning environment for individuals belonging to those groups. Even if individuals belonging to vulnerable groups do not attend the talk, it is reasonable to expect some attendees to be encouraged to adopt the words and speech behaviors of the guest speaker. Some examples of creating a hostile environment come from actual case law. Writing about harassment law, UCLA professor of Law, Eugene Volokh notes:

> A Wisconsin administrative agency has concluded that an overheard (though loud) discussion that used the word "nigger" created an illegal hostile public accommodations environment for black patrons, even though the statements weren't said to or about the patrons.[111]

Thought Box

Should campuses have the right to refuse a speaker's appearance on their campus, and if so, on what grounds? Conservatives have accused colleges of not practicing free speech, while many colleges have campus codes that reject hate speech. Given that there are vulnerable communities on most college campuses, including people of color, religious minorities, and LGBTQ individuals who feel threatened by certain speeches, should the rhetoric of some speakers be prohibited on college campuses, or should all forms of speech be accepted with the caveat that protesters would be allowed to respond in kind?

Extrapolating this decision onto other vulnerable minority groups, a speaker who may denounce LGBTQ people, particularly using slurs, or who stereotypes Muslim people as terrorists who are trying to destroy America can be viewed as creating a hostile and potentially dangerous environment to individuals belonging to these groups. Similarly, men calling women 'bitches', 'sluts', 'cunts', or calling for the mistreatment of feminists, as many men's rights activists do, qualifies as creating a hostile and dangerous environment for women. As just one example, Paul Elam, widely considered to be the most prominent men's rights activist in America, quipped,

> I find you, as a feminist, to be a loathsome, vile piece of human garbage. I find you so pernicious and repugnant that the idea of fucking your shit up gives me an erection.[112]

This is bro speech 101. But imagine being a young feminist on a college campus subjected to this kind of speech and being told the person issuing the hate speech must be accommodated on campus in the interest of free speech. Knowing that many men attend and support speeches of this kind is not 'inclusive' and cannot be 'welcoming' to the women and men on campus who identify as feminists.

The 2015 *Counter Terrorism and Security Act* affirms universities' requirement to protect freedom of speech, but also issues requirements for universities to have "due regard" of the potential risk of radicalization among students.[113] *Radicalization* has been a term used to describe extremist religious groups and particularly Islamic groups affiliated with ISIS. But political groups can become radicalized as well if they begin to demonize certain communities on the basis of race, ethnicity, gender identity, sexual orientation, or religion. The disparaging of LGBTQ communities, for example, has been part of the rhetoric of certain conservative politicians for decades, while Muslims have been stereotyped and come under fire from Trump and many who support Trump. Bros get into this discussion by being a segment of male culture that often celebrates the undermining of others and particularly, but not exclusively, women and LGBTQ people. If radicalization is dangerous and alarming, bro culture might be considered a radicalized community about which there should be concern.

GAY, WHITE BROS AND THE ALT-RIGHT

One of the strangest political alliances witnessed in the time of Trump is the recruitment of gay, white men into the alt-right movement, the most famous of whom is British sophisticate Milo Yiannopoulos.[114] During the gamergate controversy, where a harassment campaign was organized by gamer-bros who encouraged other gamers to "virtual attack" gamer-culture critic Anita Sarkeesian and other female gamers,[115] Yiannopoulos joined the attack, alleging that critics were,

> an army of sociopathic feminist programmers and campaigners, abetted by achingly politically correct American tech bloggers.[116]

Stranger still was Yiannopoulos' claim that "gay rights have made us dumber."[117] While boasting that gay men are smarter than heterosexual men, Yiannopoulos encourages gay men to marry women, stay in the closet, and produce smart children with their smarter DNA.[118] Unfortunately for Yiannopoulos' theory, intelligence is considered to be a complex interaction of biology and environment with many geneticists hypothesizing that any parental contribution to intelligence is coming mainly from one's mother due to the amount of information found on the X-chromosome as opposed to the Y-chromosome.[119] That aside, a main point about Yiannopoulos that has been made by many is that it is not his homosexuality that caused him to join the alt-right; rather, it was his white-male sympathies, evidenced by his close association with white nationalists.[120] For instance, Yiannopoulos devised a college "privilege grant" for which only white men qualified.[121] Of this grant, UC Berkeley law professor Ian Haney Lopez notes that the purpose of college grants is to,

> welcome historically excluded and dehumanized groups into every school, neighborhood and workplace, [while] affirmative action for white men is not social repair. Affirmative action for white men is a stunt to mock the moral and social importance of integration and to increase social strife.[122]

As a spokesperson for gay, white bros, Yiannopoulos is able to place his whiteness above his sexual orientation to participate in the advantages that exist for white men. He can then use his sexual orientation to appear sympathetic to other gay, white men who can shed their oppressed status in favor of a privileged status and all of the goods that go with it. A way to do this is to, like Yiannopoulos, promote the view that white men are under attack by feminists people of color, and LGBTQ communities. The *attacks*, presumably, are found in the slow but steady progress of women, people of color, and members of LGTBQ communities.

Not surprisingly, Yiannopoulos often refers to Trump as 'daddy' and claims, "The only thing I wanted from a Trump presidency is the complete extinction of political correctness in America."[123] Yiannopolous' short-lived fame came to an abrupt end when he claimed that sexual relationships between 13-year-old boys and adult men can be consensual because, he insisted, some 13-year-old boys are mature enough to consent to sex with adults.[124] In 2017, Yiannopoulos resigned, under pressure, from Brietbart.[125]

It should not be too surprising that there are gay bros who have entered the alt-right when we consider that gay activists of color have been calling out the racism within gay, male culture for years. One example is sociologist C. Winter Han of Middlebury College, who has published pieces on the ways that gay men of color are often treated by those in leadership positions at publications and other media made by and for gay men.[126] In his book *Geisha of a Different Kind*, Han argues that the muscular, white gay man is exalted as being the most attractive archetype in the gay community to the detriment of many gay men of color.[127] According to Han, gay, Asian men are often viewed as effeminate and submissive and are relegated to second-class status in terms of attractiveness when compared to the Caucasian ideal.[128] As such, gay, Asian men are a marginalized minority group within a marginalized minority group.[129]

One example of this marginalization is the pushback to those gay men of color who desire more visibility within gay and queer circles and advocated for this visibility by recommending a change to the rainbow flag famously associated with LGBTQ communities. Han notes in the 2021 documentary film, *How Does It Feel to Be a Problem?* that gay men of color pushed for a revision of the flag that included stripes of brown and black. However, a backlash was immediate. Writing for *Medium,* M.J. Murphy claims that while the desire to add a black and brown stripe to the flag comes from a sincere place that calls attention to "real and serious problems," the original flag represents "the concepts of sex, life, healing, sun, serenity with nature, art, harmony, and spirit," and should remain for purely practical reasons.[130] Murphy also claims that the brown and black stripes create an ethnocentric form of racism by reducing groups of people to the color of their skin.[131] Murphy further notes that the colors black and brown do not exist in actual rainbows in nature and that ultimately, the increase in color creates a flag that violates "good flag design principles of simplicity, meaningful elements, minimal number of colors, and originality."[132]

Han responds that "gay leaders" have promoted the rainbow flag as a symbol of diversity within LGBTQ communities, but that in fact, the colors of the original flag represent sex (pink), life (red), healing (orange), sun (yellow), nature (green), art (turquoise), harmony (indigo), and spirit (violet), and in no way represent racial diversity.[133] Han goes on to note that the backlash to the extended rainbow flag has come almost exclusively from gay, white men who dominate most of the public spaces of gay visibility in America:

> Rather than a multiplicity of colors, whiteness dominates contemporary gay life. Where racial integration takes place, it takes place only at venues where men of different races come together specifically for the purpose of seeking sexual partners of a given race while mainstream gay organizations, visibly gay spaces, and its political aspirations remain largely white. In the contemporary gay imagination, race is not something to be incorporated but to be set apart as a sexual fetish. And given the centrality of whiteness for contemporary gay life, and the muted forms of white supremacy practiced by some gay white men, it isn't surprising that the Alt-Right has managed to recruit gay white men in surprising numbers.[134]

A person like Milo Yiannopoulos aptly fits Han's description. Some gay, white men cling to their white privilege and view racial diversity as a disruption to white dominance that has come to identify what Han terms "the organizing principle of gay life."[135] If he is correct, it should not be surprising to find some gay, white men joining alt-right groups even if it appears contradictory at first sight. Alt-right politics has grown with the ascendancy of Trump, and this movement has attracted bros of various kind, from white nationalists and separatists to gay, white men who see an opportunity for power in a culture that is often marginalized by homophobia.

Thought Box

What do you think about the rainbow flag debate? Do scholars like C. Winter Han make a good case for the inclusion of a black and brown stripe or is the original flag sufficient?

POSTSCRIPT

Trump has been described as "the first porn president," after many unseemly details of his infidelities with porn performers and three appearances in porn films.[136,137] Yet, one of the more surprising aspects of the Trump presidency is the fact that even in the face of open misogyny, 23 allegations of sexual misconduct from harassment to rape, sexual payoffs to porn performers, and continued verbal attacks on women, Evangelical Christians continue to support him. To many, this support lays bare the hypocrisy of conservative Christianity, a group that has long claimed moral high ground in a nation they view as being in moral decline. The intersection of politics and religion has been contentious, yet pronounced in America, where church and state are separated, while many conservative Christians either deny this fact or bemoan its truth. Since bros are defined, in part, by their infamous denigration of others, and particularly women, the final chapter of this book will take up religion, as perhaps an unlikely but rich source of bro thinking and behavior.

Notes

1. History Editors, "Equal Rights Amendment," *History*. https://www.history.com/this-day-in-history/equal-rights-amendment-passed-by-congress
2. Douglas Martin, "Phyllis Schlafly, 'First Lady' of a Political March to the Right, Dies at 92," *The New York Times*, September 5, 2016.
3. BBC Ethics Guide, "Attempts to Justify Slavery," *BBC*. http://www.bbc.co.uk/ethics/slavery/ethics/justifications.shtml
4. PBS, "The Conditions of Antebellum Slavery 1830–1860," *PBS Resource Bank*.
5. Rosemarie Zagarri, "The Rights of Man and Woman in Post-Revolutionary America," *Omohundro Institute of Early American History and Culture*, Vol. 55, Issue 2, April, 1998, pp. 203–230.
6. Chris Nyland, "John Locke and the Social Position of Women," *University of Wollongong Australia*, 1990. https://pdfs.semanticscholar.org/4535/643da313d874c14dcd266f2348a1311c5ff4.pdf
7. Anna Irrera, "Wall Street Wants More Female Traders, But Old Perceptions Die Hard," *Reuters*, June 13, 2018. https://www.reuters.com/article/us-banks-trading-gender/wall-street-wants-more-female-traders-but-old-perceptions-die-hard-idUSKBN1JA0DF
8. Nancy Weiss Malkiel, "When Women Were Admitted to Ivy League Schools, the Complaints Sounded a Lot Like a Trump Tweet," *Los Angeles Times*, October 21, 2016. https://www.latimes.com/opinion/op-ed/la-oe-malziel-when-women-claim-male-roles-20161021-snap-story.html
9. Ibid.
10. Casey Burgat, Charles Hunt, "Congress in 2019: The 2nd Most Educated and Least Politically Experienced House Freshman Class," *Brookings*, December 28, 2018. https://www.brookings.edu/blog/fixgov/2018/12/28/congress-in-2019-the-2nd-most-educated-and-least-politically-experienced-house-freshman-class/
11. Ibid.
12. Michael Morella, "The Top 10 Colleges for Members of Congress," *U.S. News & World Report*, August 16, 2010. https://www.usnews.com/news/slideshows/the-top-10-colleges-for-members-of-congress?slide=2
13. Jon Marcus, "Why Men Are the New College Minority," *The Atlantic*, August 8, 2017. https://www.theatlantic.com/education/archive/2017/08/why-men-are-the-new-college-minority/536103/
14. Michael B. Katz, Mark J. Stern, Jamie J. Fader, "Women and the Paradox of Inequality in the Twentieth Century," *University of Pennsylvania Scholarly Commons*, September 2005. https://repository.upenn.edu/cgi/viewcontent.cgi?article=1047&context=spp_papers
15. Isabelle Bilton, "Women Are Outnumbering Men at a Record High in Universities Worldwide," *SI News*, March 7, 2018. https://www.studyinternational.com/news/record-high-numbers-women-outnumbering-men-university-globally/

16. Richard Whitmire, Susan McGee Bailey, "Gender Gap: Are Boys Being Short-changed in K-12 Schooling?" *education Next*, Vol. 10, No. 2, Spring 2010, p. 50+. Accessed 24 Sept. 2020. https://www.educationnext.org/gender-gap/
17. "Ella Grasso: First Woman Elected State Governor". Essortment. May 16, 1986. Archived from the original on March 28, 2010. Retrieved August 12, 2015.
18. Rutgers Eagleton Institute of Politics, "History of Women in the U.S. Congress," https://cawp.rutgers.edu/history-women-us-congress
19. Ibid.
20. Congressional Research Service, "Women in Congress, 1917–2020: Service Dates and Committee Assignments by Member, and Lists by State and Congress," January, 15, 2020. "Women in the United States Congress: 1917–2011" (PDF).
21. Ibid.
22. The White House, "Established in Article II, Section 2 of the Constitution, the Cabinet's Role Is to Advise the President on any Subject He May Require Relating to the Duties of Each Member's Respective Office," https://www.whitehouse.gov/the-trump-administration/the-cabinet/
23. Nicole Gaudiano, "New 'Year of the Woman'? Over 100 Female Candidates Set to Win Seats in Congress, Make History," *USA Today*, November 7, 2018. https://www.usatoday.com/story/news/politics/elections/2018/11/06/women-candidates-midterms/1845639002/
24. Rutgers Eagleton Institute of Politics, "Women in Elective Office, Women of Color in Elective Office," *Center for American Women and Politics*. https://www.cawp.rutgers.edu/current-numbers
25. Danielle Kurtzleben, "Almost 1 in 5 Members Are Women. Here's How Other Jobs Compare," *NPR*, June 11, 2016. https://www.npr.org/2016/06/11/481424890/even-with-a-female-presumptive-nominee-women-are-underrepresented-in-politics
26. BallotPedia, "Sexual Assault and Harassment in American Politics (2017–2018)," https://ballotpedia.org/Sexual_assault_and_harassment_in_American_politics_(2017-2018)
27. Ibid.
28. Eliza Relman, "The 25 Women Who Have Accused Trump of Sexual Misconduct," *Business Insider*, October 9, 2019. https://www.businessinsider.com/women-accused-trump-sexual-misconduct-list-2017-12
29. Morgan Brinlee, "8 Regressive Quotes about Women's Rights from Male Politicians," *Bustle*, May 20, 2017. https://www.bustle.com/p/8-regressive-quotes-about-womens-rights-from-male-politicians-in-2017-59199
30. Delany Dvorak, "Actual Quotes from 21st Century Politicians about Women," *Odyssey*, September 18, 2016. https://www.theodysseyonline.com/quotes-about-womens-right
31. Nina Bahadur, "22 Sexist Things President Donald Trump Has Said about Women," *Self*, June 29, 2017. https://www.self.com/story/sexist-president-donald-trump-comments
32. Kaitlan Collins, "Rush Limbaugh Awarded Medal of Freedom in Surprise State of the Union Move," *CNN Politics*, February 4, 2020 https://www.cnn.com/2020/02/04/politics/rush-limbaugh-donald-trump-medal-of-freedom/index.html
33. Marlow Stern, "Rush Limbaugh's Sexist Beyonce Rant and Gross History of Women Bashing," *Daily Beast*, July 12, 2017. https://www.thedailybeast.com/rush-limbaughs-sexist-beyonce-rant-and-gross-history-of-women-bashing
34. Ibid.

35. Simran Khurana, "Quotes to Mark International Women's Day," *LiveAbout*, January 14, 2020. https://www.thebalancecareers.com/sexist-comments-made-by-media-3515717
36. Zak Cheney-Rice, "Tucker Carlson and the Folly of Debating Bigots on Their Terms," *New York Magazine*, March 12, 2019. http://nymag.com/intelligencer/2019/03/tucker-carlson-debate-me.html
37. Andrew Kirell, "Eric Bolling's Sexism Goes Beyond Calling a Guest 'Dr. McHottie.'" *Daily Beast*, September 8, 2017. https://www.thedailybeast.com/eric-bollings-sexism-goes-beyond-calling-a-guest-dr-mchottie
38. Andrew Kirell, 'Penis Pic' Probe Ends in Eric Bolling's Odious Run at Fox News," *Daily Beast*, September 9, 2017. https://www.thedailybeast.com/penis-pic-probe-ends-eric-bollings-odious-run-at-fox-news
39. Brendan Gauthier, "Sean Hannity Goes Full Sexist Jackass: 'I guess you could argue that Bill Cosby probably helped women in their careers,'" *Salon*, January 5, 2016. https://www.salon.com/2016/01/05/sean_hannity_goes_full_sexist_jackass_i_guess_you_could_argue_that_bill_cosby_probably_helped_women_in_their_careers/
40. Glenn Beck on his webcast explaining that women shouldn't vote. https://www.youtube.com/watch?v=Pd1osAWbti8
41. Fox News, "He Said, She Said: What Is the Downside of Having a Female President?" January 14, 2015. https://www.foxnews.com/story/he-said-she-said-what-is-downside-of-having-female-president
42. Vox List of 262 Celebrities, "Politicians, CEOs, and Others Who Have Been Accused of Sexual Misconduct Since April, 2017," *Vox*, January 9, 2019. https://www.vox.com/a/sexual-harassment-assault-allegations-list/sean-hannity
43. Stephen Battaglio, "Eric Bolling Is Out at Fox News over Sex Pictures, While Charles Payne Returns to Fox Business," *Los Angeles Times*, September 8, 2017. https://www.latimes.com/business/hollywood/la-fi-ct-payne-fox-harassment-20170908-story.html
44. Mike Snider, "Sexual Harassment at Fox News: Murdoch's Overhaul Culture with Eyes on Sky," *USA Today*, July 17, 2017. https://www.usatoday.com/story/money/business/2017/07/17/sexual-harassment-fox-news-murdochs-overhaul-culture-eyes-sky/460303001/
45. Emily Steel, Michael S. Schmidt, "Bill O'Reilly Is Forced Out at Fox News," *The New York Times*, April 19, 2017. https://www.nytimes.com/2017/04/19/business/media/bill-oreilly-fox-news-allegations.html
46. Tracie Powell, "How Not to Be Sexist When Covering Female Candidates," *Columbia Journal Review*, February 26, 2014. https://archives.cjr.org/minority_reports/wam_women_running_panel.php
47. Christina Vuleta, "A Pink Wave: The Record Number of Women Heading to Congress Include Fighters, Founders, and First-Timers," *Forbes*, November 7, 2018. https://www.forbes.com/sites/christinavuleta/2018/11/07/a-pink-wave-the-record-number-of-women-heading-to-congress-include-fighters-founders-and-first-timers/#428f35e29873
48. Jennifer Hansler, "A Brief History of Female Politicians Being Told to Smile," *CNN Politics*, January 31, 2018. https://edition.cnn.com/2018/01/31/politics/women-politicians-told-to-smile/index.html
49. Tracie Powell, "How Not to Be Sexist When Covering Female Candidates," *Columbia Journal Review*, February 26, 2014. https://archives.cjr.org/minority_reports/wam_women_running_panel.php

228 Chapter 9

50. Jasmine Taylor-Coleman, "The Dark Depths of Hatred for Hillary Clinton," *BBC News*, October 12, 2016. https://www.bbc.com/news/magazine-36992955
51. Janet Reitman, "Hillary vs. the Hate Machine: How Clinton Became a Vessel for American's Fury," *Rolling Stone*, September 20, 2016. https://www.rollingstone.com/politics/politics-features/hillary-vs-the-hate-machine-how-clinton-became-a-vessel-for-americas-fury-103997/
52. Charles Derber, "Why Trump Voters and Many Anti-Trumpists Embrace Bullying," *BuzzFlash*, February 1, 2016. http://buzzflash.com/commentary/why-trump-voters-and-many-anti-trumpists-embrace-bullying
53. Matt Taibbi, "A Brief History of Everything that Happened Because of George H.W. Bush's Insecurity," *Rolling Stone*, December 7, 2018. https://www.rollingstone.com/politics/politics-features/george-h-w-bush-wimp-766076/
54. Sandra McElwaine, "Who Did Nancy Pelosi's New Face?" *Daily Beast*, July 14, 2017. https://www.thedailybeast.com/who-did-nancy-pelosis-new-face
55. Courtney Hagle, "Right-Wing Media Predictably Attack Pelosi with Sexist Remarks," *MediaMatters*, February 5, 2019. https://www.mediamatters.org/blog/2019/02/05/right-wing-media-predictably-attack-pelosi-sexist-remarks/222763
56. Ibid.
57. Ibid.
58. Amanda Fortini, "The "Bitch" and the "Ditz,"" *New York Magazine*, November 14, 2008. http://nymag.com/news/politics/nationalinterest/52184/
59. Hollie McKay, "Bill Maher Calls Sarah Palin a Female Vulgarism, NOW Stays Mum," *FOX News*, April 8, 2016. https://www.foxnews.com/entertainment/bill-maher-calls-sarah-palin-a-female-vulgarism-now-stays-mum
60. Jennifer Pozner, "Hot and Bothering: Media Treatment of Sarah Palin, "*NPR*, July 8, 2009. https://www.npr.org/templates/story/story.php?storyId=106384060
61. Gaby Del Valle, "The Real Reason Conservative Critics Love Talking about Alexandria Ocasio-Cortez's Clothes," *Vox*, November 16, 2018. https://www.vox.com/the-goods/2018/11/16/18099074/alexandria-ocasio-cortez-clothes-eddie-scarry
62. Becket Adams, "Alexandria Ocasio-Cortez Alleges Sexism, Racism in Media Coverage of Her 'Late Show' Appearance," *Washington Examiner*, January 22, 2019. https://www.washingtonexaminer.com/opinion/alexandria-ocasio-cortez-claims-sexism-racism-in-media-coverage-of-her-late-show-appearance
63. Meghan Keneally, "'Horseface', 'Crazy', 'Low IQ': Trump's History of Insulting Women," *ABC News*, October 17, 2018. https://abcnews.go.com/Politics/trumps-long-history-calling-women-crazy-attacking-appearances/story?id=48348956
64. Susannah Wellford, "Call Out Sexism in Politics," *U.S. News & World Report*, May 24, 2017. https://www.usnews.com/opinion/civil-wars/articles/2017-05-24/women-in-politics-should-call-out-sexist-attacks
65. David Smith, "Why the Sexist 'likability test' Could Haunt Female Candidates in 2020," *The Guardian*, January 4, 2019. https://www.theguardian.com/us-news/2019/jan/03/elizabeth-warren-sexism-likable-election-2020
66. Mark Makela, "Transcript: Donald Trump's Taped Comments about Women," *The New York Times*, October 8, 2016. https://www.nytimes.com/2016/10/08/us/donald-trump-tape-transcript.html
67. Ibid.
68. Laignee Barron, "'Of Course He Said It.' Billy Bush Hits Back at Trump's Access Hollywood Tape Claim," *Tome Magazine*, December 4, 2017. http://time.com/5047223/donald-trump-access-hollywood-tape-billy-bush/

69. Marco Garcia, Bradley E. Clift, Janet Kotwas, Troy Maben, "Trump Nation," *USA Today*, 2016. https://www.usatoday.com/pages/interactives/trump-nation/#/?_k=42ggu1
70. Chris Cillizza, "The Dangerous Consequences of Trump's All-out Assault on Political Correctness," *CNN Politics*, October 30, 2018. https://www.cnn.com/2018/10/30/politics/donald-trump-hate-speech-anti-semitism-steve-king-kevin-mccarthy/index.html
71. Yascha Mounk, "Americans Strongly Dislike PC Culture," *The Atlantic*, October 10, 2018. https://www.theatlantic.com/ideas/archive/2018/10/large-majorities-dislike-political-correctness/572581/
72. Jeffrey Goldberg, "A Senior White House Official Defines the Trump Doctrine: "We're America, Bitch,"" *The Atlantic*, June 11, 2018. https://www.theatlantic.com/politics/archive/2018/06/a-senior-white-house-official-defines-the-trump-doctrine-were-america-bitch/562511/
73. Emma Brown, "California Professor, Writer of Confidential Brett Kavanaugh Letter, Speaks Out about Her Allegations of Sexual Assault," *The Washington Post*, September 16, 2018. https://www.washingtonpost.com/investigations/california-professor-writer-of-confidential-brett-kavanaugh-letter-speaks-out-about-her-allegation-of-sexual-assault/2018/09/16/46982194-b846-11e8-94eb-3bd52dfe917b_story.html
74. Susanna Heller, "Christine Blasey Ford Testified against Brett Kavanaugh Over a Month Ago – And She's Still Getting Threats," *Business Insider*, November 9, 2018. https://www.businessinsider.com/christine-blasey-ford-still-getting-threats-2018-11
75. Tim Mak, "Kavanaugh Accuser Christine Blasey Ford Continues Receiving Threats, Lawyers Say," *NPR Politics*, November 8, 2018. https://www.npr.org/2018/11/08/665407589/kavanaugh-accuser-christine-blasey-ford-continues-receiving-threats-lawyers-say
76. Susanna Heller, "Christine Blasey Ford Testified against Brett Kavanaugh Over a Month Ago – And She's Still Getting Threats," *Business Insider*, November 9, 2018. https://www.businessinsider.com/christine-blasey-ford-still-getting-threats-2018-11
77. Randall D. Eliason, "The GOP Hired a Pro to Question Ford. It Did Not Go Well," *The Washington Post*, September 27, 2018. https://www.washingtonpost.com/opinions/the-gop-hired-a-pro-to-question-ford-it-did-not-go-well/2018/09/27/d11ba5be-c289-11e8-a1f0-a4051b6ad114_story.html?noredirect=on&utm_term=.496235279a38
78. Grace Segers, "Christine Blasey Ford Is "100 Percent" Certain Brett Kavanaugh Assaulted Her," *CBS News*, September 27, 2018. https://www.cbsnews.com/news/christine-blasey-ford-is-100-percent-certain-brett-kavanaugh-assaulted-her/
79. Inae Oh, "Lindsey Graham Stages Meltdown after Christine Blasey Ford Finished Testimony," *Mother Jones*, September 27, 2018. https://www.motherjones.com/politics/2018/09/lindsey-graham-christine-blasey-ford-testimony/
80. Allie Malloy, Kate Sullivan, Jeff, Zeleny, "Trump Mocks Christine Blasey Ford's Testimony, Tells People to 'Think of Your Son,'" *CNN Politics*, October 3, 2018. https://www.cnn.com/2018/10/02/politics/trump-mocks-christine-blasey-ford-kavanaugh-supreme-court/index.html
81. Steve Peoples, Lisa Mascaro, "Republicans Are Digging in on Kavanaugh. Here's Why," *AP*, September 24, 2018. https://www.apnews.com/47cf1b289f6b46cf9229ecc0c0ec6930

230   Chapter 9

82. Zack Beauchamp, "Beach Week, Brett Kavanaugh's All-Caps Calendar Entry, Explained," *Vox*, September 26, 2018. https://www.vox.com/policy-and-politics/2018/9/26/17906426/beach-week-brett-kavanaugh-calendar
83. Yascha Mounk, "Americans Strongly Dislike PC Culture," *The Atlantic*, October 10, 2018. https://www.theatlantic.com/ideas/archive/2018/10/large-majorities-dislike-political-correctness/572581/
84. Ed Kilgore, "'Political Incorrectness' Is Just 'Political Correctness' for Conservatives," *New York Magazine*, July 17, 2018. http://nymag.com/intelligencer/2018/07/anti-pc-is-political-correctness-for-the-right.html
85. Domenico Montanaro, "Warning to Democrats: Most Americans against U.S. Getting More Politically Correct," *NPR*, December 19, 2018. https://www.npr.org/2018/12/19/677346260/warning-to-democrats-most-americans-against-u-s-getting-more-politically-correct
86. Harvey Mansfield, "Political Correctness and the Suicide of the Intellect," *The Heritage Foundation*, June 26, 1991. https://www.heritage.org/political-process/report/political-correctness-and-the-suicide-the-intellect
87. Ibid.
88. Matthew Yglesias, "Everything We Think about the Political Correctness Debate Is Wrong," *Vox*, March 12, 2018. https://www.vox.com/policy-and-politics/2018/3/12/17100496/political-correctness-data
89. Ibid.
90. Justin Murphy, "Who's Afraid of Free Speech in the United States?" *Justin Murphy Blog*, September 21, 2019. https://jmrphy.net/blog/2018/02/16/who-is-afraid-of-free-speech/
91. Ed Kilgore, "'Political Incorrectness' Is Just 'Political Correctness' for Conservatives," *New York Magazine*, July 17, 2018. http://nymag.com/intelligencer/2018/07/anti-pc-is-political-correctness-for-the-right.html
92. Mihaela Popa-Wyatt, Jeremy L. Wyatt, "Slurs, Roles, and Power," *Philosophical Studies*, 175, 2879-2906, September 30, 2017. https://link.springer.com/article/10.1007/s11098-017-0986-2
93. Julia Arciga, "Don Jr. Calls Sen. Mitt Romney a 'Pussy' for Announcing Vote to Convict Trump," *Daily Beast*, February 5, 2020. https://www.thedailybeast.com/donald-trump-jr-calls-sen-mitt-romney-a-pussy-for-announcing-vote-to-convict-trump
94. Nicholas O'Shaughnessy, "How Hitler Conquered Germany," *Slate*, March 14, 2017. https://slate.com/news-and-politics/2017/03/how-nazi-propaganda-encouraged-the-masses-to-co-produce-a-false-reality.html
95. Lori Moore, "Rep. Todd Akin: The Sentiment and the Reaction," *The New York Times*, August 20, 2012. https://www.nytimes.com/2012/08/21/us/politics/rep-todd-akin-legitimate-rape-statement-and-reaction.html
96. Anna Palmer, Tarini Parti, "Akin Un-Apoligizes," *Politico*, July 10, 2014.
97. Official Twitter Page of President Donald Trump. https://twitter.com/realDonaldTrump/status/712850174838771712
98. Emily Crockett, "The "Trump That Bitch!" T-shirt Is Emblematic of Trump's Entire Campaign," *Vox*, June 17, 2016. https://www.vox.com/2016/6/17/11953388/trump-that-bitch-t-shirt-hillary-clinton
99. Max Boot, "The GOP Is Now the Party of Neo-Confederates," *The Washington Post*, November 25, 2018. https://www.washingtonpost.com/opinions/the-gop-is-now-the-party-of-neo-confederates/2018/11/25/d5d9dd88-f109-11e8-bc79-68604ed88993_story.html?utm_term=.28c08abbc4f6

100. Rosie Gray, "Trump Defends White-Nationalist Protestors: Some Very Fine People on Both Sides," *The Atlantic*, August 15, 2017. https://www.theatlantic.com/politics/archive/2017/08/trump-defends-white-nationalist-protesters-some-very-fine-people-on-both-sides/537012/
101. Evan Smith, *No Platform: A History of Anti-Fascism, Universities and the Limits of Free Speech*, Routlegde, May 14, 2020. https://www.routledge.com/No-Platform-A-History-of-Anti-Fascism-Universities-and-the-Limits-of-Free/Smith/p/book/9781138591684
102. Lucas North, Guo Sheng Liu, Josh Salisbury, David Troy, Clare Patterson, "Do 'No Platform' Policies Threaten Free Speech at University?" *The Guardian*, October 26, 2017. https://www.theguardian.com/education/2017/oct/26/do-no-platform-policies-threaten-free-speech-at-uni-students-share-their-views
103. Associated Press, "Trump Threatens to Cut Funding for Colleges 'Hostile to Free Speech,'" *The Guardian*, March 21, 2019. https://www.theguardian.com/us-news/2019/mar/21/trump-college-university-free-speech-funding
104. Susan Dodge, "Campus Codes That Ban Hate Speech Are Rarely Used to Penalize Students," *The Chronicle of Higher Education*, February 12, 1992. https://www.chronicle.com/article/Campus-Codes-That-Ban-Hate/81110
105. Holly Epstein Ojalvo, "Do Controversial Figures Have a Right to Speak at Public Universities?" *USA Today*, April 20, 2017. https://www.usatoday.com/story/college/2017/04/20/do-controversial-figures-have-a-right-to-speak-at-public-universities/37431059/
106. Ibid.
107. U.S. Supreme Court, "Perry Education Association v. Perry Educators' Association," 460 U.S. 37, 1983. https://supreme.justia.com/cases/federal/us/460/37/
108. Holly Epstein Ojalvo, "Do Controversial Figures Have a Right to Speak at Public Universities?" *USA Today*, April 20, 2017. https://www.usatoday.com/story/college/2017/04/20/do-controversial-figures-have-a-right-to-speak-at-public-universities/37431059/
109. David L. Hudson, "Controversial Campus Speakers," *Freedom Forum Institute*, April 2017. https://www.freedomforuminstitute.org/first-amendment-center/topics/freedom-of-speech-2/free-speech-on-public-college-campuses-overview/campus-speakers/
110. University of North Carolina, Chapel Hill, "Title IX and VAWA," *UNC Chapel Hill Human Resources and Equal Opportunity Compliance*. https://eoc.unc.edu/our-policies/state-and-federal-laws/title-ix-and-vawa/
111. Eugene Volokh, "Hostile Public Accommodations Environment Harassment Law," *UCLA Law*, 1996. http://www2.law.ucla.edu/volokh/harass/pubaccom.htm
112. Jaclyn Friedman, "A Look Inside the 'Men's Rights' Movement That Helped Fuel California Alleged Killer Elliot Rodger," *The American Prospect*, October 24, 2013. https://prospect.org/article/look-inside-mens-rights-movement-helped-fuel-california-alleged-killer-elliot-rodger
113. Alison Scott-Baumann, "'No Platform' Isn't the Real Danger to Freedom of Speech on Campus," *The Guardian*, October 25, 2017. https://www.theguardian.com/higher-education-network/2017/oct/25/no-platform-and-safe-spaces-arent-the-real-dangers-to-freedom-of-speech
114. Holly Epstein Ojalvo, "Who Is Milo Yiannopoulos Anyway?" *USA Today*, February 21, 2017. https://www.usatoday.com/story/college/2017/02/21/who-is-milo-yiannopoulos-anyway/37428001/

232   Chapter 9

115. Nathan Rott, "#Gamergate Controversy Fuels Debate on Women and Video Games," *NPR*, September 24, 2014.
116. Holly Epstein Ojalvo, "Who Is Milo Yiannopoulos Anyway?" *USA Today*, February 21, 2017. https://www.usatoday.com/story/college/2017/02/21/who-is-milo-yiannopoulos-anyway/37428001/
117. Milo, "Gay Rights Have Made Us Dumber, It's Time to Get Back in the Closet," *Breitbart*, June 17, 2015. https://www.breitbart.com/politics/2015/06/17/gay-rights-have-made-us-dumber-its-time-to-get-back-in-the-closet/
118. Ibid.
119. Lauren Smith, "Research Indicates that Kids Get their Intelligence from Mom," *MSN*, July 3, 2019. https://www.msn.com/en-us/health/wellness/its-official-kids-get-their-intelligence-from-their-mother/ar-AADNxWr
120. Jaclyn Friedman, "A Look Inside the 'Men's Rights' Movement That Helped Fuel California Alleged Killer Elliot Rodger," *The American Prospect*, October 24, 2013. https://prospect.org/article/look-inside-mens-rights-movement-helped-fuel-california-alleged-killer-elliot-rodger
121. Charlie Nash, "Applications Open for the Yiannopoulos Privilege Grant," *Breitbart*, January 31, 2017. https://www.breitbart.com/social-justice/2017/01/31/applications-open-yiannopoulos-privilege-grant/
122. Natalia Wojcik, "Breitbart Editor's College Grant for White Men Draws Fire," *CNBC News*, February 2, 2017. https://www.cnbc.com/2017/02/01/breitbarts-milo-yiannopoulos-creates-college-grant-exclusively-for-white-men.html
123. Tanya Gold, "The Fall of Milo Yiannopoulos," *Spectator*, April 6, 2018. https://spectator.us/fall-milo-yiannopoulos/
124. Associated Press, "Milo Yiannopoulos: Who Is the Alt-Right Writer and Provocateur?" *BBC News*, February 21, 2017. https://www.bbc.com/news/world-us-canada-39026870
125. Sydney Ember, "Milo Yiannopoulos Resigns from Breitbart News after Pedophilia Comments," *The New York Times*. ISSN 0362-4331. Retrieved 21 February 2017.
126. https://journals.sagepub.com/doi/full/10.1177/1536504217742397
127. C. Winter Han, *Geisha of a Different Kind: Race and Sexuality in Gaysian America*, NYU Press, New York, 2015.
128. Ibid.
129. Ibid.
130. M.J. Murphy, "We Don't Need a New Pride Flag," *Medium*, June 27, 2018. https://medium.com/@emjaymurphee/we-dont-need-a-new-pride-flag-efc883e0817b
131. Ibid.
132. Ibid.
133. C. Winter Han, "On Adding More Colors to the Rainbow," *NYU Press*, June 21, 2017. https://www.fromthesquare.org/pride-rainbow/
134. Ibid.
135. Ibid.
136. Brett Neely, Domenico Montanaro, "Trump Admits to Authorizing Stormy Daniels Payoff, Denies Sexual Encounter," *NPR*, May 2, 2018. https://www.npr.org/2018/05/02/607943366/giuliani-says-trump-did-know-about-stormy-daniels-payment
137. Itay Hod, "Note to Rudy Giuliana: Trump Appeared in 3 Playboy Videos," *The Wrap*, June 8, 2018. https://www.thewrap.com/note-rudy-giuliani-trump-appeared-3-soft-core-porn-videos/

10 RELIGIOUS BROS

> **Key Points**
> - Complementarianism
> - Keeping Women "in their place"
> - Benevolent Sexism
> - The Billy Graham Rule
> - Policing Women's Bodies
> - The Purity Movement
> - Policing Women's Choices
> - Family Values
> - The Gospel of Prosperity: Bro Paradise
> - Atheist Bros

Religion is one of many institutions where positions of authority are dominated by men. Most religions place men in positions of authority and power out of the belief that men were designed by God to lead. In fact, according to scriptural authority, God is male as are the prophets.

However, within the various denominations of Christianity, Islam, and Judaism, there are liberal and progressive groups that do not hold to the patriarchal traditions of the past, and instead embrace a more diverse interpretation of divine will. These groups have elevated women to positions of authority and no longer cling to the beliefs and policies of the past. At the same time, there has been a great deal of interdenominational debate over whether women should be elevated to positions of authority within the church. Conservative or orthodox versions of Judaism, Islam, and Christianity have held to rigid roles for women where leadership or authoritative positions are out of the question. We will focus mainly on Christianity in this chapter due its numerical prominence in America, but similar points can be made about other Western religions that subordinate and relegate women to lower levels of ecclesiastical duties.

This chapter is called "Religious Bros" because bro behaviors and beliefs have been wrapped around alleged scriptural authority for millennia. The edict given to women to "obey your husbands" is one of many such instructions.

The doctrinal glue that holds together the sexist-bro-thinking of conservative religion is known as complementarianism.

COMPLEMENTARIANISM

Western religions practice the doctrine known as complementarianism, which is the view that God created men and women for different purposes. Specifically, complementarianism expresses the view that men are to be the leaders at church and in the home, and women are not.[1] To the complementarian, women's proper roles are to support men by raising children and taking care of domestic chores, but that women should never compete with men at home or in the workplace.[2] Christians base this view on scripture found in I Timothy 2:12–13, which reads, "But I do not allow a woman to teach or exercise authority over a man, but to remain quiet. For it was Adam who was first created, and then Eve."[3,4] Because people of faith turn to scripture to ground their beliefs and actions, these two verses, for many, establish the role of women as supportive, but not competitive with men, and have been used to restrict women's roles to remaining at home raising children, while men work to support the family.

But as with most religious views, there is contention due to what appears to be competing scriptural messaging and of course, different ways of interpreting scripture. For instance, Miriam (Exodus 15), Huldah (2 Kings 22), and Deborah (Judges 4–5) are prophets, while Deborah also served as a judge in Israel.[5] In addition, there are a number of women who were instrumental in Jesus' ministry (Luke 8: 1–3, Luke 10: 38–42, Matthew 15: 21–28, Luke 7: 36–50, John 4: 39–42, Matthew 28: 1–10, Mark 16: 1–8, Matthew 28: 18–20, Acts 1:8). Women were also instrumental in the creation, expression, and explication of the early church (I Cor. 11:5, Acts 18:26, Romans 16: 1–8).

The thing is, regardless how one interprets scripture, there will be other people of faith who interpret the text differently, and each interpreter will be convinced that they have *the truth from on high*. When one truly believes he has captured *the will of God* accurately through a particular scriptural reading, there is little-to-no chance he will negotiate his position with those who disagree with him. In fact, by definition, if one truly has captured the will of God accurately, in his mind, a move in any other direction would be a move into falsehood. This mentality paralyzes any efforts to break through the glut of disagreement to reach a consensus, since coming to agreement oftentimes requires compromise, negotiation, and reassessment, something about which few devout people of faith are interested.

One constant problem for religion is the famous inclination to cherry-pick passages to create versions of God's will that conform to one's preferred position. So, if one person views God as mainly a figure of love, one can construct that model; if another person views God as mainly a figure of wrath, that person can construct a model of scripture that conforms to that reading. In fact, what we have witnessed in America is the establishment of different Christian churches with widely different orientations. Some churches emphasize a syncretism of Christianity and capitalism, while others emphasize a syncretism of Christianity and social justice.

Throughout the past two centuries, there has been an explosion of new Christian denominations. According to *World Christian Encyclopedia*, there are six major ecclesiastico-cultural blocs, divided into 300 major ecclesiastical traditions, composed of over 33,000 distinct denominations stretched out over 238 nations.[6] Between many denominations there are a great number of consistencies, and the differences may be small. But with other denominations, the differences are vast. For instance, salvation is determined by Calvinist traditions in a very different way than the view of salvation according to Roman Catholic traditions.[7,8] But the point of this chapter is not to debate Christian apologetics. The point is that bro culture has been greatly aided by religion and particularly Western religion. It is one thing to couch one's sexism in personal anger such as that found in the statements of many men's rights activists, but it is another thing to frame one's sexism as being an extension of God's will. When men like Pat Robertson utter wildly sexist and racist statements, they represent an authority to their followers that is considered to be superior to the sexist ramblings of Donald Trump or Mel Gibson.[9]

The merger of religion and a variety of bigotries is nothing new. The Ku Klux Klan is a Christian organization, although adherents of other forms of Christianity do not recognize it as legitimately Christian.[10] But then, the KKK and other reactionary splinter groups do not view mainstream Christianity as legitimately Christian.[11] What you end up getting is a diverse group of people identifying as Christian, but with considerable differences in doctrine. Yet, until recently, Christianity, as well as Islam and Judaism, remained firmly patriarchal. Examples can be seen throughout society. Pop-cultural curiosity and anachronism Phil Robertson of the defunct reality TV show *Duck Dynasty*, with Bible in hand, recently stated,

> Mainly because these boys are waitin' 'til they get to be about 20 years old before they marry 'em…you got to marry these girls when they're about 15 or 16.[12]

It isn't that bros are recommending child marriage, necessarily, but that once again we have a suggestion of subordinating girls' autonomy for the interests of men, as though men's desires are authoritative and the ambitions and goals of girls and women are irrelevant. The formula is an old one: make wildly sexist statements, wrap them around the Bible, and come off as a minister of goodwill who is simply trying to preach the *Word of the Lord*. This allows religious bros to reject all criticism that their views are sexist, racist, homophobic, or xenophobic as coming from ungodly atheists, heretics, and apostates who do not understand or care about God's will. This recipe allows religious figures like Franklin Graham, son of famous Christian Evangelist Billy Graham, to claim that "God is not politically correct," which opens the door to any form of sexism, racism, and homophobia as "Biblical truths" that cannot be questioned or challenged in any way.[13]

So, when calling for ending the gendered pay gap, creating greater educational and career opportunities for girls and women, protecting equal treatment for women by passing an equal rights amendment, or simply encouraging girls to pursue their dreams, complementarians often reject all of it as violating "Biblical truths" and insist that their resistance to the empowerment of women is not sexist in nature, but adherence to the will of God. This is also why there has been such great resistance to feminism by conservative religious figures, since the beliefs and teachings of feminism support the empowerment of women in ways that these religious figures believe directly challenge the divine order that instructs men to lead and women to support and follow.

KEEPING WOMEN "IN THEIR PLACE"

Christian leaders in America have long attempted to hold women down and done so by using threats, insults, and so-called Biblical authority. Famed televangelist Pat Robertson once stated of married women,

> You always have to keep that spark of love alive. It isn't something to just lie there and think "Well I'm married to him, so he's got to take me slatternly-looking." You have got to fix yourself up, look pretty, look alert.[14]

Robertson, like many older, conservative Evangelical Christians, views women as do most bros: that the most important contribution women make to society is aesthetic, beyond which they should be baby-machines and domestic servants. On *proper* gender roles, Robertson quips,

> I know this is painful for the ladies to hear, but if you get married, you have accepted the headship of a man, your husband. Christ is the head of the household, and the husband is the head of the wife, and that's the way it is, period.[15]

Naturally, when asked about husbands who cheat on their wives, Robertson pulls out this primitive bit of patriarchal wisdom:

> Males have a tendency to wander a little bit. And what you want to do is make a home so wonderful he doesn't want to wander.[16]

To the men who run most of Christendom, and particularly conservative versions of Christendom, Robertson's advice is music to their ears. Men *can't help themselves when they inevitably cheat* and so it is the responsibility of women to keep their husbands from doing what husbands naturally do by being the perfect housekeeper, while spending any spare time making yourself look like Angelina Jolie.

While it is easy to write off the ramblings of a minister whose prominence in the Evangelical community has waned, Robertson's advice and pronouncements are not at all out of step with the conservative Christian decrees of today. In fact, many conservative Christian men today practice what is known as **the Billy Graham Rule**:

Do not spend time with women to whom you are not married.[17]

Famously, Vice President Mike Pence practices a version of this rule, making sure never to have dinner alone with any woman other than his wife.[18] The rule has the egalitarian advantage of being sexist against both women and men. It implicitly assumes that men are constantly filled with lustful urges that may rupture out of them at the slightest provocation from a woman, but it also assumes that women are natural temptresses of men. This view is literally ancient. The woman as *temptress* can be traced back to Eve in the Genesis account in *The Bible*, where a serpent, later associated with Satan, is able to use Eve as a willing vessel to get herself and her husband, Adam, to violate God's command not to eat the fruit of a tree that will give them the ability to know the difference between right and wrong.[19] The *Garden of Eden* story gets the bro narrative of women up and running: *men are weak and vulnerable to women's seductive ways*, hence Mike Pence's need to stay away from women who are not his wife. Victim blaming is built into any lapses in men's judgment. When men inevitably screw up, it is not due to acting on their own selfish desires, but to women's natural ability to *make men lose control*.

Keeping women "in their place" has long been a goal of organized religion. Mike Pence's adherence to the Billy Graham rule is a good example. While Pence has the luxury of possessing political power while adhering to the rule, single women do not. Imagine being a single woman trying to rise through the patriarchal halls of government in search of a career in politics, while living by the rule that you cannot dine with a married male politician without his wife being present. Single men who are trying to create a career in politics would have no such barrier, since the rule works only if one accepts the underlying premise of men as *naturally* selfish and easily beguiled and women as *naturally* seductive and looking to sexually entice men as necessary ingredients in falling from grace.

But the Graham rule is particularly sexist. It treats women as a class instead of as individuals. Would Pence be *at risk* by having an unaccompanied supper with a woman who happens to be a single octogenarian? By universalizing the rule, women are placed in a class of beings who are problems for men. It casts women in the role of seductress and men in the role of victim, thereby avoiding any culpability when men cross the line. This has long been the rallying cry of men's rights activists, that women are to blame for men's bad behaviors. The latest angry man to take up the men's rights mantle is University of Toronto professor of psychology Jordan Peterson, who claims that women should be forced into monogamous, sexual relationships with men.[20] His reasoning is based on the idea that women left to their own choices will opt for rich, powerful men, leaving most of the male population without sexual partners.[21] Blaming women for men's "understandable" misconduct is built into both Peterson's and Pence's rules. The misogyny of both rules is found in the core message,

> *If women would only know their place, men would behave better.*

It is a banal, well-worn rule that has accompanied bro culture throughout time, and continues to be a go-to decree whenever men do stupid, sexually irresponsible, and even violent things against women.

POLICING WOMEN'S BODIES

Keeping women in their place by policing reproductive rights is another long-standing tactic of the religious right. Ironically, bros tend to support abortion rights, since it takes away potential parental responsibilities from men. But conservative religion has policed women's bodies and choices in numerous ways. The **purity movement** is one particular movement that is dedicated to policing girls' and young women's sexual choices. In her book, *Pure: Inside the Evangelical Movement That Shamed a Generation of Young Women and How I Broke Free*, author Linda Kay Klein documents her experiences that were fueled by the belief that,

> Girls and women were responsible for keeping male sexual desire in check by wearing modest clothing, maintaining a sexless mind and body and taking a "purity pledge, " in which they promised to remain virgins until marriage.[22,23]

Klein notes that "being a good Christian" entailed "protecting men from you," because your body is a threat to men, since it can *cause men* to act out sexually.[24] Once again, the bro message is clear: it is a woman's responsibility to keep men in check, since men are incapable of controlling themselves in the presence of women. As we have seen with other bro rules, the purity movement is based on sexism in both directions: women are blameworthy for having female bodies, while men are mindlessly sexual in the presence of such bodies. Beliefs of this kind also breed intense forms of shame and guilt when young people inevitably follow the urgings of nature. As documented in Chapter 8, when those urgings lead to unprotected sex, as a result of abstinence-only sex education where young people do not receive accurate information on how to protect themselves, you create a template for higher rates of teen pregnancy.

In what may be one of the most straightforward examples of religion's role in keeping women "in their place," a common refrain from conservative pastors is that women should "obey their husbands," as though women are children who must follow the dictates of their parents. Mark Harris, pastor and North Carolina Republican politician, stated during a sermon in 2014,

> What's the message to the wives? Well, God instructs all Christian wives to submit to their husbands. You see wives, please hear me

this morning. The message is not from your husband to submit, the message is from the Lord. You're not to ever submit ma'am because your husband demands it, but you do it because the Lord ordained it.[25]

We once again witness men using their place of religious leadership to support the subordination of women to men, and the command given to women to submit to men is delivered around a complementarian framework:

> Submission is not about inferiority in any way, any shape and any form. It simply reflects a God-ordained design of things.[26]

This bro-friendly ordination is convenient to a patriarchal structure like that found in most churches. Women who resist are placed in the category of heretic who are disobeying not their husbands, but God himself.

But it gets worse. Imagine you are the Christian wife of an abusive husband. A 12-month ABC News investigation revealed that Catholic, Anglican, Baptist, Pentecostal, and Presbyterian women who were subject to domestic violence at the hands of their husbands were told to forgive them and to remain in the abusive relationship rather than divorce their abusive husbands.[27] Lynne Baker, author of the book *Counseling Christian Women on How to Deal with Domestic Violence*, argues,

> Biblical principles and scriptures may be used by the perpetrator as a point of authority to condone his actions, or perhaps to 'prove' to the victim that she is not fulfilling her marital obligations.[28]

Abusive religious men often cherry-pick very specific passages in scripture to condone their abuse, such as the passages in I Peter discussed earlier,[29] or I Corinthians, where women are instructed that the man is "the head of the woman just as God is the head of Christ."[30] One can engage in scriptural interpretation debates forevermore, but these passages have opened the doctrinal door for centuries of unabated physical and sexual abuse of women at the hands of their husbands.

POLICING WOMEN'S CHOICES

Yet another way that women are "kept in their place" by conservative religion is by restricting women's career ambitions. Rarely are women told that they are disallowed from gaining employment outside of the home, but conservative religion monitors their motives to assure that those motives comport to the dictates of the church. In an article published by Christian Apologetics & Research Ministry (CARM), women are advised:

> A nurturing home life always outweighs momentary material accumulation that is not necessarily required. The pattern in the Bible is

for a wife to maintain the home. If a family is struggling financially, it may be preferable for a wife to first consider if she can find a job that keeps her closer to home, has convenient hours for the family, or is run out of her home.[31]

Naturally, no such corollary instruction is offered to men. Women are informed that their primary responsibility is to have babies, take care of children, take care of their husband, cook, clean, look good, and do everything necessary to create a model home. Those women who pursue careers are often shamed and chastised for violating their primary purposes of mother and homemaker. Yet, 47% of the American workforce is composed of women.[32] Many young women today are choosing to put off having a family until their education is complete and they have established themselves in careers, with most educated women foregoing motherhood until sometime in their 30s.[33]

A typical bro does not necessarily want his wife to stay home and not work, since two incomes afford a better standard of living than one income. But bros are often uncomfortable with the idea of their wives making more money than they make. Today, more than 40% of American families find the wife as primary breadwinner and these numbers are expected to increase as women currently outnumber men in colleges and universities.[34,35] The bro is a man who views women as secondary in importance to men, but since most men have been told since childhood that providing for the family is one of their most important roles, many men now find themselves having to redefine their role as father and husband. In fact, according to research from the University of Chicago, once a woman starts making more money than her husband, divorce rates increase.[36] According to the research,

> The percentage of people who report being "very happy" with their marriage declines when a woman earns more money than her husband. A woman out-earning her husband could even doom the marriage, as this "increases the likelihood of divorce by 50 percent."[37]

This increase in divorce could be the result of men feeling inadequate in fulfilling their expected role as provider, but it could also be the result of women realizing that they do not have to put up with bad behaviors from their husbands when they are no longer financially dependent on them. For generations, bros have been able to financially extort women by threatening to cut off funding if their wives leave them or otherwise disobey them. This sort of threat is slowly becoming obsolete as more women enter the workforce in positions of management, and could be the factor that threatens bro-hood more than any other risk.

But the fact that women are becoming more educated and financially independent from men is the very fact that may also threaten religion's deep-rooted stranglehold over women. Millennials, both women and men, are leaving organized religion in record numbers, nearly quadrupling over the past

30 years.[38] Those women who remain in organized religion are seeking more authoritative roles and in some cases, they are getting them.[39]

To this day, women are often counseled by church leaders that their career choices should conform to work that *suit women* such as nursing, daycare, or teaching in elementary schools. Careers of this sort align with the gender essentialism held by many conservatives that women are *designed* for nurturing and raising children, while men are *designed* for leadership, but also for work that requires physical strength, great intelligence, or bravery, such as careers in the military, as police officers, or fire-rescue personnel. Consider the contentious debate over whether women should serve in the military in combat forces. *The Counsel on Biblical Manhood and Womanhood* issued a guideline on this issue, stating,

> The pattern established by God throughout the Bible is that men, not women, bear responsibility to serve in combat if war is necessary.[40]

This edict is followed by a list of scriptural passages that serve as *proof* to the faithful that denying women positions in combat is God approved. These sorts of views are particularly bro-friendly, since many bros feel that women have been *encroaching* for years on areas of life they consider to be male-sacred such as policing, construction, and even STEM. Lynn Billman, President of *Christian Women in Sciences* argues,

> Christian women in STEM careers, or young women who hope to pursue such careers, are a vulnerable minority. Their churches often fail to validate their interests and ambitions, and their more secular, often atheist peers denigrate them for being religious.[41]

What Billman fails to state is that because STEM fields continue to be male dominated, those within STEM fields who may denigrate women of faith are usually men, due in large part to the fact that hierarchies favoring men over women in fields of science and technology have been sewn into the fabric of American culture. The upshot is that whether a woman is religious or not, there are forces within male culture that attempt to belittle, intimidate, and shame those women who challenge the patriarchal structure of society.

BENEVOLENT SEXISM

Benevolent sexism seems to be an oxymoron. How can something like sexism, racism, or other problematic forms of bigotry count as benign or worse, coming from a place of goodwill? There are several versions of benevolent sexism, one being the view that women need protecting by men from a hostile world. It is often contrasted with **hostile sexism,** which is any antagonism, including violence toward women.[42] But benevolent forms of sexism start from the assumption that women are less competent than men in a host of areas such that men must protect and guide women for their own good. It is, in other words, thoroughly patriarchal in nature, since benevolent sexism compromises the agentic status of women.

Conservative religion has helped itself to this form of sexism, which flows directly from complementarianism.[43] With the view that women should maintain and enjoy supportive roles to men's leadership, a hierarchy of power is established that places women in subordinate roles to male authority. According to self-described Christian, feminist author Ashley Easter, benevolent sexism in the church has three consequences:

- It leads to women being judged as less competent.
- It negatively affects women's performance.
- It makes women less likely to want to be leaders.[44]

Conservative churches do not mind this third consequence, since in general, the male leadership found in conservative religious groups do not believe that women should be leaders. The consequences for women of faith who work in conservative religious institutions are predictable. Women who are professors at conservative, religious universities, for instance, are less likely than their secular counterparts to receive opportunities for advancement.[45] Professors Elizabeth Hall, Brad Christerson, and Shelly Cunningham from Biola University, an Evangelical Christian university in Southern California, co-authored the article, "Women Faculty at an Evangelical University: The Paradox of Religiously Driven Gender Inequalities and High Job Satisfaction" to document the challenges for women who teach at conservative, Christian institutions.[46] In an interview with *Christianity Today*, the authors noted,

> Many women faculty reported feeling undermined at work by implicit assumptions that they should be home with their children, or that the qualities that are valued in academia—intelligence, assertiveness, and confidence—are not traits appropriate for Christian women.[47]

Additionally, at conservative, Christian institutions, women are not encouraged to participate in groups created by male colleagues where job-related information is discussed out of a concern over "sexual temptation" that can "result from too much contact with the opposite sex at work."[48] Much like the Billy Graham rule, women are viewed as problems for men. So, the solution to assure that no inappropriate sexual contact occurs between male and female colleagues is to discourage women from participating in collegial work with male colleagues, which could benefit their careers. But because women are expected to place their careers in a secondary role to what is considered to be their primary role as mothers and housekeepers, any negative effect to their careers is thought to be necessary to preserve the complementary structure of "God's divine plan."

While even women of faith recognize their treatment as being sexist in nature, they paradoxically report that their job satisfaction is high.[49] This counter-intuitive report is likely due to the fact that conservative women of faith accept their complementary status as a product of divine will. Writing for the *New York Times*, senior correspondent Susan Chira notes that "Sisterhood doesn't override partisanship or deeply held moral views."[50] Chira relays the view of a stay-at-home wife from Mississippi that is no doubt echoed by many women across the nation,

> In the Bible it says that a man is responsible for leading his household. And a woman's only supposed to step up if he's not willing. Aside from that, women are just too emotional. I feel like it would be dangerous to have a woman in a position to potentially start a war.[51]

Mapping religious sentiments onto political sentiments is a common reprise among people of faith. In this case, women who believe in the complementary relationship of women to men are more likely to not only accept their own subordinate status to men, but also to view women as a class of people who are incompetent to lead. The traditions of bro culture fully agree.

University of Delaware professor of political science, Erin C. Cassese found in her research that Republican men and women, particularly low-income, Evangelical Christian voters, were much more likely to engage in hostile sexism than their Democrat or Independent counterparts.[52] Cassese also discovered in her research with colleague Mirya R. Holman that those who embrace hostile forms of sexism showed greater support for Trump in the 2016 election, while those who embraced more benevolent forms of sexism supported Clinton in greater numbers.[53] Cassese noted in her research with colleague Tiffany D. Barnes that white women were far more likely to vote for Trump than women of color, concluding that the sexist beliefs held by white women were "strong determinants of their vote choice in 2016."[54] The religious views one holds have also been shown to be a strong predictor of political candidate choice.[55] In fact, NYU professor Patrick Egan argues that Americans increasingly align their intersectional identities with their political alliances.[56] People of faith who identify as Evangelical Christian, for example, will accommodate their Christian commitments to their politically conservative commitments. One way of putting this is that one's political values are often used as a filter to parse scriptural readings so that certain forms of the identity "Christian" are viewed as *naturally* coextensive with the identity "conservative," causing one's political identity to drive and interpret one's religious identity. Benevolent sexism, and sometimes hostile sexism, is a result of these interpretations coupled with a history of unchallenged patriarchy in religion.

But despite the fact that many men of faith are not happy with women's slow, but steady increases in power, including clergical power, women are gradually attaining positions of authority. When men have been instructed that women are of less value than men, increases in power can be viewed as a threat to the natural order of things. The more toxic forms of bro-hood are often found among political conservatives for the very reasons we have discussed above: that those who accept the complementary relationship of women to men often devalue the role women play in areas of leadership, while elevating the value of men in these same roles. Those men who elevate the masculine over the feminine, however they define these descriptors, are also those who commit the highest levels of domestic violence. In Australia, researchers were able to show that "Evangelical Christian men who attend church sporadically" are the men most likely to abuse their wives.[57] In fact, according to the research conducted by Lynne Baker, 22% of men who go to church regularly also engage in abusive behaviors toward their wives.[58] Other studies have shown similar levels of abuse by Muslim men.[59] Because much of domestic violence goes unreported out of understandable feelings of fear,[60] it can be difficult to accurately gauge levels of abuse, but multiple studies report that approximately one out of four women globally will experience domestic abuse in their lifetimes.[61] In many cases, religious men who abuse their wives will victim blame, claiming that their wife was disobedient and therefore in violation of the dictates of scripture.[62] The slippery slope from benevolent sexism to hostile sexism is not so slippery when men are instructed that women have less value than men and should therefore "know their place."

FAMILY VALUES

The expression 'family values' has been code for "men should be in positions of authority," "homosexuality is a sin," "there are two and only two genders," "single mothers cannot adequately raise children," and "comprehensive sex education is immoral by teaching kids it is okay to have sex" for generations. The phrase suggests that certain religious people hold copyrights on morality and that by contrast, the morality of the secular world is in reality immoral. In fact, 'family values' is often conflated with "Biblical values" as a way to distinguish the nonsecular from the secular. But the patriarchy embedded in the phrase 'family values' is and has been part of conservative Christianity for centuries.

Writing for *The American Prospect*, Jamelle Bouie notes that the phrase 'family values' has come to mean "moral superiority" that is grounded in an opposition to women's autonomy and the alleged *ethical truth* of patriarchy.[63] For years, the phrase was synonymous with the equally sinister notion, *the sanctity of marriage*, which was itself code for the rejection of marriage equality for same-sex couples.[64] Law professor Twila L. Perry writes that those who tout *family values* are often the same people who tout Trump's slogan, *Make America Great Again*, as the dream of a mythical America in the past when culture was properly aligned with the *Christian values* they believe in.[65] Those particular values often include the racist notion that people of color should know their place and not challenge the status quo of segregation and white supremacy, of times when gay people were in the closet out of fear for their safety, and when women were home baking cookies and changing diapers instead of dreaming of college educations and fulfilling careers.

These alleged *Christian values* of the past are draped in white, heteronormative patriarchy. But then much of the bro beliefs and attitudes found among white, middle-class frat-bros echo these same sentiments. Beyond the high rates of sexual harassment and assault, many fraternity bros are caught in videos making remorseless racist, sexist, and homophobic comments, or acting out bigoted behaviors as an implicit appeal to the past when words and actions of these kinds were permissible.[66,67] It isn't that these young men are unaware that these behaviors are not acceptable, but that the unacceptability itself makes the actions cooler by engaging in taboo rituals that run against today's prevailing attitudes. By framing certain bigoted beliefs and behaviors as a return to times when *things were good*, and wrapping these actions around either the American flag, *The Bible*, or the repetitive and pernicious incantation *boys will be boys*, patriarchs and bigots of various kind can attempt to justify their bigotry as a return to family or Biblical values.

One group that frames the *family values* ethos of conservative Christianity is the group known as *Promise Keepers*, which is made up of men who hold rallies, while claiming to adhere to seven promises:

- A Promise Keeper is committed to honoring Jesus Christ through worship, prayer, and obedience to God's Word in the power of the Holy Spirit.
- A Promise Keeper is committed to pursuing vital relationships with a few other men, understanding that he needs brothers to help him keep his promises.
- A Promise Keeper is committed to practicing spiritual, moral, ethical, and sexual purity.
- A Promise Keeper is committed to building strong marriages and families through love, protection, and biblical values.
- A Promise Keeper understands his authentic identity in Christ and lives in unequivocal integrity through Christ. He understands that Jesus calls him to be His hands and feet. He actively gives of his time and resources and purposefully lifts up the leadership of the church and his nation in prayer.
- A Promise Keeper is committed to reaching beyond any racial and denominational barriers to demonstrate the power of biblical unity.
- A Promise Keeper is committed to influencing his world, being obedient to the Great Commandment and the Great Commission.

With each promise, a set of appropriately cherry-picked scriptural passages are provided to assure the men of Promise Keepers that Biblical authority has anointed these promises as God's will.[68] But carefully worded phrases are found in several of the promises that can be interpreted through a patriarchal and homophobic lens such as "practicing moral, ethical, and sexual purity," and "building strong marriages through Biblical values." The word 'purity' has long been used by many people of faith to denote either *virginal* in the case of women or *heterosexual* to assure that women's sexual choices are properly policed and that LGBTQ identities are not recognized as pure or expressing Biblical values.[69,70] In fact, "Biblical values" itself is a phrase highly subject to interpretation. Denominational arguments have revolved around just such disagreements in scriptural hermeneutics, but Promise Keepers, like many conservative Christian groups, believe that they have captured God's will with great accuracy and have no interest in debating, let alone compromising, that view.

It should be noted before wrapping up this segment that Promise Keepers do not allow women to attend their rallies.[71] Like many patriarchal groups and clubs, the men of Promise Keepers believe that it is up to men to figure out how best to navigate the rules and regulations of home life, which centers around men as leader of the household and women being happy and content to follow. Revered M. William Howard, president of the New York Theological Seminary writes of Promise Keepers and their attitude toward women,

> They are saying that you as a woman should be adored and put on a pedestal and loved for the not-so-serious person you are.[72]

Tony Evans, one of Promise Keepers' most visible spokesmen urges men, "Treat the lady gently and lovingly, but lead!"[73] The complementarianism in a statement like this is palpable. Men should lead the household and women should know, and be happy about, their place of subordination to men.

THE GOSPEL OF PROSPERITY: BRO PARADISE

A longstanding rule in bro culture is the notion that men should strive for wealth. Placing one's wealth on display and boasting about it has been a commonly practiced trait for bros as diverse as Donald Trump to music artist Pitbull. Placing your wealth on display means to flash money, drive expensive cars, wear expensive jewelry, attend elaborate parties and special events, flaunt to others pictures of yourself with "beautiful women," and live in a 17,000 square foot mansion worth $17 million as does Houston-based prosperity pastor and televangelist Joel Osteen.[74]

So-called *prosperity theology* is a religious bro's dream come true.[75] Prosperity theology or the gospel of prosperity is the view that God rewards those who are faithful with financial success. Beyond the charges of hypocrisy, cherry-picking scripture, and using religion to pursue self-interest, men of faith can now live the life of a bro, while claiming to simply be following God's will. It is a marvel of capitalism that is can creep into every aspect of life, including one where its savior claimed that "it is easier for a camel to pass through the eye of a needle than for a rich man to enter the kingdom of God."[76]

In sociologist Michael Kimmel's book *Guyland: The Perilous World Where Boys Become Men*, Kimmel notes that being wealthy or at least appearing to be wealthy is a pervasive message that is driven into men at young ages.[77,78] Wealth is a marker of masculine success because it exudes one's ability to possess power over others. Being in control, possessing the freedom to do anything you want to do, having the ability to wield influence over others, and appearing to be more important than others are all cultural indicators in a capitalist society that a man has success. Men who achieve monetary success do not necessarily have to be athletic, muscular, physically intimidating, or even good-looking by societal standards since their power is abstract in the sense that its visible symptoms are expensive homes, cars, vacations, jewelry, and other conventions of external wealth.

But a capitalist culture also works on the assumption that wealth as power attracts romantic and sexual partners one could not otherwise attract. Sociologist Elizabeth McClinton argues,

> It would be very hard to separate out class and attractiveness, because they're just so fundamentally linked. I can't control for that—I don't see how anybody could.[79]

Men are taught, whether true or not, that good-looking partners will be more attracted to you if you are wealthy. It is an assumption that may not be true for millions of men and women, but it is a persistent generalization that has been around for centuries. In actuality, it is yet another way that women's accomplishments are discredited. When bros see very good-looking women who drive expensive cars or wear expensive clothing and jewelry, they assume that her wealth came either from her family or husband. This stereotype also promotes the sexist view to girls and young women that it is your looks, not your accomplishments, that will best serve you in your quest for success. In the end, bros are instructed that they can trade their wealth for beauty, while women are instructed that they can trade their beauty for wealth.

The gospel of prosperity plays right into this stereotype. The megachurches of Joel Osteen, T.D Jakes, Benny Hinn, Rick Warren, and Creflo Dollar (his actual name), sell a very bro-friendly version of religion. They syncretize Judeo-Christianity with capitalism to form conglomerations where one can feel pious and devout, while enjoying the lifestyles of the rich and famous. The megachurches are typically conservative in their theology, while appealing to feel-good messages of personal wealth and empowerment. Megachurches are defined as churches with congregations of 2,000 or more parishioners.[80] The pastors are often charismatic leaders who could double as motivational speakers. According to University of Washington professor of American religion James Wellman, "Megachurches, which rarely refer to heaven or hell, are worlds away from the sober, judgmental puritan meetinghouses of long ago." The nonjudgmental, party atmosphere of megachurches is another main draw that amalgamates the cherry-picked, feel-good scriptural passages with American capitalism. The result is a bro-friendly party church that caters to the interests of an upwardly mobile, consumer-minded congregation.

Joel Osteen's Lakewood Church in Houston, Texas draws 30,000 faithful each week and helps contribute to Osteen's reported net fortune of $40 million.[81] Osteen's car collection includes a Ferrari 458 Italia, a Porsche 911, and a Mercedes G-class sedan.[82] He has sold out Madison Square Garden seven times, and travels in private jets, which places him in the company of rappers and rock stars more than it does that of a typical preacher.[83] Everything about Osteen's lifestyle is bro-friendly. It infuses hyper-capitalism with patriarchy and then weds the entire goulash to God's will. All that is missing, so far as we know, are the sex-themed, beer-pong parties.

More recently, and unsurprisingly, megachurches have been investigated for reports of sexual harassment. The Willow Creek Community Church in Illinois, one of the first to gain national attention as a megachurch, has come under scrutiny as its pastor, Bill Hybels, has been accused by multiple women of sexual harassment.[84] An independent investigation made up of Christian leaders concluded that the accusations were credible and Hybels stepped down as pastor.[85] But it cannot be surprising that abuse of this kind is found in institutions where leadership is comprised almost entirely of men. At the Grace Community megachurch in Sun Valley, California, for instance, which instructs women to submit to men, the pastor, deacons, and elders are all men.[86] In fact, Grace Church features an all-male group entitled *Men of the Word,* which is designed to "glorify God by equipping and encouraging men to fulfill their God-ordained roles as leaders in the home, the church, and the world."[87] If you are a man who was raised throughout boyhood to view women as not having the qualities required for leadership, conservative megachurches of this kind continue the training and wrap their sexism around scripture so that you can feel good about your sexism, while living the life of a rock star.

ATHEIST BROS

It is debatable whether atheism is actually a religion, since it holds no official doctrines other than the unremarkable metaphysical assumption that there is no God. But given that atheists often hold themselves to be *more rational* than theists and offer their views as being in contrast to those religious complementarians who subordinate women to a second-class role to men, we might expect more progressive views about women. However, contemporary atheism has had a sexism problem for a long time, starting with late author, polemist Christopher Hitchens, who many viewed as the patron saint of chauvinism. Hitchens rode his many book sales and television appearances to global fame and was known as a fierce champion of atheism by agreeing to debate religious leaders around the world, but garnered backlash for his infamous claim that "women aren't funny."[88] This is a harangue that has been around before Hitchens from the late comedian Jerry Lewis and acerbic comedian Adam Carolla.[89,90] But Hitchens carried a swagger of white, male, British intellectual elitism that carried credibility in the minds of many bros who looked up to him. Hitchens also peppered his cynical dry-wit with the b-word on many occasions.[91] At the same time, and with great irony, Hitchens also stated during a debate with former British Prime Minister Tony Blair at the University of Toronto,

> The cure for poverty has a name: it's called 'the empowerment of women'. Now, name me a religion that stands, or has ever stood, for that![92]

How does one reconcile what appears to be Hitchens' support of women's empowerment alongside his liberal use of the b-word? Like many bros, he used words to suit his audience. In Hitchens' case, as a master of debate, he was able to topple his opponent by arguing that religion holds women down in countless ways, but appearing on an episode of Bill Maher's show *Real Time*, Hitchens was offered an opportunity to play to a different audience, including Maher himself, who has a history of trashing women in the name of comedy.

In one instance, Maher stated of Trump, "If Trump was a man, he'd stop whining like a little bitch," followed by the hashtag #LadyTrump.[93] Maher, a fierce opponent of religion wrote and starred in the 2008 film entitled *Religulous*, where he attempted to show the absurdities of religious belief and religious culture.[94] But when the occasion arises to knock a public figure like Hillary Clinton or Donald Trump, Maher has not hesitated to use sexist slurs to make his point and then pull out the most hackneyed bro excuse of all time, "it's just a joke," when critics call him out.

Along with Christopher Hitchens who died in 2011, British evolutionary biologist Richard Dawkins is easily one of the most visible and vocal atheists of our time. In 2014, Dawkins tweeted about rape victims, "If you want to be in a position to testify against a man, don't get drunk."[95] Dawkins went on to defend the tweet as simply sage advice to women who might not have other corroborating evidence to prove they were raped, but the backlash was intense. Bros have been blaming women for their being raped for generations, and one of the favorite tactics is to suggest that a woman's drunkenness contributed to the rape by placing oneself in the vulnerable position of being raped, followed by an inability to prove an act of rape took place because their inebriated condition creates reasonable doubt as to the veracity of their memory. While Dawkins was not claiming that it is a woman's fault if she gets raped while under the influence of alcohol, he was placing the onus on women to remain sober at all times when around men in the event that one of them rapes you.

Ironically, Dawkins advertises himself as a "passionate feminist," but laments that he is misunderstood.[96] In one instance, Dawkins stated,

> I occasionally get a little impatient with American women who complain of being inappropriately touched by the water cooler or invited for coffee or something which I think is, by comparison, relatively trivial.[97]

This is a sarcastic swipe at #metoo by reducing the charges against men brought by some women who have been sexually harassed at work to an overreaction or worse, to a non-harassing moment such as being invited to have coffee. It is wildly dismissive of #metoo or at a minimum, an accusation that #metoo has gone too far.

Neuroscientist and best-selling author Sam Harris has also made a name for himself as one of the more prominent skeptics of our time.[98] Appearing on numerous episodes of Bill Maher's *Real Time*, Harris has distinguished himself as a conspicuous critic of political correctness.[99] One such criticism took place when Harris had a confrontation with Michelle Boorstein of the Washington Post.[100] When Boorstein asked Harris why he thought his work was supported largely by men, Harris responded,

> I think it may have to do with my person[al] slant as an author, being very critical of bad ideas. This can sound very angry to people...People just don't like to have their ideas criticized. There's something about that critical posture that is to some degree intrinsically male and more attractive to guys than to women. The atheist variable just has this—it doesn't obviously have this nurturing, coherence-building extra estrogen vibe that you would want by default if you wanted to attract as many women as men.[101]

Later, defending his response, Harris noted that Boorstein's objections were appeals to political correctness and that his response was simply meant for laughs.[102] As noted in this book several times, the "it's just a joke" excuse coupled with "I don't care about being politically correct" explanation has become a mantra for bros. Men can say incredibly sexist, racist, homophobic, or xenophobic things and with a wave of a wand, make it all disappear by sarcastically uttering the magical words, "it's just a joke," and if that doesn't get the results you were hoping for, slide in the rationalization, "I don't believe in political correctness" to make your opponent appear to be a stodgy, rule-worshipping boor who isn't smart enough to appreciate the subtle nuances of language to create levity and entertainment.

Thought Box

Boorstein's question to Harris and Harris's response raises an interesting question. While there are plenty of women who are atheists, why is it that the most famous atheists of our time are men? Why is it that atheists like Dawkins, Harris, and Hitchens find their greatest support among men? The sexism these men have placed on display speaks to their understanding that the majority of their audience are men, but we witness strong defensive pushbacks from these men when they are accused of being sexist. That is, they do not want to be perceived publicly as being sexist even though some of their words court sexist themes with great gusto. What do you think? Why is atheism so male?

Ultimately, a pervasive problem in atheist circles is the male-centricity of the movement, which does itself no favors when high-profile atheists like Harris suggest that the argumentative approach of atheism turns women off. It plays to a longstanding stereotype that men are rational and women are emotional that can be found among the most zealous religious devotees in the world.

POSTSCRIPT

Religious faith comes in almost every imaginable form. From politically liberal, LGBTQ- affirming churches to racist, homophobic, misogynist-embracing churches and everything in between, religion has something for almost everyone. With respect to gender, the online publication *Newsmax* recently published the "100 most influential Evangelical Christians in America" list, and unsurprisingly, only 14 of the 100 are women, and this low number is being heralded as progress.[103] This means that religion is overwhelmingly patriarchal in nature, even with the slow advances made by women in certain notable denominations. This also means that organized religion has been a place where many bro beliefs, as we have identified them, are cultivated and flourish. Complementarianism is perhaps the most infamous of those beliefs, since it provides men with what they believe is a scriptural basis for their sexism. As such, women can be subordinated and mistreated by men, while culpability is placed on God and often women themselves, which is fantastic in bro culture, since bros have always been fond of scapegoating anyone other than themselves for their own sexist and misogynistic behaviors.

Notes

1. Matt Slick, "What Is Complementarianism?" *Christian Apologetics & Research Ministry*. https://carm.org/questions-complementarianism
2. Ibid.
3. 1 Timothy 2:12, *Biblica*. https://biblia.com/bible/nasb95/1%20Tim.%202.12
4. 1 Timothy 2:13, *Biblica*. https://biblia.com/bible/nasb95/1%20Tim.%202.13
5. Bruce Ware, "Summaries of the Egalitarian and Complementarian Positions," *The Council on Biblical Manhood and Womanhood*, June 26, 2007. https://cbmw.org/uncategorized/summaries-of-the-egalitarian-and-complementarian-positions/
6. "The Facts and Statistics on 33,000 Denominations," *Center for the Study of Global Christianity*. http://www.philvaz.com/apologetics/a106.htm
7. John Calvin on Predestination, *Theology*. http://www.theologian-theology.com/theologians/john-calvin-predestination/
8. Dave Hunt, "Calvinism's Surprising Catholic Connection," *The Berean Call*, July 1, 2012. https://www.thebereancall.org/content/july-2012-classic
9. For Trump, see Chapter 9; for Gibson, one of many sexist and racist rants were captured on tape, in one instance stating to his then girlfriend, "You look like a fucking pig in heat, and if you get raped by a pack of niggers, it will be your fault," https://www.huffpost.com/entry/mel-gibson-playboy-interview_n_581a2ea7e4b0c43e6c1d92c0
10. Joela Brown, "The Klan, White Christianity, and the Past and Present," University of Chicago, *Religion & Culture*, June 26, 2017. https://voices.uchicago.edu/religionculture/2017/06/26/the-klan-white-christianity-and-the-past-and-present-a-response-to-kelly-j-baker-by-randall-j-stephens/
11. Timothy Kelly, "Modern Hate's Anti-Catholic Roots," *NCRON*, October 17, 2018. https://www.ncronline.org/news/people/modern-hates-anti-catholic-roots

12. Fred Clark, "Franklin Graham: Racism, Misogyny, Homophobia Are 'Biblical Truths We Stand For,'" *Patheos*, January 2, 2014. https://www.patheos.com/blogs/slacktivist/2014/01/02/franklin-graham-racism-misogyny-homophobia-are-biblical-truths-we-stand-for/
13. Ibid.
14. Hayley Peterson, "Christian Conservative T.V. Host Pat Robertson Blames 'Awful-Looking' Women for Failed Marriages," *Daily Mail*, January 16, 2013. https://www.dailymail.co.uk/news/article-2261361/Pat-Robertson-says-women-look-pretty-husbands-blames-awful-looking-girls-failed-marriages.html
15. Leslie Bentz, "Facebook 'Vomit' Buttons for Gays and Other Pat Robertson Quotes," *CNN*, July 9, 2013. https://www.cnn.com/2013/07/09/us/pat-robertson-facebook-remark/index.html
16. Ibid.
17. Monica Hesse, "The 'Billy Graham Rule' Doesn't Honor Your Wife. It Demeans Her – and All Women," *The Washington Post*, July 11, 2019.
18. Brendan Showalter, "Mike Pence Ridiculed for Practicing 'Billy Graham Rule'," *The Christian Post*, March 30, 2017. Retrieved April 2, 2017.
19. J.Y. Yang, "Genesis, Chapter 3," *MIT*. http://web.mit.edu/jywang/www/cef/Bible/NIV/NIV_Bible/GEN+3.html
20. Nellie Bowles, "Jordan Peterson, Custodian of the Patriarcy," *The New York Times*, May 18, 2018. https://www.nytimes.com/2018/05/18/style/jordan-peterson-12-rules-for-life.html
21. Ibid.
22. Linda Kay Klein, *Pure: Inside the Evangelical Movement That Shamed a Generation of Young Women and How I Broke Free*, Atria Books, New York, 2018.
23. Terry Gross, "Memoirist: Evangelical Purity Movement Sees Women's Bodies as a Threat," *NPR*, September 18, 2018. https://www.npr.org/2018/09/18/648737143/memoirist-evangelical-purity-movement-sees-womens-bodies-as-a-threat
24. Ibid.
25. Brian Murphy, "In Sermons, NC Congressional Candidate Called on Women to 'Submit' to their Husbands," *The News & Observer*, October 10, 2018. https://www.newsobserver.com/news/politics-government/article216246845.html
26. Ibid.
27. Julia Baird, Hayley Gleeson, "'Submit to Your Husbands': Women Told to Endure Domestic Violence in the Name of God," *ABC News*, October 21, 2018. https://www.abc.net.au/news/2017-07-18/domestic-violence-church-submit-to-husbands/8652028
28. Ibid.
29. 1 Peter 3: 1–2, *Biblica*. https://biblia.com/bible/nasb95/1%20Pet%203.1-2
30. 1 Corinthians 11:3, *Biblica*. https://biblia.com/bible/nasb95/1%20Cor%2011.3
31. Shelley Poston, "Should a Christian Wife Work Outside of the Home?" *Christian Apologetics & Research Ministry*, August 17, 2009. https://carm.org/should-christian-wife-work-outside-home#main-menu
32. Bureau of Labor Statistics, "Women in the Labor Force: A Datebook," December, 2018. https://www.bls.gov/opub/reports/womens-databook/2018/home.htm
33. Gretchen Livingston, "For Most Highly Educated Women, Motherhood Doesn't Start Until the 30s," *Pre Research Center*, January 15, 2015. https://www.pewresearch.org/fact-tank/2015/01/15/for-most-highly-educated-women-motherhood-doesnt-start-until-the-30s/

34. Sarah Jane Glynn, "Breadwinning Mothers Are Increasingly the U.S. Norm," *Center for American Progress*, December 19, 2016. https://www.americanprogress.org/issues/women/reports/2016/12/19/295203/breadwinning-mothers-are-increasingly-the-u-s-norm/
35. Isabelle Bilton, "Women Are Outnumbering Men at a Record High in Universities Worldwide," *Study International News*, March 7, 2018. https://www.studyinternational.com/news/record-high-numbers-women-outnumbering-men-university-globally/
36. Emily Lambert, "When Women Earn More than their Husbands," *Chicago Booth, Media Relations and Communications*, February 18, 2013. https://newschicagobooth.uchicago.edu/about/newsroom/news/2013/2013-02-18-bertrand
37. Ibid.
38. Jana Riess, "Why Millennials Are Really Leaving Religion (It's Not Just Politics, Folks)," *Religion News*, June 26, 2018. https://religionnews.com/2018/06/26/why-millennials-are-really-leaving-religion-its-not-just-politics-folks/
39. David Crary, "Women Strive for Larger Roles in Male-Dominated Religions," *Religion News*, January 15, 2019. https://religionnews.com/2019/01/15/women-strive-for-larger-roles-in-male-dominated-religions/
40. Joe Carter, "Women in Combat," *The Gospel Coalition*, January 27, 2013. https://www.thegospelcoalition.org/article/the-faqs-women-in-combat/
41. Lynn Billman, "Christian Women in STEM Are a Vulnerable Minority," *Huff Post*, December 6, 2017. https://www.huffpost.com/entry/christian-women-in-stem-a_b_4854540?guccounter=1&guce_referrer=aHR0cHM6Ly93d3cuZ29vZ2xlLmNvbS8&guce_referrer_sig=AQAAALh9yc36D2IwyWXQ2LeAQAVnESUuP98ZK9N5yWlrHsN8pDEw6bwAkMpAgJb32Fa-oZ6O1EotKlxi45OuIOEsVMyyWtB_WIub5KjRia4mPVD9ahuibdp5ikETiQlDjDwt8vWt-gofI1TFCnT87oJ613f2Ej0xXsQanerpcNaoUzGF
42. Jacqueline Yi, "The Role of Benevolent Sexism in Gender Inequality," *New York University*. https://wp.nyu.edu/steinhardt-appsych_opus/the-role-of-benevolent-sexism-in-gender-inequality/
43. Elizabeth Lewis Hall, "When Love Damages: The Case of Benevolent Sexism," *Biola University Center for Christian Thought*, February 20, 2017. https://cct.biola.edu/benevolent-sexism/
44. Ashley Easter, "The Hidden Sexism in the Church: Why "Benevolent" Sexism Does More Harm Than We Realize," *Ashley Easter Blog, The Courage Conference*, April 18, 2018. http://www.ashleyeaster.com/blog/hidden-sexism
45. Kristin Larson, "Benevolent Sexism at an Evangelical University," *Juicy Ecumenism*, November 15, 2012. https://juicyecumenism.com/2012/11/15/benevolent-sexism-at-an-evangelical-university/
46. Brad Christenson, M. Elizabeth Lewis Hall, Shelly Cunningham, "Women Faculty at an Evangelical University: The Paradox of Reliously Driven Gender Inequalities and High Job Satisfaction," *Journal of Religion & Education*, Vol. 39, Issue 2, July 2012, pp. 202–229. https://www.tandfonline.com/doi/abs/10.1080/15507394.2012.648574?journalCode=urel20#preview
47. Interview by Karen Swallow Prior, "The 'Benevolent Sexism' at Christian Colleges," *Christianity Today*, November 9, 2012. https://www.christianitytoday.com/ct/2012/november-web-only/benevolent-sexism-at-christian-colleges.html?utm_source=feedburner&utm_medium=feed&utm_campaign=Feed%3A+christianitytoday%2Fctmag+(Christianity+Today+Magazine)
48. Ibid.

49. Kristin Larson, "Benevolent Sexism at an Evangelical University," *Juicy Ecumenism*, November 15, 2012. https://juicyecumenism.com/2012/11/15/benevolent-sexism-at-an-evangelical-university/
50. Susan Chira, "Women Don't Think Alike. Why Do We Think They Do?" *The New York Times*, October 12, 2018. https://www.nytimes.com/2018/10/12/sunday-review/conservative-women-trump-kavanaugh.html
51. Ibid.
52. Erin C. Cassese, Tiffany D. Barnes, Mirya Holman, "How 'Hostile Sexism' Came to Shape Our Politics," *The Washington Post*, October 2, 2018. https://www.washingtonpost.com/news/monkey-cage/wp/2018/10/02/who-supports-kavanaugh-after-last-weeks-angry-hearings-our-research-helps-explain/?utm_term=.b2e44d8509b6
53. Erin C. Cassese, Mirya R. Holman, "Playing the Woman Card: Ambivalent Sexism in the 2016 U.S. Presidential Race," *Political Philosophy*, September 21, 2018. https://onlinelibrary.wiley.com/doi/full/10.1111/pops.12492
54. Erin C. Cassese, Tiffany D. Barnes, "Reconciling Sexism and Women's Support for Republican Candidates: A Look at Gender, Class, and Whiteness in the 2012 and 2016 Presidential Races," *Political Behavior*, 2018. http://tiffanydbarnes.weebly.com/uploads/3/7/2/1/37214665/cassese_barnes_pobe.pdf
55. Leigh A. Bradberry, "The Effect of Religion on Candidate Preference in the 2008 and 2012 Republican Presidential Primaries," *PLOS ONE*, April 4, 2016. https://journals.plos.org/plosone/article?id=10.1371/journal.pone.0152037
56. Patrick J. Egan, "Identity as Dependent Variable: How Americans Shift their Identities to Align with their Politics," *New York University*, June 19, 2019. https://www.dropbox.com/s/3tjpfg50hwex82i/egan.identity.as.dv.aug.2018.pdf?dl=0
57. Julia Baird, Hayley Gleeson, "'Submit to Your Husbands': Women Told to Endure Domestic Violence in the Name of God," *ABC News*, October 21, 2018. https://www.abc.net.au/news/2017-07-18/domestic-violence-church-submit-to-husbands/8652028
58. Ibid.
59. Pamela Constable, "For Some Muslim Wives, Abuse Knows No Borders," *The Washington Post*, May 8, 2007. http://www.washingtonpost.com/wp-dyn/content/article/2007/05/07/AR2007050701936.html?hpid=topnews
60. Enrique Gracia, "Unreported Cases of Domestic Violence against Women: Towards an Epidemiology of Social Silence, Tolerance, and Inhibition," *Journal of Epidemiology & Community Health*, Vol. 58, Issue 7, June 11, 2004. https://jech.bmj.com/content/58/7/536
61. Donald L. Uden, J.A. Hazey, "American Medical Association Diagnostic and Treatment Guidelines on Domestic Violence," *Archives of Family Medicine*, 1992. https://pdfs.semanticscholar.org/d3fd/8f15635c120aae74699db1419280b2355fa9.pdf
62. Julia Baird, Hayley Gleeson, "'Submit to Your Husbands': Women Told to Endure Domestic Violence in the Name of God," *ABC News*, October 21, 2018. https://www.abc.net.au/news/2017-07-18/domestic-violence-church-submit-to-husbands/8652028
63. Jamelle Bouie, ""Traditional Values" Is Just Code for 'Men Can Do Whatever They Want,'" *The American Prospect*, May 19, 2011. https://prospect.org/article/traditional-values-just-code-men-can-do-whatever-they-want
64. Sandra Earnest, "Commentary on Family Values," *Los Angeles Times*, October 18, 1992. https://www.latimes.com/archives/la-xpm-1992-10-18-me-921-story.html

65. Twila L. Perry, "Race, Feminism, and Public Policy," *Santa Clara University*. Markkula Center for Applied Ethics. https://www.scu.edu/ethics/focus-areas/more/resources/family-values/
66. Maggie Astor, "Syracuse Fraternity Suspended for 'Extremely Racist' Video," *The New York Times*, April 18, 2018. https://www.nytimes.com/2018/04/18/nyregion/syracuse-fraternity-suspended.html
67. https://ncore.ou.edu/media/filer_public/25/91/25917772-920d-4d56-af9f-9ecc6db360a9/02_jcscore_32__f17_the_influence_of_whiteness___fraternity_men__.pdf
68. S. Brian Joyce, Tony Cawthon, "The Influence of Whiteness on the Group Socialization of Fraternity Men," *Journal Committed to Social Change on Race and Ethnicity*, Vol. 3, Issue 2, 2017. https://promisekeepers.org/promise-keepers/about-us/7-promises/
69. Dianna Anderson, "Purity Culture, and Male Entitlement to Women's Bodies," *Rewire News*, June 17, 2014. https://rewire.news/article/2014/06/17/purity-culture-male-entitlement-womens-bodies/
70. Elizabeth Shively, "Christian 'Purity' Gur's Loss of Faith May Signal a Coming Reckoning for Conservative Christianity," *Rewire News*, August 5, 2019. https://rewire.news/religion-dispatches/2019/08/05/christian-purity-gurus-loss-of-faith-may-signal-a-coming-reckoning-for-conservative-christianity/
71. Laurie Goodstein, "Women and the Promise Keepers; Good for the Gander, but the Goose Isn't So Sure," *The New York Times*, October 5, 1997. https://www.nytimes.com/1997/10/05/weekinreview/women-and-the-promise-keepers-good-for-the-gander-but-the-goose-isn-t-so-sure.html
72. Ibid.
73. Ibid.
74. Staff Writer, "Joel Osteen Builds $17 Million Mansion on Foundation Made of Sand," *Babylon Bee*, July 22, 2019. https://babylonbee.com/news/joel-osteen-builds-37-million-mansion-on-foundation-made-of-sand
75. Harvard Divinity School, "The Prosperity Gospel," *Harvard University*. https://rlp.hds.harvard.edu/faq/prosperity-gospel
76. Matthew 19:23–26. *Biblica*. https://www.biblica.com/bible/?osis=niv:Matthew.19:23%E2%80%9319:26
77. Michael Kimmel, *Guyland: The Perilous World Where Boys Become Men*. Harper Perennial, New York, 2009.
78. Kiefer Roberts, "Guyland Addresses Challenges of Growing Up Male," *The College Voice*, February 28, 2011. https://thecollegevoice.org/2011/02/28/guyland-addresses-challenges-of-growing-up-male/
79. James Hamblin, "The Myth of Wealthy Men and Beautiful Women," *The Atlantic*, July 15, 2014. https://www.theatlantic.com/health/archive/2014/07/the-myth-of-buying-beauty/374414/
80. American Sociological Association, "God as a Drug: The Rise of American Megachurches," *Phys Org*, August 19, 2012. https://phys.org/news/2012-08-god-drug-american-megachurches.html
81. Karen Bennett, "The Shocking Net Worth of These 10 Richest Pastors Will Blow Your Mind," *Showbix Cheat Sheet*, January 31, 2019. https://www.cheatsheet.com/entertainment/net-worth-richest-pastors-will-blow-your-mind.html/
82. KTEN-Taxoma Report, "Joel Osteen's House Photos, Net Worth, and Books," *ABC News, Texoma*, May 16, 2019. http://www.kten.com/story/40490669/wow-joel-osteen-house-photos-net-worth-books

83. Dwight Adams, "Joel Osteen in Indianapolis: Why Televangelist Is So Beloved and Controversial," *Indy Star*, August 19, 2018. https://www.indystar.com/story/news/2018/08/09/joel-osteen-house-net-worth-lakewood-church-wife-why-televangelist-so-beloved-and-controversial/935789002/
84. Emily McFarlan Miller, "Independent Report Finds Allegations against Willow Creek Founder Bill Hybels Credible," *Religion News Service, February 28, 2019*. https://religionnews.com/2019/02/28/independent-report-finds-allegations-against-willow-creek-founder-bill-hybels-credible/
85. Ibid.
86. Chuck Queen, "Finding Courage to Challenge Churches' Patriarchy," *Ethics Daily*, July 19, 2010. https://ethicsdaily.com/finding-courage-to-challenge-churches-patriarchy-cms-16384/
87. Grace Church, Official Website, "Men of the World," https://www.gracechurch.org/motw?AspxAutoDetectCookieSupport=1
88. Peter McGraw, Joel Warner, "Gender and Humor: Was Christopher Hitchens Right When He Said Women Aren't Funny?" *Huff Post*, March 4, 2012. https://www.huffpost.com/entry/gender-and-humor_b_1181696
89. Anita Bennett, "Jerry Lewis Says Female Comedians Can Be Funny, Just Not When They're Crude," *The Wrap*, August 4, 2014. https://www.thewrap.com/jerry-lewis-clarifies-comments-female-comics-women-can-funny-theyre-crude/
90. Alyssa Rosenberg, "Adam Carolla, Sexism, and the Failure of the Hollywood Meritocracy," *Think Progress*, June 19, 2012. https://thinkprogress.org/adam-carolla-sexism-and-the-failure-of-the-hollywood-meritocracy-ed705386ccdf/
91. Rebecca Traister, "A Woman Should Run for President against Hillary Clinton. Or Many Women," *The New Republic*, June 25, 2014. https://newrepublic.com/article/118389/hillary-clinton-needs-female-primary-opponent-2016
92. Christopher Hitchens, Tony Blair, "Be It Resolved, Religion Is a Force for Good in the World," *Hitchens Debate Transcripts*, November 26, 2010. http://hitchensdebates.blogspot.com/2010/11/hitchens-vs-blair-roy-thomson-hall.html
93. Emily Q. Hazzard, "Bill Maher Has Been a Public Racist for a Long Time. Here Are the Receipts," *Think Progress*, June 3, 2017. https://thinkprogress.org/bill-maher-racist-history-b1d9c74283cd/
94. John Leland, "Cameras Roll, and Faith Hasn't a Prayer," *The New York Times*, September 26, 2008.
95. Richard Dawkins, Official Twitter Page, September 12, 2014. https://twitter.com/richarddawkins/status/510656024169447424?lang=en
96. Kimberly Winston, "Richard Dawkins Stands by Remarks on Sexism, Pedophilia, Down Syndrome," *The Washington Post*, November 18, 2014. https://www.washingtonpost.com/national/religion/richard-dawkins-stands-by-remarks-on-sexism-pedophilia-down-syndrome/2014/11/18/a2915cd8-6f64-11e4-a2c2-478179fd0489_story.html?utm_term=.a20857695821
97. Ibid.
98. Andrew Anthony, "Sam Harris, the New Atheist with a Spiritual Side," *The Guardian*, February 16, 2019. https://www.theguardian.com/books/2019/feb/16/sam-harris-interview-new-atheism-four-horsemen-faith-science-religion-rationalism
99. Ian Schwartz, "Sam Harris: "Liberals Want to Grade Islam on a Curve," Political Correctness Is Stifling Conversation," *Real Clear Politics*, October 14, 2014. https://www.realclearpolitics.com/video/2014/10/14/sam_harris_liberals_want_to_grade_islam_on_a_curve_bigotry_of_low_expectations.html

100. Michelle Boorstein, "Can Atheist Sam Harris Become a Spiritual Figure?" *The Washington Post*, September 12, 2014. https://www.washingtonpost.com/news/local/wp/2014/09/12/can-atheist-sam-harris-become-a-spiritual-figure/
101. Ibid.
102. Ibid.
103. Jen Krausz, "Newsmax's 100 Most Influential Evangelicals in America," *NewsMax*, November 17, 2017. https://www.newsmax.com/bestlists/evangelicals-influential-america-list/2017/11/15/id/826258/

INDEX

Note: *Italic* page numbers refer to figures.

abstinence-only programs 196–197
action-adventure films 140
advertising: boys and men sexism marketing 105–107; Dove 116; eurocentric models of beauty 119–120; femvertising 115–117; gay masculinity marketing 118–119; gender-normality 112–115; gender stereotypes 120; Heinz tomato soup 106; heteronormative supply-demand economics 111; heteronormativity 117–118; male-power *vs.* female-power 110; Mercedes-Benz 115; pornography 107; power imbalance 108, 109; product ads 104; Schlitz beer 106; self-objectify 111–112; sexual exploitation, women 111; soft-drink 105; subvertising 109–110; Van Heusen clothing 106; Weyenberg shoe 106; women's self-esteem 109
Affleck, Casey 3
Aguilera, Christina 14
Ailes, Roger 33, 210
alcohol-related hazing rituals 62
Alpha Epsilon Pi 65
Alpha Nu 54
Alpha Tau Omega 66
alt-right movement 222, 223
Altwies, Nick 61
American Psychological Association reports 17–18
American racism 127
Anderson, Jacob 65
anti-Semitic beliefs 218
apathy-based silence 90
Arceneaux, Michael 119
asshole effect 4
atheist bros 248–250
The Atlantic (Smith) 161

Bacharach, Burt 15, 153
The Bachelor 131, 132
Ballinger, Wolfgang 66
Banks, Azealia 14

Bannon, R. Sean 64
Barker, Deborah 134
Barnes, Tiffany D. 243
Bechdel, Alison 12, 126
benevolent sexism 241–244
Bernstein, Elizabeth 32
Beta Theta Pi 62, 64
Biblical authority 236
Biblical values 245
Billman, Lynn 241
Billy Graham rule 237, 242
bitch–ditz dichotomy 211–214
Black-Feminisms 166
Black Greek Letter Organizations (BGLO) 57, 58
Black Lives Matter 124
Blackstone, Amy 32
Blair, Karen 193
Blair, Tony 248
Bleecker, E. Timothy 64
Blurred Lines 14–15, 74, 156–157
Bogosian, Rob 90
Bowden, Mark 129
Bowen, Sesali 160–161
boy code 10–11
boys' behaviors 10–11
Breslin, Susannah 187
Breuer, Johannes 145
bro code of silence 43, 61–62; active gender inclusion 96; alexithymia 98; deafening silence, #metoo 88–91; gender segregation 87; 'gold-diggers'/'liars' 86; hostility 99; implied silence 87–88; legitimate male allies 95; medical and emotional intervention 85; medical intervention/counseling 96–97; #metoo backlash 91–93; "no girls allowed" rule 87, 88; passive gender inclusion 95; sexual abuse victims 94–95; sexual misconduct victims 86; SWAN 98
bro comedies/dramas: about sex 138; action-adventure films 140; gross-out humor 139; homophobic content

138–139; *Jackass-Hot-Tub-Time-Machine* model 141; male politician attacks 140; as protagonists role 140; risk-taking behaviors 139; sexual/romantic partner 140; women emotionalism 140–141
bro-country 167–168
"bro-flicks" 137–138
bro-ho-themed party 70–71
Brosi, Matthew W. 64
Brown, Chris 155–156
Brown, Jerry 42
Brown v. Board of Education 5
The Brute 131
Bryant, Kobe 3, 92
Bureau of Justice Statistics, sexual harassment 34–35
Burke, Tarana 29, 93
Burnett, Leo 115
Bush, George H.W. 56, 212
Bush, George W. 56
Bushman, Brad 17
bystander intervention programs 90

Caitlin Flanagan 68–69, 74
Calogero, R.M. 111
Cara, Alessia 14
Carter, Gregory Louis 37, 38
Carter, Nick 3
Cassese, Erin C. 243
Cauterucci, Christina 68
Chambers, Ali D. 57
'chick-flick,' Rom-Com and Dram-Com as 134–137
Chira, Susan 243
Chrisler, Joan C. 108
Christian Apologetics & Research Ministry (CARM) 239
Clark, Kenneth B. 5
Clark, Mamie Phipps 5
Clinton, Hillary 211–212, 219, 249
Clooney, George 115
Coard, Michael 63
Common Sense Media report 13
complementarianism 234–236, 242, 251
conservative refutation, whitewash bigotry 217–219
contrapower sexual harassment 36
Cookman, Liz 9–10
Corpse, Cannibal 14, 168
Cosby, Bill 3, 89, 210

Cox, David 134
Crane, Betsy 34
Crow, Jim 5
Crüe, Mötley 14, 167, 197–198
cultivation theory 11–12, 131
cultural appropriation 163–164
Currington, Billy 167
Cuthbert, Kate 142

dark triad personality 37, 38
Dashnaw, Daniel 188
Davis, Kiri 5
Dawkins, Richard 249
Delta Kappa Epsilon 60, 66
Delta Sigma Phi 60, 66
De Palma, Brian 130
Derby Days 59
DeSouza, Eros 36
DeVos, Betsy 68
Diaz, Junot 3
dichotomized gender training 142–143
digital gaming 16–17
Dines, Gail 189
Disney's awkward attempts, diversity and female empowerment: *Aladdin* 127; Disney princesses 126; *Frozen 2* 126; *The Incredibles* 125; male characters 127; *Moana* 126–127; *Mulan* 126; *Peter Pan* 127; *The Princess and the Frog* 126; *Snow White and the Seven Dwarves* 125; *Song of the South* 127
divestment rituals 113
"The Divine Nine," black fraternities and sororities 56–58
Donald, Athene 135
Doyle, Sady 132
Drouin, Michelle 185
DuBois, W.E.B. 57
Dyson, Michael Eric 165

economic privilege 4
Egan, Patrick 243
Elam, Paul 93, 221
emotional vulnerability 136
empathy 17, 31, 34, 38, 39, 124, 142
The Empathy Gap: Masculinity and the Courage to Change 5, 6
Engel, Beverly 67
Equal Employment Opportunity Commission (EEOC) 35, 44, 45

eurocentric models of beauty 119–120
Evangelical community 236–237
Everyday Feminism (Fabello) 194
exchange rituals 112
explicit consent 42

Fabello, Melissa A.: *Everyday Feminism* 194
Fansler, A. Gigi 36
fear-based silence 90
female empowerment 115–116
femininity 7, 8, 235
femvertising 115–117
fetishizing lesbians 193–194
Fey, Tina 136
Force, Taylor 66
Fortini, Amanda 212
Foubert, John 64, 74, 75
Fox, Richard 208
Franco, James 3
fraternity life: benefits 59; "The Divine Nine," black fraternities and sororities 56–58; ethnic and religious diversity 58; Frat-PAC 71–72; gender inequality 70–71; hazing rituals 62–64; Kappa Alpha Society 56; men and rape 64–70; multiculturalism 72–73; Phi Beta Kappa 55; pledging 61–62; Sigma Nu 54, 60; Sigma Phi 56; themed parties 70–71, 71; Theta Pi Sigma 73–74; workshop-oriented programs 74–75
Frat-PAC 71–72
Freeman, Morgan 3
Futrelle, David 20

gamer culture 144–145; sexist instruction 16–17
gamergate 16, 144
Gamma Phi Gamma 63
Garner, Eric 195
gay bros 21–22
gay masculinity marketing 118–119
Gaynor, Gloria 14
GBTQ 21
gender: balance 12; disparity 31–32; displays 113–115; egalitarians 184; equality 2, 12; essentialism 7–8, 10; freedom 12–13; identity 5; inequality 7–8, 69, 70–71; parity 208; safety 12, 13; sexual slurs 34; social justice 12, 13

gender-based violence 90–91
gendered Clark experiment 5–7, *6*
gendered porn gap 188–189
gender-flip movies 142–144
gender-inclusive fraternity 73–75
gender-normality: divestment rituals 113; exchange rituals 112; gender displays 113–115; grooming rituals 113; possession rituals 112–113
Gentile, Douglas 192
gentlemen's clubs 187–188
Gerbner, G. 11, 131, 192
Gilleon, Dan 195
Gillibrand, Kristin 211
Global Early Adolescent Study 14
Goffman, Erving 104, 113–114
Goldstein, Ari 65
gonzo porn 182
Graham, Franklin 235
Graham, Lindsey 216
Grand Theft Auto (GTA) game series 17, 191
Graves, Earl 57
Greek life *see* fraternity life
Greenfield, Lauren 6–7, 115
Griffith, D.W. 131
Grimes, David Robert 43
grooming rituals 113
gross-out humor 139
The Guardian 3–4

Haigh, Kirsty 15
Halberstam, Jack 118
Han, C. Winter 119, 223, 224
Hankes, Keegan 20
Harris, Joel Chandler 127
Harris, Mark 238
Harrison, Genie 44
Harrison, Todd 44–45
hashtag feminism 115
Haubegger, Christy 40
Haze, Angel 161
Hechinger, John 61
Heflick, Nathan A. 152
Hefner, Hugh 132, 133, 180–181
Helms, Angela 157
The Heritage Foundation 217
heteronormativity 11, 117–118
Hilton, Zoe 185
#himtoo movement 40–41, 92

Hitchens, Christopher 248, 249
Hoffman, Dustin 3
Hollywood film-narratives 125
Holma, Mirya R. 243
homophobia 138–139, 194; hazing rituals 64
hostile sexism 241
Houser, Kristen 41
Howard, M. William 246
Hubbard, Shanita 166
The Huffington Post 166, 183, 189
Hughes, Langston 57
Hunter, Margaret 166
Hurren, Wanda 95
Hurt, Byron 162
Hyacinth, Flora 57
hypermasculine models 16, 154, 165

implied consent 42
incel rebellion 20–21, 169
intellectualism 55
intimate-partner violence 32–34
Ivy League universities 207

Jackass-Hot-Tub-Time-Machine model 141
Johnson, W. Brad 89
Johnston-Robledo, Ingrid 108
Jones, Alex 211
Jordan, Michael 57
Jotanovic, Dejan 118–119
Judeo-Christianity 247

Kaepernick, Colin 159
Kahf, Christian 66
Kappa Alpha Society 56
Kappa Delta Rho 60
Kappa Psi Kappa 54
Kappa Sigma 66, 178
Katehakis, Alexandra 18–19, 179
Katz, Jackson 37, 46, 75, 88, 89, 94, 164
Keltner, Dacher 31
Kerry, John 56
Kilbourne, Jean 109, 111, 114
Kilgore, Ed 217
Kimmel, Michael 246
Kirk, David Anthony 66
Kitwana, Bakari 163
Klein, Linda Kay 238
Kowert, Rachel 145

Lake, Celinda 213
Lambda Chi Alpha 65
Lambert, Mary 171
Lauer, Matt 3
"lean-in" philosophy 135
Leary, Mary Graw 185
Lee, Shannon 161
Lehmiller, Justin 183, 184
LGBTQ 14, 128, 129, 220–222, 245; in advertising 118; communities and individuals, #metoo movement 30, 41–42; gay leaders 223; misogyny music 151; pornography 179; Theta Pi Sigma 73–74
Lieberman, David 33
Lisak, David 68, 94
Lofgreen, Ashton M. 39–40
Lopez, Ian Haney 222

McCarthy, Meghan 60
McClintock, Elizabeth 9
McClinton, Elizabeth 247
McCracken, Grant 112, 113
McCreary, Gentry 61
MacFarland, Seth 86–87
McGowan, Rose 21–22
McGraw, Tim 167
Machiavellianism 37
McInnes, Gavin 19, 20
McKee, Kathryn 134
McLaughlin, Heather 32
Madison, Holly 180, 181
Madle, Zachary 66
Magee, Joe 39
Maher, Bill 212, 249–250
mainstreaming 11–12
Maisy test 12–14
male dominance 4
male entitlement 34
male privilege and entitlement 3–5
Manne, Anne 3–4
mansplaining 8–9
manterrupt 9
mask of masculinity 10
Mason II, Byron 165
mass media 11–13
Mattson, Richard 43
media sexism 211
Mehta, Vinita 37
men's rights activists 92–93

men's sexual behaviors 36
#metoo movement 85, 93; backlash 91–93; deafening silence of men 88–91; LGBTQ communities and individuals 30, 41–42; men's roles 46; sexist socialization 29; sexual assault 29; sexual harassment 29, 30 (*see also* sexual harassment); Time's Up 40; verbal exchange 30
Meyer, Iian 94
Meyers, Seth 136
Mikkelson, Jill 168–169
Miller, Dennis 212
Minamore, Bridget 164
misogyny music 14–15, 47, 191; Black men 164; bro-country 167–168; cultural appropriation 163–164; hypermasculine 165; intersectional feminism 165; LGBTQ communities 151; love songs 172; male-centricity 170–171; of metal 168–170; rap music 160–163; socioeconomic classes 165; spillover effect 152; Wanton sexism, pop music (*see* wanton sexism, pop music); women's empowerment and equality 151
moral superiority 244
Moran, Rachel 184
multiculturalism 72–73, 167
Murnen, Sarah K. 64
Murphy, M.J. 223
Murray, Dwayne 57
musical misogynists *see* misogyny music
Musiqology (Vilanova) 159
Muslim fraternity 72

narcissism 37
National Association of Latino Fraternal Organizations (NALFO) 58
National Longitudinal Study of Adolescent Health 197
National Multicultural Greek Council 73
National Violence against Women Prevention Research Center 91–92
Ndegeocello, Meshell 14
Newberry, Johnathan 74
Nifong, Mike 68
Nu Phi Zeta 54

Ocasio-Cortez, Alexandria 213
Ocean, Frank 14

Ojeda, Monica 186
O'Neal, Shaquille 57
O'Reilly, Bill 44
orgasm gap 190
Osteen, Joel 247

Palin, Sarah 212–213
Pascoe, C.J. 194
Paura, Catherine 142
Pautz, Michelle C. 130–131
Pence, Mike 237, 238
Perfect White skin cream 120
Perry, Twila L. 244
Peterson, Jordan 237
Phadke, Shilpa 214
Phi Beta Kappa 55
Phi Delta Theta 62, 65
Phi Kappa Tau 64
Phi Sigma Nu 58
Pi Alpha Kappa 62, 63
Piff, Paul K. 4
Pi Kappa Phi 66
"Pimps and Hoes" Party 71, *71*
Plank, Liz 44
Playboy Clubs 133
playboy philosophy 132–133, 180–181
political sexism: alt-right movement 222, 223; American colonization 207; bitch–ditz dichotomy 211–214; B-word 215; conservative refutation, whitewash bigotry 217–219; elite universities 208; gay recruitment 222; gender parity 208; Ivy League 207; media attacks on women 210–211; media sexism 211; misogyny 214–217; no platforming 219–222; N-word 215; sexist bigotry 210; slaves and non-slave women 206
Pollack, William 10
Popa-Wyatt, Mihaela 218
pop culture 3, 14–15, 235; pornification 190–193
pornography 3, 17–19, 47, 107; degradation and humiliation 189; fetishizing lesbians 193–194; gendered porn gap 188–189; gender egalitarians 184; gentlemen's clubs 187–188; gonzo porn 182; homophobic slurs and behaviors 178; *The Huffington Post* 183; hyper-subordinated women 183; Kappa Sigma 178; LGBTQ

communities 179; orgasm gap 190; Playboy philosophy 180–181; pornification, pop culture 190–193; power-imbalance porn 183; racism 194–195; sex education 179, 181–182, 195–197; sex-positive education 182; sexting 185–186; sexual orientation 179; strip clubs 187; *The Sundial* 187
possession rituals 112–113
Potter, Claire 33
Potter, Shawna 169–170
power-threat model: " bros before hoes" 32; gender disparity 31–32; intimate-partner violence 32–34; male entitlement 34; quid-pro-quo harassment 30–31; sexual misconduct versions 31, 33; street harassment 33–34; Title VII of the Civil Rights Act of 1964 33
Pozner, Jennifer 116, 132, 213
Price, Lisa 57
Promise Keepers 245–246
Prosecutorial Remedies and Other Tools to End the Exploitation of Children Today (PROTECT) Act 185
prosperity theology 246–248
Proud Boys 19–20
Psi Upsilon 66
psychopathy 37
Public Enemy 162
Pulp Fiction 137–138
purity movement 238
Puzder, Andy 105–106

quid-pro-quo harassment 30–31
Quinn, Beth A. 38
Quinn, Zoe 16, 144

racial segregation 5
racism charges 19
radicalization 221
Ramirez, Rafael 73
rape culture 65
rape supportive attitude scale (RSA) 64
rap music 160–163
Rashad, Phylicia 57
Reagan, Ronald 181
reality TV 131–134
Recher, Jen 73

religious bros: atheist bros 248–250; benevolent sexism 241–244; Biblical authority 236; Billy Graham rule 237; complementarianism 234–236; Evangelical community 236–237; family values 244–246; prosperity theology 246–248; scriptural authority 233; women's bodies policing 238–239; women's choices policing 239–241
Relopez, Jason 66
reproductive competition 37–38
Reyes, Daisy Verduzco 58
Rey, Rosario Del 186
Richie, Guy 127
Rivas, Luis 187
Robertson, Pat 236, 238
Robertson, Phil 235
Rodger, Eliot 20
Romney, Mitt 218
Ronell, Avital 45
roofies 61
Rose, Charlie 3
Ross, Lawrence 57
Rowden, Kehoe 12

Sandberg, Sheryl 33
Sarkeesian, Anita 16, 144, 222
Savage, Michael 212
Scarface 137
Scarry, Eddie 213
Schlafly, Phyllis 206
Schwartz, Dana 9
scriptural authority 233
Seacrest, Ryan 3
self-conscious 119–120
self-esteem 109, 119
self-gratification 189
self-objectify 111–112
Service Women's Action Network (SWAN) 98
sexism 1–2; *Blurred Lines* 14–15; boy code 10–11; cultivation theory 11–12; digital heroin 16–17; frat-guy 2; gay bros 21–22; gendered inequality 7–8; gender equality 2; gender essentialism 7–8, 10; heterosexual guys 2, 22; Incel Rebellion 20–21; mainstreaming 11–12; Maisy test 12–14; male privilege and entitlement 3–5; mansplaining 8–9; manterrupt 9; pop culture 3; pornography 3, 17–19;

Proud Boys 19–20; sexual assault 3, 4, 23; sexual harassment 3, 4, 23; STEM 2–3, 8; womanterrupt 10
sexist bigotry 210
sexting 185–186
sexual abuse victims 94–95
sexual assault 3, 4, 23, 29, 91, 92
Sexual Assault Expected (SAE) 66
sexual conquest 21
sexual dominance 38
sexual harassment 3, 4, 16, 17, 23, 91, 209, 211; *bros before hoes* 43; contrapower 36; hybrid model 39–40; LGBTQ communities and individuals 41–42; power-threat model 30–34; sexual drive and conformity 36–39; socioeconomics 34–36
sexual intimacy 188
sexual liberation 15, 180
sexual temptation 242
sexual violence victims 95
Shakur, Tupac 161
Sheppard, Elena 167
Shpancer, Noam 36
Sifferlin, Alexandra 17
Sigma Alpha Epsilon 66, 128
Sigma Chi 59–60, 65
Sigma Nu 54
Sigma Phi 56
Sigma Phi Beta 54
Sigma Theta Epsilon 58
Simmons, Russell 3
Simz, Little 161
Sinatra, Frank 152
Skinner, B.F. 154
slurs 218
Smith, David G. 89
Smith, Jack Ryan 66
Smith, Mychal Denzel: *The Atlantic* 161
Smith, Pamela 39
Smith, Sam 14
Smith, Stacy 170
social cognition 142
social fraternities 56
socialization process 7
social justice activism 116, 235
Solnit, Rebecca 9
Southern Poverty Law Center 19, 20
Spacey, Kevin 3, 41
spillover effect 152

Sprenkle, Preston 97
Stagliano, John 189
Stemple, Laura 94
Strasser, Annie-Rose 10
street harassment 33–34
Strudwick, Patrick 22
subvertising 109–110
Summer Blockbusters: antihero 129–130; cult of self mentality 129; de facto teaching tools 128; *Fast & Furious* 130; *The Joker* 129; lead character 128; superhero features 129

Tabberer, Jamie 21
Taft, William Howard 56
Taneja, Amit 21
Tatum, Jerry 74
Theron, Charlize 143
Theta Pi Sigma 73–74
Thicke, Robin 15, 156
Thorpe, Hayden 154
Time's Up movements 40–41, 85
Title VII of the Civil Rights Act of 1964 33
tough guise 37
Trump, Donald 3, 11, 44, 91, 92, 106, 110, 124, 127, 159, 195, 206, 235, 249; *see also* political sexism
Tufnel, Nigel 107

Uggen, Christopher 32

Van Deventer, Leena 144
Vilanova, John: *Musiqology* 159
Vincke, Eveline 37
Vittar, Pablo 14
Volokh, Eugene 220

The Wall Street Journal 32
wanton sexism, pop music: *Blurred Lines* 156–157; domestic violence 158; Eminem's homophobia 159; gender and sexual liberation 153; hypermasculine models 154; operant conditioning 154; rehabilitation treatment 155; teaching tools and templates, behavior 152
Wayne, Bruce 132
Weiner, Anthony 186
Weinstein, Harvey 3, 31–33, 43, 44, 86, 88, 89, 95

white fraternity 57
whiteness marketing 120
Whitson, Jennifer 39
Williams, Carla Marie 171
Willow Creek Community Church 248
womanterrupt 10
women abusers 44
women dehumanization 65
women emotionalism 140–141
women's bodies policing 238–239
women's choices policing 239–241

World Health Organization (WHO) 16
Wu, Brianna 16
Wyatt, Jeremy 218

Yafi, Faysal A. 97
"yes means yes" campaign 42
Yiannopoulos' theory 222
Young M.A 161

Zeigler, Cyd 63
Zimbardo, Philip 19

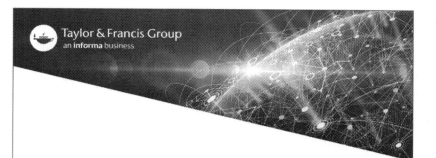

Printed in the United States
By Bookmasters